Spokesperson Milton

Spokesperson Milton

Voices in Contemporary Criticism

Edited by
**Charles W. Durham
and Kristin Pruitt McColgan**

Selinsgrove: Susquehanna University Press
London and Toronto: Associated University Presses

© 1994 by Associated University Presses

All rights reserved. Authorization to photocopy items for internal or personal use, or the internal or personal use of specific clients, is granted by the copyright owner, provided that a base fee of $10.00, plus eight cents per page, per copy is paid directly to the Copyright Clearance Center, 222 Rosewood Drive, Danvers, Massachusetts 01923. [0-945636-65-2/94 $10.00 + 8¢ pp, pc.]

Associated University Presses
440 Forsgate Drive
Cranbury, NJ 08512

Associated University Presses
25 Sicilian Avenue
London WC1A 2QH, England

Associated University Presses
P.O.Box 338, Port Credit
Mississauga, Ontario
Canada L5G 4L8

The paper used in this publication meets the requirements of the American National Standard for Permanence of Paper for Printed Library Materials Z39.48–1984.

Library of Congress Cataloging-in-Publication Data

Spokesperson Milton: voices in contemporary criticism / edited by Charles W. Durham and Kristin Pruitt McColgan.
    p.   cm.
    Includes index.
    ISBN 0-945636-65-2 (alk. paper)
    1. Milton, John, 1608-1674—Criticism and interpretation.
I. Durham, Charles W.   II. McColgan, Kristin Pruitt.
PR3588.S67   1994
821'.4—dc20   93-47329
                                                    CIP

To John T. Shawcross,
superb scholar, wise counselor,
and dear friend:
"Be strong, live happy, and love."

Contents

Acknowledgments	ix
Introduction	xi

Part I. Spokesperson Milton

Spokesperson Milton JOHN T. SHAWCROSS	5

Part II. Spokesperson for Theological and Spiritual Concerns

The Fruitless Tree in *Paradise Lost*: Symbol of Sin ALICE M. MATHEWS	21
No Fortunate Fall, No "Unfeared Second Fate": Satan and the Critique of Meliorism, *Paradise Lost*, Book 2 CATHERINE GIMELLI MARTIN	31
"By Faith to Stand": Faith in the Theodicy of *Paradise Lost* JOHN S. TANNER	47
Dodging the Dragon's Tail: Apocalyptic Combat in *Paradise Regained* SAMUEL SMITH	57

Part III. Spokesperson for Political Views

Jubilee in Scripture and History: Reading Milton's "At a Solemn Music" STEPHEN M. BUHLER	71
Milton's Royalist Reflex: The Failure of Argument and the Role of Dialogics in *Eikonoklastes* JANE HILES	87
The Cardinal and the King: Milton's State Letters to France ROBERT THOMAS FALLON	101
"Under Thir Head Embodied All in One": Milton's Reinterpretation of the Organic Analogy in *Paradise Lost* STEVEN JABLONSKI	113

A Fissure in the Milton Window?: Arnold's 1888 Address
DAVID BOOCKER 126

Part IV. Spokesperson for Authority of Author and of Text

Meddling with Authority: Inspiration and Speech Acts in Milton's Prose
ANGELA ESTERHAMMER 141

The Creative Self and the Self Created in *Paradise Lost*
ALBERT W. FIELDS 153

Conflicts of Authority: Interpretation of Events in *Paradise Regained* and *Samson Agonistes*
DANIEL T. LOCHMAN 165

Authorial Providence and the Dramatic Form of *Samson Agonistes*
JANE COLLINS 179

Part V. Spokesperson for Tradition and Change

Comus: Milton's Re-Formation of the Masque
J. ANDREW HUBBELL 193

Milton's Vergilian Epigraphs of 1637 and 1645
NATALIE JOY WOODALL 206

"Nature Taught Art": The Topos of Art and Nature in *Paradise Regained*
PETER M. MCCLUSKEY 217

Part VI. Spokesperson for Women

Beneficent Hierarchies: Reading Milton Greenly
DIANE MCCOLLEY 229

"Grateful Digressions" and "Casual Discourse": Eve's Rapport-Talk
JOAN F. GILLILAND 249

Discourse and Danger: Women's Heroism in the Bible and Dalila's Self-Defense
HOPE PARISI 260

Contributors 275

INDEX 279

Acknowledgments

We owe thanks to many for their contributions to the completion of this project: to the Middle Tennessee State University Faculty Research Committee for a generous grant that facilitated the editing of this book; to Cindy Duke and Gail Spake, for willingly putting aside other responsibilities when we appealed to them; to John N. McDaniel, Larry Mapp, and Roger Easson for assistance along the way; to Kevin J. Donovan and Frank Ginanni, for their commitment to the idea of a Milton conference that helped make it happen, and to all the participants for making it a success; to colleagues for continually reminding us of why we love teaching and to students for continually reminding us of why we love Milton; to Donald P. McDonough and James P. Shea, friends forever, for never tiring of talking about Milton; to our families, especially Raymond Pruitt, for always believing in the power of love and poetry, Ed, Carrie, and Andrew McColgan, Janie and Elliott Durham, for loving us in spite of Milton; and most of all, to the contributors to this volume, without whose voices we would be silent.

Introduction

> [A]s I had from my youth studied the distinctions between religious and civil rights, I perceived that if ever I wished to be of use, I ought at least not to be wanting to my country, to the church, and to so many of my fellow-Christians, in a crisis of so much danger.
> —John Milton, *Second Defense*

Clearly, Milton saw himself as a spokesperson for political and religious causes, a view documented in biographical and critical studies. What has perhaps not been adequately emphasized are the variety and scope of Milton's expressions of cultural, religious, political, and artistic concerns, from the poetry of his youth, such as "At a Solemn Music" and *A Mask Presented at Ludlow Castle*, and his stated intention to write a work "doctrinal and exemplary to a nation" (*The Reason of Church Government*), through the plethora of prose tracts—both defenses and allegations—issued during years of national and international crisis, to the artistic achievements of *Paradise Lost, Paradise Regained,* and *Samson Agonistes.* Such expressions have allowed Milton to become spokesperson, as John T. Shawcross suggests, "for many people, even those espousing diametrically opposite causes." Although the critical voices represented in this collection examine Milton's poetry and prose from different perspectives, they all challenge earlier critical assumptions and reveal that spokesperson Milton's voice was not one but many, as he ever sought "By winning words to conquer willing hearts" (*Paradise Regained*, 1.221–22).

In Part I, the title essay, John T. Shawcross lays the groundwork for exploration of Milton's role as spokesperson, first, according to eighteenth-century standards, then, in light of modern attention to issues of politics, feminism, and hierarchy. His cogent references to Milton's detractors and idolaters, to those who would "kill" the oedipal father and those who would venerate him as sire, support his claim that "Milton as spokesperson for ideas presents a . . . bifurcation of approval and disapproval in both the eighteenth century and the twentieth."

In Part II, the contributors address and interpret religious views in *Paradise Lost* and *Paradise Regained*. Alice M. Mathews explores the "alarming implications" of the poet's presentation of the "fruitless tree" from which Adam and Eve select leaves to cover their nakedness after the Fall. She concludes that the tension inherent in the epic simile "[defines] the spiritual condition of Adam and Eve in geographical and scientific terms" and "gives . . . a precision and objectivity to the abstract concept of sin." Both Catherine Gimelli Martin and John S. Tanner reject the *felix culpa* as an expression of Milton's theology. Martin analyzes the demonic council scene in book 2 as the "satan-speak" of a "self-deluded philosophic system," meliorism, in dramatic contrast to a "corrected" Adam's recognition that "true victory demands both an initial acknowledgment of sin and a lifelong confrontation with it." Likewise, Tanner critiques "simplistic notions of a fortunate fall" as undermining the tone of the conclusion of *Paradise Lost* that "works in part because . . . [the poem] 'solves' the dilemmas of theodicy not only conceptually, with answers and arguments, but dramatically, with confessions by Adam and Eve of their renewed willingness to obey, love, and walk by faith." Samuel Smith examines *Paradise Regained* to demonstrate that "Christ's final apocalyptic victory over Satan . . . figures prominently in Milton's retelling of Jesus's temptation." He argues that an "apocalyptically alert reader realizes" at the poem's conclusion "that the final conflict between Christ and the dragon has been typologically and prophetically battled out in the victory of Jesus over Satan in the desert wilderness of Judea."

The essays in Part III suggest the extent to which political views inform Milton's poetry and contribute to the shaping of his prose; they also consider the effect of these political views on Milton's contemporary audience and on later generations of readers. Stephen M. Buhler probes the "interconnections between poetry and power, religion and politics" in his analysis of the term *jubilee* in "At a Solemn Music." Such an approach highlights the seventeenth-century "debate over the political lessons to be derived from scripture" and reveals Milton's "tendency . . . toward responding and reshaping, toward engagement in and with history." In her examination of *Eikonklastes* as a "surprisingly unrhetorical response" to *Eikon Basilike*, Jane Hiles attributes Milton's "failure" to what she terms his "royalist reflex," the

> propensity to follow the royalist pattern of shifting the blame for the king's crimes to advisors or others, minimizing the king's offenses by failing to elaborate on them, and focusing on the literary aspects of the conflict to the near exclusion of larger ideological issues.

Milton's state papers to France are the subject of Robert Thomas Fallon's essay, which compares "the power sharing arrangement" between the young King Louis XIV and the power behind him, Cardinal Jules Mazarin, to "that to be found in the realms of *Paradise Lost*," maintaining that "From his State Letters . . . we learn what Milton knew of the political events of his time, and thereby gain an important key to the understanding of his poetic achievement." Similarly, Steven Jablonski posits a relationship between politics and art in his discussion of Milton's exploitation of the royalist analogy of the body politic to the heavenly order in *Paradise Lost*. However, he speculates that "Milton suggested such a parallel only to expose its failure and thereby employed the example of the Son's headship as a critique of rather than a sanction for [human] monarchy." In short, "Christ as head suffers for his people; the people suffer for a king as head." David Boocker shows how a nineteenth-century spokesperson for cultural values, Matthew Arnold, divorced Milton's political stance as a supporter of the Puritan cause from an assessment of the stylistic achievement of Milton's poetry. Ironically, Arnold was himself "making an explicitly political statement on the relationship between art and politics," on their "incompatibility." Boocker concludes that "our job as readers of Milton is to rediscover and reintegrate [the poet's] political languages into literary text" and thus "repair the fissure in the Milton window."

In Part IV, the contributors investigate ways in which Milton as author establishes his own authority within texts and encourages readers to choose between conflicting models of authority. Angela Esterhammer asserts the preeminence of "inspired individuals" over "church officials" in Milton's autobiographical digression in *The Reason of Church Government* and claims that, in his prose, Milton "is 'meddling with authority,' both in the sense of interfering with recognized power structures and in attempting to secure a new mandate for such interference." Albert Fields sees a pattern in *Paradise Lost* in Milton's authoring of the text and in his presentation of God as author of Adam and Adam as author of his own identity. Arguing that "the most powerful ongoing and universal creative impulse emanated from the Logos, the controlling principle, the 'word' invested in the Son," Fields concludes that "in the poet, formed in the image of God, the 'word' might be the most powerful expression of the Self creating." Daniel T. Lochman explores the parallel movements of the Son in *Paradise Regained* and Samson in *Samson Agonistes* and contends "that the interior self is the only reliable authority for truth in a world filled with multiple perceptions and distortions of reality." Despite significant contrasts between "the rude and uncivil Samson" and "the refined, genuinely learned, and inspired Son," both are destroyers and deliverers, testimonies to the authority of "a new world order, rooted in the Bible and one's inner light." Jane Collins believes that Milton offers the reader "interpretive keys" to *Samson Agonistes*, a means of locating authority in the text through Milton's use of dramatic form that clarifies "a tragic flaw in his characters and in his time—the self-serving interpretation of events as signs of divine providence without interrogation of their meaning." Milton, she suggests, "[warns] against an easy, convenient reading of the text" that would mirror the chorus' "ritualized interpretation."

Milton's adaptation of traditional literary motifs and forms is addressed in the essays of Part V. Looking at literary, religious, and political ramifications in *Comus*, J. Andrew Hubbell indicates that "Milton changed the masque's primary function from honoring the king to honoring the poet" and thereby exalted "The poet's myth" as "superior to the king's." This "re-formation" of the masque, with its "prophetic paradigms," calls attention to the "self-aware poet," to "the arrival of a man chosen by God to prepare a nation for its glorious ascent to divine favor." Natalie Joy Woodall considers possible reasons for Milton's change of Vergilian epigraphs from the 1637 edition of *A Mask Presented at Ludlow Castle* to the version that appeared in the 1645 volume of his poetry, hypothesizing that the substitution "illustrates his increasing abhorrence of Greek and Roman mythological characters" and his repudiation of "paganism" in favor of the Bible as "ultimate truth." In his investigation of the nature/art topos in *Paradise Regained*, Peter M. McCluskey demonstrates Milton's awareness of traditional models in Ovid, Tasso, and Spenser and his subtle manipulation of literary antecedents "to meet the unusual needs of his brief epic." In the banquet temptation, McCluskey asserts, "Milton deliberately clouds the question of whether the 'pleasant Grove' is natural in order to use the topos without raising ... questions," either "theological or motivational."

In Part VI, issues of gender and hierarchy are explored in light of Milton's portrayals of the relationships between Adam and Eve and Samson and Dalila. Diane McColley uses patterns of heavenly hierarchy to illuminate the role of Adam and Eve as "hierarchs, or ministers, to nature" who "[seek] a balance between personal and ecological relations" and to support her claim that "Paradisal hierarchies are beneficent, flexible, and reciprocal." McColley points out that Adam and Eve's language "expresses the nature of Nature" in its variety and unity, and claims that Eve "most clearly makes practical applications of ... ecological conscience." The differences between male "report-talk," with its emphasis on status and content, and female "rapport-talk," with its emphasis on creating and maintaining relationships, serve as the basis for Joan F. Gilliland's study of Eve before, during, and after the Fall. The prelapsarian Eve reveals her preference for language that builds consensus, whereas after she eats the forbidden fruit, she "[plays] the masculine game of establishing a dominant position" over Adam. Her plea for forgiveness in book 10 marks her return to the language of rapport and may, Gilliland suggests, further Adam's "education in conversation." Hope Parisi explores Dalila's role as hero and mediator in *Samson Agonistes* from the seemingly disparate perspectives of biblical prototypes and seventeenth-century views of women's heroism. "An ancient Near Eastern intercessor for her people, Dalila mediates in a way that conflicts with domestic 'strategies' proper to seventeenth-century women" even while she acts and reacts in "a world of dangerous male anger" and the "repressive family structure of Milton's day." Parisi concludes that "Dalila's scriptural prototypes require her to stand outside the gendered heroisms of the seventeenth century."

The contents of this collection, originally presented in shorter forms at The First Southeastern Conference on John Milton at Middle Tennessee State University, Murfreesboro, Tennessee, 24–26 October 1991, are evidence of the energizing dialogue that occurs when readers converse with each other and engage in dialogue with the many voices of a spokesperson such as John Milton.

# Spokesperson Milton

Part I
Spokesperson Milton

Spokesperson Milton

JOHN T. SHAWCROSS

For a number of years I have been compiling a bibliography of John Milton's works in the eighteenth century and of works touching upon his presence as poetic mentor, as authority figure, and as spokesperson for ideas that another author wanted to assert or refute. In our century we have seen a rejection of Milton as poetic mentor and authority figure, although today he is acknowledged by many poets, if not all critics, as a significant predecessor to their own creative achievements—for example, John Berryman, Gary Snyder, Allen Ginsberg, and Howard Nemerov—or he is regarded by many critics, if not all poets, as an oedipal father figure who must be symbolically killed before poetic individuation can be achieved. Some, like T. S. Eliot, Hart Crane, James Joyce, or George Bernard Shaw, "killed" this poetic father by negative critical assertions, while constantly reflecting their inheritance from the poetic father. In the mid-eighteenth century the William Lauder affair, abetted by Dr. Samuel Johnson, attempted to stem the Miltonic progeny, including the poetasters and their frequently dismal excursions into blank verse or octosyllabic couplets, with "sublime" language and "poetic" images employed relentlessly, by accusing Milton of forging *Paradise Lost* out of the work of others. Lauder's proof of plagiarized sources, for the most part, lay in lines interpolated into the poem written supposedly by people like the mid-seventeenth-century Jacob Massenius, but these cited lines were often from William Hog's 1690 Latin translation of Milton's epic. Milton as poetic mentor and authority figure was, for a while at least, called into question, and James MacPherson's Ossian texts and Thomas Chatterton's bid for fame a quarter of a century later—as also William Ireland's production of "William Shakespeare's" manuscripts—are obverse fallout from the notoriety of Lauder's forgeries.[1]

Milton as spokesperson for literary activity and authorization had perhaps been shaken as much as Satan shook God's throne (*Paradise Lost*, 1.105).² Lauder's defense in his "dubious Battel" (*Paradise Lost*, 1.104) was the commendable enough desire to make the British poetic world aware of the achievements of Scottish poetry and particularly that of Allen Ramsay. But a psychological impetus for Lauder's actions seems more likely: a kind of satanic envy and its source in self-hate, and the attempt to kill the oedipal father and couple the widowed muse. A classical scholar who was crippled in a sporting accident, Lauder was also an inept versifier. He was thus reacting to the physically impaired yet major sublime poet of the age. Milton, of course, remained poetic mentor, authority figure, and spokesperson for ideas.

More interesting and more psychologically involved in this attempt to undermine Milton's influential voice are the actions of Dr. Johnson, who as an editor of *Gentleman's Magazine* had helped persuade the original publication of Lauder's series of charges (1747) and then aided in their book appearance (first issue 1749 but dated 1750). Once the fraud had been revealed by the Reverend John Douglas (in November 1750 but dated 1751), Johnson insisted on Lauder's confession, and was actually the author of the preface and epilogue to it (in the second issue of 1750), though unattributed. While Lauder accused Milton of forgery, and while it was he who was actually guilty of this, Johnson additionally made Lauder a kind of forger by ghostwriting these items.³ The episode is not one that Johnsonians like to hear about. Johnson's relationship with Milton, his works, and his ideas, while the subject of much scholarship, still needs further analysis from objective critics. Some in the past have been fairly objective, like Johnson's friend Sir John Hawkins in the eighteenth century and, for one instance, Stephen Fix in ours—but some have been excusatory like Arthur Murphy or incensed like James Burnet, Lord Monbaddo. We are well aware of Johnson's praise of Milton, particularly for *Comus* and *Paradise Lost*, in his often reprinted *Life of Milton*, and also of his scathing dismissal of *Lycidas* and the sonnets. Yet Johnson has not always been well served by modern critics—not by Miltonists, but also not by Johnsonians, who have too frequently been regrettably narrow and protective—because many commentators seem to forget such important criticism as the 1751 *Rambler* essays on *Samson Agonistes* and on versification in *Paradise Lost*, or seem ignorant of the influence of Milton on "London" (1738), "The Vanity of Human Wishes" (1749), and even on *Irene* (1736 but produced in 1749), all shortly before or in the midst of the Lauder affair.⁴

Johnson is far from the Eliot camp of criticism: his praise seems to be of his literary "father"; his dispraise does not seem to be of an oedipal father. Rather those negative evaluations of *Lycidas* and the sonnets, and other comments in the essays and *Life,* tell us about Johnson's aesthetics and politics, not really his reaction to Milton the poet. The problem of literary history has been that Johnson's aesthetics have been made to prevail in our critical views of eighteenth-century literature by his idolaters of this century. Forgotten thus have been important and good women writers—poets and novelists; dismissed have been important and good male writers; and assumed has been the death of the sonnet and the persistence of only a few "private" lyrical forms for the so-called Romantics, who were emerging in the last years of the century, to build upon and continue. We have had the incompetent term *pre-Romantic* offered to us, in order to include such Miltonic sons as Edward Young and James Thomson, but there were many more precursors of Wordsworth and Coleridge (let alone Robert Southey, Robert Burns, and Samuel Rogers), with the attributes that one expects from the handbook definition of "Romantic." Yet their poems—I think of the work of poets like Mary Robinson or Charlotte Smith, Robert Merry or William Parsons—are not different from "Michael" or various sonnets or even the Lucy poems. Milton as poetic mentor and authority figure had a steady presence in eighteenth-century literature, without a hiatus, up to the time "Lyrical Ballads" appeared. That title, of course, is a generic oxymoron, but it is one also describing the work of predecessors, who write narrative forms lyrically and lyrics with story elements, not unlike "Michael," and all reflect the presence of Milton. Indeed some of these writers produced the contemporary poetry that Wordsworth and Coleridge, and Byron, Shelley, and Keats would have been reading outside the classroom when they were impressionable schoolboys.[5]

I run over these eighteenth-century matters to suggest, first, that there is much still to be investigated and evaluated in that century's literature and aesthetics, in which much will be found owing to Milton as a literary spokesperson, and second, that the twentieth-century literary scene has been ripe for a similar investigation as that proposed for this earlier period, an investigation that moves past the Ezra Pound/F. R. Leavis/T. S. Eliot antagonisms and looks at the novelistic, critical, and poetic achievements of, say, Aldous Huxley/Charles Williams/Gwendolyn Brooks, for all of whom Milton has been a strong, though sometimes subtle, poetic mentor or spokesperson.

Milton as spokesperson for ideas presents a similar bifurcation of approval and disapproval in both the eighteenth century and the twentieth. Reanalysis of both centuries' approaches is in order in this arena of dispute as well. Perhaps today the most frequent areas of Miltonic critical discussion are the political arena, feminist issues, and their relation with the third, which involves hierarchies or subordinationism. Indeed, those are the general subjects or themes of many essays presented in this collection. The eighteenth century also paid attention to these matters, although the line of division was the political, a major cause of diatribe levied at the same time that encomium of the sublime poet was sung. The issue was simple enough: Milton was associated with the regicides (or was one) and he argued against monarchy and specifically Charles, soon to be Royal Martyr of Blessed Memory. The issue of whether Charles wrote *Eikon Basilike* remained viable even through 1824 with Christopher Wordsworth's "*Who Wrote Eikon Basilike?*" *Considered and Answered.* (He was William Wordsworth's youngest brother.) The next year, because his positive answer to the question had been refuted, he published a documentary supplement to that discussion.[6] Today Milton is still detested by some British because of his association with the regicides: "But they didn't have to kill the king!" we will still hear, and this has aided in putting him out of favor as both poet and prose writer, regardless of whether his "message" is a precursor of the most fervently held liberal or conservative ideas. (That last statement will raise questions for some people, for generally today Milton is looked upon as radical, not only for his day but even for ours, except to those who view him as a male chauvinist or as nondemocratic in his seeming lack of regard for the "people," the workers, women, Jews, and Roman Catholics.)

For Joseph Addison, talking of *Paradise Lost* in 1694, "What tongue, what words of rapture can express / A vision so profuse of pleasantness," but then immediately he laments,

> Oh had the Poet ne'er profan'd his pen,
> To vernish o'er the guilt of faithless men;
> His other works might have deserv'd applause!
> But now the language can't support the case;
> While the clean current, tho' serene and bright,
> Betrays a bottom odious to the sight.[7]

Clearly Addison was showing his own attitudes and political position, not weighing Milton's arguments or the felicity of their expression in regards to intended audience or circumstance. A stylistic analysis shows the great contrasts in such works as *The Tenure of Kings and Magistrates* against *Brief Notes Upon a Late Sermon*, or *A Treatise of Civil Power* against *Of True Religion, Heresie, Schism, and Toleration*. The writing deserves applause as calculated rhetoric at least, even though the conclusion or opinion the reader is trying to be persuaded to accept be unacceptable to that reader. Just as Addison deplored Milton's brand of "republicanism," his "antimonarchianism," so too did Thomas Yalden (1698):

> But when thy impious mercenary pen
> Insults the best of princes, best of men,
> Our admiration turns to just disdain,
> And we revoke the fond applause again.
> ... So thou profane'st his image here below.
> Apostate bard! may not thy guilty ghost,
> Discover to its own eternal cost,
> That as they heaven, thou paradise hast lost![8]

Of Johnson's criticism of *Samson Agonistes,* Sir John Hawkins wrote, "he seems to have been prompted by no better a motive, than that hatred of the author for his political principles which he is known to have entertained, and was ever ready to avow," although Hawkins, manifesting his own political posture, goes on to agree that Milton "was a political enthusiast, and, as is evident from his panegyric on Cromwell, a base and abject flatterer."[9] (A more careful and subtle reading of that panegyric, included in a second defense of the interregnum government and therefore rhetorically apt, would suggest that Milton harbored fears that Cromwell's earlier, rather uncommendable life could again emerge if Cromwell did look back at what had been ploughed and thus defied the message of Luke 9.62 and Milton's Sonnet 16.) On the other side of the fence from Johnson and Hawkins was the political enthusiast Thomas Hollis, who admonished Edward Holyoke, president of Harvard, for a slight toward Milton's prose: "Milton, or the warmest common-wealth man, never thought of altering the antient form of government, till Charles the First had sinned flagrantly and repeatedly against it, and had destroyed it by his violences." Rather Hollis claims, "that it is to Milton, the divine Milton ... that we are beholden for all the manifold and unexampled blessings which we now every where enjoy."[10]

Today we hear from Frederic Jameson that Milton did not "imagine genuine human equality";[11] but from Annabel Patterson, in a clearly better informed study, we hear that Milton and the Good Old Cause he espoused "gave us the principles of modern democracy."[12] We discover that the radical side of such groups as the antinomians, as Joan Bennett has demonstrated,[13] had close connections with the ideas assumed and developed by Milton, but also that, according to Reuben Márquez Sánchez's decidedly pro–Roman Catholic position, he is devious, contradictory, and inconsistent in his uncompromising attitude toward toleration, falsely argued through false postures of liberty.[14]

On feminist issues we learn from Joseph A. Wittreich's researches that earlier women readers of *Paradise Lost* "held in their arms a text full of seemingly dead ideas, a text that was pronounced a corpse by their male counterparts, but they then proceeded to pronounce otherwise: 'Look there! look there! It lives.'"[15] Yet others like Anna Juhnke discover "remnants of misogyny" in the epic, largely because of a misreading of its last two books and a lack of understanding of the achievement of Milton's Eve.[16] Mary Wollstonecraft, I would point out, was a much better reader of Milton than some of our commentators today. In her first novel, for instance, she has her title character Mary remark, paraphrasing *Paradise Lost* 8.591-92: "That earthly love is the scale by which to heavenly we may ascend."[17] Like Raphael, Wollstonecraft has seen in Adam's intemperate statement just preceding this line a precursing of the Fall in his emphasis at both times upon the bodily. Wollstonecraft, of course, wants her reader to reject the societal commonplaces about women and men, not to champion one and condemn the other. One must ask after looking at much recent feminist argumentation against Milton and Milton's Eve (and Diane McColley's study and William Shullenberger's review of the matter provide excellent and defensible counters to such argumentation[18]) whether the argument is really with Milton—and whether he has really been read—or is the argument rather with the world of society, and business, and education, that is still dominated by patriarchal powers. If so, such a mindset does not allow for a defensible reading of his work. (In similar fashion the alleged problem of Milton's God is Empson's God and Empson's rejection of this concept of the godhead. Milton's God may not be your or my God but he is also not, in my case, the God Empson forged into Milton's epic. A justified view of Milton's God can emerge from Dennis Danielson's Good God and Michael Lieb's explorations of the Holy as well as of the dialogue in Heaven and the *odium Dei*. It is a god that Joan Webber so well discerned.[19])

That brings me to the third area noted earlier: the question of hierarchies and subordination. It has its pertinency to government, to man and woman, and to the interrelationships of all beings, including the angels, faithful or fallen, and even the godhead. Annabel Patterson has indicated the relationship of these seemingly separate issues of politics and genderizations when she writes, "the proto-feminist project of *Paradise Lost*, wherein Eve's desire to be 'more equal perhaps' (9:823) offers the reader (perhaps) yet another model of a future politics."[20] The usual male attitude—of the eighteenth century, at least—may be seen in Dr. John Trusler's (unpublished) remarks on women: "We have seen women lovely without beauty & handsome without being lively; it is gracefulness that causes this variation & strews a brilliancy over features that would be otherwise disagreable, as the Sun paints a showery Cloud with the colours of the rainbow. / Milton speaking of Eve says / Grace was in all her steps, Heav'n in her Eye / In all her gestures, dignity & Love."²¹ Milton, of course, can be one's spokesperson for such a view. But then, also in the eighteenth century, there is "The Maid's Soliloquy," which has as epigraph: "Hail wedded Love! mysterious Law! &c. / Our Maker bids—Increase!—who bids abstain, / But our Destroyer—Foe to god and Man!"

> It must be so!—MILTON, thou reason'd well!
> Else, why this pleasing hope, this fond desire,
> This longing after something unpossess'd!
> Or, whence this secret dread, and inward horror,
> Of dying unespous'd? Why shrinks the soul
> Back on itself, and startles at Virginity?
> 'Tis Instinct, faithful Instinct, stirs within us,
> 'Tis Nature's self that points out an alliance,
> And intimates an Husband to the Sex.
> Marriage! thou pleasing, and yet anxious thought!
> Thro' what variety of hopes and fears,
> Thro' what new scenes and changes must we pass!
> Th' unchanging state in prospect dies before me;
> But shadows, clouds, and darkness rest upon it.
> Here will I hold. If Nature prompts the wish,
> (And, that she does, is plain from all her works)
> Our duty and our int'rest bids indulge it;
> For the great end of Nature's laws, is Bliss!
> But yet—in Wedlock, WOMAN must OBEY!
> I'm weary of these doubts—the Priest shall end 'em!
>   Nor rashly do I venture loss and gain;
> Bondage and pleasure meet my thoughts at once;
> I wed—my Liberty is gone for ever;
> But, Happiness from time itself secur'd;
> Love first shall recompense my loss of freedom;
> And when my charms shall fade away, my eyes
> Themselves grow dim, my stature bend, with years;
> Then, virtuous Friendship shall succeed to Love;
> Then, pleas'd, I'll scorn infirmities and death,
> Renew'd, immortal, in a filial race!²²

One suspects that the author may have been a man, but there is nothing here that might not also suggest a woman facing the issue of the patriarchal state of life. The problems raised for woman are that in wedlock she "must OBEY!" and that though she loses liberty she may find happiness, which in time will transform "love" into "virtuous Friendship," and all of this within "a filial race!"

Milton and Milton's Eve as well as the "subordination" of the Son to the Father and also the position of Milton's Adam in the "filial race"—and we can extend this to the poetic sons and oedipal fathers—all suggest both hierarchy and independence, a political mix that I find in all of Milton's thought, a combination that has allowed him to be spokesperson for many people, even those espousing diametrically opposite causes. The unknown author of *The Censure of the Rota* (1660) took Milton to task for what he calls Milton's "seeming absurd and Contradictory" arguments concerning political, spiritual, and civil liberty. For example, he finds Milton contending "That every man may do what he pleases in matters of Religion, but onely those that are in Authority, who ought not to meddle in such matters."[23] If this epitome is accurate, it posits a person who argues for what would be considered freedom of thought and action but who also believes that two kinds of limitation exist for those exercising such thought and action. There is a separation of those who have the authority to exercise such thought and action from those who do not, and this implies some kind of hierarchical order for those with authority. While he would argue theoretically for freedom for all, he likewise recognized differences among people to the extent that some are incapable of exercising freedom intelligently. We might be thinking of those who mean license when they cry for liberty. Accordingly, he recognizes the need for doers and shakers and those who follow—"obey" perhaps the "doer," "serve" by standing and waiting to "obey" the shaker. Politically there is at least an administrative hierarchy in *Paradise Lost* and *The Ready and Easy Way to Establish a Free Commonwealth*, to name two obvious examples, and his own governmental employment moved in such hierarchical areas without, apparently, a demurral.

The seeming contradiction of liberty for all, though only some are capable of fulfilling the demands of liberty, and the conflict that hierarchy inflicts on those enjoying supposedly equal freedom are not uncommon phenomena. The fact of the matter is that Milton espouses the ideal concept of freedom for all when thinking theoretically; but when thinking practically, he recognizes the need for controls by those of warranted and capable authority. And as soon as the practicality of action is raised, delegation of duty—administrative position and interaction—becomes necessary, with a hierarchical chain of command emerging. At the head may be a Council of State, or a leader of such a group—and Oliver Cromwell's assumption of the Lord Protectorship in 1653 caused difficulties for Milton if we read his remarks in the *Second Defense* carefully—but the theoretical overview of Common Cause is supposed to nullify superiorities within that hierarchical chain. The concept of checks and balances that was to emerge after his death (and through the eighteenth century), and the further reliance on constitutionalism, were not specifically within his vision, although

George Sensabaugh has demonstrated his importance as That Grand Whig behind the forging of the new British political institution that exists on such checks and balances and sense of constitutionalism.[24]

The question of hierarchy, particularly in a work like *Paradise Lost*, is perhaps too colored by the implications of the term. While God stands at the head, he divides into a triune being with a subordinationism clearly stated between God the Father and God the Son, the division representing different functions of the godhead. In subordinate position are the angels, but these are in a military ordering (for whatever it is angels did before the rebellion of Satan), some kind of grouping with at least one individual angel (like Lucifer or Michael) having position over others. The position is administrative and military: such "hierarchy," if we can call it that, does not dispense with an equality of all in the group in matters other than whatever the administrative action controls. Yet the organization also sustains the contradictory view that there are some with and worthy of authority and some without, and those with position over the mass appear to be more than only one. The action of Abdiel poses the difference between hierarchy and equality, hierarchy being an administrative/military imposition on the group while equality is maintained in individual thought and being. Charles W. Durham has been pursuing the nature of the precedence that such individual thought and being has over the concept of hierarchical authoritarianism for Milton, through the example of Abdiel.[25] Diana Treviño Benet has examined both the Abdiel episode and the separation scene of book 9 to establish for us the realization that Eve does not err in exercising her individual being. Rather, she is a good example of what Milton would have praised, even though such an action leads to her innocent deceit by the experienced Father of Lies.[26]

While hierarchy may exist through separation of intelligence, ability, and the like, it is finally only administrative, setting up a chain of command based on function and ability. It is broken when a function is not carried out properly, when there is any usurpation that reduces individual equality of the group, when it exists only because of custom and self-interest—two important concerns of *The Tenure of Kings and Magistrates*. But subordinationism as a concept remains, not only by way of administrative hierarchies of function and ability.

We surely agree with William Kerrigan that the oedipal being of Milton is both celebratory and belligerent, as epitomized in the seeming opposition of father/son relationships of God and his Son and of God and Satan.[27] While the ego may act as rival to the father, the ego-ideal may rise to a dominant position in the structure of conscience, delimiting the superego, or, rather, making it part of the ego-ideal. But for the Son and for Satan, and thus for all sons of God, a question of the righteousness of the Father underlies the relationship. This has been stated often enough as the difference between the true and the false God, and true or false or half gods. The Son in book 3 of *Paradise Lost* celebrates the Father, but prior to his offer of himself, there is an underlying question about the Father's position, his attitude toward humankind. Belligerence is not the right word, of course, but the Son's is not a nonthinking acceptance. The Father rises to the occasion and shows himself, in the Son's eyes, a whole god, the true god. This is akin to Milton's relationship with his father in *Ad Patrem*; the record of Milton's life from 1638 shows that his father rose to establish himself as whole father, true father. The Son in *Paradise Lost* takes on the being of the Father as his surrogate, takes on the superego of the Father, that is, in his dealings with humankind in the Creation, the Judgment, and the Incarnation. The superego of the Father has become the ego of the Son. This, too, defines the poet's ego as an assumption of the superego of the oedipal father-poet.

Movement upward or downward within the hierarchical structure depends upon the worthiness of the respective persons within that hierarchy. Abdiel's challenge to Satan, his hierarchical superior, is a case in point—once Abdiel recognizes Satan's abrogation of his position under God. "Equality" exists in the essences that the three persons of God are, in the essences that Raphael and Michael and Gabriel are individually, and in the essences that Eve and Adam are individually. They are their individual selves, just as Milton is his individual self, in matters of self; but in matters of community, a hierarchy of administration cuts through. The positioning within the human hierarchy depends on abilities (or should), and so some are leaders who take on the concerns of those who are led. While Milton recognizes godly women who should lead and ungodly men who should not, he also believed in the subordination of woman to man since "Paul ends the controversy by explaining that the woman is not primarily and immediately the image of God, but in reference to the man," mixing divine and human subordinations.[28] Equality in a commonplace sense today does not appear in Milton's thinking in the realms of political or governmental life, social or family life, or indeed religious life: there continues for him the existence of a "rabble," and a subordination of son (or children) to true father and of wife to husband. The individual not only needs the proper regard for self and the selflessness toward others exhibited by the Son, but also the determination to act. This may lead to confrontation, which in turn will uncover falsity and reveal truth. In Milton's thinking, the political organization will allow human beings to keep in their ways by creating a force that will counter the opposition to this. (I refer, of course, to Psalm 91.11–12 and Satan's fraudulent misstating of it in the Temptation in the Wilderness in *Paradise Regain'd*.) Politically, Milton's belief may be epitomized thus: the worthy individuals should exercise their "ways," but an organization of able servants should exist to "keep them in their ways" against the forces that would lead to death, real or metaphoric, all under the subordination that he on high has set by his love.

It can be seen in my remarks, despite arguments that might be raised, that Milton provides varying kinds of evidence to be spokesperson for this group or that, this attitude and belief or that. As poetical mentor, he can be a father siring a Gerard Manley Hopkins, who does not need to "kill" his father in oedipal strife, or a William Mason, who should have. As religious and political mentor he can be the creative father of a Satan that John Wesley admonishes us to reject or of a Satan whom William Godwin saw as having "a sense of reason and justice . . . stronger in his mind, than a sense of brute force," one with "real compassion and sympathy for his partners in misfortune."[29] With that in our remembrance we better understand Godwin's *Caleb Williams* and his daughter's *Frankenstein* (has she rejected, as Freud would have us believe she might, her mother's teaching?), as well as Blake's assignment of Milton to unconscious brotherhood with the devil's party. We can lament that some readers will miss Milton's indictment of Adam as the more grievous disobeyer of his Father, who completed the act that "Brought Death . . . and all our woe" (*Paradise Lost*, 1.3) into being, those readers who do not comprehend the significance of Eve's being the last to speak in the epic, as the one who leads the repentance, as the one through whom salvation will come. We can lament that the two grandparents setting off on their solitary way indicates a oneness that equates equality, though each has a separate function, a separate essence, but a subordination in Milton's thinking that extends from God through all creation.

Notes

1. Among references for further information concerning this and the next two paragraphs, see Joan Webber, "Walking on Water: Milton, Stevens, and Contemporary American Poetry," *Milton and the Line of Vision*, ed. Joseph A. Wittreich (Madison: University of Wisconsin Press, 1975), 231–68; John T. Shawcross, "The Poet in the Poem: John Milton's Presence in *Paradise Lost*," *The CEA Critic* 48/49 (Summer/Fall 1986): 32–55; Shawcross, "Influence for the Worse? Hart Crane Rethinks Milton," *The Visionary Company* 1/2 (1983): 71–89; Shawcross, " 'They that dwell under his shadow shall return': Joyce's *Chamber Music* and Milton," *New Alliances in Joyce Studies: "When it's Aped to Foul a Delfian,"* ed. Bonnie Kime Scott (Newark: University of Delaware Press, 1988); Shawcross, "Further Remarks on Milton's Influ-

ence: Shelley and Shaw," *Milton Quarterly* 20 (1986): 85–92; Shawcross, *Milton 1732–1801: The Critical Heritage* (London: Routledge & Kegan Paul, 1972), 26–29, 135–47, 171–98.

2. John Milton, *Paradise Lost, The Complete Poetry of John Milton*, ed. John T. Shawcross, rev. ed. (New York: Doubleday, 1971). All references to Milton's poetry are to this edition and are cited parenthetically in the text.

3. See for references in these two paragraphs William Lauder, "An Essay on Milton's Imitations of the Moderns," *Gentleman's Magazine* 17 (1747): 24–26, 82–85, 189, 285–86, 363–64; Lauder, *An Essay on Milton's Use and Imitations of the Moderns in His "Paradise Lost"* (London, 1750); John Douglas, *Milton Vindicated From the Charge of Plagiarism, Brought against him by Mr. Lauder* (London, 1751); Lauder [and Samuel Johnson], *A Letter to the Rev. Mr. Douglas, Occasioned by his Vindication of Milton* (London, 1751); Lauder, *An Apology for Mr. Lauder* (London, 1751).

4. For additional references in this paragraph, see Shawcross, *The Critical Heritage*, 342–43 (Hawkins), 28 and 33 (Murphy), 259–84 (Monbaddo), 290–310 (Johnson), 217–22 and 200–16 (Johnson); and Stephen Fix, "Johnson and the Duty of Reading *Paradise Lost*," *ELH* 52 (1985): 649–71. Johnson's works are: "Life of Milton," *Prefaces, Biographical and Critical to the Works of the English Poets* (London, 1779), vol. 60 of *Works* and vol. 2 of *Prefaces*; [*Samson Agonistes*], *The Rambler*, no. 139 (16 July 1751) and no. 140 (20 July 1751); [Versification of *Paradise Lost*], *The Rambler*, no. 86 (12 January 1751), no. 88 (19 January 1751), no. 90 (26 January 1751), no. 94 (9 February 1751).

5. Some of these particulars are discussed in John T. Shawcross, *John Milton and Influence: Presence in Literature, History and Culture* (Pittsburgh: Duquesne University Press, 1991).

6. Christopher Wordsworth, *"Who Wrote Eikon Basilike?" Considered and Answered. In Two Letters, Addressed To His Grace the Archbishop of Canterbury* (London, 1824), and *Documentary Supplement to "Who Wrote Eikon Basilike?"* (London, 1825).

7. Joseph Addison, "An Account of the Greatest English Poets," *The Annual Miscellany: For the Year 1694. Being the Fourth Part of Miscellany Poems*, ed. John Dryden (London, 1694), 321–23.

8. Thomas Yalden, "On the Reprinting of Mr. Milton's Prose-Works," *Oxford and Cambridge Miscellany Poems*, ed. Elijah Fenton (London, [1709?]), 177–78.

9. Sir John Hawkins, *The Life of Samuel Johnson* (London, 1787), 243–44.

10. Thomas Hollis, *Memoirs of Thomas Hollis, Esq.*, ed. Francis Blackburne (London, 1780), 92–94.

11. Frederic Jameson, "Religion and Ideology," *1642: Literature and Power in the Seventeenth Century*, ed. Francis Barker et al. (University of Essex, 1981), 336.

12. Annabel Patterson, "Imagining New Worlds: Milton, Galileo, and the 'Good Old Cause,'" *The Witness of Times*, ed. Katherine Keller and Gerald Schifshorst (Pittsburgh: Duquesne University Press, 1993), 238–60.

13. Joan S. Bennett, *Reviving Liberty: Radical Christian Humanism in Milton's Great Poems* (Cambridge: Harvard University Press, 1989).

14. Reuben Márquez Sánchez, "'The Worst of Superstitions': Milton's *Of True Religion* and the Issue of Religious Tolerance," *Prose Studies* 9 (1986): 21–38.

15. Joseph A. Wittreich, *Feminist Milton* (Ithaca: Cornell University Press, 1987), 153.

16. Anna K. Juhnke, "Remnants of Misogyny in *Paradise Lost*," *Milton Quarterly* 22 (1988): 50–58.

17. Mary Wollstonecraft, *Mary: A Fiction* (London, 1788), 107.

18. Diane Kelsey McColley, *Milton's Eve* (Urbana: University of Illinois Press, 1983), and William Shullenberger, "Wrestling with the Angel: *Paradise Lost* and Feminist Criticism," *Milton Quarterly* 20 (1986): 69–85.

19. See William Empson, *Milton's God*, rev. ed. (London: Chatto & Windus, 1965); Dennis Danielson, *Milton's Good God: A Study in Literary Theodicy* (Cambridge: Cambridge University Press, 1982); Michael Lieb, *Poetics of the Holy: A Reading of "Paradise Lost"* (Chapel Hill: University of North Carolina Press, 1981); Lieb, "The Dialogic Imagination," chapter 6, 76–97, *The Sinews of Ulysses: Form and Convention in Milton's Works* (Pittsburgh: Duquesne University Press, 1989); Lieb, "'Hate in Heav'n': Milton and the *Odium Dei*," *ELH* 53 (1986): 519–39; Joan Webber, "Milton's God," *ELH* 40 (1973): 337–41.

20. Annabel Patterson, "The Good Old Cause," address at the University of Central Florida's Conference on the Arts and Public Policy.

21. John Trusler, "Essays on the Affairs of Life," British Library. MS Additional 28121, f. 11.

22. Anonymous, *South-Carolina Gazette*, 4 March 1751.

23. Anonymous, *The Censure of the Rota* (London, 1660), 11–12.

24. George Sensabaugh, *That Grand Whig, Milton* (Stanford, Calif.: Stanford University Press, 1952).

25. Charles W. Durham, "'To stand approv'd in sight of God': Abdiel, Obedience, and Hierarchy in *Paradise Lost*," *Milton Quarterly* 26 (1992): 15–20.

26. Diana Treviño Benet, "Abdiel and the Son in the Separation Scene," *Milton Studies* 18 (1983): 129–43; Benet, "'No Outward Aid Require': A Note on Eve in Separation," *ANQ* 2 (1989): 90–94.

27. William Kerrigan, *The Sacred Complex: On the Psychogenesis of "Paradise Lost"* (Cambridge: Harvard University Press, 1983).

28. John Milton, *Tetrachordon* (London, 1645), 3.

29. William Godwin, *An Enquiry Concerning Political Justice* (Dublin, 1793), 242.

Part II
Spokesperson for Theological and Spiritual Concerns

The Fruitless Tree in *Paradise Lost*: Symbol of Sin

ALICE M. MATHEWS

In *Milton: Poet of Exile*, Louis Martz examines John Milton's kinship with Ovid, particularly in a shared vision of the poet as creative exile. In developing his thesis, Martz discusses those heroic similes in *Paradise Lost* that reflect the "chearful waies of men," thereby asserting Satan's failure to destroy the human spirit.[1] One of the similes that Martz cites is the account of the fig tree in book 9. This passage, says Martz, "somewhat alleviates the effect of the Fall," because it describes the tree's benefit to humankind.[2] The validity of Martz's claim, however, is somewhat questionable because it ignores the alarming implications of some of the simile's allusions.

The context of the passage is Adam and Eve's recognition of their nakedness and search for a tree with leaves that can be fashioned into garments. The simile begins with their choice of the fig tree:

> there soon they chose
> The Figtree, not that kind for Fruit renown'd,
> But such as at this day to Indians known
> In Malabar or Decan spreads her Armes
> Branching so broad and long, that in the ground
> The bended Twigs take root, and Daughters grow
> About the Mother Tree, a Pillar'd shade
> High overarch't, and echoing Walks between;
> There oft the Indian Herdsman shunning heat
> Shelters in cool, and tends his pasturing Herds
> At Loopholes cut through thickest shade: Those leaves
> They gather'd, broad as Amazonian Targe,
> And with what skill they had, together sew'd,
> To gird thir waist, vain Covering if to hide
> Thir guilt and dreaded shame; O how unlike

> To that first naked Glory. Such of late
> Columbus found th' American so girt
> With feather'd Cincture, naked else and wild
> Among the Trees on Isles and Woody Shores.
> (9.1100 –18)³

The tree that Adam and Eve select is likened to a particular species that grew on the Persian Gulf. Europeans knew it as the banyan tree, so called because the Hindu traders, or Banians, built pagodas under its umbrellalike structure.⁴ In the seventeenth century, there were numerous accounts of the tree such as John Gerarde's *Herball*, Ben Jonson's *Neptune's Triumph*, and Sir Walter Ralegh's *History of the World*—all of which Kester Svendsen cites as possible sources for Milton's description.⁵ However, determining a specific source is less significant than examining how the poet used the information—which is my purpose here.

In the comparison of the fig tree in Eden to the Indian fig tree, the first relationship they share is negative; both trees are barren of fruit. Ascribing fruitlessness to the tree contradicts other accounts of the tree,⁶ such as Gerarde's, which specifically describes the "fruit, of the bigness of a man's thombe, in shape like a small Fig . . . of a sweete taste."⁷ Milton's departure from such accounts is highly provocative, particularly in light of the rich meanings associated with the word *fruit*, which Jean Graham has catalogued. As Graham notes, "to limit our understanding of 'fruit' to a merely literal level . . . would be to imitate Satan, who comprehends nothing of the total structure of meanings inherent in 'fruit.'"⁸ Although Graham shows that Milton sometimes uses "fruit" to mean both good and evil results,⁹ biblical references to the fig tree associate fruitlessness only with evil. In Habakkuk 3.17 the fig tree's barrenness reveals God's indictment and punishment of humankind's wickedness: "the fig tree *shall* not blossom, neither *shall* fruit be in the vines."¹⁰ Numerous references in the New Testament extend the analogy between fruitfulness and righteousness. Christ calls himself the vine and his followers the branches, who "bringeth forth much fruit" (John 15.5). When Christ tells the parable of the vineyard owner who condemns the barren tree—"I come seeking fruit on this fig tree, and find none: cut it down"—Christ clearly draws on the parallel between fruitlessness, and spiritual impotence and decay (Luke 13.7). A barren tree, therefore, is ironically apt, for its leaves are used to cover the sexual organs of Adam and Eve: a fruitless tree to conceal the reproductive organs of the pair, now shorn of virtue by their violation of the forbidden fruit.

Another likeness that the fig trees share is luxuriant growth, broad branching "Armes," the twigs of which take on a life of their own by rooting in the ground. The description is one of fecundity, for the twigs, still part of the mother, fall to the earth, take root, and "rise again as daughters."[11] The fig tree then represents the paradoxical conditions of barrenness and fertility. These contradictory positions are verbalized just before the Fall when Satan takes Eve to the forbidden tree. She describes their coming as "Fruitless to meè, though Fruit be here to excess" (9.648). In the sense of fruit as representative of righteousness, her following of Satan is indeed "fruitless." Christopher Ricks observes another truth in Eve's pun, that "there is indeed fruit 'to excess.'"[12]

The tasting of the fruit has other implications. One of the maxims from *Regimen Sanitatis Salerni* of 1634 is that figs produce lust, and Ralegh mentions the opinion of Becanus, that the Tree of Knowledge is the Indian fig tree. Although Milton employs the traditional apple as the forbidden fruit and denies the fruitful condition of the banyan, the existence of such traditions imbues the tree with rich possibilities—one tree for sin and for the evidence of sin.[13] In its fecundity the tree yields no fruit but only daughter-reproductions, as lust produces not righteousness but offspring. As had been promised, Eve's womb is still fruitful although her spiritual condition is barren.

Anticipation of the tree as a microcosm of sexuality occurs in earlier passages, as in the description of Adam and Eve about their nurturing duties:

> On to thir morning's rural work they haste
> Among sweet dews and flow'rs; where any row
> Of Fruit-trees overwoody reach'd too far
> Thir pamper'd boughs, and needed hand to check
> Fruitless imbraces: or they led the Vine
> To wed her Elm; she spous'd about him twines
> Her marriageable arms, and with her brings
> Her dow'r th' adopted Clusters, to adorn
> His barren leaves.
>   (5.211–19)

Here the trees and vine are imbued with sexual powers, rendering them fertile or, if misdirected, barren. Later in book 9 when Eve proposes dividing their tasks, she argues the need for more efficient labor:

> what we by day
> Lop overgrown, or prune, or prop, or bind,

> One night or two with wanton growth derides
> Tending to wild.
>
> (209–12)

According to Christopher Ricks, "wanton" at first means "undisciplined, disobedient" but ends with the connotation of lustful, thereby combining the reason for the Fall and its immediate effects.[14]

Another common quality of the fig trees is the picture of pastoral life that they embody. This quality is most likely what leads Martz to attribute an optimistic view of humankind's destiny to the simile. Note the lines that describe the effects of the tree's unusual growth:

> a Pillar'd shade
> High overarch't, and echoing Walks between;
> There oft the Indian Herdsman shunning heat
> Shelters in cool, and tends his Pasturing Herds
> At Loopholes cut through thickest shade.
>
> (9.1106–10)

The picture is one of serenity, of cool respite amid the heat of the day, and an apparent answer to Adam's agonizing cry for refuge from the bright radiance of heaven:

> Cover me ye Pines
> Ye Cedars, with innumerable boughs
> Hide me.
>
> (9.1088–90)

Milton's use of Gerarde's *Herball* is suggested by the description of "echoing Walks," the Indian herdsman, and the loopholes:

> Through the thickest part [of the tree] ... they cut certaine loope holes or windowes in some places ... that they may see their cattle that feedeth thereby ... from which vault or close walke, doth rebound such an admirrable eccho, or answering voice.[15]

The scene, however, is no mere pastoral painting but an example of highly charged irony. As James Whaler has observed, the peacefulness depicted in these few lines brings into sharp relief the inward turmoil of Adam and Eve, the "high Passions, Anger, Hate" (9.1123), which have replaced their once calm state.[16] One recalls a previous use of the phrase "shade high overarch't," when Satan and his legions were compared to

> Autumnal Leaves, that strow the Brooks
> In Vallombrosa, where th' Etrurian shades
> High overarch't imbow'r.
> (1.302–4)

Shade there was not a respite but a threat. Just as no Arcadia awaited Satan in Hell, there is no haven for Adam and Eve within the leafy walls of the tree. Only the Indian herdsman can find sanctuary here.

As the peacefulness of the scene is deceptive, so is the security that the tree appears to offer. The Indian herdsman who rests within its leafy interior cuts holes in the foliage to allow him a view of his herds, a practice also mentioned in *Herball*[17] and in *Comus* (138–40). While protected, the herdsman can watch his flocks. Recalling the wolf who easily invades the pen of the "secured" sheep in book 4, the reader concludes that security is an illusion. As Eden is "Ill fenc't for Heav'n to keep out such a foe / As now is enter'd" (*Paradise Lost*, 4. 372–73), so are Adam and Eve "ill fenc't" to resist the suffering engendered by the foe's treachery.

The "protective" nature of the tree extends to its leaves, "broad as Amazonian Targe" (9.1111), and broad enough to guard the shame of Adam and Eve. In comparing the size of the leaves to the shield or target of Amazons, Milton is not original. Jonston's *History of the Wonderful Things of Nature* notes the same similarity.[18] However, in the context of the passage, the comparison is particularly suitable. The comparison of the leaves to the defensive instrument of the shield is consistent with the tree's protective quality. Furthermore, the size of the leaves is stressed by the reference to Amazons, a fabled race of great, female warriors. A Greek legend told of the Amazons' destroying the right breast to prevent its interfering with the bow; they mutilated their bodies to enhance their own security.[19] The irony of their enterprise parallels that of Adam and Eve's use of the leaves: "vain Covering if to hide / Thir guilt and dreaded shame" (9.1113–14).

One of the most interesting passages in the fig tree account is the comparison of Adam and Eve to the American Indian:

> O how unlike
> To that first naked Glory. Such of late
> Columbus found th' American so girt
> With feather'd Cincture, naked else and wild
> Among the Trees on Isles and Woody Shores.
> (9.1114–18)

Technically this is a separate simile, but it serves to expand the meanings suggested by the fig tree. At first there seems to be a confusion in the use of "Indian." Identifying America with the Orient was common in the seventeenth century and probably resulted from seamen's habit of calling all remote and rich countries by the name of India.[20] However, Milton does not adopt generalizations unless they suit his purpose, so one must look for reasons apart from tradition.

A "fit" reader of Milton's day would recognize the references to Malabar and Deccan as locations in India and the fig tree as indigenous to that area. The herdsman tending his flocks would also be associated with that part of the world. Why then does Milton evoke the East only to transfer the scene to the opposite side of the globe, to the American native, "With feather'd Cincture, naked else and wild"? (9.1117).

John Rumrich's rebuttal of Stanley Fish's argument concerning the similes of the first two books suggests one explanation. Observing the frequency of "indefinite exclamations of dismay" such as "How unlike!" "how fall'n! how chang'd!" in those similes, Rumrich disagrees with Fish's contention that the first two books exalt Satan and his cause.[21] Instead, Rumrich argues, the similes of these books seem to "express the shiftiness of a locale" governed by ambiguity. The effect is one of continual instability and confusion, qualities that Milton thus associates with the fallen.[22]

Rumrich's observation of a shifting of locale as suggestive of the fallen also pertains to the passage about the Native American, as indicated in the "How unlike!" exclamation and in the more literal geographical movement. I contend, however, that Milton's shift in place has significant historical meaning as well as the psychological meaning that can be deduced from Rumrich's argument.

To discover the historical meaning, one must determine what qualities Milton might have associated with both India and America. One possible source of his information is the popular seventeenth-century book on cosmography by Peter Heylyn. Heylyn describes the people of Malabar who "are of coal-black colour" and who wear "about their middle a cloth, which hangeth down to conceal their nakedness." He then relates the treachery and barbarity of these inhabitants, who war with poisoned arrows and who sacrifice the virginity of their daughters by impaling them upon a gold bodkin of their idol.[23] In his account of Deccan, he describes the fantastic wealth of that area but adds that the people are "a Mongrel body of Chiftians, Mahometans, and Centiles, acknowledging no common Parent, nor agreeing in Language, Customs, or Religion." The word *Decan* represents this amalgamation in its meaning of "illegitimate brood, or a body of Bastards."[24] Therefore, in at least one account of Milton's day, Deccan and Malabar are associated with vulgarity, at best, and savagery, at worst.

Seventeenth-century notions of the Native American are strikingly similar. Benjamin Bissell explains that because America was commonly confused with China and India, many of the marvels attributed to the East were naturally transferred to the new land.[25] Peter Heylyn even suggests that the natives of America descended from the Tartars, whose barbarity they emulate. Like the seventeenth-century view of the Tartars, the image of the American native is primarily one of cruelty and savagery. Early histories relate frightening encounters with Native Americans and accounts of cannibalism and human sacrifice to the devil. Pictures of the half-naked savage bedecked with feathers and indulging in unspeakable atrocities are found in much of the travel literature of Milton's time, such as Theodore DeBry's *Discovering the New World*. Debry's collection, published in Frankfurt between 1590 and 1634, was an important influence on the European aesthetic conception of the Native American, a conception that has, in its notion of vulgarity, barbarity, and paganism, features common to their image of India.[26]

Despite the image of the American as a fierce savage, there was also among Milton's contemporaries a tendency to regard the American Native as a simple, harmless being, exploited and provoked to brutality by adventurers. In 1658 Sir William Davenant's opera, *The Cruelty of the Spaniards in Peru*, brought Native Americans to the stage in a production that focused on their suffering.[27] Although the opera's run was unsuccessful, the existence of such a sympathetic approach suggests a mitigating attitude toward the Native American.

Benjamin Bissell mentions another mitigating factor in shaping the seventeenth-century image of the American—the legend of an earthly paradise vaguely located far out in the western ocean, a paradise where inhabitants lived in peace and harmony. Parts of this legend appeared in the *Decades* of Peter Martyr, a work quite popular all over Europe by the early 1600s. With the increasing awareness of America, this legend was easily applied to the Native American, and the western land, imagined as a kind of "primitive Arcadia."[28]

The comparison of Adam and Eve to the American is thus wonderfully appropriate, from the more superficial similarities of their nakedness and crude attempts to cover their bodies to the more profound charge of heathenish debauchery. The barbarity attributed to the savage is that of the human race—a legacy of the Fall. In the description of the savage, naked and wild, "Among the Trees on Isles and Woody Shores" (1118), one is reminded of Adam and Eve's seeking refuge among the trees in the garden. The use of the *New* World mirrors the original new world of Eden, and the phrase "of late" emphasizes this quality of "newness." (As John Leonard points out, in *Paradise Lost* "late" usually means "recently."[29]) Also, tempering the negative connotations associated with the pair and with the savage is a compassion for their naiveté and their suffering and a grief for their paradise, now corrupted.

The effect of the simile is heightened by a retrospective view of the poem. As Jonathan Collett has observed, a noticeable phenomenon of *Paradise Lost* is the rich use of classical myths in the prelapsarian similes,[30] one of which compares Adam and Eve to Jupiter and Juno:

>   hee in delight
> Both of her Beauty and submissive Charms
> Smil'd with superior Love, as Jupiter
> On Juno smiles, when he impregns the Clouds
> That shed May Flowers; and press'd her Matron lip
> With kisses pure.
>   (4.497–502)

The contrast of such a passage with the savage, "naked else and wild," is arresting. From god and goddess to naked savages, their transformation recalls the metamorphosis of the fallen angels from "Earth's Giant Sons / Now less than smallest Dwarfs" (1.778–9).

The noble carriage and naked dignity that mark the appearance of Adam and Eve in book 4 evaporate in the figure of the feather-clad pagan, the fulfillment of Adam's earlier plea:

>   O might I here
> In solitude live savage, in some glade
> Obscur'd.
>   (9.1084–86)

As the savage reflects their degradation, so does the fig tree correspond to their fallen state. Milton's previous use of plant imagery, "the Garland wreath'd for Eve / Down dropp'd, and all the faded Roses shed" (9.892–3), and the description of Eve, "Defac't, deflow'r'd, and now to Death devote" (901), prepare for the fig tree as a symbol of sin.

The allusions to India and to the American native, as well as the lust and barrenness associated with the fig tree, thus seem to contradict Martz's optimistic reading of the simile. The disparity is not surprising given the large critical consensus that the epic simile in *Paradise Lost* is "Milton's most conspicuous device for eliciting and then correcting fallen response."[31] Although Stanley Fish and his adherents find that tension most common to the first two books, where the majority of the great similes are found, the fig tree passage also produces a similar effect, that of raising and then defeating expectations. If the passage contains a glimmer of hope concerning the human condition, it lies not in the pastoral serenity provided by the branching arms of the tree, but rather in the reference to the American. The tree of sin will never bear fruit, but Adam and Eve, even as naked savages, will. And it is their fruit—the Son—who will ultimately redeem humanity.

In defining the spiritual condition of Adam and Eve in geographical and scientific terms, Milton gives a literal sense to inward experience, a precision and objectivity to the abstract concept of sin. And in the linking of East and West, the poet achieves a kind of wholeness that suggests not humanity's "chearful waies" but its universal woe.

Notes

1. Louis L. Martz, *Milton: Poet of Exile* (1980; New Haven: Yale University Press, 1986), 88.
2. Martz, *Poet of Exile,* 90.
3. John Milton, *Paradise Lost, John Milton: Complete Poems and Major Prose*, ed. Merritt Y. Hughes (New York: Odyssey Press, 1957). All references to Milton's poetry are to this edition and are cited parenthetically in the text.
4. *Oxford English Dictionary*, 1:652.
5. Kester Svendsen, *Milton and Science* (Cambridge: Harvard University Press, 1952), 31.
6. Svendsen, *Milton and Science,* 31.
7. John Gerarde, *The Herball or Generall Historie of Plantes* (1597; Norwood, N.J.: Walter J. Johnson, 1974), 2:1331.
8. Jean E. Graham, "Fruit So Various: A Word Analysis in *Paradise Lost,*" *Milton Quarterly* 24 (1990): 26.
9. Graham, "Fruit So Various," 27.
10. All biblical references are to the King James Version and are cited parenthetically in the text.
11. Svendsen, *Milton and Science,* 135.
12. Christopher Ricks, *Milton's Grand Style* (Oxford: Oxford University Press, 1963), 74.
13. Svendsen, *Milton and Science,* 134.
14. Ricks, *Milton's Grand Style,* 145.
15. Gerarde, *Herball,* 2:1331.
16. James Whaler, "The Miltonic Simile," *PMLA* 46 (1931): 1058–59.
17. Gerarde, *Herball,* 2:1331.
18. Svendsen, *Milton and Science,* 32.
19. Guy Cadogan Rothery, *The Amazons in Antiquity and Modern Times* (London: Francis Griffiths, 1910), 26.
20. Peter Heylyn, *Cosmographie in foure Books . . .* , 5th ed. (London: Anne Seile, 1677), 3:204.
21. John Peter Rumrich, "Uninventing Milton," *Modern Philology* 87 (1990): 259.
22. Rumrich, "Univenting Milton," 260.
23. Heylyn, *Cosmographie,* 3:204.
24. Ibid., 3:202–3.

25. Benjamin Bissell, *The American Indian in English Literature of the Eighteenth Century* (New Haven: Yale University Press, 1925), 1.
26. Bissell, *American Indian*, 4–5.
27. Ibid., 118–19.
28. Ibid., 3–4.
29. John Peter Leonard, "Language and Knowledge in *Paradise Lost*," *The Cambridge Companion to Milton*, ed. Dennis Danielson (Cambridge: Cambridge University Press, 1989), 104.
30. Jonathan Collett, "Milton's Use of Classical Mythology in *Paradise Lost*," *PMLA* 85 (1970): 94.
31. Rumrich, "Uninventing Milton," 250.

No Fortunate Fall, No "Unfeared Second Fate": Satan and the Critique of Meliorism, *Paradise Lost*, Book 2

CATHERINE GIMELLI MARTIN

> Henceforth I learn, that to obey is best,
> And love with fear the only God, to walk
> As in his presence, ever to observe
> His providence, and on him sole depend,
> ... that suffering for Truth's sake
> Is fortitude to highest victory,
> And to the faithful Death the Gate of Life.
> (12.561– 64, 569–71)[1]

These final, sobering words of Adam, a summary of what he has learned from the lengthy course of Michael's biblical history, cast a considerable shadow over his celebration of the Redeemer's final victory a hundred lines earlier. Dennis Danielson has argued that this later attitude expresses the predominant mood of *Paradise Lost*'s conclusion, a cautious optimism scarcely compatible with the complete vindication implied by the doctrine of the fortunate fall. Alternating between intuitive accuracy and enormous error in his response to Michael's visions, Adam's earlier exclamation must thus be understood as a naturally joyful but not fully considered response to the human condition:

> O goodness infinite, goodness immense!
> That all this good of evil shall produce,
> And evil turn to good; more wonderful
> Than that which by creation first brought forth
> Light out of darkness!
> (12.469–73)

Not only does a close reading of this exclamation fail to support Arthur Lovejoy's claim that the poem endorses the theology of the *felix culpa* (a claim that has become a somewhat pernicious "cliché of Milton studies"), but also helps to explain why Lovejoy regarded Milton's theology as "amazingly superficial."[2] Regarding Adam's fall as fortunate destroys the Arminian or "free will" defense of God, conflicts with the broader context of the poem, and undermines its theodicy. Yet even in the immediate context of the passage in question, Adam quickly qualifies his hope of complete exculpation:

> *full of doubt* I stand
> Whether I should repent me now of sin
> ... or rejoice
> Much more.
> (12.473–76; emphasis mine)[3]

Later his perplexity is further intensified when he reflects upon the fate of the faithful remnant (479–84) who, because of his sin, will frequently fall prey to "th' unfaithful herd, / The enemies of truth" (481–82). Beset by the overwhelming opposition of the many, the few cannot hope even figuratively to reassemble the scattered body of truth in the present social order—the redemptive aim implicit in the quasi-sacramental doctrine of *felix culpa*, but rejected by the Protestant individualist as at once deluded and idolatrous.[4] Milton's goal is almost precisely the opposite: to shatter premature optimism about our rehabilitation in order to promote a self-denying fortitude, the true path "to highest victory."

Yet in charting the poem's uniquely "middle flight" between Catholic optimism and Calvinist pessimism, Danielson eschews speculation upon the more concrete ethical objectives of its sobering yet not hopeless course. Observing that *Paradise Lost* does *not* provide a "comic" justification of Adam's fall that would make ours "the best of all possible worlds"—a perspective more compatible with Dryden or Pope than with Milton—he omits any consideration of the factors that virtually require the poem to satirize such views.[5] Like that of Voltaire's Candide, the epic quest of Milton's Satan is as concerned with exposing pseudophilosophies as with promoting its own. In the process, optimism, meliorism, "preordained harmonies," and every other form of the myth of progress are traced to the fallen Panglosses of the world, the silver-tongued "enemies of truth" whose original "gloss" is Satan himself.[6] In contrast to these adversaries of humnity and God, the "corrected" Adam neither glosses over the hardships nor diminishes the prospects of the human journey. Thus as Christopher Hill remarks, like Samson's, his objective is to escape from history as circular treadmill . . . [to] become free to choose the good [since] . . . there will be no miraculous intervention by an external Saviour merely because we impatiently expect it. It is Satan who offers short cuts.[7]

Ethically as well as philosophically, then, satanic meliorism and Miltonic pragmatism offer two diametrically opposed attitudes toward the human condition.[8] Like a good Calvinist, Satan regards himself as already fated to be either "doomed" or "saved"; he can only play out his sense of himself on the vast stage of the *theatrum mundi*; whether hero or villain/victim, the transcendental aloofness of the divine puppet-master allows the suffering sinner to take on attributes of either or both alternatively. The Miltonic hero has no such excuses. Not actor, but coauthor of an improvised performance, he does not merely display but vitally transacts his role in the arena of moral, spiritual, and social salvation.[9] Of course, neither view is without its price. The first offers at least the illusion of a limitless subjectivity, as well as the imminent expectation of a triumphant round of applause—unless, like Satan, we are peremptorily hissed off the stage (10.545–47). Inevitably, then, it leads from romantic self-assertion to an unbounded cycle of objectification, a denial of legitimate otherness due to the demands of the illegitimate self.[10] The latter view, on the other hand, pays its price first; its freedom is founded upon acceptance of transcendental loss and the recovery of only a "wand'ring" form of revelation (11.335–54). Yet while accompanied with the shedding of some "natural tears," it yields a "higher" and less dependent selfhood capable of encountering the limitless horizon wherein "The World was all before them, where to choose / Thir place of rest, and Providence thir guide" (12.646–47).

Thus the pleasures of this ending, if not as pure as worldly optimists like Dryden might wish, are ultimately as real as the pleasures of the "paradise within."[11] Because this resolution entails the rejection of either fully comic *or* tragic "solutions" to the questions of history, it provides an alternative escape, an Other *as well as* Self-actualizing means of avoiding the "wand'ring mazes" in which the demons are lost (2.561). Nevertheless, before they are lost in these mazes, the demons serve the useful purpose of demonstrating the wrong responses to the unavoidable questions that all fallen creatures must ask: Can an apparently *un*fortunate fall be rectified, and if so, what *kind* of "second fate" will take its place? Since an understanding of the wrong answers to these questions provides the necessary background both to an understanding of Adam's fall and of Michael's historical overview of fallenness, the consequences of these wrong answers are appropriately illustrated first in the microcosm of Milton's Hell. There the reader first begins to grasp why any doctrine providing an "automatic" escape from the treadmills of history is actually opposed to authentic optimism and freedom. Instead, it produces not only "woe to mankind" through satanic misappropriation, but woe to demonkind through a self-deluded philosophic system that seems to support but only enslaves them.

While the working of this woe is ultimately no more simple than that of the truth that sets humanity free, its first manifestations already show signs of the relativism and reductivism that will eventually engulf all of Satan's subjects along with himself. Almost at once the demons begin to compose pagan epics lamenting the "injustices" of "Fate" (2.550) and to invent circular exercises in dialectical theology. Too early to mock Leibnitz or the other eighteenth-century meliorists, Milton nevertheless manages to satirize many of their predecessors and perhaps their progeny. In particular, Hell, home of the father of philosophical lies, is portrayed also as the mother of the *felix culpa*, the queen of its theological muddles. Assuming a privileged status similar to that of Sin, whose "attractive graces" subdue even the most skeptical demons, this doctrine springs full-grown from the head of Satan, its chief benefactor and beneficiary (2.755–67). Summoning it into existence through a process of rhetorical inflation and inverted logic that resembles his daughter's in both style and substance—the substance being their policy of mutual increase—Satan rallies his troops to further resistance by turning a bitter acknowledgment of defeat (1.84–93) into a virtual assurance of victory (1.118–24). Part false prophet, part falsifying politician, this forebear of the historical Caesars and Antonys—and dramatic descendant of Shakespeare—must perform a seemingly impossible task: not only of convincing his army that they remain undefeated, but that their quite visible loss is actually a gain. With appropriate irony, Satan bases his "proof" of his victory on what he has lost, his immortal, god-given condition:

> For since no deep within her gulf can hold
> Immortal vigor, though opprest and fall'n,
> I give not Heav'n for lost.
>
> (2.12–14)

This leap of logic provides the groundwork for his later "justification" of the demonic doctrine of the fortunate fall. Not hesitating to soar where Adam later fears to tread, he further claims that

> From this descent
> Celestial Virtues rising, will appear

More glorious and more dread than from no fall
And trust themselves to fear no second fate.
(2.14 –17)

Yet the most insidious aspect of Satan's proclamation that a Phoenix-like, unearned glory will spontaneously arise from the ashes of their "Immortal vigor" (13) is not its illogic but its tendentiousness. Thus while neither their former substance nor the fact of their fall can prove anything but their now terminated connection to the divine source of light and life, the success of Satan's boasts do demonstrate the demons' continuing allegiance to the promises of inalienable privilege that first won them to his cause. What this in effect means is that Satan can be a Caesar without fearing the opposition of a Brutus. Nevertheless, like any good politician, he is always on guard against counterrevolutionary applications of his own doctrine. In order to disarm potential challenges to his dubious conflation of free assent/ascent, these rhetorical stratagems thus lay the basis of an empire disguised in the trappings of a democracy, a totalitarian domain of doublespeak made possible by the mental and moral sloth of his subjects. If only in this ironic sense, his "election" *does* then proceed from "just right and the fixt Laws of Heav'n" (18), just as he claims: their common wrongs and his greater vigilance have made these subjects "rightfully" his. Additionally, not only "in Counsel or in Fight" (20) has he won his title to this hellishly "safe unenvied Throne / Yielded with full consent" (23–24), but won it through his ability to conceal in council the actual *aftermath* of their fight. Hence his half-truths serve to conceal the potentially damaging fact that since their consent has *always* been conditional upon his ability to thwart real or apparent dangers to their status—either through the leveling effect of the Son's "promotion," or the far graver consequences of their "second fate"—his rule inevitably *remains* conditional upon his ability to supply at least the illusion of ascent.

Because of his awareness of these precarious conditions, both the military strategies and strategic propaganda planned in conjunction with Beelzebub are designed to circumvent the weaknesses inherent in his position. Both demons understand the hollowness of his claim that since the War in Heaven was glorious and their current enterprise yields only the "greatest share / Of endless pain" (29–30), his supremacy will necessarily remain uncontested. Not only did *all* their pains begin with their first blows against God (6.327, 452– 64), but like any defeat incurred by a usurper or tyrant, this one could lead to a challenge of the losing general's authority. As a result, Satan's aim is to recall, only to blur and bury, these events in the half-light of meretricious hope and spurious honor, rousing them to the tyrant's tune of military pomp and circumstance and enlisting their allegiance to a nationalist program founded upon his "divine right" and their "manifest destiny." Of course, the moral price of these anodynes is ruinously high: an easeful death that ushers them into oblivion, not millennium; and a deathful ease that ensures their compliance in exchange for their complicity. Politically the price is equally as high, as the scenes set in the secret chambers of Pandemonium have already suggested. Based upon a purported "unity" already undermined by its secret conclaves, Satan's promises of limitless fellowship and prosperity are obviously intended to gain the abject inequality and vassalage that are at once his goal and, in the last analysis, his fate:

> where there is then no good
> For which to strive, no strife can grow up there
> From Faction; for none sure will claim in Hell
> Precedence, none, whose portion is so small
> Of present pain, that with ambitious mind
> Will covet more. With this advantage then
> To union, and firm Faith, and firm accord,
> More than can be in Heav'n, we now return
> To claim our just inheritance of old,
> Surer to prosper than prosperity
> Could have assur'd us.
> (2.30–40)

From this starting point, the same brilliant sophistry that here allows Satan to pose as the idol of liberté, egalité, and fraternité, inevitably *requires* him to become the golden calf of the myth of progress. By conflating authentic faith and freedom with the advance of a "surer prosperity," he successfully distracts the "ambitious minds" of potential rivals and conveniently directs them toward less strenuous, if nominally "heroic," paths. In this sense, at least, his linguistic strategies accurately reflect his political aims; both proclaim a "firm Faith" whose real accord lies in a mutually agreed upon distortion of the facts. The most superficial of inquiries would reveal that Satan's "just inheritance" is an egregious euphemism for just punishment, and that his promises of "prosperity" depend upon a reductive definition of the word: it can no longer mean "increasing in fortune or happiness," but merely *increasing*. Yet once they accept these linguistic substitutions, Satan can "honestly" assure them that they will prosper better *without* prosperity—that is, without divine favor. By thus twisting etymologies and promoting an empty work ethic, Satan's mind indeed becomes "its own place" (1.254), the rhetorical placeholder of Hell.

Further, by converting the meaning of *union, faith*, and *harmony* to connote unquestioning servitude to him, he parodies and displaces the real communion modeled by the Father and Son, a dialogue in which harmony is based upon difference.[12]

Thus book 2 begins first by foreshadowing the later devolution of the Prince of Hell and then focuses on the first effects of Satan-speak among his followers. These effects are shown to be greater both in proportion to their victims' literalistic investment in them and to the mental or moral sloth that encourages that investment. Yet ironically, the most consistent effect upon the adherents of satanic meliorism is nihilism, an effect easily seen among all the orators who speak in the council of Hell. It is perhaps most obvious in Moloch, a spirit readily inclined to violent and extreme remedies. Nevertheless, Moloch's motive in advocating a renewal of "open War" (51) also stems from the influence of the satanic doctrine of manifest destiny, the idea that "descent and fall / To us is adverse" (76–77). If the pun on *adverse* is *inadvertent* on the part of the fallen angel, it is scarcely so on the part of the poet. Moloch is above all adverse to "descent and fall," but only his nihilistic self-delusion can convince him that it is therefore adverse to him. In the long run, this simplification of an already reductive case is a potential source of embarrassment to Satan, in that it actually hinders his disguised intent—not the direct retaliation, but the complicit consolidation of his forces. To accomplish this, he needs to assure his cohorts that "ascent is easy" (81), and then to delay them from putting the proposition to the test. This plan can be furthered not by facing, but only by *appearing* to face, realities that must be indefinitely avoided; any actual confrontation is an "event [to be] fear'd" indeed (82). These designs are particularly jeopardized by Moloch's stoical definition of success; he prefers dying forever rather "Than miserable to have eternal being" (98), and punishing himself rather than awaiting punishment. Even more ironically, because his straightforward assessment has more in common with the newly fallen Adam's honest fears than with Satan's tortured rationalizations, it too obviously displays the hollow core of their shared escapism. Lacking real hope or purpose, both succumb to despair; if unable to ascend, they can resolve only to fall quickly and finally into oblivion (2.99–101, 10.852–56).

Yet if baldly nihilistic, impolitic, and inopportune, Moloch's guess that their semideferred engagement with God must ultimately be resolved one way or the other is close enough to the truth that the more optimistic of the self-deluded demons automatically repress it. This is, of course, no mean feat, since even in abeyance, the Almighty's power over them is hardly nonexistent; not only does it debar them from light and its attendant joys, as here, but it later forces them to perform a yearly repetition of their own and humankind's fall, as they discover when their "victory" celebration turns into a writhing, hissing imitation of Satan's deceit (10.515–21). In this respect Moloch's perception that neutrality is impossible as well as undesirable only underscores the even more fantastic escapism that Satan's doctrine of the fortunate fall typically produces in his peers. These delusions are especially embodied in the character of the next speaker, Belial, the unrepentant advocate of the deathful ease that will lead them all to gradual destruction. Taking up satanic ideology from the extreme opposite position, he recommends making the best of what is at least not the worst of all possible worlds, "for his thoughts were low; / To vice industrious, but to Nobler deeds / Timorous and slothful" (2.115–17). Yet precisely because Belial promotes an unheroic form of meliorism remote from that envisioned by either Satan or Moloch, his remarks shed light on the inherent fatalism of the philosophy even when divorced from militarism or imperialism. For much the same reason, his approach eloquently illuminates its universally degrading consequences.

In contrast with Adam's final resolve to endure despite the hardships of his "second fate," Belial's solution is paradoxically less pragmatic and less truly optimistic. Despite, and even because of, the stoical sentiments in which he disguises his epicurean sensuality, his disbelief in God's continuing opposition only thinly conceals his own failure of will and lack of integrity. His commitment to a policy of neutrality thus rests upon two related errors: a disbelief in divine justice and a disbelief in the need for individuals to come to terms with it. By this means, the vision of a "necessary" or spontaneous rather than a just basis for ascent is linked to a dream of irresponsibility, a puerile fantasy less realistic but not ultimately more nihilistic than Moloch's. Yet at the same time that Belial errs in thinking that an unassailed Almighty might "forget" to exact full justice, his cowardice at least makes him fully cognizant of Moloch's chief oversight, the fact that since God *remains* almighty and unassailable,

> our great Enemy
> All incorruptible would on his Throne
> Sit unpolluted, and th' Ethereal mould
> Incapable of stain would soon expel
> Her mischief.
>
> (2.137–41)

This undeniable truth, one that the reader will actually see enacted as God's "immortal Elements" "purge off" our Grand Parents from Eden (11.50–54), results in a deadlock between the two positions. If Moloch's is impracticable, Belial's is illogical. Nor is this parallelism surprising, given that both make the error of conflating two incompatible objectives: a reascent to heaven, and a continuing rejection of its dictates. The parallel extends to their final outlook, which in either case resembles the position Belial complains of in Moloch: "our final hope / Is flat despair" (2.142–43). Thus both demons propose programs too obviously fatalistic and self-destructive to be palatable to the others. Moloch's fanatic aggression is as objectionable as Belial's blithe passivity, his cringing acceptance of the fact that

> since fate inevitable
> Subdues us, and Omnipotent Decree,
> The Victors will. To suffer, as to do,
> Our strength is equal, nor the Law unjust
> That so ordains.
>
> (2.197–201)

Thus thinking to illuminate the hidden power, Belial reveals only the hidden weakness of stoicism, the same philosophy scornfully rejected by the Redeemer of *Paradise Regained*.[13] The reasons for that rejection are even clearer here, where Belial's banal equation of individual fortitude and eternal Law parody the complex coordinates of Christian integrity. By placing its hope in inevitable historical cycles, it seeks actually *only* to suffer, not to do. Here as elsewhere, the demonic tendency to objectify the more mysterious ways of God's "second fate" causes sound inferences to yield empty conclusions. Hence Belial's groundless hope that the Almighty may "remit / His anger" (210–11) and "Not mind us not offending" (212) degenerates into circuitous, vapid doggerel:

> these raging fires
> Will slack'n, if his breath stir not thir flames.
> Our purer essence then will overcome
> Thir noxious vapor, or enur'd not feel,
> Or chang'd at length, and to the place conform'd
> In temper and in nature, will receive
> Familiar the fierce heat, and void of pain;
> This horror will grow mild, this darkness light,
> Besides what hope the never-ending flight
> Of future days may bring, what chance, what change,
> Worth waiting, since our present lot appears
> For happy though but ill, for ill not worst.
>
> (2.213–24)

Here stoical meliorism becomes its own parody, its vague expectations of automatic ascent exhibiting only Belial's downward spiral into ever greater accommodation of evil, as long as evil can be redefined as good—thus fusing the emotional corruption of a *Brave New World* with the linguistic corruption of a *1984*. Belial's audience thus immediately perceives that his advice is inauthentic:

> words cloth'd in reason's garb
> [that] Counsell'd ignoble ease, and peaceful sloth
> Not peace.
>
> (226–28)

All too accurately this counsel reflects his complete alienation from a divine ray that only in his imagination will ever make "this darkness light."

As if to underscore the point that there can be no redemption apart from divine mercy and individual acceptance of "the better fortitude / Of Patience and Heroic Martyrdom" (9.31–32), the next demon's counsel falls between the horns of the dilemma created by the arguments of the preceding speakers without actually extricating himself from either. Although Mammon not only spots but even "corrects" the more glaring errors in Belial's logic, his proposal is no real improvement. In the place of "ignoble ease," he proposes a more energetic and worldly-wise yet equally futile form of meliorism—an active in place of a passive plan of self–incrimination. However, superficially Mammon's program is not only more appealing but far more practicable; so practicable, in fact, that it is destined to supply an important ingredient in Satan's general design. Shrewdly isolating the common weakness in the positions of both previous speakers, Mammon points out that both rely upon an unrealistic assessment of Chance, a force that can hardly be depended upon to supply their recovery (2.229–37). Yet because Mammon is a kind of secular Calvinist, one who proposes to "seek / Our own good from our selves . . . to none accountable" (2.252–53, 255), he is especially singled out to illustrate the most subtle of the dangers inherent in self-made forms of meliorism: its false assessment of worldly pleasure as opposed to godly pains. As Adam's corrected understanding later attests, only those of contrite heart and "sorrow unfeign'd" (10.1092) can know the authentic joy and hope of repentance, and only they can see that in their Judge's face, "When angry most he seem'd and most severe, / What else but favor, grace, and mercy shone?" (1095–96).

Mammon thus becomes a central figure in the debate both because he improves upon and also because he shares the delusion of the other two. Rejecting the "servile Pomp" of Heaven (2.257), he nevertheless hopes not merely imaginatively but materially to replicate, even to outdo, its splendors. Like the voice of worldly ambitions and worldly gods that he is, he improves upon Belial's pseudo-Stoicism by cloaking its self-aggrandizing aims in a pseudo-Christian work ethic. He thus claims that their "greatness will appear" (257)

> when great things of small,
> Useful of hurtful, prosperous of adverse
> We can create, and in what place soe'er
> Thrive under evil, and work ease out of pain
> Through labor and endurance.
> (258–62)

This noble rhetoric, already suspect in the mouth of Mammon, the chief contractor of Pandemonium, will later be fully discredited as the exact inversion of the reeducated Adam's ideal, always "with good / Still overcoming evil, and by small / Accomplishing great things" and thereby *subverting* "worldly strong, and worldly wise / By simply meek" (12.565–69). Like Adam's irrevocable expulsion from ease without pain, the circumstances of his renewed resolution thus expose the inherent weakness of Mammon's progressivism, plainly refuting the fallen assumption that creatures may live well, in fact thrive, in alienation from God, by taking advantage of the divine "calling" to rise inherent in God's "one first matter" (5.472). As Raphael explains to Adam, the internal limitation placed upon this matter's tendency to return to God is his subjects' refusal to be "deprav'd from good" (5.469–71). By extrapolation, then, Mammon's meliorism is tenable only on the basis of a neoclassical or Calvinist dualism, a divorce of spiritual from material works that the inspired poet everywhere rejects. Because in *Paradise Lost* the workings of the spirit represent *tendencies* but not fully visible *or* invisible realities (except in time),[14] any work ethic that separates worldly pleasures from divine grace is as distorted as one that conflates them. Both may be regarded as a reversed Manichaeanism: a supposedly beneficial but actually detrimental separation of the spiritual and material forms of the Good.

Like other heresies, the inherent lack of viability of this reversed Manichaeanism does not prevent its power; its ethical and political consequences are as real as those of other forms of delusion. Thus not only does it produce a "splendid" Pandemonium, but *will* produce all those other edifices of human pomp and tyranny from Babel to the present. Although these will, Babel-like, ultimately fall, their final extermination is neither especially imminent nor especially progressive. Michael's history reveals a saga of erratic recurrences, an ongoing yet concretely unpredictable succession of peaks and valleys, a nightmare with but one certain escape. Hence like the doctrine of the fortunate fall, the demonic creed that time will somehow "remove / The sensible of pain" (2.277–78) contains a dangerous form of half-truth. Both doctrines place their faith in a guaranteed *temporal* recovery based solely on the "miracles" of individual effort or external circumstance, and both expect the restoration of lost glory without an authentic struggle for reconciliation either with God's laws or their correct application in his material universe.[15] Therefore, both demean the Son's act of atonement even while taking advantage of its temporal dispensation. Like the demons who "hail the Horrors" of Hell and welcome their newfound "freedom," the adherents of these doctrines conveniently forget the extent to which redemption bestows greater glory *only* upon God and his Son, not on either his opposers, for whom it creates pains innumerable, or even on his forgiven progeny, who gain fruits of love without loss of pain. The latter, too, will suffer and die; even the faithful remnant cannot expect more from divine sacrifice than an uneven balance of hardship and good will (12.477). In the very best of circumstances, glory can be gained only at the hard price of *two* "heroic martyrdoms," their own and the Son's.

While the most successful demagogues always grasp this painful truth, they use it only to further their own destructive ambitions. Unlike the naive and slothful Belial, they understand this situation in order to control it, and to retain their power have struck the devil's bargain: to sacrifice the true ascent accorded the few for the approval and consent of the many. Hence unlike the more naive meliorists who precede them in the council of demons, Beelzebub and Satan do not so much subscribe to the sanguine platitudes of the *felix culpa* as find it useful in extending their reign in Hell and on Earth. They know that like Belial and Mammon, most of the demons will prefer comfortable platitudes to the truly strenuous requirements of "Hard liberty" (2.256). Although by now they cannot repent, their fate parallels that of human philosophers who will not; their dream of prospering in terms of a purely evanescent prosperity will make them easy prey for tyrants and demagogues of varying hues. Beelzebub's next task is thus a relatively simple one. Calling attention to the fatal flaw in even Mammon's scheme—its failure to account for the opposing forces of the Almighty—he "corrects" this flaw by offering them a substitute Savior. Because without *some* god on its side—chance, fate, or Satan—the myth of progress collapses, and since the former two have been examined and found wanting, Beelzebub's maneuver thus rounds out the reader's understanding of the inevitably idolatrous basis of the myth and its origins. Finally, it also draws attention to the inevitability of warfare between the "unfaithful herd" and the lovers of truth, for, as Beelzebub warns them, no "peace will be giv'n / To us enslav'd, but custody severe" (2.332–33).

Of course, like Satan himself, Beelzebub is adept at drawing his audience's attention to harsh realities in order to placate them with false solutions. To the slothful herd who desire no "dangerous expedition" (342) but "Some easier enterprise" (345), the luxury of believing that they are not "Hatching vain Empires" (378) will turn out to depend upon remitting their sovereignty into Satan's hands, the final move finessed by the Father of Lies in league with the Lord of the Flies (378–80). It finds its appropriate climax in an acceptance speech whose repeated double entendrés raise the self-parodic element of the performance to a deafening crescendo. Yet ironically, the promises founded upon these double meanings disclose as much as they conceal about the actual fate that awaits those putting faith in a fortunate fall. Since *like what they are*, the demons have "Great things resolv'd" (392), Satan predicts that their "resolve"

> Will once more lift us up, in spite of Fate,
> Nearer our ancient Seat; perhaps in view
> Of those bright confines, whence with neighboring Arms
> And opportune excursion we may chance
> Re-enter Heav'n; or else in some mild Zone
> Dwell not unvisited of Heav'n's fair Light
> Secure, and at the bright'ning Orient beam
> Purge off this gloom; the soft delicious Air,
> To heal the scar of these corrosive Fires.
> (2.393–401)

This glorious misalliance of realism and utter fabrication allows us to see Satan himself as the fullest flower and finest satire of the meliorist impulse. Characteristically substituting the euphemism "fate" for any more direct and thus dangerous allusion to the "Almighty," he ultimately traps himself in his own circumlocutions in a way that unintentionally reveals their consequences. As he promises, his imperialistic expedition will allow them to enter the more "soft delicious Air" of a milder zone, a place in fact "nearer our ancient Seat." Yet not only will this "ascent" merely succeed in making earth more hellish, but in the process Satan will discover that its psychic pains increasingly follow him *everywhere* (4.75). For this and a number of related reasons, he cannot heal but only worsen the scarred substance of those to whom "all good . . . becomes / Bane" (9.122–23). Once these qualifications are taken into consideration, Satan's myth of progress not only loses considerable attraction, but becomes a "second fate" actually to be feared—a fall both more agonizingly fatal than the first, and of far greater duration than the quick end Moloch had envisioned.

Thus Satan's pose as the redeemer who makes a self-sacrificing journey through "the coasts of dark destruction" in order to win "Deliverance for us all" (2.464 – 65) is exposed as a hollow substitute both for Christ's redemption and for the individual *struggle* necessary to avail oneself of it. Those who place their faith in this kind of progress reap not only the hollow reward they sow, but pains far greater than those they sought to avoid: the pains of godly repentance and faith. In contrast, true victory demands both an initial acknowledgment of sin and a lifelong confrontation with it, whether in the form of external "enemies of truth," or the internal enemy within, the easeful, sensual self. Yet its benefits are actually incomparably greater than its costs: both in this world and the one to follow, false hope produces slavery and death, while true hope yields freedom and life. Finally, then, the darkest aspect of our "second fate" is that defeat will always be most probable when most palatable, when posed as some false assurance or false messiah offering easy victory along with easy slavery.[16] Yet its bright side is equally assured, if not equally easy to grasp: that divine mercy and justice will still be available to direct the "wand'ring steps and slow" of imperfect humans, who, with their assistance, will still advance in freedom and grace (3.185–97). Thus our sad "second fate" can be overcome—not by accepting the premature bliss of the *felix culpa* or any of its melioristic progeny, but only by acknowledging the consequences of Adam's most unfortunate fall.

Notes

This work originally appeared as "Self-Raised Sinners and the Spirit of Capitalism: *Paradise Lost* and the Critique of Protestant Meliorism" in *Milton Studies* 30 (1994): 109–133. This revised version is published by permission of University of Pittsburgh Press.

1. John Milton, *Paradise Lost*, *John Milton: Complete Poems and Major Prose*, ed. Merritt Y. Hughes (New York: Odyssey Press, 1957). All references to Milton's poetry are to this edition and are cited parenthetically in the text.
2. Dennis Danielson, *Milton's Good God: A Study in Literary Theodicy* (Cambridge: Cambridge University Press, 1982), 202. Arthur O. Lovejoy's general remark on Milton's theology appears in *The Great Chain of Being: A Study of the History of an Idea* (New York: Harper & Row, 1936), 212.
3. Lovejoy of course does not deny that Adam expresses this initial doubt, but somewhat hastily decides that "an intelligent reader could hardly have failed to conclude that the doubt was to be resolved in favor of the second [celebratory] alternative" (168). See Arthur O. Lovejoy, "Milton and the Paradox of the Fortunate Fall,"

ELH 4 (1937): 161–79. Danielson's critique of this essay appears in *Milton's Good God*, 224–27.

4. Danielson notes that the majority of sources Lovejoy uses in establishing Milton's use of the doctrine are Roman Catholic, the most prominent of these of course being the *Exultet* from the Roman liturgy. Further, the Protestants who embraced the doctrine were chiefly Calvinists who differed from Milton on this as on a number of other theological points; see *Milton's Good God*, 207–10.

5. Danielson, *Milton's Good God*, 205–7.

6. Although Voltaire's Pangloss is not satanic per se, it is hardly far-fetched to link him to an institution that both Milton and Voltaire considered a force for evil, the Church of Rome. Thus while "comic" readings of the epic have been attempted, as in F. W. Grandsen's article, "Milton, Dryden, and the Comedy of the Fall," *Essays in Criticism* 26 (1976): 123, they face virtually insurmountable problems, as I show below. The opposite or "tragic" approach taken by Frank Kermode, if equally extreme, is actually far more convincing from a textual point of view. See "Adam Unparadis'd" in *The Living Milton*, ed. Frank Kermode (London: Routledge and Kegan Paul, 1960), 85–123.

7. Christopher Hill, *Milton and the English Revolution* (London: Faber and Faber, 1977), 386.

8. For an excellent examination of Milton's skeptical pragmatism, see Donald L. Guss, "Enlightenment as Process: Milton and Habermas," *PMLA* 106 (1991): 1156–69.

9. Here I am assuming a continuity between traditional religious and secularized or progressivist optimism; for Milton, both appear to be satanic in source, the former because of its transcendental escapism, the latter for its politico-social escapism. For an important examination of the changing meaning of the *theatrum mundi* in the late Renaissance, see Jean-Christophe Agnew, *Worlds Apart: The Market and the Theatre in Anglo-American Thought 1550–1750* (Cambridge: Cambridge University Press, 1986).

10. This aspect of Satan is skillfully examined by Keith Stavely in *Puritan Legacies: "Paradise Lost" and the New England Tradition, 1630–1890* (Ithaca: Cornell University Press, 1987), 92ff.

11. Earlier efforts to discredit the idea that the poem promotes the optimistic theology of the *felix culpa* include Earl Miner, "*Felix Culpa* in the Redemptive Order of *Paradise Lost*," *Philological Quarterly* 47 (1968): 43–54, and Virginia R. Mollenkott, "Milton's Rejection of the Fortunate Fall," *Milton Quarterly* 6 (1972): 1–5. However, while valuable, these relatively brief treatments overlook the point at issue here, that Milton prepares the reader to reject this concept from the very beginning of the poem, in Hell itself. The preeminence given this rejection thus confirms its central importance in Milton's theology as a whole, a facet of the "Unfortunate Fall" that Danielson acknowledges, but is only tentatively able to make; see *Milton's Good God*, 226–27.

12. For an excellent discussion of this "alternate" dialogue, see Michael Lieb, "Milton's 'Dramatick Constitution': The Celestial Dialogue in *Paradise Lost*, Book III," *Milton Studies* 23 (1987): 215–40.

13. Hence, although Malcolm Kelsall convincingly argues that the hero of *Paradise Regained* is a historically and biblically informed *type* of stoic individual, *contra* Christ's, Belial's stoicism is shallow, corrupt, and *mis*informed. See Kelsall on "The Historicity of *Paradise Regained*," *Milton Studies* 12 (1978): 235–51.

14. For Time, though in Eternity, appli'd
   To motion, measures all things durable
   By present, past, and future.
   (5.580–82)

15. Of course, in spite of this similarity, there are many differences; the temporal recuperation envisioned by the *felix culpa* is sacramental, while that of secular Calvinism is a complex blend of material and social distinction. However, as I suggest, both promise a species of symbolic reward that the poem frames as both illusory and insubstantial.

16. Thus Joan S. Bennett argues that the chorus of *Samson Agonistes* remain unregenerate due to the same mistake made by Satan and his deluded demons. Seeing Samson's victory, the chorus facilely conclude that "All is best," and that "God must have wanted Samson to sin all along so that he could engineer the catastrophe." However, Bennett argues that although Samson *is* regenerated, the choral exultation in his *felix culpa* remains unjustified: "A subsequent event cannot justify a former event, an event cannot by itself justify a means." For this reason, the chorus remain chained to the letter rather than the spirit of the law. See *Reviving Liberty: Radical Christian Humanism in Milton's Great Poems* (Cambridge: Harvard University Press, 1989), 138ff.

"By Faith to Stand": Faith in the Theodicy of *Paradise Lost*

JOHN S. TANNER

Fifty years ago, C. S. Lewis summarily pronounced the concluding books of *Paradise Lost* to be "an untransmuted lump of futurity," a "grave structural flaw" in Milton's grand design.[1] Since then, as William Kerrigan remarks, there has been a sea change in critical opinion: "today we know for certain, in a manner that Lewis himself would have admired, that 'futurity' has been transmuted with all the architectural power one expects from this poet: Milton hath quit himself like Milton."[2] Kerrigan cites with approval Samuel Richardson's lavish praise of the poem's power to "calm and purify the mind . . . to exalt and fix it to the mysteries, sublimities and practices of religion; to a state of tranquility and happiness, the uttermost mortality is capable of."[3] Somehow Milton's conclusion induces even ideologically disparate readers to make peace with the world—a world the final books explicitly acknowledge to be infected with suffering, sin, sorrow, and death. Somehow the conclusion dispels the theological problem of evil not solely (or even, perhaps, mainly) by convincing its readers so much as by moving and calming them, as Richardson attests. The conclusion works in part because, like the Book of Job, *Paradise Lost* "solves" the dilemmas of theodicy not only conceptually, with answers and arguments, but dramatically, with confessions by Adam and Eve of their renewed willingness to obey, love, and walk by faith.

To establish the importance of faith in Milton's theodicy, I shall focus on two climactic passages in book 12: Adam's outburst of joy upon learning that, through the Atonement, good shall finally triumph over evil; and Adam's second, more subdued exclamation that closes his discourse in the poem. Milton's ending succeeds as theodicy, I believe, because it couples the eschatological consolation of the first speech with the existential solace of the second; because it moves from the distant promise of a paradise to come to the immediate task of creating a "paradise within." Ironically, Milton defends Heaven less effectively when he *justifies* God's ways argumentatively, in a voice from on high, than when he *asserts* Eternal Providence artistically, in a voice at our shoulder of a vulnerable narrator or of a contrite Adam and Eve. Adam's meek concluding expressions of love and commitment are more eloquent and sustaining responses to alienation than any propositional distillation of Milton's "great argument" could be. Surely this is one reason why Milton's poem is more satisfying as a theodicy than is Pope's. Milton's ending saturates the mystery of evil with faith in this world and in the next. It does *not* presume to answer all the questions that vex theodicy, but sends forth its readers, like Adam and Eve, into a harsh world better prepared to walk by faith. Faith is the essential, but often overlooked, element in Milton's theodicy.

Before pursuing this point, let me first express a word of caution about the concept of *theodicy*, an Enlightenment coinage from Leibnitz for an intellectual enterprise that often does more mischief than good. It is easy to strike a false note when discussing the so-called problem of evil. One must always remember that theodicy is more than a logical conundrum requiring some cleverly worked out moral algebra to balance God's goodness on the one hand with human suffering on the other. Theodicy is made humanly urgent, even imperative, because personal spiritual concerns agitate intellectual dilemmas. Therefore, one should never speak abstractly about death, disease, alienation, and so forth—as I must in this essay—unless the human realities summoned forth by such terms shadow the discourse at every point.

For this reason, when presenting an oral version of this essay in Tennessee, I began by evoking names I had just taken off tombs of a nearby Civil War graveyard. Walking through the cemetery, with Ken Burns's documentary enlivening the somber autumn scene, I felt again the familiar stabbing pain in my heart that has often caused me and countless others to cry, "Why, God, why!" I ached for the dead soldiers and for the parents, wives, children, and friends they left behind to make sense of mortality. Such anguish should never be far from any reflection about theodicy. Nor is it far from Milton's great epic about loss and restoration, which from the opening lines situates itself in the midst of "all our woe" (1.3).[4] Milton's text aims at reconciling its readers to such woe. It does this most frontally in the final vision of salvation history Adam and Eve receive from the archangel Michael.

The emotional climax of Michael's history (and, some readers feel, of the entire poem) occurs for Adam when Jesus' redemptive mission of atonement is finally made plain. Then Adam rejoices to "understand

/ What oft my steadiest thoughts have searcht in vain" (12.376 –77). Having learned of the Lord's promised victory at the end of the world, Adam is beside himself with wonder and joy. In one of the poem's most famous passages he expostulates:

> O goodness infinite, goodness immense!
> That all this good of evil shall produce,
> And evil turn to good; more wonderful
> Than that which by creation first brought forth
> Light out of darkness! full of doubt I stand,
> Whether I should repent me now of sin
> By mee done and occasion'd, or rejoice
> Much more, that much more good thereof shall spring,
> To God more glory, more good will to Men
> From God, and over wrath grace shall abound.
> (12.469–78)

Echoing Paul's dictum "where sin abounded, grace did much more abound" (Romans 5.20), Adam's talk of *felix culpa* lifts the poem from the somber, tragic notes (9.6) occasioned by the Fall, to a mood more like the original peace and bliss of Paradise, if not more joyful.

Yet Adam's joy does not warrant attributing to the poem simplistic notions of a fortunate fall, which, largely through the influence of Arthur O. Lovejoy, had "become a kind of cliché of Milton criticism" until Dennis Danielson's impressive critique.[5] Adam's speech articulates neither the full nor final utterance in *Paradise Lost* about the conditions characterizing human salvation. Note, for example, how fleeting is Adam's ecstasy. Even by the end of his colloquy with Michael, Adam is much more subdued. Moreover, despite the elation he expresses in this joyful *felix culpa*, Adam never fully recovers a "paradise within . . . happier far" in the course of the poem (12.587). This paradise remains only a bright possibility that Michael locates specifically on the horizon of Adam's expectation, a condition toward which he is urged to strive rather than a blessedness he has yet attained (12.574 – 87). Michael's prophecy that

> the Earth
> Shall all be Paradise, far happier place
> Than this of Eden, and far happier days
> (12.463– 65)

similarly remains a prospect set in the future, in this case in a far distant eschatological future. Not till the end of time will Earth become a new Eden.

In the meantime, Adam and his posterity have to live by faith amid adversity. Michael's prophecies fail to fully dispel the great grief Adam and Eve have traversed; indeed, the final vision actually alloys their tranquility with sorrow. Adam descends from the mountain of vision "greatly instructed," "greatly in peace" (12.557, 558)—but such peace as he enjoys has had to be won in a world of woe. Adam's postlapsarian peace must survive deeply disturbing visions—of Abel "Rolling in dust and gore" (11.460), of a ghastly catalogue of human maladies in the Lazar-house (11.477–93), and of the sad and sorrowful saga that constitutes fallen history. Adam has also had to find solace despite his personal alienation and guilt. Similarly, Eve awakens from her "gentle dreams" "calmed" and "composed" yet also subdued and chastened. Michael predicts that she will live "cheer'd" "though sad" (12.595–605).

Truly, then, Adam's joyous outburst "O goodness infinite, goodness immense!" provides neither the last nor a complete measure of his or the text's concluding tone. Rather, *Paradise Lost*'s closing tone resembles that of Shakespeare's final plays. It blends extremities of grief and joy, encompassing feelings aroused by a world ransomed and one destroyed (cf. *The Winter's Tale* 5.1.15). Adam and Eve are cast out of Eden exactly as per the charge God gave to Michael: "sorrowing, yet in peace" (11.117); not singing "Happy Days" but wiping away "Some natural tears" (12.645). Within the poem's final consolation, there remains ample room for death, sickness, betrayal, heartache, and the whole gamut of human anguish as we now know it. Milton's closure makes place for the world that lies between Genesis and the Book of Revelation—for history, for us.

If the world that lies "all before them" (12.646) as Adam and Eve leave Eden looks familiar, it is because it *is* our world. As Wayne Shumaker aptly observes, the final books turn *Paradise Lost* "homeward" (12.632), "toward Milton and his seventeenth-century readers and toward us": "Milton sensed, as the best writers have always done, that literature ought ultimately to reconcile and strengthen, to return the audience to the everyday world with enhanced willingness to meet the stresses of living."[6] Another, perhaps deeper, term for "enhanced willingness" is *faith*, the consummate consolation *Paradise Lost* has to offer either Adam and Eve or the reader.

"To the faithful," says Adam, "Death [is] the Gate of Life" (12.571). These sentiments come near the end of Adam's second outburst of hope, his final speech in the poem. I find this speech and Michael's exhortation that follows it far more affecting than Adam's earlier outburst of *felix culpa* ("O goodness infinite . . ."). Adam's final exclamation, beginning "How soon hath thy prediction" (12.553), is quieter, less grandly cosmic, and more firmly situated in the human than the first. The first expostulation belongs to a discourse of metaphysics; the joy it anticipates pertains to an eschatological paradise not to be realized till the end of history. The second speech anticipates a paradise located in history and within pitiable, fallen, recognizably human creatures, who must make their lonely way through an alien world. This second consolation belongs to a discourse of faith in and for the world—a faith that has made peace with this harsh world without despising it, a faith that embraces human experience with gratitude and hope. I quote Adam's speech at length:

>   and thus Adam last repli'd.
> How soon hath thy prediction, Seer blest,
> Measur'd this transient World, the Race of time,
> Till time stand fixt: beyond is all abyss,
> Eternity, whose end no eye can reach.
> Greatly instructed I shall hence depart,
> Greatly in peace of thought, and have my fill
> Of knowledge, what this Vessel can contain;
> Beyond which was my folly to aspire.
> Henceforth I learn, that to obey is best,
> And love with fear the only God, to walk
> As in his presence, ever to observe
> His providence, and on him sole depend,
> Merciful over all his works, with good
> Still overcoming evil, and by small
> Accomplishing great things, by things deem'd weak
> Subverting worldly strong, and worldly wise
> By simply meek; that suffering for Truth's sake
> Is fortitude to highest victory,
> And to the faithful Death the Gate of Life;
> Taught this by his example whom I now
> Acknowledge my Redeemer ever blest.
>   (12.552–73)

From first to last, this poised and gracious response to the divine is firmly emplaced in the human. Adam commences by specifically recognizing his human limitation and concludes by taking strength from the humble example embodied in the human ministry of a suffering, meek Jesus (in contrast to the conquering, triumphant Christ who animated Adam's initial joy). As mere mortals, Adam admits, there is much we do not comprehend of "Eternity, whose end no eye can reach." What we need, in our weakness and ignorance, is to obey, to love, to trust in God's merciful providence and to cooperate in his work of bringing good out of evil. Compared to the "worldly" great, strong, and wise, the faithful may seem small, weak, and foolish, but precisely through these despised qualities they shall prevail. This, however, does not mean good people will be successful in a superficial sense. Just the reverse. The meek and faithful often will suffer and die, as did their Redeemer, whose praise comprises the last lines Adam speaks in the poem. Yet somehow, through a coalescence of human fortitude and divine grace, the Lord will turn defeat into victory and death into life.

This promise of renewed life includes, but is not limited to, hope for a "blissful eschaton" at the resurrection.[7] Hence, Adam's consolation eludes the Nietzschean critique, as William Kerrigan summarizes it, "that the postulate of a transcendent world debases and devalues this world."[8] Adam's faith in an afterlife cannot be construed as "another of the poisons that taint this life"; nor does it denigrate this life as something to be "tolerated because of a life to come."[9] Rather, while properly overjoyed at the prospect of the world's ultimate renewal, Adam receives back the fallen world as a graced heavenly gift, to be embraced in love, in the same way he and Eve receive each other after Michael's visions. Like them, the world is flawed but also blessed.

The poem's conclusion meets the challenge of theodicy most effectively not by addressing questions of why there should be death and disease but by renewing, in Adam and Eve and in the reader, a sense of gratitude for this flawed world, such as it is. An inverse relation exists between feelings of gratitude and the emotions that energize complaints against Heaven. Louis Mackey's comments on the relation between gratitude and theodicy illuminate the final posture of Adam and Eve: "life itself, whatever it may contain of happiness or of misery, is a gift of God . . . which man should receive with gratitude." Gratitude leaves little room, Mackey continues, for "attempts to figure out what He [God] meant by pain and evil." In fact, though it is entirely understandable that rational creatures should desire theodicy, "what such a man wills is the death of God" by the reduction of life into fully transparent moral categories. Our religious duty is to love God and the life we are given, through "weal and woe," and to trust that all things shall ultimately work together for the good of those who love God.[10]

By the end of *Paradise Lost* Adam likewise learns to trust. He learns that by faith, virtue, patience, temperance, and love, *this life*—whatever its hardships—may become more abundant, even paradisal. As Michael tells Adam, completing the poem's climactic concluding insight:

> only add
> Deeds to thy knowledge answerable, add Faith,

> Add Virtue, Patience, Temperance, add Love,
> By name to come call'd Charity, the soul
> Of all the rest: then wilt thou not be loath
> To leave this Paradise, but shalt possess
> A paradise within thee, happier far.
> (12.581–87)

Drawn from the 2 Peter 1.4–8, this sublime comfort is specifically aimed at fitting Adam to live blessedly in a fallen world. By the end of the poem Adam, like Milton, has assimilated loss and is learning to trust—sometimes "in spite of" rather than "because of" life's experiences, but always with hope rather than contempt for this life.

Michael's final counsel educates Adam in the kind of knowledge Israel's God cares most about: faithfulness. The Hebrew prophets regularly conflate knowledge with faith and fidelity; to know God is to love him.[11] So taught the prophet Hosea. So Jesus would later teach his disciples, and they the early church.[12] So, too, Milton begins his *Christian Doctrine*, whose first chapter conjoins faith ("or the knowledge of God") with love ("or the worship of God"): "These two divisions, though they are . . . put asunder for convenience of teaching, cannot be separated in practice." "Besides," adds Milton, "obedience and love are always the best guides to knowledge, and often lead the way from small beginnings" (*Christian Doctrine*, 904). Similarly, what Michael calls "the sum / Of wisdom" (*Paradise Lost,* 12.575–76) is "not a speculative answer . . . but a way of consecrated living."[13] Hence Michael exhorts: "only add / Deeds to thy knowledge answerable, add Faith."

Faith in the midst of bewilderment and seemingly senseless suffering is ever the surest, and sometimes the only, consolation available for believers when life conspires to make theodicial questions painfully urgent. For the soul struggling against a sense of godforsakeness, faith envelops every explanation, however logically compelling. No explanation ever gets beyond faith. Moreover, as Kierkegaard astutely observes, no generation begins ahead of another in the religious task of living by faith.[14] This ancient wisdom about the problem of evil, embedded in the Book of Job, is equally inscribed in the final vision of Milton's theodicy.[15] Michael counsels Adam that only those "built by Faith to stand, / Thir own Faith not another's" (12.527–28) can hope to endure. To stand in the right relationship to God—vigilant, alert, willing, patient, obedient, faithful—is to obtain "the sum / Of wisdom" (12.575–76), "the ultimate knowledge of God."[16]

So what shall we say of Milton, the erudite justifier of God's ways to men? Judged by this definition of knowledge, Milton paradoxically shows himself to be wisest where he is least conventionally wise.

Like fallen Adam or blind Samson, whose true strength lies in dependence on God, Milton as narrator stands firmest when he is most vulnerable. As Kierkegaard says, "man's need of God constitutes his highest perfection."[17] Accordingly, Milton never seems stronger than when, acknowledging his weakness, he implores: "What in me is dark / Illumine, what is low raise and support" (1.22–23). In a provocative discussion of this subject, Kerrigan reminds us that an aged Milton occasionally signed his name affixing the motto "My strength is made perfect in weakness."[18] Similarly in his *Second Defense*, Milton writes, "There is, as the apostle has remarked, a way to strength through weakness. Let me then be the most feeble creature alive . . . then, in proportion as I am weak, I shall be invincibly strong, and in proportion as I am blind, I shall more clearly see" (826). In this sense, the poet resembles his own faithful angels whose vulnerability signals their dependence on the one who can make them invulnerable (cf. *Paradise Lost*, 6.595).

Similarly, Milton's theodicy leaves its protagonists and readers still vulnerable to vicissitude. Rather than obviate the need for faith, the poem imparts the deep gnosis that we walk by faith. Its concluding discourses leave polemics behind and engage in the language of confession. Its rhetoric bespeaks faith in him "whom I now / Acknowledge my Redeemer ever blest" (12.572–73). The final lines sing with confidence in "Eternal Providence" (1.25), our sure guide through "this dark world and wide" (12.647; Sonnet 19, line 2). What the ending asserts poetically does as much or more to reconcile us to the enigmatic "ways of God" than what the rest of the poem justifies rationally (see 1.22–26).

For, paradoxically, Milton's God feels more truly present in the poem when he is addressed than when he is pictured. Thus most readers sense the divine presence more in Milton's invocation to book 3— with its humble query ("May I express thee unblam'd?"), its tender complaint about blindness ("but thou / Revisit'st not these eyes, that roll in vain / To find thy piercing ray, and find no dawn"), and its heartfelt supplication for inward sight ("that I may see and tell / Of things invisible to mortal sight")—than in the direct presentation of God that follows (3.3, 22–24, 54–55). Similarly, *Paradise Lost* seems more persuasive to me as a humanly situated poem by a man, like Adam, "fall'n on evil days" (7.25) than as theologically-situated theodicy by a man who has all the right answers as from on high. For the best consolation *Paradise Lost* offers Adam or its readers—and this consolation is considerable—is new (or renewed) faith in the ancient hope that, though "sin is behovabil [inevitable]," through Christ "all shall be well and all shall be well and all manner of thing shall be well."[19]

Notes

This work originally appeared in *Anxiety in Eden: A Kierkegaardian Reading of "Paradise Lost"* (New York: Oxford University Press, 1992). This revised version is published by permission of Oxford University Press.

1. C. S. Lewis, *A Preface to "Paradise Lost"* (New York: Oxford University Press, 1961), 129.
2. William Kerrigan, *The Sacred Complex: On the Psychogenesis of "Paradise Lost"* (Cambridge: Harvard University Press, 1983), 271–72.
3. Samuel Richardson's *Explanatory Notes and Remarks*, cited in Kerrigan, *Sacred Complex,* 270–71.
4. John Milton, *Paradise Lost, John Milton: Complete Poetry and Major Prose*, ed. Merritt Y. Hughes (New York: Odyssey, 1957). All references to Milton's poetry and prose are to this edition and are cited parenthetically in the text.
5. Dennis Richard Danielson, *Milton's Good God: A Study in Literary Theodicy* (Cambridge: Cambridge University Press, 1982), 202. Lovejoy's thesis is set forth in "Milton and the Paradox of the Fortunate Fall," *ELH* 4 (1937): 215–40. I should note that Danielson's case against a fortunate fall was not unprecedented. It is forcibly anticipated in Virginia Mollenkott's essay, "Milton's Rejection of the Fortunate Fall," *Milton Quarterly* 6 (1972): 1–5. In this volume, both Catherine Gimelli Martin and I continue the revaluation of a fortunate fall in *Paradise Lost*.
6. Wayne Shumaker, *Unpremeditated Verse: Feeling and Perception in "Paradise Lost"* (Princeton: Princeton University Press, 1967), 224, 216. For other fine comments on the "homeward" movement of Milton's final books, see Joseph H. Summers, *The Muse's Method: An Introduction to "Paradise Lost"* (1962; reprint, New York: Norton, 1968), 223–24, and Mary Ann Radzinowicz, "'Man as a Probationer of Immortality': *Paradise Lost* XI–XII," *Approaches to "Paradise Lost,"* York Centenary Lectures, ed. C. A. Patrides (Toronto: University of Toronto Press, 1968), 31–51.
7. Kerrigan, *Sacred Complex,* 279.
8. Since my argument partly parallels the conclusion of *The Sacred Complex* (esp. 275–86), I want to register my difference with Kerrigan. Both of us distinguish between what I term the poem's eschatological and existential consolations—that is, between the paradise envisioned on Earth at the end of time and the paradise within us in time. Like Kerrigan, I am most moved by the consolation the poem offers (through faith) in and for *this* world. But unlike Kerrigan, I do not intend to dismiss or disparage as "surrender to literalism" the hope offered by the promise of a Second Coming (275–76) or future heavenly bliss (279–80), or a literal resurrection. "[U]nless the reader can believe or achieve the illusion of believing," Kerrigan remarks, "that the sky will one day part, and Christ, returned as judge, will reward and punish the human race, leading the just to immortal bliss, the kerygma of Milton's [eschatological] consolation is a dead letter" (275–76). These are not dead hopes for me or for Milton, who would surely concur with Paul: "If in this life only we have hope in Christ, we are of all men most miserable" (1 Corinthians 15.19). I do not suggest, nor does Milton require, that we must choose between an eschatological and existential paradise. Both are important to the conclusion of *Paradise Lost*. However, since we can do nothing but hope for the literal renewal of Eden on Earth, Milton's vision of an existential paradise moves me more. It speaks to the central purpose of Christian life as I understand it—which is the *imitatio Christi*.
9. Kerrigan, *Sacred Complex,* 279–80, 285.
10. See Louis Mackey, *Kierkegaard: A Kind of Poet* (Philadelphia: University of Pennsylvania Press, 1971), 98–100.

11. A number of biblical studies have explored the rich significance of *knowledge* in the Hebrew Bible, especially the covenant dimensions of the term. Introductions to the topic may be found in *The Interpreter's Dictionary of the Bible: An Illustrated Encyclopedia*, 4 vols., ed. George Arthur Buttrick et al. (New York: Abingdon, 1962) in O. A. Piper's entry under "Knowledge" and Elizabeth Achtemeier's entry "Righteousness in the Old Testament," as well as in Bernhard W. Anderson's *Understanding the Old Testament*, 3rd rev. ed. (Englewood Cliffs, N.J.: Prentice-Hall, 1975), 287–89.

12. See, for example, Hosea 4.1–2 and 6.6, John 14, and 1 John 2.3–4.

13. Both these phrases come from observations about the Book of Job. In *Essays on Biblical Interpretation* (ed. Lewis S. Mudge [Philadelphia: Fortress Press, 1980]), Paul Ricoeur avers, "What is revealed [by Job] is the possibility of hope in spite of . . ." (87). In "Introduction and Exegesis to Job" (*Interpreter's Bible*, [Nashville, Tenn.: Abingdon, 1954], 3:877–905), Samuel Terrien observes that the Book of Job proposes "not a speculative answer . . . but a way of consecrated living" (902). I have discussed these dimensions of Job in "Job and the Prophets," *Cithara* 26 (1986): 23–25.

14. See the preface and epilogue of Kierkegaard's *Fear and Trembling: Dialectical Lyric*, trans. with intro. and notes by Howard V. Hong and Edna H. Hong (Princeton: Princeton University Press, 1983).

15. Kant makes this point in his trenchant little essay "On the Failure of All Attempted Philosophical Theodicies" (1791), *Kant on History and Religion*, trans. Michel Despland (Montreal: McGill-Queens University Press, 1973), 291–97. Kant exempts the Book of Job from failure because it does not attempt a strictly philosophical solution. In this regard, consider Kerrigan's comment about Milton's oft-noted use of Job in *Paradise Regained*: "It is astonishing to realize that Milton the justifier turned for inspiration to the book that offers the most powerful refutation we have of the theodicial project of *Paradise Lost*. . . . Life, not doctrine, is central to the latest Milton" (*Sacred Complex*, 312n). I would argue that the conclusion of *Paradise Lost* has also assimilated some of the wisdom implicit in Job. In this way as in others, the final books align themselves with Milton's sequel poem on paradise.

16. See the chapter "The Ultimate Knowledge of God" in Lee A. Jacobus, *Sudden Apprehension: Aspects of Knowledge in "Paradise Lost,"* Studies in English Literature 94 (The Hague: Mouton, 1976), 197–212. "In *Paradise Lost*," observes Jacobus, "faith, obedience, and love are the ultimate ways of truly knowing God" (197). On Milton's use of *stand* in *Paradise Lost*, see John T. Shawcross, *With Mortal Voice: The Creation of "Paradise Lost"* (Lexington: University Press of Kentucky, 1982), 159–65.

17. As Kierkegaard entitles a lecture in *Edifying Discourses: A Selection*, ed. Paul L. Holmer, trans. David F. and Lillian Marvin Swenson (New York: Harper Torchbooks, 1958), 136–76.

18. See Kerrigan, *Sacred Complex,* 134; compare William Riley Parker, *Milton: A Biography* (Oxford: Clarendon Press, 1968), 1:479.

19. From Dame Julian of Norwich; echoed in the conclusion of T. S. Eliot's *Four Quartets*, *The Norton Anthology of English Literature*, 5th ed., ed. M. H. Abrams (New York: W. W. Norton, 1986), 2:2204n. Cf. the final chorus of Milton's *Samson Agonistes*:

> All is best, though we oft doubt,
> What th' unsearchable dispose
> Of highest wisdom brings about
> And ever best found in the close.

(1745–48)

Dodging the Dragon's Tail: Apocalyptic Combat in *Paradise Regained*

SAMUEL SMITH

One of the most significant Puritan typologies in Milton's England was the threefold conflict between Christ and Satan. In *The Rise of Puritanism* William Haller remarks that three pivotal encounters between good and evil—Adam and the serpent (eisegetically identified as Satan) in Eden, Jesus and Satan in the Judean wilderness, and Michael (identified with Christ) and the dragon (identified with Satan) in the Apocalypse—demonstrated for Puritans that "all existence and very human life" was a "phase of conflict between Christ and Satan."[1] Any biblically literate reader of Milton's brief epic will recognize the allusions to Genesis in the opening of the poem and those to Revelation in its close. Most readers also recognize the prominence of humanity's Fall in *Paradise Regained*'s reversal of the events of *Paradise Lost*. But I would like to suggest that Christ's final apocalyptic victory over Satan also figures prominently in Milton's retelling of Jesus' temptation, appearing in a typological and prophetic manner that Milton's contemporaries would recognize.

The adumbrated presence of the apocalyptic dragon in a narrative about the temptation of God's Son would have neither surprised nor eluded many readers in Milton's first audience. Popular seventeenth-century exegetes William Perkins, Thomas Taylor, David Pareus, and Daniel Dike followed Luther's lead in connecting the devil in the desert with the great red dragon who wars against God and his people in Revelation. In *The Tenure of Kings and Magistrates*, Milton aligns himself with this tradition when he links the devil's offer of worldly power to Jesus in Luke 4 with the dragon's empowering of the beast in Revelation 13 to mark tyrannous monarchy as satanic government.[2] Of the many Puritan discussions of the apocalyptic dragon, one with important implications for Milton's poem is Thomas Taylor's *Christs Victorie Over The Dragon or Satans Downfall* (1633). In this long, discursive commentary on the twelfth chapter of Revelation, Taylor delineates the nature of the dragon in great detail, outlining and exposing the dragon's combative strategies for effecting the fall of God's prophets and ministers, symbolized by the dragon's sweeping the stars out of the sky with a swing of his awe-ful tail.

Taylor identifies three primary means of attack represented by the dragon's tail: its violent strength signifies physical persecution ("force and tyranny"), its marvelous aspect suggests "flattery and faire persuasions," and its stinging poison symbolizes the heresies of false prophets (*Christs Victorie*, 229–30). Following Luke's sequence, *Paradise Regained* presents three temptations in three successive days; these three temptations match the three strategies listed by Taylor. The first day's stones-to-bread temptation reveals the dragon's hope of luring Jesus into assuming a false prophethood, emphasized by Jesus' counterthrusting exposure of Satan as a false prophet. The second day entails Satan's various "faire perswasions" and flattering offers of earthly kingdom, a strategy designed to bring Jesus' kingdom under his own draconic authority. The third day, climaxing with Satan's malevolent setting of Jesus on the temple pinnacle after a night of apocalyptic storm, reveals the dragon's desperation as he resorts to physical persecution and force.

The dragon cloaked in the appearance of the old man on the first day discovers himself in his means of attack—heresy and false prophecy—as the poison in the dragon's tail. Uncovered and wounded by Jesus' wielding of God's word ("God'sword"), the dragon in Satan seeks to ally himself with God's servants and prophets, recalling his willingness to be God's instrument of judgment against "the proud King Ahab" (1.368–77).[3] Jesus incisively qualifies this sophistical argument by identifying Satan's true nature and motivation: "fear" and "pleasure to do ill" (1.422–29). Milton's allusion to Ahab's four hundred lying prophets (1 Kings 22) both negatively defines Satan as a false/evil prophetic inspiration and clearly reveals him as the apocalyptic dragon. While the earlier allusion in this passage to Satan's attack on Job has received much attention, the purpose and meaning of the allusion to Ahab's false prophets has not been sufficiently understood. According to Puritan exegesis, the typological meaning of this puzzling biblical incident resides in the context of the final struggle between Christ and the dragon. Taylor's prime example of the dragon's past successful strikes with a tail envenomed with the poison of false prophecy is 1 Kings 22.21. "He [the dragon] offereth himselfe to be a lying spirit in the mouth of Ahabs prophets; and striketh down with his taile 400 [prophets=stars] at once" (*Christs Victorie*, 232). Perkins makes the same connection in his exposition of Matthew 4:

> And when Ahab went to fight against the King of Syriah, Satan became a lying spirit in the mouth of 400 Prophets & moe [*sic*], I King. 22.22. This is that *great red dragon, that with his taile drew downe the third part of the starres of heaven* . . . Revel. 12.3.4.[4]

Ironically, by offering this particular illustration of his past prophetic "service" to God as an attempt to defend himself, Satan inadvertently undercuts himself, identifying his true nature as the heinous dragon who strikes down God's prophets by seducing them with false prophecies. He will repeat this mistake, exposing his draconic evil intent to both Jesus and the biblically informed reader who would identify with the elect who fight against the dragon in the Apocalypse.

When Satan returns on the second day, "Not rustic as before, but seemlier clad, / As one in City, or Court, or Palace bred" (2.299–300), he appears cloaked as Taylor's dragon once again: "Although he be a dragon . . . he commeth commonly as a friend, and in the habit of a good counsellor" (*Christs Victorie*, 152). His method of temptation on this second day accords with Taylor's description of the second way the dragon swings his tail against the stars of Heaven:

> By flattery and insinuations, by which, as by a dragons tayle the Pastors were beaten down: for as dogs do use to fawne and flatter their masters with their taile; so the dragon not by open force onely, but by secret fraud and insinuation assaileth the stars; namely by many faire promises, and sugred perswasions, making offers of wealth and preferment, favor, and whatever else the world can bestow on her favorites. (*Christs Victorie*, 228)

Milton's dragon is full of "flattery, faire promises, and sugred perswasions" on this second day. The sugared persuasion of the banquet spread "in *regal* mode" (2.340; emphasis mine) is followed by a blatant offer of "wealth and preferment" that "rais'd Antipater the Edomite, / And his Son Herod plac'd on Judah's Throne" (2.422, 423–24). Satan's illustration of his success in this vein—Herod—is ironically devastating, again revealing and affirming his true identity as the great red dragon. Herod's function as a type of the dragon who appears in Revelation 12 to persecute the woman and devour her son is clearly remarked by Taylor: "How *Herod* the dragon stood before the woman seeking to slay the childe Jesus so soone as he was born, appeareth Mat. 2.16" (*Christs Victorie*, 248).[5]

Satan unwisely chooses another such revealing example when he tries to lure Jesus into accepting an earthly kingdom on his terms by emphasizing the oppression of Israel by foreign conquerors in a way that gives a strong sense of urgency to the need for the Messiah. Appealing to Jesus' sense of duty, Satan tries to move Jesus by portraying the current Roman emperor Tiberius as a kind of Antiochus Epiphanes, who is here a prophetically and typologically significant analogue. Antiochus Epiphanes' blasphemous desecration of the Jewish temple in the second century BCE resulted in a long tradition of commentary identifying him with the sacrilegious king responsible for "the abomination that maketh desolate" in the apocalyptic prophecy of Daniel 11.31–36. Antiochus thus becomes a type of the blaspheming beast who receives his power from the dragon as described in Revelation 13.4 – 6:

> And they worshipped the dragon which gave power unto the beast: and they worshipped the beast, saying, Who is like unto the beast? who is able to make war with him? And there was given unto him a mouth speaking great blasphemies; and power was given unto him . . . And he opened his mouth in blasphemy against God.[6]

David Pareus pushes this common type a bit further, observing that in a historical interpretation of Revelation 12, the dragon whose swinging tail knocks stars out of Heaven alludes to Antiochus Epiphanes, who is a "type of Antichrist."[7] The apocalyptic context evoked by Antiochus as a type of Antichrist enables Jesus and Milton's readers to recognize that the kings whom Satan sets up for Jesus to topple and replace are the dragon's own beasts and puppets, and the dragon's ploy is to make a beast and puppet of Jesus as well.

Satan renews his attempt to bring Jesus' kingdom under his draconic authority by offering him the military power of Parthia. But Milton's description of the violent, conquering force of the Parthian army parallels the military might of the dragon's beast in Revelation. In the preface to Milton's friend Samuel Hartlib's edition of *The Revelation Reveled*, John Dury asserts that the government of the beast will "do all things by a Brutish and bodilie violence and force, rather than in a friendlie and amiable waie." Indeed, the vision of Parthian destruction presented by Satan corresponds to the character of the beastly government described by Dury: it will "destroie without mercie all that stands in the waie of [its] will."[8] When Jesus refuses this form of the kingdom offered by Satan, he in effect refuses to become the beast who receives power from the dragon.

Satan's subsequent bold offer of the Roman empire subsumes all of the means he has used to tempt Jesus to receive an earthly kingdom from him on this second day. The offer of Rome also enhances the apocalyptic context. Rome was categorically identified by nearly all seventeenth-century protestant theologians with the Antichrist,[9] and the initial description of that city in Milton's poem suggests the Whore of Babylon from Revelation 17–18:

> The City which thou seest no other deem
> Than great and glorious Rome, Queen of the Earth
> So far renown'd, and with the spoils enricht
> Of nations.
> (4.44–47)

Here is the great Harlot who considers herself "a queen" to all the "kings of the earth" (Revelation 18.7–9), who "reigneth over the kings of the earth" (Revelation 17.18), and who enriches and is enriched by "the merchants of the earth" (Revelation 18.11). Seductive as this Whore, Milton's dragon again swings his alluring tail of "faire promises and sugred perswasions," flattering Jesus and putting the offer in terms of achieving a good and desirable end: Jesus can demonstrate his own virtue and supplant the evil tyrant Tiberius at the same time, expelling a "monster from his Throne" (4.100). Jesus' reply exposes the dragon's game, marking Satan's attempt to become the draconic authority behind a "beastly" kingship:

> I shall, thou say'st, expel
> A brutish monster; what if I withal
> Expel a Devil who first made him such?
> (4.127–29)

"A brutish monster" fits the apocalyptic beast and the word *Devil* could be functionally replaced by *Dragon* if it would not counter the apocalyptic method of revealing truth by concealing it under images and words that can be penetrated only by the initiated.

Despite Jesus' pointed allusion to the apocalyptic image of Daniel's "stone that shall to pieces dash / All Monarchies besides throughout the world" (4.149–50), prophesying Jesus' destruction of all beasts empowered by the dragon (Taylor identifies Daniel's stone with Christ who "breake in pieces the power of the dragons" [*Christs Victorie*, 387]), Satan still pushes brutishly forward with the blatant offer that most clearly marks him as that dragon:

> The Kingdoms of the world to thee I give;
> For giv'n to me, I give to whom I please,
> No trifle; yet with this reserve, not else,

> On this condition, if thou wilt fall down,
> And worship me as thy superior Lord.
>
> (4.163–67)

As I have demonstrated, Milton and his contemporaries identify this act with the dragon of Revelation. In the poem it is a desperate maneuver, revealing the dragon's utter inability to penetrate the truth of Jesus. But perhaps Satan's desperate repetition of his kingdom offer signifies a nascent or even unconscious apprehension of the spiritual nature of the Messiah's kingdom. Satan's demand that Jesus bow down and worship him in return for the kingdoms of the world can be interpreted as a request for spiritual worship. Taylor notes this as another mark of the dragon:

> If Christ require spirituall worship, being a spirituall king, the dragon will require the same, Math. 4, If thou fall downe and worship me; And that which he could not obtain of Christ he winneth of all the wicked in the world, who worship the beast and the dragon, Rev. 14.3. (*Christs Victorie*, 203)

Satan's desperate request may also spring from his enmity toward Jesus: "Satan's malice and contrariety to Christ and Kingdome, and all he claimeth" means that "If Christ be Lord of all, the dragon will claim all. Math. 4. All these things will I give thee, for they are mine" (*Christs Victorie*, 203). Viewing Satan's uncloaked offer as the malicious act of the child-devouring, star-felling dragon would both explain and justify—if justification is needed—Jesus' particularly scathing response to Satan. His apocalyptic judgment of Satan as "That Evil one, Satan for ever damn'd" (4.194) is singularly appropriate. God's "Morning Star" (1.294, cf. Revelation 22.16) is not about to bow down, either physically or spiritually, and worship the dragon.

At this point, given this rather climactic action in the context of the typology of the Apocalypse enacted here, the inclusion of a temptation to rule a kingdom through pagan knowledge and wisdom[10]—a temptation that has puzzled more than one generation of *Paradise Regained* readers—may seem anticlimactic and unnecessary. Why include it then? Satan's nascent recognition of the true nature of Jesus' kingdom as a spiritual one could be one reason for this surprising maneuver. But this form of the kingdom temptation also rounds out the tradition evident in William Perkins and Thomas Taylor. Perkins, taking some liberty with the biblical account of Satan's offer of the kingdoms of the world in an applicative (not interpretive) way, remarks that Satan's use of pagan wisdom as a means of redirecting the God-willed course of God's young prophets should be both expected and anticipated:

even in Gods church the Devill workes mightily in this way, by stealing away the affections of yong students from the Bible, and ravishing them with delight in the writings of men; for thus he keepes them from the fountain of truth, that they either fall into error themselves, or be less able to discerne and confute it in others. (*Christs Victorie*, 393)

Milton's Jesus echoes this sentiment when he responds that the one who receives "Light from above, from the fountain of light, / No other doctrine needs" (4.289–90), and then proceeds to expose the error of the ancient philosophers: "Much of the Soul they talk, but all awry" (4.313). Taylor directly links Perkins's observation to the dragon's "faire promises and sugred perswasions," and his tactic of promoting evil ends by good means and "handsomely apparrell[ing]" what is evil to make it seem good. Taylor's illustration of this tactic is a learning that would direct a person away from studying and relying on God's word:

To neglect the study, & preaching of Gods word, and to carry men from the simple truth to toyes, and froth of human spirit and wit, is profoundness and depth of learning. Revel. 2.24. for how else came schoole-learning to banish the scriptures, for many hundred yeares, but under pretext of deeper learning? (*Christs Victorie*, 160)

Of Education's author could certainly accommodate these anti-scholastic sentiments, and there seems to be an echo of Taylor in Jesus' denunciation of pagan wisdom in favor of the sufficiency of the scriptural tradition. His important qualification on the use of learning includes a use of the word *toys* in a way reminiscent of Taylor's passage:

> who reads
> Incessantly, and to his reading brings not
> A spirit and judgment equal or superior
> (And what he brings, what needs he elsewhere seek)
> Uncertain and unsettl'd still remains,
> Deep verst in books and shallow in himself,
> Crude or intoxicate, collecting *toys*,
> And trifles for choice matters, worth a sponge.
>   (4.322–29; emphasis mine)

Jesus' response reveals that the dragon has spent the entire day wielding his alluring tail in vain.

After remonstrating with Jesus for his rejection of his offer of the kingdom and prognosticating a fate of suffering for Jesus, which Jesus himself has already acknowledged, Satan returns Jesus to the desert wilderness and leaves him, "Feigning to disappear" (4.397). But he returns to attack Jesus as he sleeps, fulfilling once again the paradigm of draconic behavior as Taylor delineates it. Taylor remarks that the dragon will "dissemble flight when he need not, when he doth not," departing "but for a season" only to "renew his forces and assaults" after the believer has fallen into a metaphorical sleep of security (*Christs Victorie*, 175). The dragon also characteristically takes advantage of believers by attacking them in their literal sleep (*Christs Victorie*, 155). Thus Milton's Satan returns like Revelation's dragon, attacking Jesus as he sleeps, assaulting him with a frighteningly apocalyptic storm of cosmic disorder followed by a horrifying demonic assault. When Satan forces the winds to rush forward "From the four hinges of the world" (4.415), he counters the angel of God who holds back the four winds in Revelation 7.1. Even the thunder, coming from "either Tropic" and "both ends of Heav'n" (4.409–10), suggests apocalyptic judgment from the four corners of the earth. The hideous demons tormenting Jesus in a dream can be compared to the hideous locusts that issue forth from the bottomless pit to torment humanity in Revelation 9. It is as if, realizing he is losing the future apocalyptic battle in this present encounter, Satan attempts to turn the Book of Revelation's destroying power against the very one it reveals: Jesus Christ (Revelation 1.1).

"Swoln with rage" (*Paradise Regained,* 4.499), Satan makes a last defense of all his previous actions; he then uses "Another method" (4.540) identifiable as the dragon's tail swung with "force and tyranny" (*Christs Victorie*, 277). In an act of tyrannic violence, Satan places Jesus on a pinnacle, in peril of his life. The image of Jesus and Satan high in the sky at the point of the highest pinnacle's spire suggests the image of the War in Heaven, and Satan's temptation correlates to the dragon exposed in Taylor's commentary. Satan's use of Psalm 91 renders him a "preaching dragon," which is "the most dangerous" of false preachers, "who will winde us in by Scripture, and by that which is the only preservative against sinne, draw us into sinne" (*Christs Victorie*, 153). In this way the dragon attempts to turn the Christian's own weapon—God's word—against him (*Christs Victorie*, 173). One of Taylor's many examples of this is the dragon's attempt to "bring Christ to presumption" by breaking off before quoting that part of Psalm 91 that would enable Jesus to defeat him during the pinnacle temptation. The part of Psalm 91 that Satan leaves unsaid is poignant:

> Thou shalt tread upon the lion and the adder: the young lion and the *dragon* shalt thou trample under feet. Because he hath set his love upon me,

therefore will I deliver him: I will set him on high, because he hath known my name. (Psalm 91.13–14; emphasis mine)

Jesus has indeed set his love upon God and known his name: "King of Kings." Buttressed by his faith in God's providence and kingdom, Jesus defeats Satan with the "sharp sword" (Revelation 19.15) that is the word of God: "Also it is written, / Tempt not the Lord thy God" (*Paradise Regained,* 4.560–61). As Jesus continues to stand by the grace and power of God, Satan is "smitten with amazement" (4.562) and falls, evoking the image of the falling dragon in Revelation 12.

At this point Milton's poetic power focuses on the theme of the eternal life depicted at the close of Revelation after Christ has overcome the dragon and his evil forces. Immediately after his victory, Jesus is presented with a celestial banquet from the true Giver and an angelic hymn of praise, evoking the wedding feast of the Lamb in Revelation 19 and the Elysium of Revelation 22.[11] Served by ministering angels, Jesus receives "Fruits fetched from the tree of life" (4.589) found on either side of the river of life in Revelation 22.2. More significantly, "to eat of the tree of life" is promised to "him that overcometh" Satan in Revelation 2.7. Jesus *has* overcome Satan's temptations and in eating of the tree of life he establishes the type for his own promise, since the glorified Jesus is the speaker in that verse. Jesus also drinks from the "fount of life Ambrosial" (4.590) promised "to him that is athirst" in Revelation 21.6.

The celestial banquet is appropriately accompanied by an angelic hymn of praise for the Son, a hymn that parallels the hymns of the martyred saints and the twenty-four elders in Revelation 5. The angels echo John 1.14 ("And the Word was made flesh, and dwelt among us") when they speak of the Son as being "remote from Heaven, enshrin'd / In fleshly Tabernacle, and human form" (4.598–99). But they also evoke Revelation 21.3: "And I heard a great voice out of heaven saying, Behold, the tabernacle of God is with men, and he will dwell with them, and be their God." The angels also sing of Jesus' victory over Satan in apocalyptic terms: "him long of old / Thou didst debel, and down from Heav'n cast / With all his army" (4.604–6). Emory Elliot[12] points out that this recalls both Revelation 12.9, "And the great dragon was cast out, that old serpent, called the Devil, and Satan," and Revelation 20.2–3, 10:

And he laid hold on the dragon, that old serpent, which is the Devil, and Satan, and bound him a thousand years, And cast him into the bottomless pit . . . And the devil that deceived them was cast into the lake of fire and brimstone.

The angels' warning to Satan, that "like an Autumnal Star / Or Lightning thou shalt fall from Heav'n trod down / Under his feet" (4.619–21), reinvokes the missing portion of Psalm 91 that speaks of the dragon being trod under the feet of God's servant. The future tense of the warning reminds the reader that the final battle is yet to come, and its presence in this encounter is typological and prophetic. The hymn also provides the model response for saints: praise to God for Christ's victory over the dragon:

> In that the Church rejoyceth, that now the Lord hath put forth his strength in the overthrow of the enemies, and set up his own kingdome wherre the dragon and his angels ruled in darknesse, Idolatry, cruelty, and tyranny, we learne, that *this Saints ought to rejoyce when they see Gods kingdome set up and prevaile against the dragon and his angels.* Rev. 11.15. (*Christs Victorie*, 510)

Thus the apocalyptically alert reader realizes at the close of *Paradise Regained* that the final conflict between Christ and the dragon has been typologically and prophetically battled out in the victory of Jesus over Satan in the desert wilderness of Judea, years before the crucifixion and millenia before the Second Coming of Christ and the end of human history.

Notes

This work originally appeared as " 'Christs Victorie Over the Dragon': Apocalypse in *Paradise Regained"* in *Milton Studies* 29 (1992):59–82. This revised version is published by permission of the University of Pittsburgh Press. Special thanks to Richard Strier for some helpful criticism toward the revision of this work, and to Messiah College for a generous Scholarship Supplement Grant in support of this and other work-in-progress.

    1. William Haller, *The Rise of Puritanism* (New York: Columbia University Press, 1938), 151.

    2. See William Perkins, *The Combate Betweene Christ and the Devill Expounded*, Works (Cambridge, 1609), esp. 3:373, 384, 400; Thomas Taylor, *Christs Combate and Conquest* (Cambridge, 1618), esp. 4, 8, 310, 324–25, and *Christs Victorie Over the Dragon or Satans Downfall* (London, 1633)—because of this work's significance for my thesis, subsequent quotations from this edition are cited parenthetically in the text; David Pareus, *A Commentary Upon the Divine Revelation of the Apostle and Evangelist John*, trans. Elias Arnold (Amsterdam, 1644), 291; Daniel Dike, *Michael and the Dragon, or Christ Tempted and Satan Foyled* (London, 1635), 223. For Luther see Jaroslav Pelikan, "Some Uses of Apocalypse in the Magisterial Reformers," *The Apocalypse in English Renaissance Thought and Literature*, ed. C. A. Patrides and Joseph A. Wittreich (Ithaca: Cornell University Press, 1984), 85–86. Milton's remarks

can be found in *Complete Prose Works of John Milton*, 8 vols., ed. Don M. Wolfe et al. (New Haven: Yale University Press, 1953–82), 3:210.

3. John Milton, *Paradise Regained, John Milton: Complete Poems and Major Prose*, ed. Merritt Y. Hughes (New York: Odyssey Press, 1957). All references to Milton's poetry are to this edition and are cited parenthetically in the text.

4. Perkins, *Combate*, 384.

5. See also Pareus, *Commentary*, 257, for the same identification.

6. All biblical references are to the King James Version and are cited parenthetically in the text.

7. Pareus, *Commentary*, 261.

8. *The Revelation Reveled*, ed. Samuel Hartlib (London, 1651), 48. The young Milton dedicated his *Of Education* to Hartlib.

9. See Christopher Hill, *Antichrist in Seventeenth-Century England* (Oxford: Oxford University Press, 1971), 1–40.

10. Dick Taylor, "The Storm Scene in *Paradise Regained*: A Reinterpretation," *University of Toronto Quarterly* 24 (1955): 367, has argued convincingly that the so-called "Athens" temptation is just one more form of the kingdom temptation.

11. Edward Tayler, *Milton's Poetry: Its Development in Time* (Pittsburgh: University of Pittsburgh Press, 1979), 164, calls this banquet a reminder of the *eschaton*, or last things (Revelation).

12. Emory Elliot, "Milton's Biblical Style in *Paradise Regained*," *Milton Studies* 6 (1974): 238.

Part III
Spokesperson for Political Views

Jubilee in Scripture and History: Reading Milton's "At a Solemn Music"

STEPHEN M. BUHLER

Critical and scholarly interpretations of Milton's earlier poetry have both shaped and been shaped by historical and biographical models. One's understanding of the political import of the youthful Milton's work—or the lack thereof—depends, in part, on one's ideas of the interconnections between poetry and power, religion and politics, ideology and class in one's own time, as well as in the seventeenth century. Further, recent readings have diverged dramatically in accordance with the readers' distinct, even discrete understandings of the "trajectory" of Milton's life: how soon one can detect a commitment to the radical Protestantism of the polemical middle period, and how early another can detect a hint of doubt in the Good Old Cause, deeply affects *what* each perceives as Milton's politics. The model and the evidence that supports it enter into a symbiotic, if not circular, relation. Christopher Hill's 1970s construct of an ever-revolutionary John Milton, and the refinements and critiques of that construction (including the parodic "Hillton," as Edward Chaney has trenchantly dubbed it[1]) perhaps convey a sense of the process most vividly.

I have rehearsed this outline of a recent version of the age-old hermeneutical problem not only to bring my own interpretive model under scrutiny. I also want to suggest the applicability of the outline and the model to Milton's own age and art by grounding them in the debate over the political lessons to be derived from Scripture. This debate was, perhaps, never more fierce than in the years culminating in the English civil wars, although skirmishes persist to this day. For those who could read scripture "radically" in the wake of the Reformation, the question as to how the Kingdom of God was to be realized on Earth—whether developmentally or disjunctively, through a gradual and historical process or through a metatemporal, divine intrusion—was a matter of immense concern and immediate moment. Since sacred history provides ample evidence for both sides of the argument and even for a *via media* negotiating both, the answer to that overwhelming question often depended upon the reader's own interpretive model. The model could itself undergo either developmental or disjunctive transformations, and continues to do so.

The twenty-four-year-old John Milton enters and incorporates such debates in "At a Solemn Music," a poem that, despite its brevity, nonetheless grapples with an imposing range of topics: the lessons of sacred history, the accuracy of a cosmological model of the created universe as harmonious instrument, and the limits of an architectonic art indebted to that cosmology. In the analysis that follows, I will make reference to other Miltonic works, early and late, in order to place the poem in a developmental scheme: this literary-biographical approach is, I believe, not inconsistent with the views of history suggested by the poem itself. In opposition to the grand correspondential order invoked by Ulysses in *Troilus and Cressida*—and by other apologists for a version of the status quo during the Renaissance and in our own time—Milton's speaker presents that harmonious concord as lost. In opposition to a quietist notion that the concord can be restored through exclusively divine agency, the speaker also presents the concord as recoverable through a process that includes human effort. Both the conviction of loss and the promise of recoverability help to mark Milton's political orientations, as a potentially radical Protestant, and to mark the preconditions, if not the beginnings, of his idiosyncratic radicalism. David Loewenstein is right, I think, in seeing Milton's work as operating within an intellectual space located "between responding to history dramatically and envisioning its decline tragically, between an impulse to reshape its convoluted course and an impulse to retire inwardly from its conflicts."[2] But the tendency of the writings, overall, is toward responding and reshaping, toward engagement in and with history.

In considering the question of historical action and involvement in the poet's work and thought, Stanley Fish has argued that what Milton's characters and speakers usually "desire is that someone do something, that something happen."[3] Since that desire is never fulfilled to their satisfaction or expectation, Fish concludes that Milton argues *against* action, that he presents action itself as a "temptation." I would counter that in Milton's poetry the temptation to be withstood is the invitation not to action, but to belief in *in*action: what is most dangerous and disastrous is either to conclude that resolution has already been achieved—that complete fulfillment has already been experienced—or to presume that things are not already occurring, already in process. Fish himself notes that in "At a Solemn Music" action is ongoing ("not only is everyone doing the same thing; they are doing it all the time"[4]) but suggests that the poem itself "stands still" as a result and a response to this realization, and that it counsels us to do likewise. Milton, however, both withholds the terms of resolution and also postpones a significant aural resolution until we near the end of the poem. In so doing, he suggests that something can be accomplished, even if initially on an imaginative or ideational level, in time and history. What confirms that the accomplishment is more than a matter of imagination and comprehension is the precise language employed to represent the ongoing but infinitely dynamic accord.

The phrase "perfect Diapason" appears not at the beginning of "At a Solemn Music," but on line 23 in a work totaling twenty-eight lines.[5] In that location, the words necessarily look back as much as forward in time: they refer specifically to the lost harmony of the first Creation, of Eden, even as they lead to the image of ultimate unification with God's "celestial consort." The language employed indicates the idea's complexities and richness for Milton. "Diapason" can refer not only to the harmony itself but also to the full range of elements contributing to it; "perfect," in its senses of completion and fulfillment, suggests the role that time and history must now play in the renewal of that harmony among such diverse elements. Even though it will be God himself who unites us "ere long," that temporal immediacy seems dependent upon our own immediacy and duration in the faith: "O may we soon *again* renew that Song, / And *keep* in tune with Heav'n" (25–26; emphasis mine). God, it is suggested, will respond to our own efforts, however sporadic they have been in the past; this would not be the first time the Song has been renewed, but rather the first time that renewal has been faithfully sustained. The process of renewal, then, is ongoing, as is our on-again, off-again participation in that process.

The intermittent nature of human accord with the divine will is reflected in the rhyme scheme of the poem. The opening four lines of invocation alternately rhyme, while the rest of the poem settles into iambic pentameter couplets—with four notable exceptions. Lines 8 and 15 complete their respective couplets with one or two fewer metric feet; the lines that immediately follow, 9 and 16, comprise the most widely separated rhyming pair of the poem. Not content with constructing an idealized architectonic "cosmographical glass," Milton prefers to reflect more accurately his understanding of the interrelation between human and sacred history through this deferred resolution: the concord breaks down, to be restored only in time. Milton skillfully invokes such orders by building the reader's expectations of satisfying resolution, of constant, harmonious "chiming," and then he challenges these orders by denying or delaying such resolution. David Norbrook makes a similar point in connection with other poems: Milton "built into his poems a distrust of specious harmony obtained at the expense of repression"; an example of this strategy can be found in *Lycidas* where "movements toward a closed couplet are constantly disrupted."[6] Joseph A. Wittreich has argued that *Lycidas* "drives relentlessly toward certainty and regularity achieved in the tenth paragraph and made conspicuous in the *ottava rima* stanza that comprises the poem's epilogue."[7] I would suggest that Milton's energies are also devoted to disrupting and postponing a certainty that humankind is overly eager to proclaim prematurely: much of the drive, both in *Lycidas* and in the earlier poem, is in the opposite direction to the one Wittreich emphasizes.

The short lines in "At a Solemn Music" alert the reader to take special notice of the language of the subsequent lines as well as to note the long hiatus that delays the harmonizing between "Saintly shout and solemn Jubilee" and "singing everlastingly." The brevity of the lines and the suspension of the rhyme are notable even in early drafts of the poem; by the second version that appears in the Trinity Manuscript, Milton had determined *not* to form an immediate couplet with "jubilie."[8] Also, in the partly damaged first version as in the second, one can detect evidence of these authorial decisions. In the first, Milton replaces a line concluding with "sollemne crie" with the line we have now; in the second, he marks the significance of that line with the terse "To him that sits thereon."

The delay in resolving the rhyme in "At a Solemn Music" has been variously commented upon. E. M. W. Tillyard sees it as part of a strategy governing tempo that compels a "gradual quickening of rhythm to the final trochaics": the aural isolation of *jubilee*, he argues, "impels us to go on to find its rhyme-fellow, which is carefully kept back."[9] Cleanth Brooks and John Edward Hardy, in contrast, attribute the delay to poetic instincts not yet fully developed. They insist that "the separation is too wide for the rhyme to be effective, and the inevitable impression that the two lines are *not* rhymed detracts from the effectiveness of the poem."[10] But the word *jubilee*, for Milton, demands a delay in the poetic "consort." The word appears amidst intricately woven allusions to Old and New Testament texts of strongly prophetic and apocalyptic character. In the lines surrounding the term, Milton connects the "sapphire-colored throne" from Ezekiel 1 with the jewelled throne before which the "just Spirits" sing in Revelation 14. Jubilee, then, recalls not only general notions of rejoicing and sacred festival, but also the Old Testament text in which the word first appears and the later scriptural passages that extend the term's meaning.

The Year of Jubilee is introduced to the people of Israel in Leviticus 25: the Lord directs his people to celebrate a year of restitution, remission, and release every fifty years. During this celebration, the hired servant "shall return unto his own family and unto the possession of his fathers shall he return" (41).[11] The entire nation has justice and compassion brought to mind: "Ye shall not therefore oppress one another; but thou shalt fear thy God" (17). The latter verse suggests that personal liberty and social justice have their bases in a recognition that sovereignty and awe are rightly the Lord's alone; the former depicts personal freedom in touchingly domestic detail. Some characteristics of the Puritan revolution and specific values in Milton's personal radicalism find analogues in these passages.

Jubilee takes on messianic and millennial import in Isaiah's appropriation of the "year of favor" to describe his prophetic mission, and in Christ's application of Isaiah's prophecy to himself. In Isaiah 61, the prophet announces his authority and his mission:

> The Spirit of the Lord GOD is upon me: because the LORD hath anointed me to preach good tidings unto the meek: he hath sent me to bind up the brokenhearted, to proclaim liberty to the captives, and the opening of the prison to them that are bound; to proclaim the acceptable year of the LORD, and the day of vengeance of our God. (1–2)

After Christ reads this passage in the synagogue at Nazareth, he retakes his seat and announces to his fellow worshippers that "This day is this scripture fulfilled in your ears" (Luke 4.21). No wonder, then, that jubilee took on apocalyptic import as well. During the peasant uprisings that tried to extend the impact of the Lutheran Reformation, the nineteenth-century historian Leopold von Ranke noted, "the Mosaic institution of the year of jubilee" was frequently invoked in opposition to social and economic inequities, specific and general, from the exaction of interest on loans to the crushing poverty of farm laborers.[12] In calculations of the date of the Second Coming, the fifty-year cycle of jubilee was often used: both Nicholas of Cusa and Osiander suggested that since Christ lived thirty-three years on earth, the thirty-fourth jubilee year *anno domini*—calculated as roughly 1650—might witness the establishment of his reign on Earth.[13] C. A. Patrides has credited "At a Solemn Music" with being Milton's "first elaboration of the vision of God enthroned so central to both the Apocalypse and *Paradise Lost*":[14] the apocalyptic nature of the poem is strengthened if we grant *jubilee* its extended complex of meanings within the poem.

That concession has not been forthcoming from most Miltonists, and reasons for their reluctance are suggested by the citations listed in the *Oxford English Dictionary*. Both the old and new editions turn to the pages of Samuel Purchas's compendium of cultural difference, *Purchas His Pilgrimage*, in demonstrating the primary, Old Testament meaning of the term: "Touching this yeare of Iubilee is much controversie."[15] While the passage in Purchas refers to the scholarly debate over how the year of Jubilee was to be calculated, this sentence deftly summarizes the productive tension at work in the term's usage, as well as the constant anxiety over the term's meaning. Some of the tension appears in subsequent entries: along with Ranke's observation of the more revolutionary aspect of *jubilee* (also in entry 1.a.), we find Sir Thomas Browne's famous dictum, "The First Day of our Jubilee is Death" (1.b.), with its mixture of both skeptical and accepting attitudes toward earthly orders of justice and knowledge.[16] It is in that context that we also find Milton's *Paradise Lost*, book 3, cited as a illustration of usage denoting "joyful shouting" (5.b.) and—in the new edition—references to a "Negro folk-song of an optimistic and joyful kind, often having a religious basis" (5.c.). The juxtapositioning of Milton's angelic jubilee with spirituals drawn from the experience of slaves and former slaves is appropriate, for both of these uses of the term engage with biblical precedents and with the controversy over whether God's deliverance can be realized only in the next world (as Browne suggests), or in this world as well.

One strong indication of Milton's stand on this matter is his later use of *jubilee* to characterize Parliament's increasing assertiveness in terms of both political and apocalyptic renewal. In the *Animadversions*, Milton argues against censorship imposed by the bishops:

> The Romans had a time once every year, when their slaves might freely speake their minds, 'twere hard if the free born people of England, with whom the voice of Truth for these many years, even against the proverb, hath been heard but in corners . . . if now at a good time, our time of Parliament, the very *jubilee*, and resurrection of the State, if now the concealed, the aggrieved, and long persecuted Truth, could not be suffered [to] speak. (1:669; emphasis mine)[17]

If the heathen, despotic Romans could, periodically, vouchsafe freedom of speech to their slaves, then certainly English citizens should enjoy the same degree of liberty in this period of renewed justice, a time of general resurrection for the polity and its best institutions. A similar, if subtler, use of the term may be at work in Andrew Marvell's "Music's Empire," where the biblical Jubal is credited with first tuning "Musicks *Jubilee*," and where music's "Victorious sounds" are asked to praise contemporary, Parliamentary successes.[18]

Two prose treatises of the seventeenth century also invoke the idea of a decidedly Protestant version of the Jewish festival: Lodowick Lloyd's *The Jubile of Britane*, published in 1607, and *The Jubilie of England*, written by "W. J." (perhaps "W. I.") and published in 1646. Lloyd, a sergeant-at-arms in the courts of Elizabeth and James, dedicates his pamphlet to Prince Henry. It shares in the character of most of his works, described by Thomas Seccombe in *The Dictionary of National Biography* as "consist[ing] exclusively of 'collectanea curiosa.'" But the rationale for this collection of royal ceremonies and funerary customs from antiquity is militantly religious: Lloyd proclaims that

> Our great Iubile in *England* was just upon the fifty yeare, which was between *Edward* the sixt, and Iames the sixt now our King, at his first arrivall unto England. No greater Iubile could be in *Iudah*, than in the time of young *Iosias*, who purified *Hierusalem* and all his Kingdomes from images and idols. . . . Neither can there be a greater Iubile now in great *Brittane*, then to have such a godly religious King after so good and so religious a Queene.[19]

After this strong implication that just as Josiah fought idolatry, so did Elizabeth and so should James, Lloyd proceeds to equate the enemies of Protestant England with the enemies of Israel and, in good *Actes and Monuments* fashion, the enemies of the first Christians. But despite his disclaimer that "this little treatise is not to entreate of antiquitie, which is full of errours,"[20] Lloyd decries Roman Catholics as latter-day Egyptian and Roman oppressors only by way of introducing the royal customs (and "jubilees") of Egypt and Rome, among other ancient nations, which hold such a fascination for him. Unwittingly, Lloyd has isolated many of those tensions between the reformed and the royalistic perspectives that found explosive release during the English civil war. The later work by W. J. reinforces our sense of Marvell's understanding of jubilee, as it commemorates a decisive battle in that war, the victory of Cromwell and Fairfax over Charles I and Prince Rupert at Broadmoor, near Naseby. An expanded, though not complete, version of the title makes the intent of the work clear: *The Jubilie of England, from Nasebie to the Mount in Cornwall, and round about; telling of the righteous and glorious acts of the Lord, done for us within the circle of the yeere now past.* The idea of jubilee was, at times, applied to history itself in a way that advanced a developmental model for Reformation, a model that nonetheless warned that development could be far from uniform, could indeed be sporadic.

The periodicity of the Jewish festival (akin to that of the Roman holiday) suggests that God does not expect even his Chosen Ones to maintain such harmony with his will for long; they will have to be brought back to such harmony again and again, even in an institutionalized manner. Following the divine commission, Israel itself will call for trumpets to be sounded to remind its people they have once again wandered away. The trumpets that are to announce the Jubilee (Leviticus 25.9) and that give the festival its name—from the Hebrew *ybel*, ram's horn or trumpet—correspond closely to the "loud uplifted Angeltrumpets" that herald the divine concord in Milton's subsequent lines. There is a suggestion here that Milton's readers/listeners are in need of just such a festival, such a renewal; the suggestion places the readers in the role of the ever-erring, ever-returning people of Israel. As suggested above, the revolutionary meaning of the term *jubilee* also seems to go through recurring, even overlapping cycles. Influenced somewhat by the colonial Puritan heritage, and strongly by early nineteenth-century millennial sentiment about the New Republic,[21] the abolitionist movement used the word extensively as an emblem of its goals: the liberation of slaves and the establishing of a just society. The Jubilee Singers of Fisk University, one of the first institutions of higher education established for emancipated slaves, would later draw their name from Leviticus and lend that name to the type of music most expressive of hope in liberation.[22] By the end of the nineteenth century, though, other associations began to dominate (Queen Victoria's Jubilees, for example) and "Jubilee songs" gradually became part of the minstrel show repertoire. Upbeat spirituals that had announced—if often in a coded fashion—kinship with those who first heard the Mosaic message of freedom from bondage became, too often, a form of entertainment that reassured audiences with supposed exemplars of the Negro's exuberant faith in a purely transcendent deliverance.

From the seventeenth century on, identification with Israel was far more prevalent in the Puritan camp than in the court-connected hierarchy; that is another point of connection, if not influence, between the Good Old Cause and American versions of the cause of liberty.[23] The dismissal by Milton and others of monarchy as "gentilish" was in part a response to court rhetoric: for example, in a sermon delivered in the latter years of James's reign, Launcelot Andrewes concludes his examination of the Magi by commenting that the kingly astrologers were "Gentiles: So are we."[24] Through the sermon, Andrewes implicitly distinguishes between the learned, Established clergy (compared with the Magi themselves) and the untrained, russet-cloaked preachers of the Puritan camp.[25] But such a distinction is a double-edged sword, if not a two-handed engine, since it leaves itself open to the Reformed strategy of casting those who resist reformation in the role of gentile oppressors of the faithful Israelites. Long before Milton's variation on this strategy in *Samson Agonistes*, and before Lodowick Lloyd's appropriation of it for antiquarian purposes, the Eisenach reformer Jakob Strauss pitted the year of Jubilee against the "heathenish laws of the jurists" who were intent on maintaining the status quo and their own privileged station.[26] When Milton addresses his countrymen directly, he assumes the role of the prophet chiding and inspiring the Chosen People. Milton's application of the trumpets of Jubilee to his own time and nation takes on clearly prophetic and apocalyptic overtones in *The Reason of Church Government*, written a decade after "At a Solemn Music." There he sees the call for justice as sounding harshly in the ears of many of his listeners:

> For surely to every good and peaceable man it must in nature needs be a hateful thing to be the displeaser, and molester of thousands; much better would it like him doubtless to be the messenger of gladness and contentment, which is his chief intended business, to all mankind, but that they resist and oppose their own pure happiness. But when God commands to take the trumpet and blow a dolorous or a jarring blast, it lies not in man's will what he shall say or what he shall conceal. (*Complete Prose Works*, 1:803)

The prophet's role is to be impatient with periodic reforms, and as Isaiah and Jeremiah challenged Israel, so John Milton—tacitly invoking their authority—challenges England to return to an accord with the divine will and to sustain it.[27]

While Milton is clearly at pains in *The Reason of Church Government* to reinterpret his personal and poetic history to conform with his increasing conviction that he had already served a prophetic role in English events, not much revisionism is necessary in the case of "At a Solemn Music." The "Angel-trumpets" do recall those which, scripture advises, will be heard at the Second Coming (Matthew 24.31) and at the opening of the Seventh Seal (Revelation 8 and 9). Since the Year of Jubilee was itself interpreted as a type for the final recovery and renewal of all things in and through Christ, Milton reminds his readers of the political significance of the Last Days: Christ's return will signal an end to all oppression and injustice, through a sustained reestablishment of unity between human reason and will and the divine mind and will. However discreetly presented, this characterization of the present time as iniquitous suggests that Milton was no more in the concealing vein in his 1633 verse than he was in the poetry published in 1645, 1667, or after. What does seem to undergo change is his sense of the source of the iniquity, as Milton's antimonarchism developed and then deepened. Three texts—"At a Solemn Music," *The Reason of Church Government*, and *Paradise Lost*—can trace that development and deepening. Early drafts of "At a Solemn Music" show that Milton considered, and rejected, depicting in courtly terms the angelic hosts as ranged in "princely row," as "sweet-wing'd squires," and as "Heavn's henshmen."[28] (Even this, though, could have been in keeping with the ultimate conclusion that only *"His* state / Is kingly": that is, God's alone.) In *The Reason of Church Government,* Milton is at pains to depict Charles as a dupe of the corrupt clergy (*Complete Prose Works,* 1:858–59): the king is presented, in fact, as a Samson enervated by prelatical Delilahs. He grows, in time, unwilling to grant that much virtue to most wearers of an earthly crown. In *Paradise Lost,* Milton uses *jubilee* only twice: in describing the angelic response to the Messiah's meritorious kingship of service and self-sacrifice (3.348); and in describing the heavenly response to the expulsion of the rebellious, monarchially-minded Satan and his followers (6.884). Their joy, their jubilation, is politically grounded as well as divinely inspired.

In Book 12 of *Paradise Lost,* the archangel Michael observes to Adam that political tyranny is rooted in the corruption of human will initiated by Adam and Eve themselves in their fall, and perpetuated in human emulation of diabolic hegemony. Since representative Man

> permits
> Within himself unworthy Powers to reign
> Over free Reason, God in Judgment just
> Subjects him from without to violent Lords;
> Who oft as undeservedly enthral
> His outward freedom: Tyranny must be,
> Though to the Tyrant thereby no excuse.
> (12.90–96)

The characterization of Reason as "free" and of tyrannical enthrallment as "oft . . . undeserved" suggests some question as to how necessary oppression is; after all, "necessity" is elsewhere termed the "Tyrant's plea" (4.393, 394). The younger Milton makes a similar connection in his account of what has interrupted the one-time "perfect Diapason" and what has prevented human observance of just Jubilee; he also suggests what might make that observance more likely. The Fall of humankind occurred when

> disproportion'd sin
> Jarr'd against nature's chime, and with harsh din
> Broke the fair music that all creatures made
> To their great Lord.
> (19–22)

The regeneration of humankind will progress when "we soon again renew that Song" which acknowledges where true sovereignty lies, and when we can maintain that "fair music." Again, the agency is not God's alone.

The interruption of "celestial consort"—of heavenly harmonies and of harmony with the divine will—is represented in the verse by the suspension of the *Jubilee/everlastingly* rhyme. Both resolutions are delayed, and while the aural resolution takes place, the eschatological one is yet to be. Something already here on earth, though, can typify that song of union, as the historical Jubilee typifies the arrival of Christ's just kingdom: that something is human song—but song directed, as were the trumpets of the Year of Jubilee, at communicating a prophetic message of repentance and renewal. This aspect of the power of the "Sphere-born harmonious sisters, Voice and Verse," is made clear in the reference to their Orphic ability to infuse "Dead things with inbreath'd sense" (4). In light of the direct allusion to the first chapter of Ezekiel that follows, the line is also reminiscent of Ezekiel's prophesying in the valley of the dry bones, drawing the bones together, clothing them with sinews, flesh, and skin, and breathing life into them: "So I prophesied as he commanded me, and the breath came into them, and they lived, and stood up upon their feet, an exceeding great army" (Ezekiel 37.10). The martial image, along with the chapter's subsequent interpretation of this renewed army as the "whole house of Israel," contributes a note that is "prophetic" in the conventional sense of being prescient—a sense Milton himself employed as he looked back, as in the headnote to *Lycidas*, upon his earlier work. In *The Reason of Church Government*, though, the foundation of prophecy in spiritual and social reform more fully informs his retrospection.

Milton there explains the benefits and the functions of poetic talents that "are the inspired gift of God" and that are able "to inbreed and cherish in a great people the seeds of virtue and public civility, to allay the perturbations of the mind and set the affections in right tune" (*Complete Prose Works*, 1:816–17). At this point, Milton may not be recalling the more obviously "prophetic" *Lycidas* as much as he recalls "At a Solemn Music," which asserts that the "Blest pair of Sirens" can reveal the "Song of pure concent" to human imagination, to "our high-rais'd fantasy" (5–6): in both poetry and prose we find echoes of the Sidneyan account of the "erected wit" and its relation to the "infected will" that is our inheritance from the Fall. We also find echoes of the Spenserian faith that imaginative works can circumvent "the use of these days seeing all things accounted by their showes, and nothing esteemed of, that is not delightfull and pleasing to commune sence"[29] in Milton's confidence that prophetic verse is able to reach "those especially . . . who will not so much as look upon Truth herself, unless they see her elegantly dressed" (*Complete Prose Works*, 1:818). The blest Sirens, then, can entice the fallen imagination to perceive more accurately "the paths of honesty and good life," which are "indeed easy and pleasant." But in distinction both from Spenser's skepticism and from Sidney's more conservative pessimism about how thoroughly the realms of history and eternity—mutability and sabbath—can overlap, Milton's sense of the progressive dynamic in Reformation and in Jubilee envisions the easy yoke and light burden of Christian virtue and *civitas* gradually appearing preferable, in the eyes of his fellow-citizens, to present bondages of sin and political injustice.[30] Any such progress, though, has been marked by periodicity, by renewal and relapse. As Milton winds up his catalog of poetic "abilities," he mentions the need and the duty "to deplore the general relapses of Kingdoms and States from justice and God's true worship" (*Complete Prose Works*, 1:817).

While humanity awaits the renewal of its ability to participate in the universal harmony, song that can truly be termed solemn—religious, awe-inspiring, and especially prophetic—cannot only prepare its hearers for the resolution of human and sacred history; such "solemn Jubilee" can inspire them to join in that resolution. Regina Schwartz has noted that, in Milton's understanding, hymns should "not simply *interpret* time typologically, but *enact* typology."[31] It is worth remembering that the original heading—perhaps title—of "At a Solemn Music" in the Trinity Manuscript is, simply, *Song*. In its "mixt power" of voice and verse, sacred song can remind men and women of their "first obedience and their state of good" (24) and prompt them "with undiscording voice" to "rightly answer that melodious noise" (17–18). The potentially oxymoronic *melodious noise* reinforces the sense that the proper answer at any one time may sound jarring to some ears; only as time resolves itself into the "endless morn of light," as described in the final line, will the "consort" be universally harmonious. Milton's iconoclastic approach to poetic form, embryonically present in the deferred rhyme in "At a Solemn Music," will develop into the gloriously resistant rhymes of *Lycidas*—which are all the more powerful for their being placed at the culmination of the English verses in the 1645 *Poems*, each elegantly (and respectably, to use Thomas Corns's term) balanced by its Latin counterpart. Perhaps the great culmination of Milton's experiments with form and antiform comes with the recasting of *Paradise Lost* into twelve books: while this makes the epic "conform" with the classical models it ruthlessly interrogates, it also disrupts many of the topomorphical balances that are at work in the earlier version. Joseph A. Wittreich cites seventeenth- and eighteenth-century biblical commentators to establish how prophetic utterances were thought to be marked by "too ardent a spirit to be confined by rule" and also how the scriptures themselves were not to be viewed "like an artificial Garden, wherein the Walks are plain and regular."[32] John Milton's special skill, perhaps, is his ability to invoke—and even to invent—such rules and artifice and then to defy both in order to claim the spiritual and political authority of prophecy.

I have suggested a way of reading an author's poem and, indeed, *corpus* that reflects, I hope, overriding concerns and conceptions for the author and for his age. However skeptical our own age has been about authorial functions, neither the idea of the author nor the idea of literary and scriptural authority was foreign to Milton or to the seventeenth century. At the same time, though, he and his age were deeply aware of the constructed and even contingent qualities of both ideas, even as the concepts were invoked in support of various claims to other kinds of authority. A way of reading this poem, along with other poems of the age, that takes into account both the conviction and the critical perspective such ideas provoked will provide a useful means of beginning again the process of entering into the age's understanding of itself. Jon S. Lawry's cogent remarks on the message of "At a Solemn Music" can be usefully extended to both Milton's historical moment and the critical enterprise: whether we are envisioning the end times, the just society, or the poetic craft, we all have "to move from passive rapture to active pursuit of its conditions."[33] I would add that the pursuit entails understanding of the terms employed to describe that rapture and those conditions; the history of the construction of *jubilee* is a case in point. This model of historical criticism is indebted to the dynamic process advanced by—and embodied in—Miltonic prophecy. In the case of historical criticism, of course, words inspire the process of recovering not pure "concent" but a less than harmonious age. As with Miltonic prophecy, though, the recovery is never quite complete in time, and instead occupies a curious space between being and becoming, between the synchronic and the diachronic.

Notes

1. Edward Chaney, "*Pro se et appendico Anglicano defensio*: Response to a Review of *The Grand Tour and the Great Rebellion*," *Milton Quarterly* 23 (1989): 80.

2. David Loewenstein, *Milton and the Drama of History* (Cambridge: Cambridge University Press, 1990), 119–20.

3. Stanley Fish, "The Temptation to Action in Milton's Poetry," *ELH* 48 (1981): 516.

4. Fish, "Temptation to Action," 518.

5. John Milton, "At a Solemn Music," *John Milton: Complete Poetry and Major*

Prose, ed. Merritt Y. Hughes (New York: Odyssey Press, 1957). All references to Milton's poetry are to this edition and are cited parenthetically in the text.

6. David Norbrook, *Poetry and Politics in the English Renaissance* (London: Routledge and Kegan Paul, 1984), 242, 272.

7. Joseph A. Wittreich, *Visionary Poetics: Milton's Tradition and His Legacy* (San Marino, Calif.: Huntington Library, 1979), 173.

8. See John Milton, *Poems: Reproduced in Facsimile from the Manuscript in Trinity College, Cambridge* (Menston Ilkley, England: Scolar Press, 1972), 4–5.

9. E. M. W. Tillyard, *Milton* (London: Chatto and Windus, 1949), 64–65.

10. Cleanth Brooks and John Edward Hardy, eds., *Poems of Mr. John Milton: The 1645 Edition with Essays in Analysis* (New York: Harcourt, Brace, 1951), 119.

11. All biblical references are to the King James Version and are cited parenthetically in the text.

12. Leopold von Ranke, *History of the Reformation in Germany*, trans. Sarah Austin (London: Routledge, 1905; reprint, New York: Frederick Ungar, 1966), 1:335. The anger against ecclesiastical dues and rents is noted in Abraham Friesen, *Thomas Muentzer, a Destroyer of the Godless: The Making of a Seventeenth–Century Religious Revolutionary* (Berkeley: University of California Press, 1990), 193–94. Other financial burdens on the peasantry are documented by Thomas A. Brady, Jr., *Ruling Class, Regime, and Reformation at Strausbourg 1520–1555* (Leiden: E. J. Brill, 1978), 147–52.

13. Robin Bruce Barnes, *Prophecy and Gnosis: Apocalypticism in the Wake of the Lutheran Reformation* (Stanford, Calif.: Stanford University Press, 1988), 127, 129.

14. C. A. Patrides, "Apocalyptic Configurations in Milton," *The Apocalypse in English Renaissance Thought and Literature: Patterns, Antecedents, Repercussions*, ed. C. A. Patrides and Joseph A. Wittreich (Manchester: Manchester University Press, 1984), 218.

15. In entry 1.a. for *jubilee*, the *OED* cites the second edition of Samuel Purchas, *Purchas His Pilgrimage* (London, 1614), 126; the passage also appears in subsequent versions, such as that of 1617, 108.

16. Sir Thomas Browne, *Religio Medici*, line 44, ed. L. C. Martin (Oxford: Clarendon Press, 1964), 42. Browne, however, also invokes the millennial dimensions of the term in line 46: "I am afraid that the Soules that now depart . . . groane in the expectation of the great Jubilee" (44).

17. John Milton, *Complete Prose Works of John Milton,* 8 vols., ed. Don M. Wolfe et al. (New Haven: Yale University Press, 1953–82). All references to Milton's prose are to this edition and are cited parenthetically in the text. I have modernized both spelling and typography slightly.

18. Andrew Marvell, *Poems and Letters*, ed. H. M. Margoliouth, rev. Pierre Legouis and E. E. Duncan-Jones (Oxford: Clarendon Press, 1971), 1:50–51. Margoliouth and Legouis (266–67) suggest that the "gentler Conqueror" lauded in the poem is Lord Fairfax; John Hollander, in agreement with Percy Scholes, identifies the figure as Oliver Cromwell in *The Untuning of the Sky* (Princeton: Princeton University Press, 1961), 314.

19. Lodowick Lloyd, *The Jubile of Britane* (London, 1607), 3.

20. Lloyd, *Jubile*, 2.

21. The famed Congregationalist minister Lyman Beecher—father to both Henry Ward Beecher and Harriet Beecher Stowe—celebrated the revolutionary, republican, and Puritan character of the United States in terms of jubilee. In his 1826 address, *The Memory of Our Fathers*, he foresaw the millenium's being achieved by "revolutions and overturnings," inspired by American example, that would spread "until the world

is free.... Then will the trumpet of jubilee sound, and earth's debased millions will leap from the dust, and shake off their chains, and cry 'Hosanna to the Son of David!'" See Constance Mayfield Rourke, *Trumpets of Jubilee* (New York: Harcourt, Brace, 1927), 30–31. Keith W. F. Stavely's *Puritan Legacies: "Paradise Lost" and the New England Tradition, 1630–1890* (Ithaca: Cornell University Press, 1987) does not consider the anti-slavery movement as part of "the New England tradition" he discusses and therefore does not explore the possibility of Miltonic inspirations and analogues for abolitionism.

22. Joe M. Richardson, *A History of Fisk University, 1865–1946* (University: University of Alabama Press, 1980), 29. While the name was initially selected by music director and college administrator George L. White, the members of the group ratified the choice themselves. That collaborative process is paralleled by the avidity with which the term and concept of *jubilee*, largely popularized by whites opposed to slavery, was embraced by African Americans; the most famous example is Margaret Walker's *Jubilee* (Boston: Houghton Mifflin, 1966), which employs both actual slave spirituals and songs by abolitionists such as Henry C. Work ("Marching Through Georgia" and "Kingdom Coming").

23. Nathan O. Hatch, *The Sacred Cause of Liberty: Republican Thought and the Millenium in Revolutionary New England* (New Haven: Yale University Press, 1977), 94–96. See also the early documents compiled by Conrad Cherry in *God's New Israel: Religious Interpretations of American Destiny* (Englewood Cliffs, N.J.: Prentice-Hall, 1971).

24. Launcelot Andrewes, *XCVI Sermons* (London, 1632), 147.

25. I have discussed elsewhere how Andrewes's rhetoric here participates in a tradition that endeavors to "redeem" pagan learning as compatible with—and conducive to—Christian piety; see "Marsilio Ficino's *De stella magorum* and Renaissance Views of the Magi," *Renaissance Quarterly* 43 (1990): 369. Thomas N. Corns has argued that the 1645 *Poems* is an attempt on Milton's part to demonstrate his learning, to show that his increasingly apparent radicalism was not grounded in ignorance. Milton, from this perspective, was anxious to prove that he was not one of the "russet Rabbies" or self-crowned "Doctors of the Church" dismissed by Daniel Featley in *The Dippers Dipt* (London, 1645), 129, 136; see Corns, "Milton's Quest for Respectability," *Modern Language Review* 77 (1982): 771.

26. Ranke, *History of the Reformation*, 1:335. Even as he disagreed with Strauss and others about the binding nature of Mosaic law on Christians, Martin Luther acknowledged the justice at work in Jubilee:

> Again in Moses it is also stipulated that no man should sell his field into a perpetual estate, but only up to the jubilee year [*Laut jar*]. When that year came, every man returned to the field or the possessions which he had sold. In this way the possessions remained in the family relationship. There are also other extraordinarily fine rules in Moses which one should like to accept.

Luther, though, does not think Jubilee should be obligatory; see his *Works*, ed. E. Theodore Bachmann (Philadelphia: Muhlenberg Press, 1960), 35:167.

27. William Kerrigan cites both John Calvin and Tommaso Campanella in establishing not only the contemporary significance of prophecy in the Reformist perspective, but its possible relation to monarchy. Campanella calls Tasso's poetry "almost prophetic, because the true prophet is the one who not only says future things, but who scolds princes for their wickedness and cowardice"; Calvin, in his second lecture on Jeremiah, holds that prophets and teachers may "boldly set themselves against kings and nations." See Kerrigan *The Prophetic Milton* (Charlottesville: University Press of Virginia, 1974), 52n, 70, 95.

28. Milton, *Poems . . . from the Manuscript in Trinity College*, 4.

29. Edmund Spenser, *The Faerie Queene*, ed. Thomas P. Roche, Jr. (New Haven: Yale University Press, 1981), 16.

30. As Wittreich observes: "For Spenser, eternity, though it may be glanced at from history, lies beyond it; for Milton, in contrast, history may be brought to an apotheosis" (*Visionary Poetics,* 73).

31. Regina M. Schwartz, *Remembering and Repeating: Biblical Creation in "Paradise Lost"* (Cambridge: Cambridge University Press, 1988), 82.

32. Robert Lowth, *Lectures on the Sacred Poetry of the Hebrews*, trans. G. Gregory (Boston: Joseph Buckingham, 1815), 211; Henry More, *An Explanation of the Grand Mystery of Godliness* (London, 1660), 4. Qtd. in Wittreich,*Visionary Poetics,* 28.

33. Jon S. Lawry, *The Shadow of Heaven* (Ithaca: Cornell University Press, 1968), 59.

Milton's Royalist Reflex: The Failure of Argument and the Role of Dialogics in *Eikonoklastes*

JANE HILES

Eikonoklastes is a prime example of the sometimes self-defeating oddity of Miltonic polemics. While it is not surprising, given his disdain for royalist "masking" and image-mongering, that Milton eschews the bathetic fervor of the *Eikon Basilike*, it is surprising that *Eikonoklastes* diverges so sharply from the most common argumentative strategies of its time.[1] To invoke Thomas Wilson's criteria from the *Arte of Rhetorique* (1553), Milton not only fails to excoriate the excess of Caroline misgovernment so vividly that his readers feel "as though they saw it plaine before their iyes," but he also neglects to "[heap] together" the details and "al the circumstaunces" of that wrongdoing (that is, to compound them) in order to make the king's "offence[s]" seem not just treasonable, but "so hainouse, that the like hath not been seene heretofore."[2] By Wilson's standards, therefore, *Eikonoklastes* is neither an especially passionate invective against the excesses of Charles I's reign, nor even as thoroughgoing a demonstration as it might have been of the king's treasonable unfitness as a ruler and the consequent justice of his overthrow and execution. This failure is a symptom of what one might call Milton's *royalist reflex*: his propensity to follow the royalist pattern of shifting the blame for the king's crimes to advisors or others, minimizing the king's offenses by failing to elaborate on them, and focusing on the literary aspects of the conflict to the near exclusion of larger ideological issues. The result is a surprisingly unrhetorical response, one that consistently has been criticized as strange and inadequate. William Riley Parker, for example, maintains that Milton "tried to be reasonable, and succeeded in being largely irrelevant"; it perhaps would be fairer to say that Milton's response is relevant to something other than what its readers over the years have anticipated.[3]

Eikonoklastes at times seems irrelevant because at crucial junctures it declines to engage the *Eikon Basilike* on the (rhetorical) terms its readers expect. What the seventeenth-century reader—or even the twentieth-century reader, for that matter—would anticipate is that *Eikonoklastes* either should respond to the *Eikon Basilike*'s emotional appeal with an even more heightened emotional appeal of its own, or it should provide a thoroughgoing logical demonstration of royalist misrepresentations, proved with syllogisms and copious examples. What Milton delivers, however, is not a subtle exercise in the logic of republicanism, nor is it an especially passionate invective against the crimes of Charles I's reign, nor even as thoroughgoing a demonstration as it might have been of the king's treasonable unfitness as a ruler and the consequent justice of his expulsion and punishment. Instead, Milton borrows a page from the royalist text to construct an essentially stylistic response to a work that he considered a literary fiction. The strategy for this response is at once related to fictionalization, to literary criticism, and to the citation and reply method so common in the point-by-point refutations of the seventeenth century.

Although Milton declares in the preface to *Eikonoklastes* that the king's "own guilt, not imputed any more to his evil Counsellors . . . shall be laid heer without circumlocutions at his own dore" (3:341), this blame frequently fails to materialize. Instead, at crucial junctures *Eikonoklastes* is curiously devoid of a sense of the king's agency. Behind the fraud of the king's book, for example, Milton discerns not Charles I, but the advantage-seekers of the royalist party, who "intend [the *Eikon Basilike*] not so much the defence of [the king's] former actions, as the promoting of thir own future designes, making thereby the Book thir own . . . more then his" (3:338). Even though he has caught Charles I (literally) countenancing a "Politick Fetch" more blatant than the one for which *Of Reformation* excoriated the English bishops, Milton nevertheless restrains his judgment against this "politic contriver" (343), explaining that the king's person, "or his Name at least . . . [was] made use of" by the royalist party, who "took him to set a face upon thir own malignant designes" (345). Grammatically and ideologically, Milton here allows Charles to assume the all too familiar role of the passive object of other men's political subterfuges. In so doing, Milton himself shifts the blame for the deception from Charles to the royalist party.

Similarly, in attempting to attack the king's willful misconstruction of recent history and his invocation of divine judgment in the service of royalist propaganda, Milton becomes so caught up in the agency of Charles's "reprobate thoughts" that he neglects to inveigh against the will that moves them:

> And he, who without warrant but his own fantastic surmise, takes upon him perpetually to unfold the secret and unsearchable Mysteries of high Providence ... approaches to the madness of *those reprobate thoughts, that would wrest the Sword of Justice out of God's own hand, and imploy it more justly in thir own conceit*. (564; emphasis mine)

While it brilliantly captures the essence of the proprietary struggle over authoritative interpretation, the metaphor of the reprobate thoughts simultaneously derails the accusation against the king. Thus, while Milton intends to accuse Charles of disguising his attempted usurpation of divine prerogative as just interpretation, he merely succeeds in raising curiosity about the drama of these insurgent thoughts. Not Charles, but thoughts themselves have become the usurpers here. The ad hominem is so weakened at this juncture that Milton tries to refocus his attention on Charles's overreaching in the next sentence:

> we see him doing little less then laying hands on the weapons of God himself, which are his judgements, *to weild and manage them by the sway and bent of his own fragile cogitations*. (564; emphasis mine)

Milton ends with the efficacy, not of Charles's actions, but of his thoughts, and thus the metaphor reestablishes itself even as Milton attempts to discard it. This is not an isolated instance of Milton's failure to emphatically attribute the king's deeds to the king's person. Elsewhere Milton even manages to shift the blame for Charles's undeserved reputation from his obvious attempts to control public opinion to the impugned judgment of the populace:

> By so strange a method amongst the mad multitude is a sudden reputation won, of wisdom by wilfulness and suttle shifts, of goodness by multiplying evil, of piety by endeavouring to root out true religion. (345)

Here the complicity of the "mad multitude" in its own victimization tends to exculpate the king, while Milton's suspicions about the genesis of the king's reputation balance the laudatory rhetoric of popular opinion without overcoming it. In the very attempt to confute Charles's putative virtues, Milton manages only to enumerate them.

If Milton's concern over the indecorousness of blaming the dead king militates against the effectiveness of *Eikonoklastes*, his failure to compound evidence against Charles—or, in Wilson's words, to "heap together" all the details of the king's misdeeds—is even more damaging. When Milton contends in chapter 1, for example, that "All men by thir own and thir Childrens interest are oblig'd to honestie and justice: but how little that consideration works in privat men, how much less in Kings, thir deeds declare best" (357), the assertion calls for a list, however abbreviated, of Charles's dishonest and unjust deeds in order not to beg the question. What follows, however, is no such enumeration of the king's deeds but rather a further criticism of his words, as Milton takes issue with a subsequent passage of the *Eikon Basilike*. While the whole of Milton's chapter may be retrospectively construed as proof of the king's dishonesty (and indeed, Milton implies in his preface that the very words of the *Eikon Basilike* are Charles's most horrible act of deception), the predominant localized effect of Milton's approach is to create the sense of an unsubstantiated accusation on the one hand and a non sequitur on the other.

This failure to compound the king's crimes effectively is especially striking in light of abundant proof that Milton could write cutting invective and formidable arguments. His excoriation of the martyred protestant bishops in *Of Reformation*, for example, makes *Eikonoklastes'* repudiation of Charles's false martyrdom seem generous by comparison. When *Eikonoklastes* enumerates Charles's offences, the list is succinct, almost abbreviated, and contains few rhetorical flourishes:

> such illegal actions . . . to get vast summs of Money, were put in practise by the King and his new Officers, as Monopolies, compulsive Knighthoods, Cote, Conduct and Ship money, the seizing not of one *Naboths* Vineyard, but of whole Inheritances under the pretence of Forrest, or Crown-Lands, corruption and Bribery compounded for, with impunities granted for the future. (353)

Only two elements, a tag declaring Charles's fiscal abuses illegal and a biblical simile, enlarge or comment upon an otherwise unadorned list. Milton even announces in *Eikonoklastes* his intention to avoid speaking ill of one who has "payd his final debt both to Nature and his Faults" (337). In *Of Reformation*, however, Milton had exhibited no such restraint toward the English bishops. There Latimer, Cranmer, and Ridley, despite having paid their respective debts and more, are the objects of a double-barrelled assault of logic and invective:

> The *Bishops* . . . suffer'd themselvs to be the common stales to countenance with their prostituted Gravities every Politick Fetch that was then on foot, as oft as the Potent *Statists* pleas'd to employ them. . . . But it will be said, These men were *Martyrs*: What then? Though every true Christian will

be a *Martyr* when he is called to it; not presently does it follow that every one suffering for Religion, is without exception. Saint *Paul* writes, that *A man may give his Body to be burnt,* (meaning for Religion) *and yet not have Charitie*: He is not therfore above all possibility of erring, because hee burnes for some Points of Truth. (*Complete Prose Works*, 1:530 –31, 533)

Of Reformation assails not only the judgment, but the honesty and ultimately the righteousness of the English bishops in a vitriolic argument ad hominem. The vehemence of this argument arises less from its logical content, which turns on an apt distinction between martyrdom and sanctification, than from the reiteration of pejoratives: not only have the bishops erred but, according to Milton, they have sold their consciences; they have, he insists, "prostituted" their reputations like "common stales." Repetition gives weight to the simile, and leading rhetoric ("Politick Fetch," for example, rather than "political objective") urges the reader to affirm his conclusion. While *Eikonoklastes'* list lacks the emphatic repetition to convey the scope and seriousness of the offence it decries, *Of Reformation's* castigation of the bishops abounds in vivid detail that takes the form of emphatic repetition and editorializing commentary:

> Nor was this the first time that they discover'd to bee followers of this World; for when the Protectors Brother, Lord Sudley . . . through private malice and mal-engine was to lose his life, *no man could bee found fitter* then Bishop Latimer . . . to divulge in his Sermon the *forged Accusations.* . . . *What could be more impious* then to debarre the Children of the King from their right to the Crowne? To comply with the *ambitious Usurpation* of a Traytor; and to make void the last Will of Henry 8 . . . ? Yet Bishop Cranmer . . . and the other Bishops none refusing . . . *could find in their Consciences* to set their hands to the disinabling and defeating *not onely* of Princesse Mary the Papist, *but* of Elizabeth the Protestant. (1:532–33; emphasis mine)

Evaluative tags ("ambitious Usurpation") and leading commentary ("What could be more impious") work in conjunction with semantic intensifiers ("not onely . . . but" and "Nor was this the first time") to reiterate and emphasize Milton's charges against the bishops. Such loaded rhetoric serves to compound Milton's charges and (tautologically) to imply a judgment in the very accusation. "No man could be found fitter" to scheme than Bishop Latimer, Milton contends; "Nor was this the first time" the bishops had been guilty of political maneuverings (532–33). In comparison, the texture of *Eikonoklastes* is curiously flat.

The combined effects of Milton's tendency to shift the blame and his failure to forcefully compound evidence even lend an odd flatness and irrelevancy to his description of one of the stellar outrages of Charles's reign—the king's entrance into the House of Commons with several hundred armed troops on 4 January, 1642. The House of Commons's *Declaration . . . Touching a Late Breach of Their Privileges* (17 January, 1642) demonstrates the polemical value of detail strategically used. The declaration begins with an overview of the king's actions:

> His Majesty . . . came to the said House, attended with a great Multitude of men, armed in warlike manner with halberds, swords and pistols, who came up to the very door of the House, and placed themselves there . . . to the great terror and disturbance of the members then sitting.[4]

Even in this brief passage, the parliamentary writer includes more visual detail and more editorial commentary than mere reportage requires. He describes not just many men, but a multitude; their specific armaments are bodied forth; his editorial commentary assures the reader that these very halberds, swords and pistols are the weapons of war; and lest the implication thereof be dismissed, the House's "terror and disturbance" model the reaction of the ideal reader. Having established the nature of the trespass, the *Declaration* then reiterates and elaborates upon the circumstances of the invasion in language intended to emphasize the affront to the dignity of Commons and the pugnacious hostility of the royalist troops:

> many soldiers, Papists and others, to the number of about five hundred, came with His Majesty . . . to the . . . House of Commons, armed with swords, pistols and other weapons, and divers of them pressed to the door of the said House, thrust away the door-keepers, and placed themselves between the said door and the ordinary attendants of His Majesty, holding up their swords, and some holding up their pistols . . . and they not suffering the said door according to the custom of Parliament to be shut. . . . And some . . . did likewise violently assault, and by force disarm some of the attendants and servants of the members of the House of Commons.[5]

Cast thus as an armed incursion, Charles's action appears revolutionary, an effect that the strategic mention of Roman Catholic forces is intended to reinforce. At the same time, a running editorial commentary warns that this attempt to arrest members of Commons is "a high breach of the rights and privileges of Parliament, and inconsistent with the liberties and freedom thereof," that Charles is attempting to do what "by law he cannot do," and that this threat by armed troops "was a traitorous design against the King and Parliament."[6] Thomas May's treatment of the incident includes the same sort of editorial commentary but frames it with the monarch's promises to protect the parliament:

the House of Commons . . . Petitioned him to allow them a Guard for security of their Persons while they sate. . . .

Which Petition was denied by the King; but with a solemn engagement of himself by the *Word of a King, that the security of all, and every one of them, from violence was, and ever should be, as much his care, as the preservation of himself and his Children.* . . .

The next day after that the King had thus answered the Petition . . . he gave unhappily a just occasion to think that their fears and jealousies were not causelesse. For upon that day the King came to the Parliament in Person.[7]

May transforms historical detail into an ironic narrative by juxtaposing Charles's promises of parliamentary safety against his assault on parliamentary privilege. Viewed within the context of Charles's breach of the very parliamentary safety he had just guaranteed, his subsequent promise from the unpromising locale of the Speaker of the House's chair that *"no King of England that ever was, should be more careful to maintain the Privileges of Parliament than he would be"* seems an irony worthy of Richard III.[8] May's masterful emplotment makes a final thrust at the king by enumerating the "many circumstances" by which "this great breach of Privileges of Parliament was encreased."[9] The result is a strong indictment of kingly perfidy.

Milton could have fashioned an even stronger indictment, had he made strategic use of his material. And this is precisely what he seems to do at the outset. Using Charles's own words against him, Milton reminds his audience that the king has already admitted that his entrance into the House of Commons was "a plaine breach of thir Privilege" (*Eikonoklastes*, 3:377). This admitted, Milton enlists the monarch's own criteria to convict him of treason:

> *He had discover'd as he thought unlawfull correspondencies which they had us'd, and ingagements to imbroile his Kingdomes*, and remembers not his own unlawfull correspondencies, and conspiracies with the Irish Army of Papists, with the French to land at Portsmouth, and his tampering both with the English and the Scotch Army, to come up against the Parlament: the least of which attempts by whomsoever, was no less then manifest Treason against the Common-wealth. (377–78)

Rather than build on this sound denunciation, however, Milton ultimately trivializes it by shifting from blame directed at the king's behavior to ridicule directed at the king's language:

> *That I went*, saith he . . . *attended with some Gentlemen*; Gentlemen indeed; the ragged Infantrie of Stewes and Brothels . . . and then he pleads *it was no unwonted thing for the Majesty and safety of a King to be so attended.* . . .

> An illustrious Majestie no doubt, so attended: a becomming safety for the King of *England*. ... Happy times; when Braves and Hacksters, the onely contented Members of his Goverment, were thought the fittest and the faithfullest to defend his Person against the discontents of a Parlament and all good Men. (380–81)

The stately irony of May's prosecution is here degraded to burlesque; Charles's treasonous incursion against the House of Commons is not compounded by details of the trespass, but rather downgraded to a breach of decorum. Not only does the dismissive tone of Milton's ridicule deny the importance of his topic, but his broad slaps at the royalist troops serve to promote the soldiers as the subjects of his discourse, thereby distracting attention from the real object of his invective, the king.

If Milton's decision not to attack Charles roundly can be seen as an excess of decorum, his obsession with the *Eikon Basilike* as a literary text seems an excess of subtlety. It often seems that the greatest authorial energy in *Eikonoklastes* is dedicated to delivering a sidelong jeer at an inferior literary artifact. Milton appears to have read the collection of prose set pieces that comprise the *Eikon Basilike* less as arguments than as literature—and responded to them in kind.[10] This is not to insist that Milton never enumerates the faults of Charles and his favorites, but to suggest that Milton's response to the king's book is at once less emotional, less reasoned and more artistic than its occasion would seem to warrant. Like a literary critic, Milton is preoccupied with the style of the king's book. His disdain for the *Eikon Basilike*'s belletristic flourishes is well known: "Poets indeed use to vapor much after this manner," he sneers (502). Elsewhere he treats the tropes and colors of the *Eikon Basilike* with sardonic amusement:

> The Simily wherwith he begins I was about to have found fault with, as in a garb somwhat more Poetical then for a Statist: but meeting with many straines of like dress in other of his Essaies, and hearing him reported a more diligent reader of Poets, then of Politicians, I begun to think that the whole Book might perhaps be intended a peece of Poetrie. The words are good, the fiction smooth and cleanly; there wanted only Rime. (406)

And we know what Milton thought of rhyme.[11] Despite its obvious failings, or perhaps because of them, Milton consistently demonstrates his engagement with the literary aspects of the king's book, linking the *Eikon Basilike*'s lack of artistic merit to Charles I's political demerits: "But to bad Kings, who without cause expect future glory from thir actions, it happ'ns as to bad Poets; who sit and starve themselves with a delusive hope to win immortality by thir bad lines"

(502).¹² Because such royalist fictions are Milton's grand topic in *Eikonoklastes*, his linkage of Charles's political machinations to the *Eikon Basilike*'s literary tropes is perfectly appropriate.

Too often, however, Milton seems preoccupied with the style of the king's book to the exclusion of its ideology. Even in what is perhaps *Eikonoklastes*' most vitriolic attack on Charles, Milton's preoccupation with the royalist use of metaphor distracts him from the central issue of power relations. In answer to the royalists' adoption of the metaphor of paternity, or patriarchal authority, to express the prerogatives of unlimited monarchy, Milton responds with the implication that, by asserting the masculine force of his control on Parliament's conceptions, Charles attempted to exercise unnatural (i.e., incestuous) mastery over the mother of his kingly legitimacy (467). Unfortunately, Milton attenuates his just charge of unlawful interference with Parliament by casting it in an unsustainable metaphor. While the image of the monarch forcing incestuous relations upon the Parliament has considerable shock value initially, the poor fit of the metaphor—Charles was hardly guilty of too liberal congress with parliaments—almost immediately undercuts the effectiveness of Milton's accusation and distracts from the more serious complaint about Charles's abusive refusal to call parliaments and his early dismissals of those few he did call. Cast as it is, Milton's real complaint seems to be against Charles's highly literary self-imaging as the patriarch of England and not against his attempts to disempower the Parliament.

Another of *Eikonoklastes*' specifically literary concerns is the identification of the many voices that constitute the royalist text. Pamela's prayer, which Milton identified as having been plagiarized from Sir Philip Sidney's *New Arcadia*, is the best-known example, but it is just one of many imported voices that derive from literary sources such as the speeches of Shakespeare's Richard II and Richard III or from biblical sources such as the Psalms of David and even the words of Christ. Throughout *Eikonoklastes*, Milton's aim is to display the seams in this ostensibly unified royalist discourse and to orchestrate the *Eikon Basilike*'s borrowed voices so that they interrogate each other. This situation suggests that both *Eikonoklastes* and the *Eikon Basilike* may be best understood, not in the light of traditional argument, but from the perspective of a stylistics that focuses on the interplay of voices in a given discourse. Such a perspective will reveal that Milton's response is inherently literary—and inherently subversive.

As M. M. Bakhtin explains in a monograph entitled "Discourse in the Novel," language consists in political beliefs and ideological constructs as well as in morphemes, for language as he perceives it is "ideologically saturated"; it is not merely a vocabulary but "a world view ... a concrete opinion."[13] The system of conventions and norms recognized by a society as its "common unitary language" serves, according to Bakhtin, to "unite and centralize verbal-ideological thought," and it perpetuates the status quo[14] by

> giv[ing] expression to forces working toward concrete verbal and ideological unification and centralization, which develop in vital connection with the processes of sociopolitical and cultural centralization.[15]

"Philosophy of language, linguistics and stylistics," Bakhtin maintains, "have all postulated a simple and unmediated relation of speaker to his unitary and singular 'own' language, and have postulated as well a simple realization of this language in the monologic [single-voiced] utterance of the individual."[16] He contends, however, that the "centripetal" force of unitary language is opposed by the "centrifugal" force of dissenting voices when languages enter into dialogue.[17] As a colloquy of voices or ideological "speaking consciousness[es]," dialogue is by definition the locus of multiple meaning, contradiction, influence and interpenetration.[18] Thus, genres in which more than one language or voice is obvious or latent—specifically the novel "and those artistic-prose genres that gravitate toward it"—attempt to subvert the status quo enforced by official language by introducing other voices into the official monologue. This multi-voicedness, or *heteroglossia*, is "aimed sharply and polemically against the official languages of its given time."[19] To point out the essentially multivoiced nature of the seemingly monologic official utterance called the *Eikon Basilike*,[20] as Milton does in *Eikonoklastes*, is thus at once to recognize in it an inherently literary (i.e., dialogic) quality and to use equally literary means to attempt to subvert the established political order by revealing the incipient disunity of its official language and the existence of an alternate language—and thus an alternate ideology.[21]

Chapter 25 of *Eikonoklastes*, for example, issues such a challenge to official discourse by examining the *Eikon Basilike*'s implicit comparison of Charles I to David in the light of the political subtext of the king's utterances and the moral context of their scriptural source. Striking a note of Psalmic lament, the *Eikon Basilike*'s "Penitential Meditations and Vows in the King's Solitude at Holmby" ostensibly plead for divine mercy on the English people:

> And if Thy anger be not to be yet turned
> away, but Thy hand of justice must be
> stretched out still, let it, I beseech Thee,
> be against me and my father's house; as for
> these sheep, what have they done?

> Let my sufferings satiate the malice of
> mine and Thy church's enemies.
> But let their cruelty never exceed the
> measure of my charity.[22]

The source of this purloined prayer is 1 Chronicles 21.17:

> And David said unto God, Is it not I that commanded the people to be numbered? even I it is that have sinned and done evil indeed; *but as for these sheep, what have they done? let thine hand, I pray thee, O Lord my God, be on me, and on my father's house; but not on thy people*, that they should be plagued (emphasis mine).[23]

In Chronicles, it is God's charity that is at issue, not the king's. Choosing divine mercy over human justice, David cries, "let me fall now into the hand of the Lord; for very great are his mercies: but let me not fall into the hand of man" (1 Chronicles 21.13). The *Eikon Basilike*, on the other hand, retracts its Davidic prayer for the people's welfare by submitting it to the limits of the king's dubious mercy: "But let their cruelty never exceed the measure of my charity."[24] By recalling the biblical context for this utterance, Milton constructs an implicit comparison between the limits of Charles's kingly compassion on the one hand and the unlimited bounty of divine love on the other, and he reveals that Charles's covert intention is far from the intention of David's imported voice. David's demonstration of compassion for his people is not conditional (as is Charles's) on either his subjects' behavior or the limits of his own tolerance; rather, it issues from David's acknowledgment of his error and his faith in divine compassion. Charles, according to Milton, "usurp[s] and ill imitate[s]" David's language by misapplying David's prayer to spare his people to a situation in which Charles had been unwilling to spare his own; in Milton's terms, this is "the vain ostentation of imitating *Davids* language, not his life" (3:555). "Had he borrow'd *Davids* heart," Milton complained earlier, "it had bin much the holier theft" (3:547). Thus the real issue, both in 1 Chronicles 21 and in Milton's response, is, as *The Interpreter's Bible* suggests, not royal beneficence but royal presumption—not only David's but Charles's "sin of arrogance"—that caused their respective kingdoms to suffer in the first place.[25]

In responding to Charles's purloined Davidic prayer, Milton's reflex is to borrow a page from the royalist script; he, too, invokes a scriptural voice—none other than the voice of Christ:

> His prayer is most of it borrow'd out of *David*; but what if it be answerd him as the *Jewes*, who trusted in *Moses*, were answerd by our *Saviour*. There is one that accuseth you, eev'n *David* whom you misapply. (3:446)

In much the same way that the Messiah of *Paradise Regained* turns to scripture in order to answer Satan's temptations, Milton enlists the (carefully attributed) scriptural voice of Christ to chasten the king's version of David. Thus Milton creates a dialogue between David and Christ on the right use of scripture by cleverly employing Charles's heavy-handed imitation of Christ to respond to yet another royal imposture. In the end, the fictionalized Charles I of the *Eikon Basilike* seems to rebuke himself. Through this artistic orchestration of voices, Milton seeks to fracture the seemingly unitary royalist discourse that would claim divine sanction to perpetuate unlimited monarchy. When voices are orchestrated artistically in such a dialogue, then, according to Bakhtin, the "centrifugal" force of *heteroglossia* (or multi-voicedness) breaks through the "centripetal" force of unitary language to reveal an opposing world view.[26] Therefore, merely to point out the essentially multivoiced nature of a seemingly monologic official utterance, as Milton does in *Eikonoklastes*, is at once an inherently artistic and an inherently subversive activity.

Ultimately Milton's royalist reflex is triggered by his attempt to observe decorum, by his adherence to the convention of point by point refutation, and especially by his determination to catch the king in his own literary style. Milton's odd and unrhetorical response to a masterpiece of royalist propaganda can be viewed as an attempt to compensate for the fact that, as Stanley Fish notes, "there is no adequate defence against eloquence at the moment of impact."[27] Fish's analysis of the reader's vulnerability to the eloquence of Satanic rhetoric in *Paradise Lost* applies equally to even the sophisticated contemporary reader's vulnerability to the eloquence of the *Eikon Basilike*: "from a disinterested appreciation of technique one moves easily to a grudging admiration for the technician and then to a guarded sympathy and finally, perhaps, to assent."[28] This analysis of the dynamics of assent suggests that in *Eikonoklastes*, as in *Paradise Lost*, Milton's best hope to prevent his audience's seduction by deceptive rhetoric is to attempt to discredit the speaker by disparaging his technique. If, as Milton held in *Areopagitica*, one might as well kill the man as kill his book, *Eikonoklastes*' adoption of the royalist defense of shifting the blame would allow a symbolic second regicide through disparagement of the *Eikon Basilike*.

Notes

1. Milton's dismissal of the *Eikon Basilike* as a masking scene staged by a "politic contriver" suggests his appraisal of the tract's sincerity:

quaint Emblems and devices begg'd from the old Pageantry of some Twelf-nights entertainment at *Whitehall*, will doe but ill to make a Saint or Martyr: and if the People resolve to take him Sainted at the rate of such a Canonizing, I shall suspect thir Calendar more then the *Gregorian*.

John Milton, *Eikonoklastes, Complete Prose Works of John Milton*, 8 vols., ed. Don M. Wolfe et al. (New Haven: Yale University Press, 1953–82), 3:343. All references to Milton's prose are to this edition and are cited parenthetically in the text.

    2. Thomas Wilson, *The Arte of Rhetorique*, ed. Thomas J. Derrick, *The Renaissance Imagination* (New York: Garland, 1982), 1:269.

    3. William Riley Parker, *Milton: A Biography* (Oxford: Clarendon Press, 1968), 1:131.

    4. Samuel Rawson Gardiner, ed., *Declaration . . . Touching a Late Breach of Their Privileges, The Constitutional Documents of the Puritan Revolution, 1628–60* (Oxford: Clarendon Press, 1889), 159–60.

    5. Gardiner, *Declaration*, 161.

    6. Ibid., 160, 162.

    7. Thomas May, *The History of the Parliament of England, Which Began November the Third, 1640*, ed. Francis Maseres (1647; reprint, London, 1812), 90–91.

    8. May, *History of the Parliament*, 92.

    9. Ibid., 92.

    10. There are relatively few investigations of literary strategies in *Eikonoklastes*. Joan S. Bennett, in "God, Satan, and King Charles," uses the tract as an index to correspondences between Milton's conception of Charles I's reign and the portrayal of satanic tyranny in *Paradise Lost* (*PMLA* 92 [1977]: 441–57). Bruce Boehrer's "Elementary Structures of Kingship" focuses on polemical uses of family/state metaphors in the regicide controversy (*Milton Studies* 23 [1987]: 97–117). Lana Cable explores the manner in which Milton both "attack[s] and exploit[s]" the "affective power" of the *Eikon Basilike*'s imagery ("Milton's Iconoclastic Truth," in *Politics, Poetics, and Hermeneutics in Milton's Prose*, ed. David Loewenstein and James Grantham Turner [Cambridge: Cambridge University Press, 1990], 136). Thomas N. Corns's "Imagery in Civil War Polemic" surveys a number of image clusters in *Eikonoklastes* (*Milton Quarterly* 14 [1980]: 1–6). In "Milton Reads the King's Book," Richard Helgerson compares the *Eikon Basilike*'s representations of Charles to Elizabethan self-fashioning through performance art (*Criticism* 29 [1987]: 1–25). David Loewenstein, in "'Casting Down Imaginations,'" links the visions of *Eikonoklastes* and *Samson Agonistes* to explore theatricality, violence, and poetic refashioning in Milton's iconoclasm (*Criticism* 31 [1989]: 253–70). In *Milton and the Drama of History*, Loewenstein explores "the figurative dimensions of Milton's historiography and polemical writings" ([Cambridge: Cambridge University Press, 1990], 2). Florence Sandler's "Icon and Iconoclast" examines the influence that radical Protestantism may have exercised on Milton's response to the typology of the *Eikon Basilike* (in *Achievements of the Left Hand: Essays on the Prose of John Milton*, ed. Michael Lieb and John T. Shawcross [Amherst: University of Massachusetts Press, 1974], 160–84). For the view that *Eikonoklastes'* artistic means are incompatible with its rhetorical aims, see Keith Stavely's *The Politics of Milton's Prose Style* (New Haven: Yale University Press, 1975).

    11. In the prefatory statement to the second edition of *Paradise Lost*, Milton terms rhyme "no necessary Adjunct or true Ornament of Poem or good Verse . . . but the Invention of a barbarous Age, to set off wretched matter and lame Meter"; it is a "fault avoided by the learned Ancients both in Poetry and all good Oratory," and Milton

wished to liberate the epic from "the troublesome and modern bondage of Riming" (*John Milton: Complete Poems and Major Prose*, ed. Merritt Y. Hughes [New York: Odyssey Press, 1957], 210).

12. Richard Helgerson mistakes Milton's criticisms of the style and veracity of the king's book for "disdain for poetry itself." Helgerson claims that "not only does he heap abuse on the particular practices of stage-work and masqueing, of sonneting and romance," but "he also scorns the fundamental image-making faculty on which all poetry, including his own, depends" (15). This judgment fails to take into account Milton's avowed poetic vocation or his distinction between verse and a "true poem."

13. M. M. Bakhtin, *The Dialogic Imagination*, trans. Caryl Emerson and Michael Holquist (Austin: University of Texas Press, 1981), 92.

14. As Loewenstein notes, "the icon and text of *Eikon Basilike* dramatize the stability, authority, and historical merit of Charles as rightful Stuart king" (*Milton and the Drama,* 54).

15. Bakhtin, *Dialogic Imagination,* 270–71.

16. Ibid., 269.

17. Ibid., 270–72.

18. Ibid., 427, 434.

19. Ibid., 273.

20. For a look at the issue of intertextuality from the royalist perspective, see Lois Potter's *Secret Rites and Secret Writing: Royalist Literature, 1641–60* (Cambridge: Cambridge University Press, 1989).

21. Bakhtin maintains that "novelistic discourse is poetic discourse, but one that does not fit within the frame provided by the concept of poetic discourse as it now exists" (*Dialogic Imagination,* 269). "The speaking person and his discourse," Bakhtin adds later, "is, as we have said, what makes a novel a novel" (333).

22. [John Gauden], *Eikon Basilike*, ed. Philip A. Knachel (Ithaca: Cornell University Press, 1966), 150.

23. Unless otherwise indicated, all biblical citations are to *The New Oxford Annotated Bible with the Apocrypha* (New York: Oxford University Press, 1977) and are cited parenthetically in the text.

24. [Gauden], *Eikon Basilike,* 150.

25. *The Interpreter's Bible* (New York: Abingdon Press, 1954), 413–15. See the parallel account at 2 Samuel 24. The editors of the *New Oxford Bible* explain that "taking a census was deemed an infringement upon the prerogatives of . . . God, the sole arbiter of the destinies of the nation and its people" (411n).

26. Bakhtin, *Dialogic Imagination,* 270–72.

27. Stanley Fish, *Surprised by Sin: The Reader in "Paradise Lost"* (Berkeley: University of California Press, 1967), 6.

28. Fish, *Surprised by Sin,* 12.

The Cardinal and the King: Milton's State Letters to France

ROBERT THOMAS FALLON

An examination of Milton's State Letters can cast new light on the poet's political experience, our knowledge of which is shadowy at best, and prompt a reevaluation of the political imagery of his great works. In his volume of the State Papers, published as part of the Yale *Prose*, J. Max Patrick includes 168 documents that can be reliably attributed to the poet.[1] Several features of these papers, considered in conjunction with historical and archival evidence, lead to the conclusion, as inescapable as it is significant, that he was responsible for the preparation of considerably more than that number. The inescapable I shall address first, the significant later.

After the execution of Charles I, one of the early acts of the new government was to appoint Milton to the position of Secretary for Foreign Languages, or Latin Secretary, as it was more familiarly known, to the English Republic, a post he held for virtually the entire eleven years of its existence. His chief duty in that office, and perhaps the only one he was able to perform after the dimming of his eyesight in early 1652, was the preparation of letters exchanged between England's executive bodies and foreign heads-of-state.[2] This correspondence was conducted in Latin, the accepted language of diplomatic discourse at the time, and it was Milton's task to prepare letters in the ancient tongue for dispatch abroad and to translate those received into English for consideration by his superiors.

Milton was the only Latin Secretary appointed by the government during the first four years of his tenure; but his blindness made it necessary to engage others in the post, principally Philip Meadows, who after his appointment as ambassador to Denmark in 1657, was succeeded by Andrew Marvell. In fact, however, except for occasional short periods of time, Milton was never the only translator employed by his government. There was no lack of learned translators engaged in foreign correspondence for the English Republic. The secretariat included a number of individuals who, though they had no official title, assisted from time to time as the need arose, men like Theodore Haak, for example, who was responsible for correspondence with the United Netherlands, and Rene Augier, who until his dismissal in 1655 assisted in exchanges with the French.

Milton's activity in office was, in fact, distinctly focused. Whenever possible, his superiors employed him selectively in correspondence with a particular nation over a period of time, or in diplomatic efforts with many nations to resolve a single international issue, such as the Piedmont Massacre, for however long it took. To consider only his published papers, for example, fully 70 percent of those he prepared from 1655 to 1659 were related to but three matters: the Piedmont Massacre, the War in the North precipitated by the ambitious King of Sweden, Charles X, and correspondence with France. Indeed, this focus of his activities would be even more pronounced had there not been a period of several months in 1656 when it appears he was the only Latin Secretary available and was, hence, required to prepare letters which would not otherwise have been his responsibility, ten of them, for example, to the United Netherlands and Portugal. This focus of Milton's activity has important implications for any evaluation of the scope of his government service. If the public archive contains letters that, while not attributed to him, are of the type he wrote, that is, correspondence between heads-of-state, and in substance directly related to these three concerns, then one must consider the possibility that he was responsible for them as well.

The manuscript history is equally suggestive. Modern editions of the State Papers are based on three seventeenth-century documents, the Columbia Manuscript in Butler Library at Columbia University, the Skinner Manuscript in the Public Record Office in London, and the *Literae Pseudo-Senatus Anglicani*, a volume published two years after Milton's death. Available evidence seems to indicate that the two manuscripts were transcribed under the poet's supervision; how the text of the *Literae* was compiled is still a question. Each of the three sources was prepared at a different time for a different purpose; and each includes letters not present in the others. The Skinner Manuscript, for example, contains fourteen not in *Literae* and four not in the Columbia Manuscript, while *Literae* has thirteen not in Skinner and one absent from the other two. These differences, along with a number of other features, strongly suggest that the letters in each of the three sources were in fact selected for transcription from, hence represent but a fraction of, a larger body of documents that Milton maintained in the performance of his official duties. In brief, while there is no assurance that Milton kept a copy of every document he worked on, there are significant indications that he kept copies of many more than he had transcribed.

Milton's letters to France are a case in point. Of his one hundred published letters written from 1655 to 1659, thirty are addressed to that country alone. None are dated earlier than May 1655, which would seem to indicate that he assumed responsibility for French correspondence at that time, probably from Rene Augier, who had been dismissed the previous month.[3] A unique feature of this correspondence makes it quite clear that he was responsible for more: Of the thirty published letters to France, sixteen are written in pairs, that is, companion letters of the same substance, presumably composed at the same time, a practice made necessary by the unusual situation prevailing within the French monarchy at the time.[4] During the 1650s, Louis XIV, though King of France, was still a minor; the Queen Mother, Anne of Austria, acted as regent; and the reins of government were firmly in the hands of her able chief minister, Cardinal Jules Mazarin. Therefore, any letter to the king, who was titular head-of-state, had to be accompanied by another to the cardinal, who would decide on the matter in any event. This was no easy matter. The protocol of the time dictated that such letters be couched in the language of extravagant compliment with references to ancient and honorable alliance and promises of undying affection for the addressee, even if one were provisioning a fleet to bombard the harbors at the time. Here was a challenge indeed, to compliment in companion letters a young, ambitious king, eager to assume the power to which he was heir, and an aging cardinal, who held that power firmly in his hands, especially as there was a distinct possibility that they read each other's mail. The writer had to praise the one without diminishing the other.

The eight pairs in Milton's published papers reflect a judicious diplomatic observance of the protocol. Those to Louis, then still in his teens, stress his honor, his reputation, his dignity as king, his military prowess, and the grandeur of his court. In one petition, for example, protesting the seizure of an English ship by French privateers in violation of a solemn treaty between the two states, Cromwell insists that the king's "Honour" is at stake and that those who presume "to violate the League and most Sacred Oath of their Sovereign, should suffer the Punishment due to so much Perfidiousness and daring Insolence" (W73, P111); and in another letter of similar substance Louis is advised that "your Authority it self, and the Veneration due your Royal Name, are chiefly in dispute" (W86, P120). While it was thought that such appeals would carry weight with the young king, a different approach was called for with the seasoned cardinal. He is praised for the qualities that equip him to run the kingdom. He is "the sole and onely person, whose singular Prudence Governs the most important Interests of the French Nation, and the most weighty Affairs of the Kingdom with Fidelity, Council, and Vigilance" (W74, P113); he is the one "upon whose care the Prosperity of France depends" (W125, P160). Honor, authority, and preservation of the "Royal Name," then, were considered the young king's concerns; prudence, vigilance, and fidelity the cardinal's.

Four of the eight pairs were occasioned by a single event. In the spring of 1658, a combined Anglo-French army surrounded a Spanish force in the port of Dunkirk; and Louis, then nineteen, was eager to be present for what promised to be a signal victory, so both king and cardinal joined the army in Flanders. In an earlier treaty between the two powers, France had agreed that once Dunkirk was secured, it would be turned over to English control; and Cromwell sent his son-in-law, Viscount Fauconberg, to Flanders with the mission, among other things, of ensuring that the agreement remained fresh in the young king's mind. Milton's letters follow the pattern of elaborate compliment already alluded to. In one Cromwell urges the king by his "Military Prowess [to] take speedy Vengeance of the Spanish Frauds" and assures him of the affection with which "we labour the Prosperity of your Achievements." After the surrender of the port, Cromwell writes again, praising the king's "singular Benignity and Generosity of Mind" and reminding him of the treaty in which he had given "the Word of a most Excellent King." The letters to Mazarin, again, emphasize his "Civility, Candour, and Friendship," his "Prudence and Vertue," and his well-earned reputation, from which others "may learn with equal Renown to Govern Kingdoms, and manage the most important Affairs of the World" (W118–19, P154–55).

The fact that these letters were dispatched in pairs lends substance to the proposition that Milton was responsible for many more than appear in the seventeenth-century sources of his State Papers, for among his published letters to France, written over the same period, 1655 to 1659, addressed to Louis XIV and signed by Oliver Cromwell, and after his death Richard Cromwell, there are seven that have no companion letters to Cardinal Mazarin. In addition, two of those addressed to the cardinal are without companions to the king.[5] The evidence of England's meticulous adherence to the protocol assures us that the companion letters to the nine lacking them were indeed composed and dispatched, though diligent search may have failed to bring them to light. Further, it must be assumed that if Milton was responsible for one, he was responsible for both. The poet's immediate superior, the able Secretary of State, John Thurloe, was an eminently practical man; and he would certainly not have had two different secretaries sitting at different ends of Westminster writing separate letters on the same subject to corulers of a nation, particularly if he had a John Milton hard by, one who had been observing the protocol for years.

In addition to these incomplete pairs, one can turn to the French holdings in the Public Record Office in London for documentary confirmation of the somewhat self-evident observation that the governments of the Republic dispatched many more letters to foreign heads-of-state than are to be found in the seventeenth-century sources of Milton's State Papers. The correspondence with France is one of the most complete collections of letters to and from foreign states in English archives; and nowhere else does one find more persuasive evidence that Milton was responsible for more letters, in both Latin and English, than the early sources document. In the late nineteenth century the French archivist, Armand Baschet, undertook the task to assemble, from various depositories where they lay scattered, documents from the early diplomatic correspondence between the two nations. Baschet deposited a transcript of these documents in the Public Record Office, one entitled "Lists of Despatches of Ambassadors from France to England; Henry VIII.—George I.; 1509–1714";[6] and he published a catalogue of the transcript in The Thirty-ninth Annual Report of the Deputy Keeper of the Public Records in 1878.[7] Aside from the "Despatches of Ambassadors" there are included a number of letters exchanged between the heads-of-state of the two governments. Of those from the period of the English Republic the transcript includes thirteen from Cromwell to Mazarin and Louis XIV, seven of which are Milton's.[8] There are eight additional such letters, listed in the catalogue but for some reason absent from the transcript, two of which bear the same dates as Milton's letters.[9] Thus, the Paris archives hold at least twenty-one letters that the Cromwells wrote to Louis XIV and Mazarin, dated during the years when Milton was responsible for French correspondence; but at the most only nine of them are included in his early manuscripts. Surely, not all of the remaining twelve are Milton's work; but just as surely, some of them are.

The French, of course, replied meticulously to each letter they received; and the transcript also contains twenty-five from the French rulers to the Cromwells, nine of which are of particular interest because their dates come within a period of months in the year 1658 when Milton was decidedly engaged in correspondence with France over two matters of mutual concern, the capture and transfer of Dunkirk and the transition of power after Oliver's death.[10] Further, of these twenty-five, six were answers to letters Milton wrote.[11] It can be reasonably assumed that he was responsible for translating into English, if not all, at least the majority of these letters from France.

The correspondence with France, then, was voluminous during the period when Milton was regularly employed in translating or composing the exchanges between the two nations.[12] This is not to suggest that he was responsible for all of the letters that passed between them, but there is evidence that permits us to add substantially to the number included in the seventeenth-century sources. To summarize, nine of the letters attributed to him, customarily written in pairs, are wanting the companion that the protocol of the correspondence demands. Further, those dealing with any single issue, such as the employment of English forces in France during 1658, can be attributed to him with a high degree of probability. One can also say, with some assurance, that he was called upon to translate into English the replies to letters whose Latin he had composed.

In his consummate biography of Milton, William Riley Parker finds this kind of research, leading to these kinds of conclusions, of little consequence. As he puts it, "If one set about seriously collecting on this basis, it should not be difficult to double or triple the now accepted number of letters! And to what end?" The end, I am suggesting, is to enhance our understanding of Milton's political experience. This research, for example, has persuaded me that some of these letters were, in whole or in part, *composed* by Milton; that he was certainly more than the mere "translator for monolingual bosses" that Parker would have him; hence, that some of these documents may reasonably be considered as the product of his pen.[13]

To speak further of "ends," of more significance to Milton scholarship is the question: Did this experience in any way influence his creative imagination? It is a commonplace that diplomatic correspondence requires meticulously accurate language, with deliberations in the seventeenth century often turning on the meaning of a single Latin word; and the secretary entrusted with preparing documents had to be intimately aware of the matters at issue. To perform his function competently, Milton was required to keep fully abreast of events as they developed. This combination of circumstances, the greater number of letters for which he was responsible and the evidence that some were of his composition, lends weight to the position that the events chronicled in these documents had a significant impact upon his art. This is clearly the case with the Piedmont Massacre, which inspired the famous sonnet and several passages in *Paradise Lost* where linguistic parallels between art and events reflect the influence of the shocking barbarities of the incident upon his sensibility.

As to the influence of the French letters, our focus here, I have discussed elsewhere the striking parallels between the English acquisition of Dunkirk and Satan's conquest of Adam's World.[14] Of comparable significance are the similarities between the power-sharing arrangement within the French monarchy during the 1650s and that to be found in the realms of *Paradise Lost*. In brief, all four of those realms, those in Heaven, Hell, Chaos, and on Earth, are governed by corulers.

Milton depicts a Heaven ruled by two kings; God presides, of course, but the Son does as well, once he is declared "to be Heir and to be King" (6.708).[15] They reign together, "God and Messiah his anointed King" (6.718; see also 5.664, 6.43). They sit on separate thrones, toward which the loyal angels bow with equal reverence, casting their crowns "to the ground / With solemn adoration" (3.350–51). The seemingly contradictory status, both heir and king at once, was a strategy employed by Milton and his biblical sources to circumvent the unpromising prospects of an heir to a throne occupied by an immortal father; still the heir/king arrangement is not unknown in human experience. During his minority, Louis XIV was indeed king, but only heir to the power of the throne, which was exercised by Mazarin. God in contrast transfers all authority to the Son:

> all Power
> I give thee, reign for ever, and assume
> Thy Merits.
>
> (3.317–19)

The pattern prevails in Hell, where Satan aspires to reign—a goal "worth ambition" (1.262), as he puts it—and eventually, of course he does, though not without challenge. When he arrives at the gates of Hell, he is confronted by a crowned apparition who asserts his claim to the throne. Hell is a place, Death proclaims, "Where I reign King, and to enrage thee more, / Thy King and Lord" (2.698–99). The two prepare for armed battle to decide the issue, only to have Sin intervene and reveal their relationship. Which of the two reigns, therefore, is left unresolved, though later imagery would seem to point to the dominance of Satan in the unholy Trinity. There are corulers in Chaos as well,

> Where eldest Night
> And Chaos, Ancestors of Nature, hold
> Eternal Anarchy.
>
> (2.894–96)

With that allegorical monarch

> Enthron'd
> Sat Sable-vested Night, eldest of things,
> The Consort of his Reign,
>
> (2.961-63)

"Consort" here having its now-obsolete meaning of "a colleague in office or authority," without gender connotation (the *OED* cites these lines as example). Satan addresses them as equals (2.970) and promises that upon his victory he will return the World to their realm, so that they may "once more / Erect the Standard there of ancient Night" (2.985-86).

On Earth, before the Fall at least, Adam and Eve, as "Mankind," rule as equals; according to Raphael, God intends them to

> Fill the Earth,
> Subdue it, and throughout Dominion hold
> Over Fish of the Sea, and Fowl of the Air,
> And every living thing that moves on the Earth.
>
> (7.531-34)

Adam recalls that at his birth the Creator bestowed the Earth upon him and his race: "as Lords / Possess it, and all things that therein live" (8.339-40); and as a mark of humankind's rule, Adam named all the creatures of the Earth and Eve named the flowers.

This image of corulers is enriched by other factors that find parallels in the arrangement within the French monarchy. The first of these is a family relationship that modifies the exercise of power. Louis XIV was titular king, of course, but until his majority the royal authority lay with the Queen Mother as regent. In both Heaven and Hell, the corulers are father and son, on Earth, husband and wife; and traditionally, of course, the son is subject to the father, as was, in Milton's time, the wife to the husband (Chaos and Night reflect no such family relationship). The hierarchy within the royal family does not contradict or undercut the image of corulers, so much as it embellishes it, bringing it within the scope of human experience. Indeed, some fourteen years after Milton's death, England was ruled by two monarchs, William and Mary, who reigned jointly, though the king undertook the actual exercise of power while the queen agreed that since she was his wife, "the rule and authority should be his."[16]

The image is further embellished by the presence of a third person in the formula of rule, as in France where the Queen Regent completed a triumvirate of power; and, again as in France, the third person may be feminine. In Hell, the gender of Sin is obvious. In Chaos the corulers reign, but it is a realm in which the "high Arbiter / Chance governs all" (2.909–10). One need not belabor the fact that the figure of Chance is predominantly feminine in Western culture, from the "Dame Fortune" of Milton's time to the "Lady Luck" of our own.

When one turns to Heaven, the image is not so clear, for though in his chapter on the Holy Spirit in *Christian Doctrine* Milton consistently refers to the third person with the masculine pronoun, some scholars are persuaded that in *Paradise Lost* the figure is feminine. This impression derives from an intermediate identification, however, the assumption that Milton conceived of his inspiration, that is his Muse, as the Holy Spirit. In a jointly written essay, William B. Hunter and Stevie Davies present the case for such an identification. They argue for a trinity of muses, the Father, Son, and Holy Spirit, appearing in different invocations of *Paradise Lost*, the third person most prominently in those to books 7 and 9. Citing Milton's qualification, "The meaning, not the Name I call" (7.5), they identify Urania as the Holy Spirit and propose that when the poet explicitly refers to his muse as feminine in the invocation to book 9, "my Celestial Patroness" (21), we are exposed to his true sentiments on the matter. As they note,

> Although in Christian tradition the Spirit is ordinarily understood as, or assumed to be, masculine, a substantial tradition exists that associates this person of the Trinity with the feminine gender and more expressly with a mother principle in the deity.[17]

The argument may or may not persuade, but it does suggest that in Milton's Heaven there is a feminine figure hovering in the background, sharing power with the two kings but not openly exercising it, a role much like that of the Queen Regent in France during the 1650s.

The pattern does not seem to extend to Earth, unless one can consider God himself as the third person in humankind's prelapsarian reign. After the Fall even he retires and though Adam and Eve seem no less "Lords" of all that "live in Sea, or Air, Beast, Fish, and Fowl" (8.339, 41), they are condemned to return to the dust of their dominion, and their status as corulers is severely compromised by the divine injunction that "to thy Husband's will / [Eve] shall submit, hee over thee shall rule" (10.195–96). It is as a result of the Incarnation that the celestial pattern is established on Earth, when God sends the Holy Spirit down to form a triumvirate of man, woman, and Spirit to continue the struggle against Satan. In associating with humanity, the third person seems to assume qualities of both genders, at once a "Comforter" and one who will arm the individual "With spiritual Armor" (12.486, 91).

How much of this imagery of corulers as part of a triumvirate can be traced to Milton's experience in correspondence with France and how much to other sources is, of course, impossible to say. We can be assured, however, that he was aware of such a model in a government of his own time. From his State Letters, thus, we learn what Milton *knew* of the political events of his time, and thereby gain an important key to the understanding of his poetic achievement. To inquire thus into the mind of the poet can enrich our reading of works that abound with political figures engaged in much the same activities as were those with whom he worked and to whom he wrote: kings, princes, counselors, generals, diplomats, all skilled in the language of royal compliment and parliamentary debate, the rhetoric of league and alliance, slavery and freedom, conquest and defeat.

To read *Paradise Lost* as a historical narrative is to become vividly aware of the rich diversity of the poem's political imagery. The War in Heaven is precipitated by a question of governance—is the Son to rule the angels or not? Both God and Satan are seen as rulers of separate domains, though they exercise the power of state in strikingly different ways. The fallen angels sit in a representative assembly, where policy is determined by ballot, and debate issues of peace and war. God governs by decree. The contest between good and evil is figured as a conflict between two great powers maneuvering for possession of Man's World, which is a secure part of the Kingdom of Heaven at the beginning, but falls to and is occupied by the forces of Hell at the end of *Paradise Lost*. Satan enters into diplomatic negotiations with Chaos, promising to return the World to the realm of "ancient Night" (2.986) in return for aid, and then breaks his word. When he speaks of his ambitions, it is at times in terms of warfare, of "conquering this new World" (4.391), at others of diplomacy, "League with you I seek, / And mutual amity" (4.375–76). God, like the ruler of any major power, dispatches emissaries to a smaller, dependent ally, Raphael to spell out for Adam the conditions for continued alliance between Heaven and Earth, Michael to revoke the old agreement and announce new terms. The Incarnation shifts the balance of power; Mankind is now protected by "spiritual Armor, able to resist / Satan's assaults, and quench his fiery darts" (12.491–92). In *Paradise Regained*, Christ's ordeal in the desert,

> by vanquishing
> Temptation, hast regain'd lost Paradise,
> And frustrated the conquest fraudulent.
>
> (4.607–9)

As Michael foretells, at the Resurrection

> He shall ascend
> The Throne hereditary, and bound his Reign
> With earth's wide bounds.
> *(Paradise Lost,* 12.369–71)

At the close of cosmic history, Milton predicts, the celestial political structure will undergo yet another transformation. The Son will resign his "Sceptre and Power," for "regal Sceptre then no more shall need" in a state where God is the "All in All" of creation *(Paradise Lost,* 6.730, 3.340–41). All concerned observe the protocol of elaborate compliment required in Milton's day, a language that he knew from his long service is as often employed to conceal intent as to seal allegiance.

How much of this imagery was inspired by the poet's wide reading and how much by his ten years of public service is not at issue—some measure of each, we must assume. But surely his experience in world affairs, as reflected in the events chronicled in his State Letters, will reward our study.

Notes

1. *The Complete Prose Works of John Milton*, 8 vols., ed. Don M. Wolfe et al. (New Haven: Yale University Press, 1953–82), 5:2.9–14. The Yale edition of Milton's works is hereafter referred to as *Prose*, the Columbia edition (*The Works of John Milton,* 18 vols., ed. F.A. Patterson et al. [New York: Columbia University Press, 1931–38]) as *Works*.

2. There is no record of the Council of State officially ordering Milton to write the *Second Defense*, as they had the *First*.

3. *Calendar of State Papers Domestic Series Commonwealth*, ed. Mary Ann Everett Green (Vaduz: Kraus Reprints, 1965), 8:127–28.

4. Letters are identified by the numbers assigned them in *Works* (W) and *Prose* (P). The pairs are: W112, 139, P79, 78; W56–57, P82–83; W145–46, P93–94; W73–74, P111, 113; W113–14, P146–47; W115–16, P149, 148; W118–19, P154–55; W124–25, P159–60; W143–44, P156–57.

5. The letters without companions to Mazarin are: W61, P85; W68, P97; W81, P112; W86, P120; W110, P151; W131, P166; W140, P88. Those without companions to Louis XIV are: W132, P167, and W134, P168. Two other letters, addressed to the French Ambassador and signed by the President of the Council, would not have required companions (W93, P126; W102, P136).

6. Public Record Office, London, PRO 31/3/1–203. Documents from the Interregnum are in 31/3/89–106. Original documents cited are in PRO files.

7. Appendix 8:573–826 (Interregnum records in pp. 705–16). The catalogue, however, is unreliable, listing some documents not in the transcript and failing to list some that are. A corrected copy is available in the PRO Round Room reference shelves, no. 19/42. Baschet's preliminary reports are in *The Thirty-sixth Annual Report of the Deputy Keeper of the Public Records* (1875), App. 1, no. 5, 230–58 and *The Thirty-seventh Annual Report* (1876), App. 1, no. 3, 180–94.

8. Cromwell's letters are as follows, cited by piece and folio numbers in PRO 31/3, and by language. Milton's letters are identified.

90/630 after 31 Mar 53	Cromwell to Mazarin (F)	
95/13 9 Jun 53	Cromwell to Mazarin (F)	
90/586 26 Jan 54*	Cromwell to Mazarin (E)	
98/15–16 25 May 55	Cromwell to Louis XIV (L)	W139, P78
98/17–18 25 May 55	Cromwell to Mazarin (L)	W112, P79
98/82–84 31 Jul 55	Cromwell to Louis XIV (L)	W56, P82
98/85–31 Jul 55	Cromwell to Mazarin (L)	W57, P83
98/182–83 4 Dec 55	Cromwell to Louis XIV (L)	
98/184–85 4 Dec 55	Cromwell to Mazarin (L)	
98/188–89 12 Dec 55	Cromwell to Mazarin (L)	
99/8 4 Apr 56	Cromwell to Mazarin (L)	W146, P94
100/57–58 25 Sep 56	Cromwell to Mazarin (L)	W74, P113
102/201 20 May 58	Cromwell to Mazarin (L)	P150

*Incorrectly filed with 1653 letters. The date is obviously old style, as it is signed "Oliver P." In letters prior to December 1653 the signature is "O. Cromwell."

9. These eight, all addressed by Oliver and Richard Cromwell to Mazarin, are listed in the catalogue but are not in the transcript. They bear the following dates: 29 Jun 54, 4 Apr 55, 25 Sep 55, 29 Mar 58, 1 Apr 58, 1 Jul 58, 6 Sep 58, 15 Nov 58. Of Milton's letters, W144, P157 is dated 1 Jul 58, and W125, P160, 6 Sep 58.

10. The letters, all dated 1658, are identified by folio pages in PRO 31/3/102:

126–27 6 Apr	Mazarin to Cromwell
148 12 Apr	Mazarin to Cromwell
240–41 12 Jun	Mazarin to Cromwell
242–43 20 Jun	Louis XIV to Cromwell
267 20 ? Jun	Mazarin to Cromwell
268–69 ? Jun	Louis XIV to Cromwell
273–74 25 Jun	Mazarin to Cromwell
450–51 25 Sep	Mazarin to R. Cromwell
498 24 Oct	Mazarin to R. Cromwell

11. The answers are cited, again, by piece and folio number in PRO 31/3. They are all in French:

98/40–42 12 Jun 55	Louis XIV to Cromwell	(to W139, P78)
98/43 13 Jun 55	Mazarin to Cromwell	(to W112, P79)
98/107 1 Sep 55	Mazarin to Cromwell	(to W57, P83)
102/268–69 ? Jun 58	Louis XIV to Cromwell	(to W116, P148)
102/273–74 25 Jun 58	Mazarin to Cromwell	(to W119, P155)
102/450–51 25 Sep 58	Mazarin to R. Cromwell	(to W125, P160)

12. SP 78/113 & 114, State Papers Foreign, France.

13. William Riley Parker, *Milton: A Biography* (Oxford: Clarendon Press, 1968), 2:945, 1014.

14. Robert Thomas Fallon, *Captain or Colonel: The Soldier in Milton's Life and Art* (Columbia: University of Missouri Press, 1984), 145–50.

15. John Milton, *Paradise Lost*, *John Milton: Complete Poems and Major Prose*, ed. Merritt Y. Hughes (New York: Odyssey Press, 1957). All references to Milton's poetry are to this edition and are cited parenthetically in the text.

16. Gilbert Burnet, *History of His Own Time* (New York: Dutton, 1906), 251.

17. William B. Hunter and Stevie Davies, "Milton's Urania: 'The Meaning, Not the Name I Call,'" William B. Hunter, *The Descent of Urania: Studies in Milton, 1946–88* (Lewisburg, Pa.: Bucknell University Press, 1989), 32.

"Under Thir Head Embodied All in One": Milton's Reinterpretation of the Organic Analogy in *Paradise Lost*

STEVEN JABLONSKI

When Milton entered the polemical debates of the seventeenth century, he drew upon a pool of imagery, mostly classical and biblical in origin, which he shared with friend and foe, Puritan and papist, roundhead and cavalier. Yet images, metaphors, analogies, and symbols were ideologically contested as well as shared, and it is indeed possible to speak of a typically Puritan metaphor (e.g., life as a journey) or a commonly royalist conceit (e.g., the monarchy of a beehive). With this in mind I propose in this essay to isolate one key image from Milton's account of the War in Heaven, not to fit it into any purportedly universal world picture, but rather to explore how Milton challenged its appropriation by his ideological foes.

In book 5 of *Paradise Lost*, God appoints the Son the head of the angels. The exact designation is important. Milton's scriptural model for the exaltation of the Son in Heaven is the Psalm 2, yet in Milton's own translation of this psalm, as in the Authorized Version, God anoints the Messiah not as "head" but as "king" (162).[1] Milton had God designate the Son as head of the angels in *Paradise Lost*, I maintain, for it allowed him to exploit the analogy of the body politic, an analogy that in the seventeenth century had become a favorite of apologists for monarchial authority. Whereas royalists appealed to a sovereign's role as head of his people to justify his presumptions of superiority and command, Milton revealed the Son's headship instead to be both a sign of his humility and service and a foreshadowing of the future atonement of all humanity in Christ. Both human kings and the Son may be the heads of corporate bodies, but the relation between a king and his subjects is not parallel to the relation between the Son and his angels. Milton suggested such a parallel only to expose its failure and thereby employed the example of the Son's headship as a critique of rather than a sanction for monarchy.

The traditional analogy that represented the human body as a pattern for the political state was elaborated most fully in Edward Forset's *Comparative Discourse of the Bodies Natural and Political*, published in 1606. Following convention, Forset compared the head of a person to a monarch in the state and drew from the analogy the conclusion that subjects are to serve their monarch as the rest of the body serves the head:

> The head is by the order and instinct of nature, so dearely esteemed and honored of the bodie, as every part will not onely seek his ease and health, but even expose it selfe to any perils for his sake and safetie: the inferior parts do susteine and beare him up, moving at his beck, and fast bound when he taketh rest: the hands and armes, do readily receive upon themselves the strokes and wounds intended against the head; yea, any part doth endure paine, by incision, scarifying, ligature or issue, to remedie the greevances of the head. These good duties of kingly subjection to kingly power, I leave to the consideration and conscience of every true subject, wishing him to make his best use thereof by contemplating and applying of the same in the performance of like offices of alleagiance, love and loyaltie.[2]

Forset was not the only writer to draw this implication from the analogy of the body politic. Indeed, although the concept of the body politic was long invoked in medieval England, it was not until the reign of Henry VIII that writers began generally to use it to justify monarchial authority rather than the need for the common cooperation of all members in a society.[3] The full consequences of this shift would not be revealed until the seventeenth century. As D. G. Hale explains in his study of the metaphor of the body politic in Renaissance England,

> The application of the organic analogy to national states which are slowly becoming self-conscious, is, of course, appropriate. But the doctrine of passive obedience tends to deny the traditional medieval qualities of love and charity and to deny eventually a king's responsibility for his subjects, replacing natural harmony with force. This was not a problem in sixteenth-century England: the seventeenth was another matter.[4]

Thus, James I frequently appealed to his position as head of the body politic to justify his absolutist claims. The head, said James, "hath the power of directing all the members of the body to that vse which the iudgement of the head thinkes most convenient."[5] Michael Walzer tells us that "Anglican preachers used the image of the head (or the heart or soul) to glorify the king."[6] Salmasius himself in a line quoted by Milton in his *First Defense* stated that "[i]t is for the head to give orders, and not for the limbs; the king is the head of Parliament."[7]

While the analogy of the body politic has classical antecedents, it received seemingly impeccable support from the parallel image of Christ as the head of his church, an image ultimately derived from 1 Corinthians 12.12–31. It should be noted that Paul in the passage from Corinthians does not argue that the authority of Christ is equivalent to that of the head over the body; on the contrary, he used the metaphor of the body to emphasize the diversity of people's roles within the church rather than Christ's superiority over it. Nonetheless, the conceptions of the body politic and body ecclesiastical reinforced each other according to the system of argument by analogy that dominated political discussion in Renaissance England.[8] As Ernst Kantorowicz relates, in early modern England,

> "Body politic" and "mystical body" seem to be used without great discrimination.... It is evident that the doctrine of theology and canon law, teaching that the Church, and Christian society in general, was a "corpus mysticum the head of which is Christ," has been transferred by the jurists from the theological sphere to that of the state the head of which is the king.[9]

Thus, in book 1, chapter 24 of his *Christian Doctrine*, Milton listed three metaphors for Christ's relation to his church: Christ is the Church's head, spouse, and shepherd (*Complete Prose Works*, 6: 499–501). All three of these metaphors were very strikingly invoked by James I in his first speech to the English Parliament: "I am the husband, and all the whole island is my lawful wife; I am the head, and it is my body; I am the shepherd, and it is my flock."[10]

Milton was not about to slight Christ's position as head of the mystical body of the church. On the contrary, he specifically affirmed it in his *Christian Doctrine* and in several other places in his prose.[11] He was all too aware, however, that the analogy of the body ecclesiastical could be used to sanction the authority of a monarch as head of the body politic. To foreclose this possibility, Milton in his *Ready and Easy Way to Establish a Free Commonwealth* argued that Christ's headship is fundamentally different from what he termed the "regal dominion" of an earthly monarch. He began with an expression of puzzlement:

> I cannot but yet furder admire on the other side, how any man who hath the true principles of justice and religion in him, can presume or take upon him to be a king and lord over his brethren. (*Complete Prose Works*, 7:429)

A king, Milton continued, is guilty of the following presumptions: he rules over people who are "for the most part every way equal or superior to himself," he displays "with such vanitie and ostentation his regal splendor, so supereminently above other mortal men," and he assumes "extraordinarie honour and worship to himself." Yet this is not all, as the paragraph concludes:

> All Protestants hold that Christ in his church hath left no vicegerent of his power, but himself, without deputie, is the only head thereof, governing it from heaven: how then can any Christian-man derive his kingship from Christ, but with wors usurpation than the Pope his headship over the church, since Christ . . . hath expressly declar'd, that such regal dominion is from the gentiles, not from him, and hath strictly charg'd us, not to imitate them therein. (429)

Milton's claim that Christ associated regal presumption with the gentiles followed from his gloss of Mark 10.35–42, which he explicated elsewhere in the tract. As Milton expounded these biblical verses, Christ told his disciples not to aspire to lordship over others as the gentiles did; on the contrary, Christ gave them a different ideal: "he that is greatest among you, let him be as the younger, and he that is chief as he that serveth" (*Complete Prose Works*, 7:424). No form of government comes closer to this precept, Milton went on to say, than a free commonwealth,

> wherin they who are greatest, are perpetual servants and drudges to the public at thir own cost and charges, neglect thir own affairs; yet are not elevated above thir brethren; live soberly in thir families, walk the streets as other men, may be spoken to freely, familiarly, friendly, without adoration. (425)

He contrasted this with a monarchy: "Wheras a king must be ador'd like a Demigod, with a dissolute and haughtie court about him, of vast expence and luxurie, masks and revels, to the debaushing of our prime gentry, both male and female" (425).

Milton's ideal of the republican leader as expressed in *The Ready and Easy Way* followed from his earlier castigations of tyranny in his *Tenure of Kings and Magistrates*. While in *The Ready and Easy Way* Milton depicted the republican leader as unpresumptuous and someone who acts on behalf of those below him, in the *Tenure* Milton defined the tyrant as a ruler "who regarding neither Law nor the common good, reigns onely for himself and his faction" (*Complete Prose Works*, 2:212). Milton likewise noted that since

> *Aristotle* and the best of Political writers have defin'd a King, him who governs to the good and profit of his People, and not for his own ends, it fol-

lows from necessary causes, that the Titles of Sov'ran Lord, natural Lord, and the like, are either arrogancies, or flatteries, not admitted by Emperours and Kings of best note, and dislikt by the Church both of Jews, *Isai.* 26.13. and ancient Christians, as appears by *Tertullian* and others. (202)

Far from desiring such presumptions,

no Christian Prince ... would arrogate so unreasonably above human condition, or derogate so basely from a whole Nation of men his Brethren ... among whom there might be found so many thousand Men for wisdom, vertue, nobleness of mind, and all other respects, but the fortune of his dignity, farr above him. (204–5)

In *The Ready and Easy Way,* then, Milton drew a distinction between the presumptions of an earthly king and the teachings and example of Christ. Christ may be head of the church as a monarch is head of state, yet Christ upholds a different ideal from the regal dominion of a king. This distinction that Milton made in his prose tract informed his depiction of the headship of the Son in *Paradise Lost.* As I shall now demonstrate, whereas Satan argues that the Son's headship means that the Son is assuming the regal trappings and authority claimed by human monarchs as their prerogatives as heads of the state, Abdiel correctly recognizes that the Son's headship is a sign of his humility and service.

The appointment of the Son as head of the angels is a pivotal event in *Paradise Lost.* Not only is it the earliest event in the chronology of the poem that is explicitly described, but it also furnishes the pretense for Satan's rebellion. As Raphael describes the appointment to Adam, God summons all the angelic host before him and proclaims to them,

> This day I have begot whom I declare
> My only Son, and on this holy Hill
> Him I have anointed, whom ye now behold
> At my right hand; your Head I him appoint;
> And by my Self have sworn to him shall bow
> All knees in Heav'n, and shall confess him Lord:
> Under his great Vice-gerent Reign abide
> United as one individual Soul
> For ever happy.
> *(Paradise Lost,* 5.603–11)

Satan's immediate reaction to the appointment of the Son as head of the angels is to think himself impaired in both glory and authority. As he declares,

> Another now hath to himself ingross't
> All Power, and us eclipst under the name
> Of King anointed.
>
> (5.775–77)

In his arguments to his forces, Satan accuses the Son of presumption:

> Who can in reason then or right assume
> Monarchy over us such as live by right
> His equals, if in power and splendor less,
> In freedom equal? ...
>   much less for this to be our Lord,
> And look for adoration to th' abuse
> Of those Imperial Titles which assert
> Our being ordain'd to govern, not to serve?
>
> (5.794–97, 799–802)

The reader of these lines will remember Milton's objections in *The Ready and Easy Way* to kings who presume to rule over people who are "for the most part every way equal or superior" to themselves (*Complete Prose Works* 7:29) and demand "to be ador'd like a Demigod" (425). Satan elsewhere rebukes the loyal angels by saying in mock surprise,

> At first I thought that Liberty and Heav'n
> To heav'nly Souls had all been one; but now
> I see that most through sloth had rather serve,
> Minist'ring Spirits, train'd up in Feast and Song.
>
> (*Paradise Lost,* 6.164–67)

Here Satan comes close to duplicating Milton's exasperated bewilderment in *The Ready and Easy Way* that the English "who have fought so gloriously for liberty" could wish to "change thir noble words and actions, heretofore so becoming the majesty of a free people, into the base necessitie of court flatteries and prostrations (*Complete Prose Works*, 7:428).

Satan's arguments are not wrong; they are Milton's antimonarchial arguments in *The Ready and Easy Way* and worthy of our assent coming even from Satan. Abdiel himself is willing "to grant it thee unjust, / That equal over equals Monarch reign" (*Paradise Lost,* 5.831–32). Nor should this surprise us.[12] Satan errs regarding the headship of the Son not because Satan deduces incorrectly given his premise but rather because he inappropriately applies his premise to a specific example that it does not match. In other words, Satan fails as a casuist rather than a moralist. If the Son were as Satan describes him, then Satan's arguments against the Son's supposed presumption in becoming the head of the angels would be as valid when Satan uses them against the Son as when Milton uses them against kings. But Satan misrepresents the nature of the Son by arguing as if the Son were one of the fallen human monarchs rightfully condemned by Milton. What Satan refuses to admit is that the Son's headship is proper for him precisely because the Son *is* the Son.

Abdiel has the clearer vision. He argues that Satan does not understand God's motives:

> how far from thought
> To make us less, bent rather to exalt
> Our happy state under one Head more near
> United.
> (5.829–31)

He corrects Satan by noting that the Son is decidedly the angels' superior rather than their equal:

> Thyself though great and glorious dost thou count,
> Or all Angelic Nature join'd in one,
> Equal to him begotten Son, by whom
> As by his Word the mighty Father made
> All things, ev'n thee, and all the Spirits of Heav'n.
> (833–37)

The angels are not, he continues,

> by his Reign obscur'd,
> But more illustrious made, since he the Head
> One of our number thus reduc't becomes,
> His Laws our Laws, all honor to him done
> Returns our own.
> (841–45)

Abdiel correctly recognizes that an honor that is presumptuous when grasped at by an equal or inferior is a sign of humility when accepted by a superior. To put it another way, the common headship of the Son and human kings is the point of intersection between divergent movements, downward for the Son, upward for a human king.

In a note to the lines quoted above, Alastair Fowler comments that "Abdiel appears to regard the Messiah's kingship over the angels as a kind of incarnation."[13] Although Fowler does not elaborate on this point, he nevertheless indicates a significant subtext in Milton's account of the War in Heaven. The incarnation was but one of the steps in the Son's total humiliation whereby he laid aside his godhead and lowered himself to become human. The classic statement of the Son's humiliation is found in Philippians 2.6–11. Paul tells us how Christ

> 6. Who being in the form of God, thought it not robbery to be equal with God:
> 7. But made himself of no reputation, and took upon him the form of a servant, and was made in the likeness of men:
> 8. And being found in fashion as a man, he humbled himself, and became obedient unto death, even the death of the cross.
> 9. Wherefore God also hath highly exalted him, and given him a name which is above every name:
> 10. That at the name of Jesus every knee shall bow, of things in heaven, and things in earth, and things under the earth;
> 11. And that every tongue should confess that Jesus Christ is Lord, to the Glory of God the Father.[14]

Milton specifically alluded to these verses when he described the Son's appointment as head of the angels. There God says of the Son "to him shall bow / All knees in Heav'n, and shall confess him Lord" (5.607–8). No biblically-educated seventeenth-century reader of *Paradise Lost* would have failed to hear an echo in these words of Philippians 2.10–11, quoted above. Thus the reader is reminded of Christ's humbling himself for the sake of humanity even when Milton is describing the Son's exaltation above the angels. By becoming the head of the angels, the Son not only effectively foreshadows Christ's command to his disciples quoted in *The Ready and Easy Way* ("he that is greatest among you, let him be as the younger, and he that is chief, as he that serveth"); he also upholds the ideal of a leader of a free commonwealth as represented in the same tract ("wherin they who are greatest, are perpetual servants and drudges to the public at their own cost and charges").

Milton, however, is not yet through exploiting the implications of the Son's headship. He refers to it yet once more in book 6 when the Son gathers his forces on the third day of the War in Heaven. In Milton's words, the loyal angels are "Under thir head embodied all in one" (779). The Son thereupon tells the loyal angels to "stand only and behold" (810), for he alone will drive out the rebels. Here Milton completely reversed the analogy of the body politic as used by Forset and innumerable others. Although in Forset the body will "expose it selfe to any perils for [the head's] sake and safety" and the limbs will "readily receive upon themselves the strokes and wounds, intended against the head," in *Paradise Lost* it is the Son who, as head of the angels, acts on their behalf against the rebels. Rather than demanding protection, the Son takes all the rebels' rage upon himself and personally drives them from Heaven.

Furthermore, this image of the angels embodied under the Son as their head alludes in a subtle way to Christ's future obedient service to humanity. William B. Hunter has persuasively argued that Milton's account of the War in Heaven simultaneously describes three events from the beginning, middle, and end of time.[15] These events are

> first, the surface narrative of the fall of the angels . . . second, the defeat of Satan and his fellow devils described in the book of Revelation . . . and third and most important, the exaltation of the Son of God, which took place concomitantly with his resurrection as the incarnate God-man.[16]

According to this view, the Son's defeat of the rebels in the War in Heaven elaborately parallels Christ's passion, death, and resurrection on the third day.[17] Yet although Hunter chooses to read Christ's crucifixion and resurrection in the context of his exaltation to glory, the same events can also be read as stages in Christ's atonement of sinful humanity, a process that includes Christ's incarnation and humiliation as well as his resurrection and exaltation. To read the War in Heaven as metaphor for the atonement is not to deny that Milton alluded in his account of the War to Christ's exaltation, but rather to expand the range of his allusions. Milton, I believe, signals that he has atonement in mind in his account of the War in Heaven precisely by having the loyal angels "embodied" in the Son before he defeats the forces of Satan.

Christian theologians describe the atonement as the process by which sinful humanity is once again made "at one" with God through the activity of Christ. While these theologians agree that humanity's sins are somehow atoned for, there are several different theories of how the atonement takes place. According to the second-century Church Father Saint Iranaeus and his commentators, Christ atones for humanity's sinfulness by "recapitulating" or somehow summing up all humanity into himself so that he might do battle with and conquer the forces of Satan, Sin, and Death on humanity's behalf. Christ defeats Satan by following in Adam's footsteps and obeying where Adam was disobedient. Christ is thus both the second Adam and humanity's victorious champion.[18] This theory of the atonement differs from the later "satisfaction" theory in that its emphasis is on Christ's "breaking the power of Satanic tyranny" through his obedience to God rather than on "the release of man from the legal pains and penalties of sins" through his satisfaction of divine justice.[19] The primary metaphors of the recapitulation theory are military and agonistic, whereas those of the satisfaction theory are legal and forensic. For this reason Milton appropriately alluded to the recapitulation theory in the agonistic context of the War in Heaven just as he earlier alluded to the satisfaction theory in the forensic setting of the Council in Heaven.

Both the Latin word *recapitulatio* and the Greek word *anakephalaiosis* that it translates appear to derive ultimately from roots meaning "head" (*caput, kephale*). When Iranaeus discussed the recapitulation, he implied by it the idea of Christ's collecting everything under his head. This is apparently also how Milton understood the recapitulation. The main biblical text on which the recapitulation theory is based is Ephesians 1.10. It is worthwhile comparing Milton's own translation of this text with other standard translations.

> That in the dispensation of the fulness of times he might gather together in one all things in Christ, both which are in heaven, and which are on earth; even in him. (King James Version)

> In despensatione plenitiudinis temporum, instaurare omnia in Christo, quae in coelis, et quae in terra sunt, in ipso. (Vulgate)

> ut sub unum caput recolligeret omnia in Christo, tum quae in coelis sunt. (Milton's Latin)[20]

> that he might collect together all things under a single head in Christ, the things in heaven as well. (John Carey's translation of Milton's Latin)

In the section of the *Christian Doctrine* from which Carey's translation of Milton's version of Ephesians 1.10 quoted above is taken, Milton cited this verse in regard to the Son's headship over the angels, thus bringing us back to the circumstances of the War in Heaven (*Complete Prose Works*, 6:344–45). In an interesting parallel, the Calvinist divine William Strong, a contemporary of Milton, similarly associated Christ's headship of the angels with the recapitulation when he wrote that "we know that Christ is [the angels'] head, and they make up one body in Christ with the *Saints*, for there is an [*anakephalaiosis*] *of things in heaven and things in earth, Eph.* 1.10."[21]

Milton also punningly used the word *head* when he unmistakably alluded to Iranaeus's theory of the atonement in book 3 of *Paradise Lost*; God tells the Son

> Be thou in Adam's room
> The Head of all mankind, though Adam's Son.
> As in him perish all men, so in thee

> As from a second root shall be restor'd,
> As many as are restor'd, without thee none.
> (3.285–89)

Perhaps John Calvin was making a similar pun when he wrote of the atonement that "Our acquittal is in this—that the guilt which made us liable to punishment was transferred to the head of the Son of God."[22]

If Milton alluded to the recapitulation theory of atonement by having the loyal angels embodied under the Son as their head just before the Son faces the forces of Satan, then the Son's defeat of the rebel angels foreshadows Christ's future defeat of Satan, Sin, and Death after he recapitulates all humanity under his head. In both instances the Son's or Christ's headship is not an act of self-aggrandizement but of self-sacrifice and obedience to the Father's will on behalf of creatures far inferior to himself. By alluding to the recapitulation theory of atonement in the context of the War in Heaven, Milton underscores the connection between Christ's humiliation and his exaltation, between his service and his glory, between Philippians 2.6–8 and 2.9–11.

Given the patterns of pointed antithesis in *Paradise Lost* between the heavenly and the demonic, it is not at all surprising that Satan feigns a recapitulation of his own. The parallels and contrasts that Milton established between the Infernal and Heavenly Councils have long been noted. Thus, by offering to journey to the newly-created world ostensibly on behalf of his fellow devils, Satan anticipates the Son's offer to humble himself on behalf of humanity and obediently suffer for them as their head. When Satan is apprehended on his mission by Eden's angelic guardians, Gabriel is unimpressed with the claims of this "courageous Chief, / The first in flight from pain" (4.920–21). Although Satan pretends to be acting as a "faithful Leader" who serves his followers by alone undertaking danger for them, Gabriel says the devils are an "Army of Fiends, fit body to fit head" (953). Satan, then, may be the devils' head, but he like human kings fails to follow the Son's ideal of humility and service for his people.

We have seen how Ephesians 1.10 is the scriptural basis for both the Son's headship over the angels and Christ's recapitulation of humanity. The Geneva Bible gives it yet another gloss. In a marginal note to this verse it explains, "By this he meaneth the whole bodie of the Church." We return yet again to where we started, to Christ's headship over the mystical body of the church, but we have come far indeed from any similarity between this and the regal presumption of a king's headship over the body politic.

In this essay I have asserted a triple analogy: the Son as head of the angels, Christ as head of the church, and a monarch as head of state.

While all three components of the analogy are based on the same analogy of the body, whether it be angelic, ecclesiastical, or political, Milton in both his prose and poetry shows where the analogy fails. Though a monarch may appeal to his place in the analogy of the body politic to justify his claims of superiority and command, the example of the Son and Christ do not support this presumption. Instead, their example redefines headship in terms of service and humility. Far from offering a sanction to monarchial presumption, they provide a rebuke and a contrary ideal. By drawing on the organic analogy to link the Son, Christ, and human monarchs, Milton used apparent similarities to expose real differences.

On 30 January, 1649, King Charles I, the head of the English body politic, was himself beheaded by his subjects. The next day, John Owen preached a sermon to the Rump Parliament. In the course of arguing that England had suffered divine punishment as a result of the misdeeds of its king, Owen made the following observation:

> The deposing of divine and human things is oftentimes very opposite. God himself proceeds with them in a diverse dispensation. In the spiritual body the members offend, and the Head is punished. "The iniquity of us all did meet on him," Isa. liii. In the civil politic body the head offends, and the members rue it: Manasseh sins, and Judah must go captive.[23]

"The deposing of divine and human things is oftentimes very opposite." Christ as head suffers for his people; the people suffer for a king as head. This is precisely Milton's point in *The Ready and Easy Way* and, as I have shown, in *Paradise Lost* as well.

Notes

I would like to thank Professors Claire Fowler, Victoria Kahn, and Earl Miner for reading a draft of this paper and saving me from numerous small errors. I would also like to thank Professor Victor Preller for helping me transliterate from the Greek.

1. Milton's translation, "Psalm II," can be found in *John Milton: Complete Poems and Major Prose*, ed. Merritt Y. Hughes (New York: Macmillan, 1957). All references to Milton's poetry are to this edition and are cited parenthetically in the text.

2. Edward Forset, *Comparative Discourse of the Bodies Natural and Political, The Frame of Order*, ed. James Winny (London: George Allen and Unwin, 1957), 99.

3. Leonard Barkan, *Nature's Work of Art: The Human Body as Image of the World* (New Haven: Yale University Press, 1975), 75–76.

4. David George Hale, *The Body Politic: A Political Metaphor in Renaissance English Literature* (The Hague: Mouton, 1971), 59.

5. James I, *The Political Works of James I* (Cambridge: Harvard University Press, 1918), 308.

6. Michael Walzer, *The Revolution of the Saints: A Study in the Origins of Radical Politics* (New York: Atheneum, 1969), 174.

7. John Milton, *Complete Prose Works*, 8 vols., ed. Don M. Wolfe et al. (New Haven: Yale University Press, 1953–82), 4:483. All references to Milton's prose are to this edition and are cited parenthetically in the text.

8. For a good analysis of this practice, see James Daly, "Cosmic Harmony and Political Thinking in Early Stuart England," *Transactions of the American Philosophical Society* 69 (1979): 1–41.

9. Ernst H. Kantorowicz, *The King's Two Bodies: A Study in Medieval Political Theory* (Princeton: Princeton University Press, 1957), 15–16.

10. Kantorowicz, *King's Two Bodies,* 223.

11. See the passage from Milton's *Christian Doctrine* in *Complete Prose Works* 6:499. Studies of Milton's use of the organic analogy in his earlier prose include Michael Lieb, *The Sinews of Ulysses: Form and Convention in Milton's Works* (Pittsburgh: Duquesne University Press, 1989), 21–37; Janel Mueller, "Embodying Glory: The Apocalyptic Strain in Milton's *Of Reformation*," *Politics, Poetics, and Hermeneutics in Milton's Prose*, ed. David Loewenstein and James Grantham Turner (Cambridge: Cambridge University Press, 1990), 9–40; and Hale, *The Body Politic*, 120–30.

12. The historian Blair Worden has rightly queried if it is realized

> how close is Satan's republicanism, which is accorded its most ample documentation in Book V, to the language of *The Ready and Easy Way to Establish a Free Commonwealth* early in 1660, the year when, as far as we can tell, Milton is likely, during the succeeding months, to have written Book V?

See his "Milton's Republicanism and the Tyranny of Heaven," *Machiavelli and Republicanism*, ed. Gisela Bock, Quentin Skinner, and Maurizo Viroli (Cambridge: Cambridge University Press, 1990), 235.

13. Fowler is quoted in Dennis Danielson, *Milton's Good God: A Study in Literary Theodicy* (Cambridge: Cambridge University Press, 1982), 222. Danielson provides persuasive arguments to support Fowler's position on pages 222–24.

14. All biblical references are to the King James Version, unless otherwise noted.

15. William B. Hunter, "The War in Heaven: The Exaltation of the Son," *Bright Essence: Studies in Milton's Theology*, ed. William B. Hunter, C. A. Patrides, and Jack Hale Adamson (Salt Lake City: University of Utah Press, 1973), 115–30.

16. Hunter, "War in Heaven," 123.

17. Ibid., 126–29.

18. For studies of Irenaeus and the recapitulation theory of atonement, see C. A. Patrides, *Milton and the Christian Tradition* (London: Oxford University Press, 1966), 132–33; Gustaf Wingren, *Man and the Incarnation: A Study in the Biblical Theology of Saint Iranaeus*, trans. Ross Mackenzie (Philadelphia: Muhlenberg Press, 1959); and John Lawson, *The Biblical Theology of Saint Iranaeus* (London: Epworth Press, 1948), 140–98.

19. Lawson, *Biblical Theology,* 147.

20. Milton's Latin is quoted from *The Works of John Milton*, 18 vols., ed. F.A. Patterson et al. (New York: Columbia University Press, 1931–38), 15:98.

21. William Strong, *A Treatise Showing the Subordination of the Will of Man Unto the Will of God* (London, 1657), 157. The Greek word transliterated as *anakephalaiosis* in the passage quoted is from Iranaeus; it does not appear in the text of Ephesians.

22. John Calvin, *Institutes of the Christian Religion*, trans. Henry Beveridge (Grand Rapids, Mich.: Eerdmans, 1957), 1:439.

23. John Owen, *The Works of John Owen, D. D.* (New York: Robert Carter & Brothers, 1851–53), 8:135–36.

A Fissure in the Milton Window?: Arnold's 1888 Address

DAVID BOOCKER

In February 1888 Matthew Arnold delivered his final public address, on the occasion of the unveiling of the stained-glass window in honor of Milton at Saint Margaret's Church, Westminster. Arnold was asked to deliver the address by his friend, Archdeacon of Westminster F. W. Farrar, who instigated and arranged the gift funded by American philanthropist/owner of the Philadelphia *Public Ledger*, George Childs. Farrar was concerned that the British had been neglecting one of England's great poets, writing in an essay that appeared in *Harper's New Monthly Magazine* (January 1888) that he wanted to honor Milton because there were "fewer memorials to Milton than of any Englishman of the same transcendent greatness"—the only other memorial being a bust erected in 1737 by Auditor Benson.[1] In a February 1887 letter to Childs he had expressed his belief that Milton was "so wholly uncommemorated in England" because of the poet's politics: "For one hundred and fifty years after his death the Stuart reaction against Puritanism and the adoration of 'King Charles the Martyr' caused Milton's name to be execrated."[2]

Farrar's remarks highlight an apparent inconsistency in the late Victorian attitude toward Milton's poetry and his politics—an inconsistency adumbrated by George Lyttleton in 1760 when he wrote that Milton's poetry was destined to be in and out of favor with the English public according to the politics of the times. Lyttleton wrote that the politics of Milton during the reign of Charles II

> brought his poetry into disgrace: for it is rule with the English; they see no good in a man whose politicks they dislike. But, as their notions of governments are apt to change, men of parts, whom they believe they have slighted, become their favourite authors; and others, who have possest their warmest admiration, are in turn under-valued.[3]

Given Lyttleton's and Farrar's conclusions about the effect of Milton's politics on the reception of his poetry, it might be possible to conclude that the 1888 ceremony marks a change in the Englishman's attitude toward and reception of the great Cromwellian poet. But this conclusion would be premature. Indeed, what is most interesting about the 1888 ceremony is that despite its being an event to honor Milton, the derision of Milton's politics is obvious. In her discussion of the ceremony, Lois Parker recognizes that surrounding the unveiling ceremony was the "most insistent . . . incongruity . . . of purport and presentation by Matthew Arnold and Archdeacon Farrar."[4] This incongruity is most evident in Arnold's keynote address, in which he makes every attempt to distinguish between Milton "the poet" and Milton "the politician." This distinction between the two Miltons is most important, I believe, not just because it provides us with important insights on how Milton's poetry was received by the greatest Victorian spokesman on cultural matters, but it lays the foundation for a way of thinking about Milton and his poetry that the present generation of Miltonists is attempting to rethink.

Arnold's address focuses on the importance of the "great (or grand) style," thus reiterating a theme that had been important to him since three early lectures on Homer (1861–62), which he published together as "On Translating Homer" (1862). Here he had discussed the Homeric poems with the object of analyzing the constituent elements of the "grand style," to show the extent to which various translators had succeeded in rendering the qualities of the original. He believed the "grand style" appeared in poetry "when a noble nature, poetically gifted, treats with simplicity or with severity a serious subject."[5] The best model for the grand style simple was Homer, and the best model for the grand style severe was Milton. It is important to note that for Arnold this issue of the "grand style" was not merely a literary matter; it had tremendous social significance, because for him the "grand style" was an expression of the nobility of the human spirit, and most important, Arnold felt that the conditions of contemporary life had diminished the stature of that spirit. In the 1888 address, Milton is for speakers of English "our grand source" of what he called here the "great style" (11:331).[6]

Arnold begins his address by citing an unnamed authority to give "a warning cry against 'the Anglo-Saxon contagion'" (328). Arnold feared that this "contagion," which had as its source "the ever-multiplying and spreading Anglo-Saxon race . . . would invade and overpower all nations." Of course, the contagion was spreading fastest in the United States, where "the Anglo-Saxon race is already most numerous"; where "material interests are most absorbing and pursued with most energy"; where "the ideal, the saving ideal, of a high and rare excellence, seems perhaps to suffer most danger of being obscured and lost." This "contagion" was the tendency of Americans to elevate the "average man" in status; it is Anglo-Saxon "commonness" (333). Thus Arnold complains when a lady from Ohio sends him a book of American authors, with a note praising all of the authors contained in the volume. When he replied to her that there were only a couple of authors worthy of high praise, she agreed, but added that she thought "it pleasant . . . to think that excellence was common and abundant" (329). He concludes from this experience that "excellence is not common and abundant," and warns that "whoever talks of excellence as common and abundant, is on the way to lose all right standard of excellence."

To this point, Arnold has warned us about an Anglo-Saxon contagion threatening to destroy the human spirit. In the first four paragraphs of his address, roughly a third of its length, Arnold has not mentioned Milton, not even in passing, so we have to wonder how Arnold is going relate this contagion to the occasion. Beginning with the fifth paragraph, Arnold first mentions that "we have met here to-day to witness the unveiling of a gift in Milton's honour" and, strangely enough, he points out that the gift was "bestowed" by an American. Arnold thanks Childs for his American hospitality (Arnold had stayed with the Philadelphia newspaper owner during his American tour),[7] and commends him for being one "who wishes to keep his standard of excellence high" by donating memorials to Shakespeare and Milton.

Arnold then discusses in some detail Milton's relationship with his second wife, Katherine Woodcock, who is buried with her infant at Saint Margaret's. Arnold testifies that Milton was happy during his one year of marriage to Katherine, and he compliments Katherine by suggesting that this was, perhaps, Milton's only time "of happiness in common things and in domestic relations."

At this point, roughly half-way through his address, Arnold returns to his discussion of the Anglo-Saxon contagion. It becomes more clear now that this contagion involves the degradation of the English language. He begins an extended discussion on a cure for this contagion, drawing together his two main topics, the contagion and Milton, and prescribes a kind of antitoxin for the contagion:

> If to our English race an inadequate sense for perfection of work is a real danger, if the discipline of respect for a high and flawless excellence is peculiarly needed by us, Milton is of all our gifted men the best lesson, the most salutary influence. In the sure and flawless perfection of his rhythm and diction he is as admirable as Virgil or Dante, and in this respect he is unique amongst us. (330)

Other poets who studied Milton—Thomson, Cowper, Wordsworth—adopted his form, but in Arnold's view they "fail in their diction and rhythm if we try them by that high standard of excellence maintained by Milton constantly" (330). Not even Shakespeare possesses Milton's "sureness of perfect style. . . . Milton, from one end of *Paradise Lost* to the other, is in his diction and rhythm constantly a great artist in the great style" (331).

Thus, for Arnold, to stem the spread of the Anglo-Saxon contagion, in order for men and women to regain their lost nobility of spirit, it was necessary to turn to poetry and art:

> The mighty power of poetry and art is generally admitted. But where the soul of this power, of this power at its best, chiefly resides, very many of us fail to see. It resides chiefly in the refining and elevation wrought in us by the high and rare excellence of the great style. (331)

He goes on to say that "no race needs the influences" of the great style more than the English, and that "in poetry and art our grand source for them is Milton."

Arnold spends virtually the last third of his address explaining the reasons he believes Milton is the "grand source" of the "great style." This last section is, I think, the most important part of Arnold's address because his emphasis on Milton as the source of the great style would seem to lay the groundwork for other critics of literature, such as Pater, Raleigh, and Eliot. The key to this criticism is acknowledging the artistry of a writer's work while deemphasizing his ideas and, in Milton's case, his Puritanism. In an earlier essay on Milton, "A French Critic on Milton" (1876–77), Arnold had already discussed Milton's preeminence in style while relentlessly condemning his puritanical tendencies.

Milton's ties to the Puritans provoked some of Arnold's most caustic remarks. He says about Milton in "A French Critic on Milton":

> He had the temper of his Puritan party. We often hear the boast, on behalf of the Puritans, that they produced "our great epic poet." Alas! one might not unjustly retort that they spoiled him. However, let Milton bear his own burden; in his temper he had natural affinities with the Puritans. He has paid for it by limitations as a poet.[8]

Nowhere is Milton's temper more defective, according to Arnold, than in his prose. While Lord Macaulay had regretted that the prose writings of Milton were not more read,[9] Arnold insists that those who turn to Milton's prose writings for enjoyment are "misled, and our time wasted," and he cites the French critic Scherer to confirm this:

No doubt there is, as M. Scherer says, "something indescribably heroical and magnificent which overflows from Milton, even when he is engaged in the most miserable discussions." Still, for the mass of his prose treatises "miserable discussions" is the final right word. Nor, when Milton passed to his great epic, did he altogether leave the old man of these "miserable discussions" behind him.[10]

The "contents" of *Paradise Lost*, then, are "given by Puritanism,"[11] and Arnold seems in agreement with Scherer when he quotes him:

> *Paradise Lost* is a false poem, a grotesque poem, a tiresome poem; there is not one reader out of a hundred who can read the ninth and tenth books without smiling, or the eleventh and twelfth without yawning. The whole thing is without solidity; it is a pyramid on its apex, the most solemn of problems resolved by the most puerile of means. And, notwithstanding, *Paradise Lost* is immortal.[12]

What becomes problematic is how Arnold can call *Paradise Lost* tedious and "grotesque," as well as "immortal." On the one hand we have Milton the poet, philosopher, statesman, Puritan, whose epical matter is dismissed as Puritan dogma. On the other, we have Milton the great artist, "of all our English race . . . by his diction and rhythm the one artist of the highest rank in the great style we have" (331). Arnold, then, is able to acknowledge the "immortality" of Milton's work by assuring that this fissure in Milton's personality is maintained.

This division in Milton's personality is best explained in the 1888 address. "Nature," says Arnold, "formed Milton to be a great poet" and after declaring that no "other poet has shown so sincere a sense of the grandeur of his vocation, and a moral effort so constant and sublime to make and keep himself worthy of it," Arnold distinguishes between "The Milton of religious and political controversy" and "The Milton of poetry." The Milton of religious and political controversy, "and perhaps of domestic life also" is, according to Arnold, often "disfigured by want of amenity, by acerbity" (332). And that is all he says: the political and domestic Milton is a disagreeable and distemperate man. But for Arnold the Milton of poetry

> is one of those great men "who are modest . . . because they continually compare themselves, not with other men, but with the idea of the perfect which they have before their mind." The Milton of poetry is the man, in his own magnificent phrase, of "devout prayer to that Eternal Spirit that can enrich withal utterance and knowledge, and sends out his Seraphim with the hallowed fire of his altar, to touch and purify the lips of whom he pleases." And finally, the Milton of poetry is, in his own words again, the man of "industrious and select reading." (332)

Arnold, quoting from the second book of Milton's *Reason of Church Government*, recognizes that the Milton of poetry becomes especially important in an English culture where "there will be millions, who know not a word of Greek and Latin," who, therefore, cannot read the "great poets of antiquity" in the original, but who can find the elevating power of the "great style" in the English poetry of Milton. And this, finally, is the supreme importance of Milton: he is English—important because "The English race overspreads the world, and at the same time the ideal of an excellence the most high and the most rare abides a possession with it for ever" (333). Thus, it is the "Milton of poetry" and not the "Milton of religious and political controversy" who makes a moral effort to maintain the "great style," thereby enhancing the human spirit.

In the great scheme of Arnold's work, the 1888 address may not hold that much importance. But it does hold great interest and importance to scholars of Milton, if only to show how the great Victorian spokesman on cultural matters placed Milton's work into his view of late Victorian English culture. From our present perspective, just over one hundred years after the unveiling ceremony, we can assess Arnold's views on Milton based on successive generations of literary criticism, and when we do we can see, I believe, that Arnold's statements on Milton represent a reaction against both Romantic and early Victorian ideas about Milton; at the same time, his statements at once reflect the eighteenth-century understanding of Milton and lay the groundwork for a modern literary criticism that has tended to separate the aesthetic from the religious and political.

This tendency was nothing new; indeed, as Joseph A. Wittreich demonstrates in *Feminist Milton*, "The horizon of expectations that greeted *Paradise Lost* was created largely by Milton's own political posture and manifestations of it in his prose writings." Moreover, he says

> There was also an effort to create distance between expectations of *Paradise Lost* and Milton's supposed achievement. This was done through a maneuver that, first, disengages the poem from the context of Milton's prose writings with which it enjoys an elaborate and meaningful intertextuality and that, then, realigns this poem with the literary and generally conservative tradition of the epic.[13]

Thus, eighteenth-century critics of Milton had to find a way to justify the greatness of *Paradise Lost* on some valid critical basis other than politics or theology, or invent some new "critical" basis like the sublime.[14] To do this they separated Milton the man from the work (a division that remains until William Hayley and the Romantics), making the valid critical basis a phase of classicism grounded on literary art, or aesthetic theory, and resulting in much analysis of Milton's language and versification.

This divorce between the poet Milton and the political writer Milton is seen in some of the earliest responses to Milton in the late seventeenth and early eighteenth centuries:[15]

> The bard, who next the new-born saint address,
> Was Milton, for his wondrous poem blest;
> Who strangely found, in his Lost Paradise, rest.
> "Great bard," said he, "'twas verse alone
> Did for my hideous crime atone,
> Defending once the worst rebellion."[16]

> These sacred lines with wonder we peruse,
> And praise the flights of a seraphic muse,
> Till the seditious prose provokes our rage,
> And soils the beauties of thy brightest page.[17]

Here *Paradise Lost* either redeems the poet's politics, or the pamphlets spoil our appreciation of the poet. Either way, Milton's politics and poetry are incompatible.

Certainly Dr. Johnson did more to perpetuate this division than anyone else, and his *Life of Milton* continued to be the most influential work on Milton well into the nineteenth century. The Romantics, revolting against the formalism of eighteenth-century neo-Classicism, celebrated Milton the man and his imagination and certainly recognized Johnson's antagonism toward Milton's republican and Puritan ideas, as well as the effects of this antagonism on his reputation as a poet. Byron, for example, observed that in terms of popularity, "Milton's politics kept him down."[18] The Romantics accused Johnson of telling but half the truth because of his biased opinion of Milton, looking instead at Milton as a subjective artist whose works are best understood in light of his life and career.

Coleridge observed the need to examine the conditions under which Milton composed. "The age," he writes in his "Lecture on Milton and the Paradise Lost" (1819)

> ... won him over from the dear-loved delights of academic Groves, and Cathedral Aisles, to the anti-Prelatic party—and it acted on him, no doubt, and modified his studies by its characteristic controversial spirit, no less busy in political & theological dispute.[19]

In his *Life of Milton* (1838), DeQuincey reminds his readers that Milton was, from very early on, a Puritan.[20] Examining the political and theological conditions under which Milton lived and composed, the Romantics saw a man with strong conviction, a man who sacrificed personal gain for the good of all humankind. For many, Milton became the champion of radicalism in politics, religion, and art. Being a "king-hater," as Charles Lamb labeled Milton, was no longer contemptible.[21] Thus, unlike their eighteenth-century predecessors, the Romantics believed that it was a prerequisite to understand Milton the man in order to understand his poetry.

Still, Macaulay, in his 1825 essay written to commemorate the discovery of *De Doctrina Christiana*, is quick to point out that it is still popular to "extol the poems and to decry the poet."[22] Macaulay revered "the genius and virtues of John Milton, the poet, the statesman, the philosopher, the glory of English literature, the champion and the martyr of English liberty,"[23] for his powerful and independent mind, emancipated from the influence of authority. For Macaulay, Milton's originality and personal independence made him the founder of and model for a new Victorian tradition—the model of middle-class independence—characterized by a self-made authority that provides the example for those who lack models themselves.

Macaulay's essay was extremely influential, and there appeared in the 1830s a number of authors who agreed with Macaulay and disagreed with the earlier Tory biographers, particularly Dr. Johnson. As James G. Nelson explains, these new biographies focused on "Milton's political and religious views and activities, and, of necessity, to the exposition of the prose rather than the poetry."[24] For example, Joseph Ivimey's *John Milton: His Life and Times, Religious and Political Opinions* (1833) contained an "Animadversions on Dr. Johnson's Life of Milton," in which he maintained that Johnson's "ultra-toryism and bigotry" prevented him from understanding Milton's true character and opinions. In addition, the appearance of *De Doctrina* increased the Victorians' interest in Milton's other prose, and in 1835 Robert Fletcher edited *The Prose Works of John Milton*. In the "Introductory Review" he accused Tory biographers of suppressing Milton's prose works because they were a "burthen of his song."[25]

These are only three of many examples of liberal receptions of Milton, and what is very apparent is that in his writings on Milton, Arnold was reacting very strongly against these liberal readings. Indeed, Arnold's "horizon of expectations" was clouded by the fact that he was the recipient of two major traditions of reception regarding Milton. While dissenters, Evangelicals, and Whigs approved the virtues and genius of Milton the Puritan poet, statesman, and philosopher, High Churchmen, Catholics, and Tories either damned him with faint praise or with outright scorn and disapproval. For these parties, there was no getting past the idea that Milton was a Puritan, so they pictured him as a sour, stern dissenter and republican. He may have been a great poet, but he was a bad theologian and a worse politician. This picture of Milton as stern and sour Puritan was also given validity by Arnold, who did not want to slander Milton's poetry, but who felt that it was unfortunate that he was a Puritan. It is not surprising, then, that in "A French Critic on Milton" Arnold writes that whoever reads Macaulay's *Essay on Milton* "with the desire to get at the real truth about Milton, whether as a man or as a poet, will feel that the essay in nowise helps him."[26] For Arnold, Macaulay's essay was nothing more than "a panegyric on Milton, a panegyric on the Puritans."

Thus, Arnold, hearkening back to conservative Tory conceptions of Milton, praises the aesthetics of Milton's poetry while criticizing his politics. In his study of Milton and the Victorians, Nelson suggests that it is easy to "recognize the principal shift in interest and emphasis from [Milton's] matter and thought to his manner, style, and prosody" and that "this movement from thought to art . . . was not completed by 1900."[27] This deemphasis of Milton's Puritanism and subsequent emphasis on aesthetics, coming at a time when post-Darwinian Victorian England was no longer able to relate to Milton's ideas, had a tremendous effect on twentieth-century criticism of his work. Nelson explains that one of these effects is that "late Victorian critics and poets prepared the way for the important Christian Humanist view of Milton by attempting to stress Milton's classical rather than his Puritan orientation."[28]

Even more significantly, this shift in interest resulted in the depoliticization of Milton's art. When Arnold spoke of the greatness of Milton's style, of the greatness of his rhythm and diction, while dismissing his political and religious associations, what resulted was an aesthetic reading of Milton, seemingly void of any political or religious meaning. But as Bernard Sharratt recognizes, once a poem like *Paradise Lost* is "dissociated from its context and its 'literary' qualities divorced from its political and theological dimensions its literary value is reduced to little more than a source for 'scholarly-critical fodder.'"[29] The irony is that in his efforts to depoliticize Milton's work, Arnold was making an explicitly political statement on the relationship between art and politics—a relationship that isolates literature from any association with religion or politics. In fact, Arnold's efforts anticipate the New Critics of the 1940s and 1950s who, as a result of the intensities of the Cold War, emphasized close readings of texts, a method that did not require any exchange between literature and politics.[30]

In 1908 Reverend H. G. Rosedale argued the need for readers to understand that "If Milton be true to himself, *'Paradise Lost'* ought to reflect and reproduce for us the inmost spirit of the Milton of the political period of his life."[31] In 1939 George W. Whiting proposed that readers of Milton should see a greater connection between his pamphlets and *Paradise Lost*, writing that

> Literary critics who ignore backgrounds and who insist upon treating poetry as merely an esthetic product have as a rule neglected or condemned Milton's work and interests in the period from 1640 to 1658, which they regard as an unfortunate episode in the life of the poet.[32]

Whiting's work utilized the prose primarily as a way to interpret the poems. To the modern critic this sounds simplistic because this is the way most all of us work. But both Rosedale's and Whiting's statements clearly indicate that there still remained readers of Milton who wanted to divorce the poet from the writer of pamphlets. Even today there is still a tendency to think genius and partisanship to be at odds, or to think that great art is in the sphere of the sublime, or to conclude that the best writers are those least fettered by the age in which they lived. Fortunately, recent critical theorists are coming up with ever more effective ways to reconnect the political and aesthetic realms. For example, Kevin Sharpe and Steven Zwicker argue that we should no longer distinguish sharply between epics, sermons, and political pamphlets because that fragments

> what was a common culture partaking of shared languages. At the beginning of the seventeenth century literature was humane letters; it embraced history and ethics, religion and politics. To isolate literature is not only to deprive its language of the power of these associations but also to deny the political its highest polemical mode.[33]

Once we recognize and acknowledge that Milton's greatest poetry was written at the nexus of religious and political controversy and that its language is freighted with political argument, our job as readers of Milton is to rediscover and reintegrate these political languages into literary texts, which should enable us to be more aware of the circumstances in which Milton's work was written.[34] To repair the fissure in the Milton window, our role as critics is to allow the Milton of poetry and the Milton of political and religious controversy to be the same man.

Notes

1. F. W. Farrar, "The Share of America in Westminster Abbey," *Harper's New Monthly Magazine*, January 1888, 309.

2. F. W. Farrar to George Childs, London, 4 February 1887. The letter appears in George W. Childs, *Recollections* (Philadelphia: J. B. Lippincott, 1890), 292.

3. George Lyttleton, "Dialogues of the Dead," no. 14, *Milton: The Critical Heritage*, ed. John T. Shawcross (New York: Barnes & Noble, 1972), 2:249.

4. Lois W. Parker, "The Milton Window," *Ringing the Bell Backward: The Proceedings of the First International Milton Symposium*, ed. Ronald Shafer (Bloomington: Indiana University Press, 1982), 69–73. This first appeared as "The Milton Window, The Americans, and Matthew Arnold," *Milton Quarterly* 13 (1979): 50–53.

5. Matthew Arnold, "On Translating Homer," *The Complete Prose Works of Matthew Arnold*, ed. R. H. Super (Ann Arbor: University of Michigan Press, 1960), 1:88.

6. Matthew Arnold, "Milton," *The Complete Prose Works of Matthew Arnold*. All references to the address are to this edition and are cited parenthetically in the text.

7. Matthew Arnold, "To his Sister," 26 July 1886, *Letters of Matthew Arnold, 1848–1888*, ed. George W. E. Russell (New York: Macmillan, 1896), 2:393.

8. Matthew Arnold, "A French Critic on Milton," *The Complete Prose Works of Matthew Arnold*, 8:184–85.

9. Thomas Macaulay, "Milton," *The Works of Lord Macaulay* (London: Longmans, 1898), 1:3.

10. Arnold, "A French Critic on Milton," 177.

11. Ibid., 179.

12. Ibid., 181.

13. Joseph A. Wittreich, *Feminist Milton* (Ithaca: Cornell University Press, 1987), 5.

14. See Leslie E. Moore, *Beautiful Sublime: The Making of "Paradise Lost," 1701–1734* (Stanford, Calif.: Stanford University Press, 1990).

15. John T. Shawcross, *John Milton and Influence: Presence in Literature, History and Culture* (Pittsburgh: Duquesne University Press, 1991), 140–41.

16. Alexander Oldys, "An Ode by Way of Elegy on ... Mr Dryden," (1700), Shawcross, *Critical Heritage*, 1:124.

17. Thomas Yalden, "On the Reprinting of Milton's Prose Works," (1698), Shawcross, *Critical Heritage*, 1:122.

18. George Gordon, Lord Byron, "From a Reply to Blackwood's Edinburgh Magazine, August 1819," *The Romantics on Milton*, ed. Joseph A. Wittreich (Cleveland, Oh.: The Press of Case Western Reserve University, 1970), 517.

19. Samuel Taylor Coleridge, "Lecture on Milton and the Paradise Lost [at the Crown and Anchor]," 4 March, 1819, Wittreich, *Romantics*, 240.

20. Thomas DeQuincey, *Life of Milton* (1838), Wittreich, *Romantics*, 466.

21. Charles Lamb, *The Last Essays of Elia* (1833), Wittreich, *Romantics*, 303.

22. Macaulay, "Milton," 4.

23. Ibid., 4.

24. James G. Nelson, *The Sublime Puritan: Milton and the Victorians* (Madison: University of Wisconsin Press, 1963), 127.

25. Joseph Ivimey, *John Milton: His Life and Times, Religious and Political Opinions* (New York: D. Appleton, 1833), viii; Robert Fletcher, "An Introductory Review," *The Prose Works of John Milton* (London: Westley and Davis, 1835), i.

26. Arnold, "A French Critic on Milton," 166.

27. Nelson, *Sublime Puritan,* 127.

28. Ibid., 151.

29. Bernard Sharratt, "The Appropriation of Milton," *Essays & Studies* (1982): 43.

30. See William E. Cain, *The Crisis in Criticism: Theory, Literature, and Reform in English Studies* (Baltimore: Johns Hopkins University Press, 1984), 4ff.

31. Rev. H. G. Rosedale, "Milton: His Religion and Polemics, Ecclesiastical as Well as Theological," *Milton Memorial Lectures, 1908*, ed. Percy W. Ames (London: Henry Frowde, 1909), 155.

32. George W. Whiting, *Milton's Literary Milieu* (Chapel Hill: University of North Carolina Press, 1939), 218.

33. Kevin Sharpe and Steven Zwicker, eds., *Politics of Discourse: The Literature and History of Seventeenth-Century England* (Berkeley: University of California Press, 1987), 2.

34. Sharpe and Zwicker, *Politics of Discourse*, 1–20.

Part IV
Spokesperson for Authority of Author and of Text

Meddling with Authority: Inspiration and Speech Acts in Milton's Prose

ANGELA ESTERHAMMER

> [Y]ou are very solicitous about [words] as if they were charmes, or had more in them then what they signifie: For no Conjurer's Devill is more concerned in a spell, then you are in a meer word, but never regard the things which it serves to expresse.[1]

The anonymous adversary who addressed this criticism to Milton in 1660 thought he was pronouncing judgment on Milton's immorality in valuing words more than the entities they denote, but modern readers may understand his sentence in a different context. No doubt Milton *is* solicitous about words because he believes there is "more in them then what they signifie." Yet the realm of spells and conjury suggests only one way in which words may have an effect beyond their referential aspect. Another way, which Milton recognized, is by partaking of the effectiveness of the Logos, the Word of the Lord that spoke through the writers of the Bible and inspires preachers and poets. Modern readers also recognize that language has more than referential value when considered in terms of speech-act theory, which holds that, by virtue of the conventions accepted by a particular sociopolitical community, utterances have the ability to alter existing circumstances and to enact what they describe. I suggest that both these models of effective language are at work in Milton's prose, that there are distinct connections between them, and that all this may be illustrated by a fresh look at the autobiographical digression in *The Reason of Church-Government*.

The basic development of Milton's concept of inspiration is from images of pagan Muses and oracles who impart *secret* and *hidden* knowledge (in the early poetry and the *Prolusions*), toward Christianized oracles, visions, and revelations (in works of Milton's middle and later years, notably the *History of Britain*), but also toward a more democratic idea that all Christians may be seen as inspired by the Holy Spirit.[2] In *De Doctrina Christiana*, fantastic experiences of divine revelation are assimilated, historically and theologically, to a pentecostal doctrine:

> And indeed all true believers either prophesy or have within them the Holy Spirit, which is as good as having the gift of prophecy and dreams and visions. (*Complete Prose Works*, 6:523–24)[3]

The "prophecy and dreams and visions" originate with the prophet Joel, who foretold the outpouring of God's spirit on all Israel on the day of the Lord:

> And it shall come to pass afterward, that I will pour out my spirit upon all flesh; and your sons and your daughters shall prophesy, your old men shall dream dreams, your young men shall see visions. (Joel 2.28)[4]

Joel goes on to prophesy "wonders in the heavens and in the earth" (Joel 2.30)—blood, fire, pillars of smoke, and other terrific events akin to those which signify divine visitation in the *History of Britain*. In the New Testament, Joel's words are recalled by St. Peter in a sermon on the day of Pentecost, and he identifies the Holy Spirit that has come upon the apostles in tongues of fire with the outpouring of which Joel spoke (Acts 2.16–21). So the prophet who was visited by the Word of the Lord is replaced by the apostle who has received the gift of the Holy Spirit, and the promise made to the house of Israel is extended "to all that are afar off, even as many as the Lord our God shall call" (Acts 2.39). Alluding to the words of Peter, Milton picks up their typological and inclusive qualities. Yet his choice of conjunction in the phrase "prophesy *or* have . . . the Holy Spirit" (emphasis mine) suggests that he remains aware of the potential for special revelation to chosen individuals. Rather than obliterating the distinction between prophets and spirit-filled believers, he admits only that the believers' abilities are "as good as" those of the favored individuals who have received "the [special] gift of prophecy."

A more radical figurative reading is involved when Milton extends "the term *prophet*" to "anyone endowed with exceptional piety and wisdom for the purpose of teaching" (*Complete Prose Works*, 6:572). This sentence from *De Doctrina Christiana* provides a gloss on the use made in *Areopagitica* of the famous Mosaic utterance that possessed Milton and William Blake alike:

> For now the time seems come, wherein *Moses* the great Prophet may sit in heav'n rejoycing to see that memorable and glorious wish of his fulfill'd,

when not only our sev'nty Elders, but all the Lords people are become Prophets. (*Complete Prose Works*, 2:555–56)

Milton's visionary reading of the Old Testament is not unmotivated by more immediate political and rhetorical considerations. Urging Parliament to free the publication of books from the restraints of the 1643 Licensing Ordinance, Milton argues that all Christians should now share the authority originally granted only to the "sev'nty Elders"— for which we might read the Stationers Company, the Archbishops, and the Chancellors of the Universities, those individuals who have been designated as enforcers of the Licensing Ordinance. The democratic spirit that apparently motivates the substitution of a visionary community of believers for a few elect individuals is intrinsically connected with—indeed, essential to—Milton's belief in republican government and presbyterian church order. Yet a special inspired authority seems reserved for "*Moses* the great Prophet," as marked by the adjective, the definite article, and the fact that Moses is appealed to as the authority for the entire vision. Anticipating the claims he will make in the opening invocation in *Paradise Lost*, Milton implicitly casts himself in the role of "the great Prophet," inasmuch as he echoes the words first spoken by Moses and announces their fulfillment.

Inspiration again has political significance in the *Defensio Secunda*, where that party of Englishmen which imprisoned and executed the king is described as "better instructed and doubtless inspired by heaven" (*Complete Prose Works*, 4:552). The notion that all true believers are in some sense inspired is explicitly used to vindicate a popular action of which Milton approves. Yet far more of the proem to the *Defensio Secunda* consists of self-congratulatory remarks, since Milton in particular ("I and no other") has been blessed by God with the gift of "speaking on so great a theme" and "publicly defending" the cause of Liberty (4:549); the focus is on an inspired voice that will allow Milton to perform things unattempted yet in the oratorial tradition (4:554). Milton needs to retain the concept of special and extraordinary inspiration, both when he turns from government-commissioned defenses of national policy to write strong poetry, and when he finds that he and the mass of "better instructed" Englishmen are no longer on the same side. In the political and ecclesiastical tracts, Milton's argument for freedom of speech and conscience relies on the accessibility of divine inspiration for lay believers, yet even in these texts the language of biblical prophecy tends to attach itself to the recipients of "the inspired guift of God *rarely* bestow'd" (*Complete Prose Works*, 1:816; emphasis mine).

By the time of Milton's maturity, he developed a twofold concept of general and particular inspiration. While these classifications are never made explicit, they correspond to the Ramist logic underlying Milton's theology in *De Doctrina Christiana*, which returns constantly to the opposition of general and particular: for instance, "A DECREE of God is either GENERAL or SPECIAL" (*Complete Prose Works*, 6:153); "Vocation, then, is either general or special" (6:455); "Repentance may be general . . . Or it may be particular" (6:468). As an implicit organizing principle for Milton's thoughts and pronouncements about inspiration, the separation of general and special suits well the situation of a writer arguing strenuously for republican freedoms, but asserting with equal vehemence his own talent and authority to meddle in these matters.

Nowhere in Milton's prose is his notion of inspiration more intimately connected with his sense of identity and vocation than in *The Reason of Church-Government*. In arguing for the freeing of the Church from the authority of prelates and the giving of church government over to presbyters and deacons who will manage it with reason and sanctity, Milton plainly has an interest in promoting the divine gifts of leadership and right reason possessed by lay believers. Yet the biblical and historical precedents on which he grounds his argument for presbyterian church-government repeatedly focus on the inspiration of extraordinary individuals: Moses above all, but also classical figures such as Minos and Tiresias, as well as David, Isaiah, Paul, and John of Patmos. Paraphrasing the teaching of Paul on the various gifts of the Spirit, Milton distinguishes between the ability to preach the Word of God and the practical work of church government:

> For publick preaching indeed is the gift of the Spirit working as best seemes to his secret will, but discipline is the practick work of preaching directed and apply'd as is most requisite to particular duty. (*Complete Prose Works*, 1:755–56)

If his intention is to set the two talents in balance as special and general forms of God-given ability, he does not quite convince. The gift of using language so as to convert others, bestowed on preachers according to the Spirit's "*secret* will" (emphasis mine), retains a certain mystique, and is subtly elevated over the second-order application of that verbal gift in the daily life of the church.

In the autobiographical digression at the beginning of book 2, the figural language Milton uses locates him firmly in the line of individuals who experience special inspiration. His poetic ability is likened to the "secret" and special gift of "publick preaching," being "of power beside the office of a pulpit" (*Complete Prose Works*, 1:816). The paradigm of Old Testament prophecy is subtly implicated in the language of Milton's autobiographical narrative; for instance, in *burden,* a word that recurs in several different contexts in the preamble to book 2. The opening sentence alludes with seeming casualness to a proverb that had recently appeared in a collection of George Herbert's, "Knowledge is no burden."[5] The word is then echoed several times more in an extended metaphor likening those who have spiritual knowledge to impart to traders weighed down by heavy and not easily salable wares. But the full significance of the metaphor only comes to bear when Milton builds up to the revelation that *burden,* in the Authorized Version, is the term used by the Old Testament prophets to introduce their troubling visions:

> And although divine inspiration must certainly have been sweet to those ancient profets, yet the irksomnesse of that truth which they brought was so unpleasant to them, that every where they call it a burden. (1:802–3)

The more famous allusion to Old Testament prophecy that follows sums up the development of Milton's concept of inspiration. Laying aside the pagan models for poetic frenzy—"the vapours of wine" and "the invocation of Dame Memory and her Siren daughters"—that held his interest in "the heat of youth," Milton appeals instead

> by devout prayer to that eternall Spirit who can enrich with all utterance and knowledge, and sends out his Seraphim with the hallow'd fire of his Altar to touch and purify the lips of whom he pleases. (1:820–21)

The New Testament's prayer for the Holy Spirit, which descended on the apostles and "gave them utterance" (Acts 2.4), here merges inextricably with the particular circumstances of the call of Isaiah, the most vivid image in the Old Testament of a prophet's special election. Positioning his autobiographical narrative between the images of Old Testament prophecy, the "burden" and "hallow'd fire," Milton identifies with the recipients of special inspiration while gesturing toward a more inclusive Protestant doctrine of the ministry of the Spirit.

What it means to receive such inspired power is revealed by Milton's use of performative language at this crucial point in his self-presentation. He sets the entire concluding section of his digression in the form of an elaborate promise, which frames the description of the work to be produced by the aid of the "eternall Spirit":

> Neither doe I think it shame to covnant with any knowing reader, that for some few yeers yet I may go on trust with him toward the payment of what I am now indebted ... till which in some measure be compast, at mine own peril and cost I refuse not to sustain this expectation from as many as are

not loath to hazard so much credulity upon the best pledges that I can give them. (1:820–21)

Milton engages himself to deliver the goods in a few years' time. Using formal legal phraseology, he seals a bargain; indeed, he signs a contract, this being the first of the antiprelatical tracts to which he puts his name. The venture is one in which the reader risks being thought overly credulous while Milton risks his honor and good name should he not deliver what he has promised. Milton's choice of the term *covenant* evokes the Old Testament resonances of an agreement in which both parties have responsibilities to fulfill. As if he were choosing his readership the way God chose his people, Milton repeatedly specifies the expectations he has of his covenanting partner: he addresses the digression specifically to the "intelligent and equal auditor" (1:806), the "elegant & learned reader" (1:807), the "gentler sort" of reader (1:808), and the "knowing reader" (1:820).

But *covenant* is also the term recognized in English Common Law since its medieval origins to mean "agreement," and in issuing his promise Milton is taking upon himself what the law called "the burden of the covenant." His promise to the reader actually contains all the elements required by the Common Law to make a promise actionable; according to William Sheppard in his *Touchstone of Common Assurances*, a treatise published the same year *The Reason of Church-Government* was written, the thing promised in a contract must be "lawful," "possible," "clear and certain," "serious and weighty," and it must accord with the consideration or motive the promiser has stated.[6] Should Milton not make good on his claim, a reader who had the admittedly aberrant desire to sue him could presumably bring a writ of covenant or breach of promise suit against him, a type of legal action that, according to the legal historian A. W. B. Simpson, was becoming increasingly frequent during the seventeenth century.[7]

According to Simpson, a covenant had the effect of legally defining a tort or wrong:

> the theoretical function of the covenant was to make future conduct, which would otherwise be lawful, tortious and actionable, in much the same way as an undertaking of responsibility in modern tort law may have the effect of making tortious otherwise lawful future inactivity or carelessness.[8]

In a Miltonic context, one analogy that comes to mind is God's injunction to Adam and Eve in the Garden of Eden, a performative utterance that renders the otherwise lawful activity of eating fruit from a specified tree wrong, and quite seriously actionable. In formulating his promise in *The Reason of Church-Government*, Milton is also delimiting the correctness of his future conduct. The comparison with original sin is particularly apt, and Milton's covenant particularly binding, since he offers to seal the bargain with a "pledge," a token or symbol exchanged between the covenanting parties. The "best pledges" that he offers may either be his already-existing works, perhaps including the present one, or the verbal assurances he has just given of his talent, ambition, and virtuous intent. One thing the noun *pledge* does *not* seem to mean here is a vow or verbal commitment; the *Oxford English Dictionary* does not document this sense of the word until the early nineteenth century. In Milton's time, *pledge* always designated an object handed over as surety and liable to forfeit if certain conditions were not fulfilled. In Milton's poetry, *pledge* is normally synonymous with *symbol* or *tangible evidence*: a child is the pledge of love between its parents (*Paradise Lost*, 2.818), the morning star is the pledge of day (*Paradise Lost*, 5.168), Samson's hair is the pledge of his vow (*Samson Agonistes*, 535, 1144), and, significantly, the tree of the knowledge of good and evil is the pledge of humanity's obedience to God (*Paradise Lost*, 8.323–25).[9] The traditionally tangible nature of the pledge ironically highlights the fact that, in the present case, all Milton has to offer as collateral for texts to come are more texts; despite the elaborate fiction of barter and exchange, the entire transaction rests on the reader's willingness to give credit to Milton's words.

In J. L. Austin's *How to Do Things with Words*, the central text of speech-act philosophy, the promise is the paradigmatic example of a speech act; to utter a promise is not to describe or report on an action, but to perform the action of committing oneself to do something.[10] Yet the promise is also one of the most problematic of speech acts, since the present utterance remains, in a sense, incomplete until a future fulfillment of the promise renders the speech act totally successful. The legal status of the promise or I.O.U. is historically a vexed question; it defies categorization as transfer or exchange because of the intrusion of temporality between the making of the promise and its completion. Simpson emphasizes the distinction made in Common Law between covenants and grants: the latter are contracts that require the immediate transfer of interest in lands or goods and, if violated, are actionable by writ of debt, while convenants, however specific with regard to the future exchange of property, are not understood to involve actual transfer but only promises to transfer, and are only actionable for damages under writ of covenant. Pursuing the theological implications of the temporality of promising, Regina Schwartz has pointed to the underlying affinity between the economic concept of exchange and remuneration and the theological concepts of belief and praise, citing

Emile Benveniste's investigation of the etymology of words for *belief* (*kred*, *credo*) as the action of giving something away with the certainty of getting it back. Schwartz observes that "Milton's discussions of praise are dominated by the familiar language of finance, of owing, paying, and reckoning."[11] Financial and legal parlance are equally prevalent when Milton speaks of belief, either in God or, as here, the belief that others may lodge in Milton himself. In his covenant with the reader, Milton asks for a "credulity" that is both analogous and etymologically related to financial credit; we remetaphorize the economic frame of reference when we "give Milton credit" for being sincere in his promise. Michel de Certeau analyzes belief as an exchange in which a believer, giving credit to a receiver, "creates a deficit whereby a future is introduced into the present."[12] As with the pledge, the underlying pattern is that of an object exchanged between parties in a temporal sequence by which a present transaction looks toward a future fulfillment.

In Milton's promise, present *and* future utterances depend on one another and, like his pledge, lack any external validation. This becomes clear when we examine the reason Milton gives for making his self-imposed commitment public:

> it nothing content me to have disclos'd thus much before hand, but that I trust hereby to make it manifest with what small willingnesse I endure to interrupt the pursuit of no lesse hopes then these, and leave a calme and pleasing solitarynes fed with cherful and confident thoughts, to imbark in a troubl'd sea of noises and hoars disputes. (*Complete Prose Works*, 1:821)

His anticipation of a greater work in the future reflects back on his disinclination to undertake the present task, which in turn guarantees the sincerity of what he is now writing—that is, the sincerity of his promise of a future masterpiece. The irony in this convoluted temporal relationship is intensified when Milton goes on to demonstrate—precisely by speaking out—just how loath he is to break "the quiet and still air of delightfull studies" (1:821–22).

The conflict between speaking and silence is important, and the reason for it emerges at the end of the digression, where the image reappears in an inverted form. Returning to autobiography, Milton affirms his preference for a "blameless silence" over "the sacred office of speaking bought, and begun with servitude and forswearing" (1:823)— apparently oblivious of the fact that he is by now trumpeting his blameless silence quite loudly. He now informs the reader that he intended to take orders in the Church of England, until he became aware that church government had been corrupted to the extent that one swearing loyalty to the Church would be forswearing himself, that he who would take Orders must subscribe slave, and take an oath withall, which unlesse he took with a conscience that would retch he must either strait perjure, or split his faith. (1:823)

This opens up a new perspective on Milton's pledge to produce a great poetic work. Instead of purchasing the right to preach publicly—that is, to have his utterances supported by the institutional authority of the Church—with an oath that goes against his conscience, Milton chooses to barter with the more attractive, though less substantial, currency of his future poetic achievement. He prefers a covenant with a knowing reader over a bond to an authoritarian Church that would compel the oath-taker to "subscribe slave."

William Riley Parker believes that Milton's refusal to take orders is a protest against the oath specified in Article Thirty-six of the *Constitutions and Canons Ecclesiastical* of 1604,[13] but in the context of his legal maneuvering it seems more likely that he is referring to the supplemental vow, the so-called "Et Cetera" oath, which all new and existing ministers were required to take in 1640. The subject of a topical debate at the time Milton was writing the tract, the new oath is considerably more burdensome, not least from a speech-act perspective. The 1604 version required affirmation of belief ("I believe the doctrine of the United Church of England and Ireland . . . to be agreeable to the Word of God"), assent to current doctrine ("I assent to the Thirty-nine Articles of Religion, and to the Book of Common Prayer . . ."), and a promise of conformity in behavior ("in public prayer and administration of the sacraments, I will use the form in the said book prescribed").[14] The 1640 oath, however, required candidates to bind themselves with regard to future utterances by swearing,

> *Nor will I ever give my consent* to alter the Government of this Church, by Arch-bishops, Bishops, Deanes, and Arch-deacons, &c, as it stands now established. (*Complete Prose Works*, 1:990–91; emphasis mine)

This archconservative declaration introduces the future into the present in a much more sinister way than an affirmation of belief, compelling an unknown future to adhere to the conditions of a defined and limited present. Milton may well have objected to what amounts to the signing away of *future* rights to performative speech, particularly since he would give up the right to assent to an ominously open-ended "et cetera" of possibilities. Rather than forswearing this right, Milton prefers a promise that guarantees a future verbal performance—a promise to write inspired poetry.

Milton's decision to decline ordination helps to explain the negative phrasing that characterizes his contract with the reader, in formulations like "Neither doe I think it shame to covnant" and "I refuse not to sustain this expectation." He *does* refuse the oath of ordination, since taking it *would* be shameful to him. The contract that Milton substitutes for the Church's oath is, in its negative formulation, a form of protest—protest being both a speech act ("I protest" enacts what it says), and the origin of Milton's preferred form of church government (a form of Protestantism). Yet the attempt to secure a new basis of convention for one's performative language is risky business, given the heavy reliance of successful speech acts on what is accepted by the community. The situation is akin to what Austin called "getting away with it," in reference to procedures that are not yet accepted as conventions but that someone is trying to initiate.[15] In order for Milton to get away with substituting a personal promise for an ecclesiastical oath, a community must exist that will consent to such an innovation—and this community is to be found in a Protestant readership that will accept a focus on individual rights and responsibilities, as well as on common law and economic transactions. We might read the digression as a re-enactment, on a personal level, of what it means to be a Protestant, Protestantism being a movement that is, from Luther's Ninety-five Theses and the Augsburg Confession onward, intimately involved with performative utterance.

Milton's easy translation of the oath of canon law into the economic and legal contract of common law exposes the extent to which church government and economics share a conceptual and linguistic formula, a similarity that is also implicit in the governing metaphor of Milton's self-presentation, Christ's parable of the talents. The parable in which the entrepreneurial servant is promised his reward is, like Milton's autobiography, another narrative that weighs present purchase against future payoff. Due to Christian exegesis of this parable, the word *talent,* which originally referred to a Hebrew coin of a certain weight, acquired a secondary meaning, as the value of a person's innate ability. In *The Reason of Church-Government*, Milton fully exploits the duality of meaning: the writer's talent is a commodity that can be properly or improperly marketed, or pledged for future delivery, just as oaths can be exchanged for one another.

"Throughout his mature existence Milton exhibited a wide, fairly intensive, and highly sentient knowledge of law as both a civil and ecclesiastical entity," Harris Fletcher remarks,[16] noting the frequent use of legal language and material in Milton's prose. Fletcher speculates that, having studied at least some Justinian in the course of his formal education, Milton contemplated following his brother Christopher into the legal profession from the end of his Cambridge career up to the time he left for Italy in 1638.[17] Further reasons for and documentation of Milton's legal knowledge are given by J. Milton French, who records Milton's ambiguous response to his father's vocation as scrivener and money-lender, as well as his occasional involvement in legal suits relating to his father's business.[18] The legal instincts thus developed may help to explain the final ironic twist in Milton's covenant with the reader.

Notwithstanding the deliberate legal formulation of Milton's promise, it is nicely undercut, in the end, by his use of the subjunctive. In place of the binding "I go on trust" or "I will go on trust," Milton writes "I *may* go on trust with [the reader]," a formulation matched in the final lines of the digression by the conditionality of "hence *may* appear the right I have to meddle in these matters." The subjunctive could be a courtesy, acknowledging the reader's right to decline the covenant, but it also seems to provide Milton with an "out," or with the possibility of arguing that he never made a firm commitment. In speech-act terms, a similar loophole is introduced by the seemingly innocuous prefix *"Neither doe I think it shame* to covnant" (emphasis mine), which in effect deactivates the performativity of the utterance. In the final analysis, Milton is not concluding a covenant but describing his attitude toward one. Yet both the underlying constative or propositional construction and the potential uncertainty of "may" are subsumed in the apparent certitude and performativity of the sentence as it culminates in the declaration, "I refuse not to sustain this expectation." Any awareness that the phrase "I refuse not" still evades the positivity of "I sustain this expectation" is almost obliterated by the declarative tone and the legalistic resonances of Milton's rhetoric. Like the intangible pledge and the self-referential temporality of the promise, the grammar of the sentence itself illustrates the ability of language to fabricate a new basis of authority, even out of a series of absences.

The anonymous reviewer of 1660 satirized Milton for risking chaos in church and state and asserting "That every man may do what he pleases in matters of Religion, but onely those that are in Authority, who ought not to meddle in such matters."[19] More precisely, what Milton is attempting to do in this tract is transfer the basis for authority and performative language from church officials to inspired individuals, and to accord it in varying degrees to those who are inspired in the general or the special sense. He is "meddling with authority," both in the sense of interfering with recognized power structures and in attempting to secure a new mandate for such interference. In the words of the closing sentence of the digression, Milton himself assumes "the right . . . to meddle in these matters" by rejecting ecclesiastical office as an authorizing power and substituting an individual's legal right to conclude a contract with other members of the community. With its focus on individual relationships and individual talents, the digression effectively enacts the foundation Milton is proposing for a reasonable church government.

Notes

1. *The Censure of the Rota Upon Mr Miltons Book, Entituled, The Ready and Easie way to Establish A Free Common-wealth*, W. R. Parker, *Milton's Contemporary Reputation* (Columbus: Ohio State University Press, 1940), 13.
2. Of the extensive literature on Miltonic inspiration, the most relevant works in the present context are E. R. Gregory, *Milton and the Muses* (Tuscaloosa: University of Alabama Press, 1989) and William Kerrigan, *The Prophetic Milton* (Charlottesville: University Press of Virginia, 1974), which analyze the development of Milton's concepts of "Muse lore" (Gregory) and religious prophecy (Kerrigan) in a literary-historical context. The discussion which follows is a synopsis of my argument about the speech-act quality of inspired and prophetic discourse in a work-in-progress on performative language in Milton and Blake.
3. John Milton, *Complete Prose Works of John Milton*, 8 vols., ed Don M. Wolfe et al. (New Haven: Yale University Press, 1953–82). All references to Milton's prose works are to this edition and are cited parenthetically in the text.
4. All biblical references are to the King James Version and are cited parenthetically in the text.
5. George Herbert, *Outlandish Proverbs*, *The Works of George Herbert*, ed. F. E. Hutchinson (Oxford: Clarendon Press, 1941), 344.
6. William Sheppard, *The Touchstone of Common Assurances, Being a Plain and Familiar Treatise on Conveyancing*, ed. Edmund Gibson Atherley, 8th ed. (London: Samuel Brooke, 1826); cited from A. W. B. Simpson, *A History of the Common Law of Contract: The Rise of the Action of Assumpsit* (Oxford: Clarendon Press, 1975), 506.
7. Simpson, *Common Law*, 46–47.
8. Ibid., 19.
9. John Milton, *The Complete Poetry of John Milton*, ed. John T. Shawcross, rev. ed. (New York: Doubleday, 1971). All references to Milton's poetry are to this edition and are cited parenthetically in the text.
10. J. L. Austin, *How to Do Things with Words*, ed. J. O. Urmson and Marina Sbisa, 2nd ed. (Cambridge: Harvard University Press, 1975).
11. Regina M. Schwartz, *Remembering and Repeating: Biblical Creation in "Paradise Lost"* (Cambridge: Cambridge University Press, 1988), 68.
12. Michel de Certeau, "What We Do When We Believe," *On Signs*, ed. Marshall Blonsky (Oxford: Basil Blackwell, 1985), 193; also cited by Schwartz, 68.
13. William Riley Parker, *Milton: A Biography* (Oxford: Clarendon Press, 1968), 2:776.
14. *Constitutions and Canons Ecclesiastical 1604, Latin and English*, ed. J. V. Bullard (London: Faith Press, 1934), 40.
15. Austin, *How to Do Things*, 30.
16. Harris Francis Fletcher, *The Intellectual Development of John Milton, The Cambridge University Period, 1625–32* (Urbana: University of Illinois Press, 1961), 2:530.
17. Fletcher, *Intellectual Development*, 2:475, 530–31.
18. J. Milton French, *Milton in Chancery: New Chapters in the Lives of the Poet and his Father* (New York: Modern Language Association, 1939).
19. *Censure of the Rota*, 11.

The Creative Self and the Self Created in *Paradise Lost*

ALBERT W. FIELDS

The essential character of Western thought may without much exaggeration be said to reflect, at least until recent times, a concern for the spiritual and moral well-being of a Self that is rationally capable of analyzing its own constituents, diagnosing the ills of the faculties of soul and mind, and prescribing the appropriate mental or spiritual exercise to restore lost or damaged harmony. Lack of self-knowledge, then, might be considered catastrophic, producing not only spiritual aridity and alienation from favor in a higher realm but also moral abandonment in a lower realm. Perhaps ironically, the most important adjunct to this concept of self-knowing is the assumed authority of the achieved self-knower to enjoin others less favored to search within.

Thus the *nosce teipsum* commonplace has come down to us in the second person, along the way coloring, characterizing, and in some important instances structuring the literature and philosophy of Western culture. But knowledge of the Self, along with the power of the individual to create, to shape the Self, has been considered a difficult attainment, especially in the Renaissance. In sixteenth- and seventeenth-century England, this difficulty was certainly due in some measure to the conceptualization of Self as deriving from a complex braid of Anglo-Saxon, Hellenic, and Judeo-Christian ontological attitudes—attitudes that commonly set the Self at war with its own being, delineating it as fallen but worthy, as blindly groping but capable of growth, as necessity's pawn but free-willed, as brutish but loving, as self-serving but magnanimous, as ignorant but educable.

Self-shaping was incessant, but self-knowledge was elusive. Frequently requiring external prompting, the quest for Self was not always conscious, seldom vigorous, and never painless. Walter Ralegh said that "It is . . . Death alone that can suddenly make a man to know himselfe."[1] The death's-head often graced the mantel of the Renaissance gentleman. An admonitory friend, Francis Bacon suggested, might serve as an authority in defining one's identity, particularly as the definition related to one's "faults," but, even so, "The Calling of a Mans Self, to a Strict Account, is a medicine, sometime, too Piercing and Corrosive."[2] Bacon may have recalled that Thomas More, whose tribulations were no less than his own, used a similar medical metaphor in his *Dialog of Comfort Against Tribulation* when he suggested that a man must practice the custom of the physician who, "for a whyle," must "forbeare the iudgement of himselfe" and submit the rule of his conscience "to the counsail of som other good man" if he hopes to shape himself in a healing self-awareness.[3] And when Edmund Spenser's Una enjoins Red Cross to "shew what you bee," as he faces the monster Errour in the first book of *The Faerie Queene*,[4] she is not in fact telling him to show what he has become but what he is becoming, or rather demonstrate ascendant motion in the shaping of a dragon-dealing holiness that Una envisions for him and for which his incipient Self has hopes. Although a victor over Errour, he discovers that there are incessant self-shaping encounters with her progeny; after he is separated from Una and becomes the champion of pride-engendering duplicity, his identity so fragments that the horrified Una, when she sees him again in canto 8, exclaims, "of yourselfe ye thus berobbed arre."[5] Stephen Greenblatt suggests that "there may have been less *autonomy* in self-fashioning in the sixteenth century than before." But he says that autonomy is not the central issue; rather, "the power to impose a shape upon oneself is an aspect of the more general power to control identity."[6] As Red Cross's "power to impose a shape" upon himself dissipates following his separation from Una and his falling under the malign influence of Duessa, so does his "power to control identity."

Like *The Faerie Queene*, Milton's *Paradise Lost* represents achievement of identity as difficult but not impossible; and his epic is, at least on one level, the story not only of Adam's creation and self-discovery but the story of his self-conception.[7] It is, moreover, an engaging paradigm of self-discovery and self-conception for his Christian/Everyman reader. Stanley Fish argues that the "centre of reference" of Milton's epic "is its reader who is also its subject" and that the author's purpose is the reader's education "to an awareness of his position and responsibilities as a fallen man" and to the distance separating him from "the innocence once his."[8] When in Milton's narrative the Son is sent by God to judge the fallen couple, the only accusation he makes prior to the judgment is that Adam failed to know himself "aright." And in making this accusation, he equates Adam's failure in self-knowledge with a lapse in reason, a "Subjection" of Self to passion's rule, and hence a failure to shape his emerging Self in terms of his divine paradigm, his likeness to God (*Paradise Lost*, 10.150 – 56).[9]

British Renaissance writers were absorbed with the notion of self-awareness and with problems of identification, definition, and shaping of Self. In the nineteenth century, Coleridge called the Delphic maxim of *nosce teipsum* a "prime / and heaven-sprung adage" of ancient Greece;[10] but he knew, as did his Renaissance precursors, that Christian notions of Self were Judaic as well as Greek in origin.[11] Both Étienne Gilson and Louis Bredvold credit Augustine with deriving the *nosce teipsum* concept ultimately from Genesis and giving the introspective method "its general currency in Europe."[12] In so doing Augustine followed Judaic tradition in representing the genesis of Self as God's "image," and he followed Platonic tradition in identifying Self with reason. Renaissance faculty psychology, as defined by John Davies and others, supported this notion of human reason as reflecting God's image and further represented an indeterminately free "will," as well as a passional nature that was benign, unless by wrong choices made in the emergence and shaping of Self, it usurped the rule of a naturally benevolent reason and thereby corrupted it.[13]

"To choose," said Richard Hooker, "is to will one thing before another"; and the "Will, in things tending toward any end, is termed Choice." Further, "Reason is the director of man's Will by discovering in action what is good."[14] John Milton was more succinct: "Reason also is choice," he said in *Paradise Lost* (3.108), but he had already developed this notion in *Areopagitica* ("reason is but choosing")[15] where he represents good and evil as "in the field of this world" growing up "together almost inseparably" and as "twins cleaving together" (*Complete Prose Works,* 2:514). Milton is, of course, talking about *moral* choice—options of good and evil, options that might, ultimately, have eschatological importance but were of greater immediate concern in the forging of identity. In *Christian Doctrine* Milton argues that "From the concept of freedom . . . all idea of necessity must be removed" (*Complete Prose Works,* 6:161) and that the free will "is irreconcilable with necessity" (6:165). Hence, moral choosing—not the stars—was the real "necessity" in human life and the enduring source of humanity's tragic vision—the vision that ineluctably elicits Lear's question of "Who is it that can tell me who I am?"[16] and mortises audience identification with the tragic protagonist. Humankind could *not* choose not to choose toward the shaping of Self, and this moral choosing was paramount in the control of identity.

Louis Martz says that "in Milton's universe the power of choice is essential to man's perfection and man's happiness, whether fallen or unfallen."[17] Good and evil were voluntary and required one, Milton argued in *Areopagitica*, to "sally out" to confront the "adversary," for "that which purifies us is trial, and trial is by what is contrary" (*Complete Prose Works*, 2:728). This notion of "trial" by "contrary" underlies the obsessive Renaissance concern with the "sweetness" of "adversity" as we find it in More, Spenser, Shakespeare, Bacon, Donne, and Milton—to name only a few. "Cloistered virtue" and trial by contrary were obviously incompatible; for "trial" is a self-shaping force: it is "that which purifies us" (2:515); and, conversely, the cloistering of virtue brings not "innocence" into the world but "impurity" (2:515).[18] With reference to Adam's fall and Raphael's lecture on his failure in self-awareness, Arnold Stein says that "Self-knowledge requires the test of action, in which the self and knowledge are both tried, separately and in relation to each other."[19] But Adam's trial begins at the very moment of his creation, at his first pristine perception of his quickening identity. "Strange as it may seem," Martz notes, "the problem of making the right choice, the problem of the right exercise of freedom, is shown to be as difficult before the Fall as it is afterwards."[20] Indeed, Martz argues, before the Fall, Adam and Eve "are 'frail' in the sense that their power of choice may wrongly choose; choice is difficult because 'wandring thoughts' and passions . . . are all part of the broad field in which human choice must operate."[21]

Thus having Hellenic and Judaic derivations, the Christian Self as created was defined in terms of reason and was a unique spiritual reflection of God; and God was the creator—the "author," as it were— of humanity's rational being. Milton's Adam is thus a creature "endu'd / With Sanctity of Reason" and consequently "self-knowing, and from thence / Magnanimous to correspond with Heav'n" (*Paradise Lost*, 7.507–11). Hence Adam's created Self corresponded to the heavenly pattern. In this regard, Stein says that "Self-knowledge is based on God's established order, upon man's knowing his proper place in that order and accepting his responsibility of his relationship upward and downward."[22] But the *created* Self, by urgency of its paradigm, becomes at once the *creator* of an emerging plastic Self, a Self undergoing endless shaping; and although external forces, including the hand of God, were eventful and forceful in this fashioning, the most significant emergent force was the Self's "will." Through continual moral choices, which punctuate the essential interlocking continuous experiences of rational being "in the field of the world," the ideal soul should thus fashion itself toward goals of self-control and moral perfection—goals that could, however, never be fully realized in the time-bound, sublunary world.

Although Milton, as his contemporaries, commonly defined reason in spiritual terms, and in terms of love and moral choice, reason always suggested a consciousness of anterior being, of present environment, and potentiality—hence Michael's instruction of Adam in the last two books of *Paradise Lost*. Because of his fallen nature and because his consciousness was time-bound, mankind's sequent thought was *discursive* and thus differed in this important respect from its paradigm, the more Godlike and angelic *intuitive* reason. In book 5, Raphael tells Adam that the "Soul," receives reason, "and reason is her being, / Discursive, or Intuitive; discourse / Is oftest yours, the latter most is ours" (487–90). Although Raphael says the difference is "but in degree," the degree is significant for Adam because his discursive reason is itself a creative activity not only in the generation and acquisition of knowledge but also in the endless experience of self-determinative choosing.

For Adam, moral choosing not only determined a continuous pattern of self-shaping but also defined the experience as a test of spiritual worthiness, a trial that might, however, lead to spiritual deprivation. As Raphael tells Adam,

> One Almighty is, from whom
> All things proceed, and up to him return
> If not deprav'd from good.
>
> (5.469–71)

Hence the "self-tempted" person who fails the test of rational choice becomes "self-deprav'd" (3.130). As Milton's God recalls the fall of the rebellious angels, he foresees Adam's and Eve's fall and that of their "faithless Progeny" (3.96), a fall that is the consequence of a failure in rational choice, a failure in self-"making" that rendered both the "Will and Reason" as "Useless and vain, of freedom both despoil'd." They "belong'd," God says, "to right" and "So were created" and cannot, therefore, blame "Thir maker, or thir making" (3.109–13). They are, God declares, "Authors to themselves in all / Both what they judge and what they choose" (3.122–23).

The importance of the Self's rational resemblance to God in Adam's representation as the created Self cannot be disengaged from the relevance of his representation as creator of entities external to himself. Although the word *author* was by the sixteenth century a common referent to one who wrote, the word, deriving from Latin *auctor* (to increase) or *augere* (to originate), had long been a referent to God as originator and creator and was commonly used as such in the British Renaissance. John Donne, for example, in his *Devotions* says that "all mankind is of one author,"[23] and Richard Hooker defines God as the "author" of the "law eternal" and the "Law of Nature."[24] In *Paradise Lost* Milton uses the word *author* fifteen times, and in every instance the referent is one who creates, in either a positive or negative sense. Hence the original author was God; and human beings in the image of God and in imitation of God had the capacity for external generation. With God as paradigm, the Self was defined as love-longing, as desirous of something external to itself. This generative desire was an essential quality that not only reflected the Self's paradigmatic relationship with the "author" but was essential as well to the Self's separate identity as an engenderer.

In *Christian Doctrine* Milton argues that the generation of the Son "did not arise from natural necessity" (*Complete Prose Works*, 6:208), and though the Father and Son are "not [one] in essence," they are one "in nearness and love" (6:239); and they are one in creative force, for it is in the Son that the Word, the Logos, is invested. Hence the Son, who is "alone" God's "word . . . and effectual might" (*Paradise Lost*, 3.169–70), becomes the creative voice, the creative instrument, and "to what [God] spake / His Word, the Filial Godhead, gave effect" (*Paradise Lost*, 7.174 –75).[25] In *Paradise Lost*, the Word, then, is a generative love-force, a benevolent agent of becoming. "As the manifestation of God's creative power," Michael Lieb says, "the Son becomes the Word whose utterance results in life."[26] Much like Milton's representation of the Word, the Logos for the pre-Socratic Heraclitus was "a kind of universal law of becoming."[27] James Olney notes that Carl Jung, like Heraclitus, but twenty-five hundred years later, defined *self* as "a process rather than a settled state of being." With reference to Heraclitus and Jung, Olney says that

> In every individual, to the degree that he is individual, the whole principle and essence of the Logos is wholly present, so that in his integrity the whole harmony of the universe is entirely and, as it were, uniquely present or existent.[28]

Hence in *Paradise Lost* the love of the "author" as a creative force is extended into the "begotten" Son in whose face "Divine compassion" and "Love without end" "visibly appear'd" (3.140–42). When God asks the rhetorical question of "where shall we find such love" (3.213) to mediate for humankind, the response—that is, the "words" of the Son "breath'd immortal love / To mortal men" (3.266–68) and thus defined an agapeic paradigm; for as God authored the immortal

Son, so will mortal man author the incarnate Son—as well as become "Our Author" (5.397), that is, humankind's procreator.

In the last two books of *Paradise Lost*, Adam receives the instruction that is essential to his self-discovery, and as the epic draws to a close, he exclaims to Michael: "Of utmost hope! now I clear understand" (12.376). What he understands is that from his "loins" will issue the "Virgin Mother" and from her "Womb the Son / Of God most High; so God with man unites" (12.379–82). The creative force fostering agapeic love thus extends outward from the "Author of this Universe" (8.360) through the begotten Son to humankind's created Self and from humankind back through the incarnate Son upward to love's archetypal "author."

Adam's shaping of Self reflects a three-step movement that includes (1) revelation, (2) the reflection of Self in the mirror of the external world, and (3) introspection that led not only to discovery of the Self's divine image but to the cognizance of an aspect of self unlike God.[29] In book 8, God says he created human beings in his own image, "self-knowing." After looking first "strait toward Heav'n," Adam discovers life outside him—woods, hills, plains, streams, a variety of other creatures—and then Self: "My self I then perus'd . . . / But who I was, or where, or from what cause, / Knew not" (8.267–71). The sense of humility and dependence that follows marks his first cognition of an inner nature; and the ensuing revelation by the "shape Divine" (8.295) defines God as omnipotent and Adam as aware of his own limitations and his plastic nature: "Thou in thy self art perfet . . . not so is Man" (8.415–16).

"Love is, among other things," says Arnold Stein, "a discipline in self-transcendence."[30] As humanity is a principal object of God's love, so God is the principal object of humanity's love; but this agapeic creative desire extended not only upward to God but outward toward earthly objects; and its mortal, mutable, procreative, yet corruptible counterpart was "eros," which, although essential to incarnation, paradoxically defined the imperfect mortal Self. Adam's request of God for redress from solitude expresses a sense of incompleteness—his difference from God—and intuition of his likeness to God as a creative Self: God, "already infinite," need not "propagate" (8.420–24). In *Christian Doctrine* Milton argues that God, because of his flawless essence, "stands in no need of propagation" (*Complete Prose Works*, 6:209). Adam, aware of his "single imperfection" as he compares himself to his "Author" in whom there "is no deficience found," defines himself as being in "unity defective" and longs for the "collateral love" that may allow him to "propagate," to "beget / Like of his like" (*Paradise Lost*, 8.415–27). Hence his creative Self and his knowledge of his "single imperfection" lead him to carnal knowledge and ultimately to procreation.

When the God of *Paradise Lost*, who is defined as the "world's great Author" (5.188) and "Author of all being" (3.374), proclaims that human beings must be "Authors to themselves in all," in their judging and in their choosing (3.122–23), he defines attributes of the *Self created* that may emerge as the creative Self. Made in the image of the "Author," human beings are the morally responsible creators of their own actions, but they are not, as Milton's Satan supposes himself, "self-begot" (5.860). As Adam is identified in terms of his creator, so in some measure is Milton's God defined in terms of Adam's Self. As Adam generates his own fall, so does he generate the incarnation and his salvation. Marshall Grossman notes that "Two stories—one of 'man's first disobedience' and the other of 'one greater man'—are entwined so that each provides the hermeneutic necessary for the interpretation of the other in a dialectic of personal and apocalyptic eschatologies."[31] More simply, Charles Coffin says that in book 8 Milton uses "self" to distinguish what Adam is "from the person who he is not, that is from the one who made him."[32] Though he may have, as Coffin suggests, a Faustian desire for freedom and autonomy, his intuition of a Creator generates a sense of humility in him as well.

Equal in thematic importance to Milton's delineation of the positive obverse Self is his representation of the converse, or negative Self, as having an identity that is unlike God, an identity generated and defined by passion and unreason.[33] Here notions of external authority, of external creation, are rejected in favor of self-authorship and baleful generation.[34] Interestingly, Milton's self-deluded Satan, who is the antithesis of humility, reason, and benevolent desire and who is called "Author of all ill" (2.381) and "Author of evil" (6.262), is also defined in terms of his progeny whom he does not at first recognize. Sin, who is born of Satan, consequent to an incestuous affair with Self, becomes his mirror, a reflector not only of self-lust but also its scion. Thus his Death-son is generated by his union with his Sin-daughter after, she says to her father-lover, "Thyself in me thy perfect image viewing / Becam'st enamor'd" (2.764 – 65). In his egomaniacal assertion that the Self is the originator of its own being, Milton's Satan argues that he is "self-begot, self-rais'd" by his "own quick'ning power" (5.860 – 61). "Our puissance is our own," he haughtily tells Abdiel (5.864). Stein says that "When Satan declares that his puissance is his own, he is denying the possibility of a source of power external to himself." He is, Stein suggests, "declaring that he is, or can be, at the top of the hierarchy."[35] Indeed, as God or the Son is the altruistic pattern for humanity, Satan is the negative paradigm who defines

Self in terms of passionate pride and self-delusion, rather than rational humility and personal awareness, whose shape-shifting for devious and malignant purposes contrasts with an altruistic self-fashioning; whose essential being is destructive as opposed to creative, and whose nature is defined as lustfully ravenous and devouring rather than procreative and drawn by agapeic desire.[36]

In *Paradise Lost* the following lines—

> Thou art my Father, thou my Author, thou
> My being gav'st me; whom should I obey
> But thee, whom Follow?   (2.864 – 66)

—could easily have been spoken by Adam with reference to his God; but they are not; they are spoken by Sin with reference to Satan who generated her. Milton represents Sin's Self as springing from the head of Satan (2.758) while Christ, God's only generation, emerges from God's bosom (3.169). Here Sin appears as a symbolic representation of intellectual pride, while Christ is generated in the area of the heart, the symbolic area of love. As Edmund Spenser's Arthur represents a summation of virtues (that is, Magnificence), virtues personified in the various questing knights, so Milton's Satan represents the converse, a summation of vices (that is, Pride), vices enumerated and personified in various fallen angels. Of course, the point is that Milton, as did other Renaissance writers, thematically represented fallen humanity as having the potential of defining itself in terms of either paradigm or more commonly as a Self divided between the obverse and the converse, the latter having a propensity for corruption, what in *Christian Doctrine* Milton called an "evil desire" (*Complete Prose Works*, 6:388) or evil "concupiscence" ("concupiscentia mala").[37] "The poet," Michael Lieb says, "must confront the uncreative aspects of the fall in order to create positively," for, he continues, "The same basic metaphor controls both experiences."[38]

In addition to God (the "Author of this Universe" and creative love), and Satan (the author of Sin), and Sin (the author of Death), and the Christ-son (author of mediation and redemption), and Raphael and Michael (authors of the revelation of things past and to come), and Adam ("Our Author" [5.397] who authors his own destiny, his own story), there is the author voice, the creative Poet-Self. Michael Foucault says that "The coming into being of the notion of 'author' constitutes the privileged moment of *individualization* in the history of ideas, knowledge, literature, philosophy, and the sciences."[39] Marshall Grossman suggests that in *Paradise Lost* the rhetoric that achieves "the suturing" of the stories of humankind's disobedience and redemption by "one greater Man" (1.4) "performs the conflation of reading and writing implied by the notion of 'self-authorship.'" Thus, he argues, "The revelation of history . . . is the narrative of the self authored as a subject, moving through time, capable of change, yet recognizably self-identical."[40]

But underpinning these various theories of authoring in Milton's epic is a notion inherent in, and conveyed by, the word *increate,* a word that Milton uses in book 3's invocation, a word that suggests a powerful precreational force essential to and conducive to the Self's creativity derivative from the divine paradigm. "The relationship between conscious art and divine inspiration is a major theme," Barbara Lewalski says, of the "personal" proems of *Paradise Lost*.[41] The aim of the quickening creative self should be, indeed, to become "a true Poem" (*Apology, Complete Prose Works,* 1:890). For the poet's song ought to be a

> divine song, which preserves some spark of Promethean fire and is the unrivalled glory of the heaven-born human mind and an evidence of our ethereal origin and celestial descent. (*Ad Patrem,* 83)

It is this "Promethean fire" of "ethereal origin," this quintessential potency, that Philip Sidney no doubt had in mind in his argument that all sciences "are but serving sciences" to poetry and that all are "directed to the highest end of the mistress knowledge." This "mistress knowledge" was "by the Greeks called [architecktonic], which stands," Sidney says, "in the knowledge of a man's self"—that is to say, a precreational force, a divine vigor essential to the creative Self.[42] Although humankind's most purposeful and urgent creative impulse was, as Milton's Adam discovers, procreative, the most powerful ongoing and universal creative impulse emanated from the Logos, the controlling principle, the "word" invested in the Son. And so for the poet, formed in the image of God, the "word" might be the most powerful expression of the Self creating, a mortal reflection, Milton might say, of "Bright effluence of bright essence increate" (3.6).

Notes

1. Walter Ralegh, *The History of the World,* ed. C. A. Patrides (Philadelphia: Temple University Press, 1971), 396.
2. Francis Bacon, *The Essays or Counsels, Civill and Morall,* ed. Michael Kiernan (Cambridge: Harvard University Press, 1985), 85.
3. Thomas More, *Utopia,* trans. Raphe Robynson, with *The Dialogue of Comfort,* intro. John O'Hagan, Everyman's Library, Theology and Philosophy, 461 (1910; reprint, New York: J. M. Dent, 1946), 213–14.
4. Edmund Spenser, *The Faerie Queene,* ed. F. M. Padelford, *The Works of*

Edmund Spenser: A Variorum Edition, ed. E. Greenlaw, C. G. Osgood, F. M. Padelford (Baltimore: Johns Hopkins Press, 1932), 1.1.19.

5. Spenser, *The Faerie Queene*, 1.8.42.

6. Stephen Greenblatt, *Renaissance Self-Fashioning: From More to Shakespeare* (Chicago: University of Chicago Press, 1980), 1.

7. For further discussions, see Michael Lieb, *The Dialectics of Creation: Patterns of Birth and Regeneration in "Paradise Lost"* (Amherst: University of Massachusetts Press, 1970), esp. chapters 1, 8, and 9; see also George Williamson, "The Education of Adam," *Modern Philology* 61 (1963): 96–109; Albert Cook, "Milton's Abstract Music," *University of Toronto Quarterly* 29 (1959–60): 370–85; and Albert W. Fields, "Milton and Self-Knowledge," *PMLA* 83 (1968): 392–99.

8. Stanley Fish, *Surprised by Sin: The Reader in Paradise Lost* (Berkeley: University of California Press, 1971), 1.

9. John Milton, *Paradise Lost, John Milton: Complete Poems and Major Prose*, ed. Merritt Y. Hughes (New York: Odyssey Press, 1957). All references to Milton's poetry are to this edition and are cited parenthetically in the text.

10. Samuel Taylor Coleridge, "Self Knowledge," *The Complete Poetical Works of Samuel Taylor Coleridge*, ed. E. H. Coleridge (1912; reprint, Oxford: Clarendon Press, 1957), 1:487; see also *Biographia Literaria*, eds. James Engell and W. Jackson Bate, *The Collected Works of Samuel Taylor Coleridge* (Princeton: Princeton University Press, 1983), 7: 252.

11. In pre-Socratic philosophy the tradition extends at least back to the seventh century B.C. to the gnomological works of Solon, Phocylides, Theognis, Thales, Chilon, Heraclitus, and others, for their moral precepts were "know thyself" and "nothing in excess" (Eduard Zeller, *Outlines of Greek Philosophy*, trans. L. R. Palmer, 13th ed. [New York: Harcourt, Brace, 1931], 35). Pausanias called these "useful maxims for the conduct of life" (Pausanias, *Descriptions of Greece*, trans. J. G. Frazer [New York, 1913], 1:535). In the next two centuries, the Pythagoreans perpetuated the maxim, but, oddly enough, their requirement of daily self-examination appears to have remained only a means of moral discipline without mystical or metaphysical implications (Zeller,*Outlines of Greek Philosophy*, 49). Plato's Socrates may have first given the precept an ontological turn. In *Alcibiades* Socrates argued that introspection alone cannot lead to self-knowledge, that one must see oneself mirrored in the soul of another. In *Alcibiades* and in the *Republic*, one apprehends the world as a revelation of a system of universals that ultimately become phases of Self and enable the outward and inner person to be as one (*The Dialogues of Plato*, trans. B. Jowett, 3rd ed. [London, 1892], 2:504–9; 3:180–81). In *Phaedrus* Socrates likens the Self to two chariot horses, one guided by reason and the other an insolent creature, a friend of "pride" (*Dialogues*, 1:452–53; 460–62).

12. Louis I. Bredvold, "The Sources Used by Davies in *Nosce Teipsum*," *PMLA* 38 (1923): 747; Étienne Gilson, *L'esprit de la philosophie médiévale*, études de philosophie médiéval, 33 (1944): 214–33; see also E. Gilson, *The Christian Philosophy of Saint Augustine*, trans. L. E. M. Lynch (New York: Random House, 1961), esp. chapter 1, part 2.

13. See John Davies's "Orchestra" and "Nosce Teipsum," *The Poems of Sir John Davies*, ed. Robert Krueger (Oxford: Clarendon Press, 1975).

14. Richard Hooker, *Of the Laws of Ecclesiastical Polity, The Works of Richard Hooker*, ed. John Keble, rev. R. W. Church and F. Paget, 7th ed. (1887; reprint, New York: Burt Franklin, 1970), 1:220, 222.

15. John Milton, *The Complete Prose Works of John Milton*, 8 vols., ed. Don M. Wolfe et al. (New Haven: Yale University Press, 1953–82), 2:527. All references to Milton's prose are to this edition and are cited parenthetically in the text.

16. William Shakespeare, *The Tragedy of King Lear*, ed. Tucker Brooke and W. L. Phelps, *The Yale Shakespeare* (New Haven: Yale University Press, 1947), 1.4.235.

17. Louis L. Martz, *Milton: Poet of Exile*, 2nd ed. (New Haven: Yale University Press, 1980), 127.

18. Cf. Fish, *Surprised by Sin*, 142–45.

19. Arnold Stein, *Answerable Style: Essays on "Paradise Lost"* (Minneapolis: University of Minnesota Press, 1953), 98.

20. Martz, *Milton*, 140.

21. Ibid., 127.

22. Stein, *Answerable Style*, 89.

23. John Donne, *Devotions upon Emergent Occasions* (Ann Arbor: University of Michigan Press, 1959), 108.

24. Hooker, *Laws*, 1:203–4, 239.

25. See also Milton, *Christian Doctrine*, book 1, chapter 5, esp. 204–11.

26. Lieb, *Dialectics*, 57.

27. W. K. C. Guthrie, *A History of Greek Philosophy* (Cambridge: Cambridge University Press, 1962–81), 1:425.

28. James Olney, *Metaphors of Self: The Meaning of Autobiography* (Princeton: Princeton University Press, 1972), 6.

29. See Fields, "Milton," 396. This three-step pattern may derive from such diverse writers as Aristotle, Augustine, and Richard Hooker.

30. Stein, *Answerable Style*, 115.

31. Marshall Grossman, *"Authors to Themselves": Milton and the Revelation of History* (Cambridge: Cambridge University Press, 1987), 178–79.

32. Charles Coffin, "Creation and the Self in *Paradise Lost*," *ELH* 29 (1962): 10.

33. For a full discussion of the dialectic of creation/uncreation, see Lieb, *Dialectics*, esp. part 2: "The Process of Uncreation." "Allegorically, the union of Chaos and his consort [Night] in *Paradise Lost*," Lieb says,

> suggests that through God's influence the coition of two negative qualities results in the birth of that which is positive. Such a pattern repeats in small the major pattern of the poem: out of darkness will spring forth light; out of disorder will spring forth order; and out of evil will spring forth good. (18)

See also John T. Shawcross, "The Balanced Structure of *Paradise Lost*," *Studies in Philology* 62 (1965): 696–718.

34. I first develop this notion of archetypal self-authorship in "The Shakespearean Self-Author," *The South Central Bulletin* 34 (1974): 150–56.

35. Stein, *Answerable Style*, 282.

36. Cf. E. M. W. Tillyard, *Milton* (London: Chatto and Windus, 1946), 271.

37. For the Latin original see *De Doctrina Christiana*, *The Works of John Milton*, 18 vols., ed. F. A. Patterson et al. (New York: Columbia University Press, 1931–38), 15:193.

38. Lieb, *Dialectics*, 37.

39. Michael Foucault, "What is an Author?" *The Foucault Reader* (New York: Pantheon Books, 1984), 101.

40. Grossman, *Authors to Themselves*, 178–79.

41. Barbara K. Lewalski, *"Paradise Lost" and the Rhetoric of Literary Forms* (Princeton: Princeton University Press, 1985), 25; see chapter 2, "Inspiration and Literary Art: The Prophet-Poets of *Paradise Lost*."

42. Sir Philip Sidney, *The Complete Works*, ed. Albert Feuillerat, Cambridge English Classics (Cambridge: Cambridge University Press, 1912–26), 3:9–12.

Conflicts of Authority: Interpretation of Events in *Paradise Regained* and *Samson Agonistes*

DANIEL T. LOCHMAN

A number of recent studies have drawn out the relationships between the two works published by Milton in 1671—*Paradise Regained* and *Samson Agonistes*—to demonstrate either their similar concerns with an individual involved in a transforming spiritual elevation or their contrasting means of effecting divine judgment, through the brute force of a strong man—regenerate or not—or the less obviously catastrophic yet equally vanquishing firmness of the Son of God. To suggest that such a comparison should be drawn along absolute lines, as has been implicit in some recent discussions of the works, seems to demean the subtlety of Milton's poetry and view of the world.[1] On the face of it, revisionist attempts to draw an absolute contrast between a "demonic" Samson and a divine Son seem counter to Milton's reluctance to impose limits on God or the potential range of a divinely inspired act—limits that, as Stanley Fish has argued, Milton would find casuistic and alien to the openness and plenitude of grace.[2] Whatever the significant contrasts that may—and should—be drawn between the characters of Samson and the Son, they are balanced by equally significant points of similarity, including their movement to a conviction that the interior Self is the only reliable authority for truth in a world filled with multiple perceptions and distortions of reality.

The introverted Samson is too clearly drawn in likeness to the introverted Christ for there to be no sense of positive comparison of their characters, their development, and their approach to understanding the world and acting in it. The real question becomes whether the ultimate relation between Samson and the Son, derived from the accumulated evidence of the whole works, points *more* toward similarity or dissimilarity. This question is seriously complicated—perhaps rendered unanswerable—due to the profound ambiguity that surrounds Samson at his conclusion. We hear many voices, discordant and chaotic, in the dramatic poem's final moments, and each lacks the crucial ring of authority supplied immediately in *Paradise Regained* through the voices of Satan and the Father and sustained throughout, saving only a few moments of doubt.

Yet those moments of doubt concerning the Son—few and slender though they may be—are clearly suggested by Milton's text and felt by the audience as what Fish calls "disappointments of expectation," these latter calling into question the sources of authority brought to bear by the audience and claimed by the characters: Fish's phrase applies equally to Samson's view of himself and the doubts, both internal and external, that surround the public identity of the Son.[3] The Son's ego-centered and seemingly hesitant soliloquy in book 1 too closely echoes the psychology of the helpless and depressed Samson for the comparison to be dismissed as products of alien and opposed divine and satanic motive forces.

The relationships, both for comparison and contrast, are especially strong at two key points in *Paradise Regained*: (1) the Son's "revolving" of his self-identity in book 1; and (2) the distinction between words and things in the discussion of learning and eloquence in book 4. Ultimately, the Son is distinguished by his differences from Samson, Satan, and the rest of humankind, which looks in vain for evidence of specifically Christian heroism in the tragic spectacle of death in *Samson Agonistes*. Yet differences in his acuity and will do not completely rupture links between the Old Law and New, between heroism predicated on brutal deliverance and heroism rooted in the Christian paradox of deliverance through "heroic" weakness: the power of the Father draws good from the Old as well as the New despite the contrary force of evil. Finally, for both Samson and the Son, a willing acceptance of providence serves to separate delusive views of reality from truer "motions" rooted in self-cancellation and a view of reality founded in the motive force of providence.

At both moments in *Paradise Regained*, Milton drives home the force of the Son's kenotic acceptance of God's will, even against the force of those things which Milton apparently sees—from the point of view of his contemporaries as well as his modern readers—as most central to a virtuous life: goods, the world, power, intellectual play, and persuasion. Hence it is that the Son's exploration of Self in language begins and ends with *revolution* in its fullest sense: the revolving of words may be demonic for Satan or ambiguous for Samson, yet it is through *revolution*, through the thorough revaluing of the signification of words such as *Messiah* and *hero*, that the Son comes to terms with his own nature and purpose (*Paradise Regained*, 1.185–88; *Samson Agonistes*, 1638.)[4]

The placement and development of the Son's revolution of purpose in book 1 points to significant differences from Milton's dramatic poem. Given the narrative frame and the epic sense of the opening to *Paradise Regained*, the reader approaches the Son's soliloquy with a firmer sense of the polarities of good and evil than is the case in *Samson Agonistes*.[5] The latter introduces a world of dust, grind, toil, and affliction from external and internal sources—placing the reader in the midst of a world with confused direction; in contrast, the Son is first seen in the desert after a series of voices—the narrator's, Satan's, the Father's—have already established the grounds of good and evil. Moreover, the Son emerges from the desert by virtue of his freely enjoining temptation; Samson ironically leaves the dust and enters the life of the court seemingly serendipitously and tragically, after his departure from a mental desert of self-perpetuated blindness. Although the definition of *heroic* may be in doubt in *Paradise Regained*, no one has seriously argued that Satan is the hero of this work or that its hero has ambiguous motives.

Paradise Regained lays the groundwork for the appearance of the Son through the narrator's exordium and description of the son of Joseph's baptism, the satanic interpretation of the same, and the Father's prophecy of his Son's imminent validation of divinity. This series of prefaces hardens the affiliations of the central parties, with the Son serving as the pivotal subject of understanding. Milton plays upon the anticipations of a Christian audience perhaps complacent in its understanding of the nature and purpose of the Son: he reconsiders the Son's depth of humanity and participation in human weakness. But whatever the doubts Milton sows in book 1 regarding the Son's nature, there is no doubt of his alignment with good or evil as there is constantly in the case of Samson. Whereas the question throughout *Samson Agonistes* is how the follower of God may extend *beyond* himself to exercise a divine as opposed to demonic will, the question in *Paradise Regained* is how the Son may come to terms *with* himself within the evil and necessarily limited confines of a material world, bodily flesh, and the devil's temptations.

In the preface, the audience of *Paradise Regained* receives a variety of perspectives describing the public declaration of the Son's filial relation to God at his baptism revealed in the gospel accounts.[6] In *Paradise Regained* the first two voices, first the narrator's and then Satan's, address and variously inflect the meaning of John the Baptist's act in baptizing the yet unknown man from Nazareth:

> Now had the great Proclaimer with a voice
> More awful than the sound of Trumpet, cried
> Repentance, and Heaven's Kingdom nigh at hand
> To all Baptiz'd: to his great Baptism flock'd
> With awe the Regions round, and with them came
> From Nazareth the son of Joseph deem'd
> To the flood of Jordan, came as then obscure,
> Unmarkt, unknown: but with him the Baptist soon
> Descried, divinely warn'd, and witness bore
> As to his worthier, and would have resign'd
> To him his Heavenly Office, nor was long
> His witness unconfirm'd; on him baptiz'd
> Heaven open'd, and in likeness of a Dove
> The Spirit descended, while the Father's voice
> From Heav'n pronounc'd him his beloved Son.
>   (1.18–32)

> Before him [the "Seed of Eve"] a great Prophet, to proclaim
> His Coming, is sent Harbinger, who all
> Invites, and in the Consecrated stream
> Pretends to wash off sin, and fit them so
> Purified to receive him pure, or rather
> To do him honor as their King; all come,
> And he himself among them was baptiz'd,
> Not thence to be more pure, but to receive
> The testimony of Heaven, that who he is
> Thenceforth the Nations may not doubt; I saw
> The Prophet do him reverence; on him rising
> Out of the water, Heav'n above the Clouds
> Unfold her Crystal Doors, thence on his head
> A perfect Dove descend, whate'er it meant,
> And out of Heav'n the Sovran voice I heard,
> This is my Son belov'd, in him am pleas'd.
>   (1.70–85)

The language of the narrator and of Satan cuts different ways, even though both speakers refer to the same event. The narrator's record parallels the disciples' shifting understanding of Christ's role as Messiah from the warrior-champion to meek exponent of filiation and love; the narrator's language moves from suggestions of warfare and military glory, associated with the Baptist's prophecies, to filial language describing the "Unmarkt, unknown," yet "beloved Son." Satan's perception moves in the opposite direction, with his sense of the Baptist's call seen not as a proclamation implying future glories but as an "invitation" to an event whose witness is intended to provide a self-serving recognition of God as "Sovran," not filial, authoritative, not loving. This discrepancy in point of view clearly marks the interpretation of events as central to *Paradise Regained*: it is no accident that the same event is read from a number of angles since reality appears to be relative, as in *Samson Agonistes*, so that what one sees depends in large measure upon what one intends to see—unless one may discover the "inward Oracle" that speaks "all truth" (*Paradise Regained*, 1.463–64).

A similar problem of interpretation appears in *Samson Agonistes*, when the chorus, Samson, Manoa, Dalila, and Harapha successively try to integrate the promise of the proposed deliverer into a framework consistent with his debased personal experience: for each, the problem becomes the squaring of prophecy with an apparently discordant reality. John T. Shawcross is not quite correct when he asserts that for *Samson Agonistes*, in contrast to *Paradise Regained*, "Futural significance is not important for the reader . . . since the reader is concerned only with Samson, now dead, not with Manoa, Dalila, Harapha, or even the people of Dan, despite the irony of their continued subservience"; although it is true that after the catastrophe the "Deliverer" is dead, the implications of his deliverance for all parties extend out to the future, whether or not Danites or Philistines have the will to act upon the spiritual freedom God offers.[7] For both Samson and the Son, especially prior to his temptation, the central problem is the reading of events, the meshing of reality with destiny, the interpretation of Self in relation to the world and one's promise.

In contrast to the narrator's, Satan's version of the baptism shows a sharper, more curious and critical eye, though ultimately a more ignorant one. The Adversary is acutely observant of significant detail—significant that is from his limited point of view. He carefully notes the "consecrated" character of the stream and rites that he describes with a sense of "reverence" that seems staged and artificial—exactly the sort of persuaded reverence that Satan seeks from his adorers in Hell. True to his obsession with power and the Son as a military and political threat, Satan focuses on the Son's kingly bearing (or the perceived lack thereof), his identity among the "Nations" and, most disturbing from a demonic point of view, his possession by "Sovran voice." Despite his attention to detail, however, Satan is handicapped by profound ignorance that apparently results from his lack of inside information after the Fall: ironically, he fails to understand the symbol of the "perfect Dove"—he is removed (has removed himself?) from the inner circle of knowledge whence, presumably, he had first heard intimations of the planned human creation. If the Spirit was "produced of the substance of God . . . probably before the foundations of the world were laid, but later than the Son" (*Christian Doctrine*, 973) and if the world was created shortly after the War in Heaven (*Paradise Lost*, 2.345–49), Satan may be ignorant of this "minister of God" (*Christian Doctrine*, 973). Despite his intellectual curiosity and clever observation of detail, Satan lacks the fundamental knowledge to derive accurate interpretations of reality.

The disjunctions between these perceptions of reality are compounded by the Son's more direct witness of the event, recounted during his "revolution" of mind, often cited as parallel to Samson's circular mullings about the relation between current state and prophesied destiny:

> The Baptist (of whose birth I oft had heard,
> Not knew by sight) [was] now come, who was to come
> Before Messiah and his way prepare.
> I as all others to his Baptism came,
> Which I believ'd was from above; but hee
> Straight knew me, and with loudest voice proclaim'd
> Mee him (for it was shown him so from Heaven)
> Mee him whose Harbinger he was; and first
> Refus'd on me his Baptism to confer,
> As much his greater, and was hardly won.
> But as I rose out of the laving stream,
> Heaven open'd her eternal doors, from whence
> The Spirit descended on me like a Dove;
> And last the sum of all, my Father's voice,
> Audibly heard from Heav'n, pronounc'd me his,
> Mee his beloved Son, in whom alone
> He was well pleas'd; by which I knew the time
> Now full, that I no more should live obscure,
> But openly begin, as best becomes
> The Authority which I deriv'd from Heaven.
> (1.270–89)

Note the contrasts in the accounts of what happened at the Jordan: in this version, the Son is drawn to the preaching of the Baptist "as all others," and he is recognized spontaneously and quickly—"Straight"—with no intimation of an event planned and staged for effect, as implied by Satan, whose Baptist invites "all" purposefully with the intent to single out the Son as preeminent and as the promised (or threatened) successor to divine sovereignty. Implicit in the Son's discussion is his self-awareness: he understands his immediate purpose—to begin his work "openly" as God's Messiah—even if, as MacCallum observes, there is no evidence that the Son understands either the general meaning of that labor for his life or the particular acts he must undertake.[8]

Like Samson's split between promise and reality, the Son's felt gap between a sense of himself as Son of God and the expectations that devolve upon him from his and his fellows' interpretations of scripture pose a challenge and distraction:

> O what a multitude of thoughts at once
> Awak'n'd in me swarm, while I consider
> What from within I feel myself, and hear
> What from without comes often to my ears,
> Ill sorting with my present state compar'd.
> (1.196–200)

In these first words of the Son's soliloquy—a soliloquy whose form echoes the self-centeredness of Satan's in *Paradise Lost* and the examination of Self in *Samson Agonistes*—Milton suggests the dangerous stinging and tormenting thoughts of the Danite judge, yet the Son's discord of what is without and within is predicated not upon a profound revulsion and denial of the Self, as in Samson's desperate early attempts to turn blindly from all that he was or was promised to be (606–51); rather, the Son confidently takes stock of—indeed has already taken stock of—"What from within I feel myself" and simply observes the existence of apparent discord. Whereas Samson strongly felt the disparity between his helpless state and the promise of his destiny (see, for instance, 564–76), the Son recognizes his undiminished potential in spite of the clash between conventional prophecies of a military and political Messiah and the reality of his impoverished and weak station. Unlike the Danite judge, the Son returns to divine authority as a means of achieving certain confirmation, not new sources of doubt and reinterpretation; learning his promise from his mother, the Son

> again revolv'd
> The Law and Prophets, searching what was writ
> Concerning the Messiah, to our Scribes
> Known partly, and soon found of whom they spake
> I am.
> (1.259–63)

The Son's adept interpretation is apparently stimulated in part by the concerns of his mother, who, perceiving the "high" thoughts of her son in his passion for "heroic acts" of deliverance mitigated by a "more humane" desire to "conquer willing hearts" with "winning words" rather than the sword, encourages him to continue to grow by performing "matchless Deeds." Though self-motivated and independent, the Son remains more open than Samson to the love, concern, and guidance of others, especially when such care is given freely and without emotional strings: Mary knows her son's fulfilled promise will produce only pain yet counsels him to proceed anyway (2.66–104). Had Manoa approached his son with a less self-centered fear of poor reputation and had Samson been more open to his paternal benevolence, the outcome of Samson's drama may have been less emotionally painful for its hero even if its catastrophic outcome remained the same.

The disparate perceptions and interpretations of the meaning of events at the Son's baptism reflect the perceivers' varying abilities to apprehend truth and, while it is safe to say that the Son has a closer understanding of the event and its meaning than the narrator or Satan, it is also clear that his comprehension of his public manifestation is incomplete. His "revolving" of the prophets has helped him to understand his nature, and it will aid him in his arguments with Satan, but this unfolding sense of purpose is still opaque when he places himself blindly, though confidently, under the will of God:

> now by some strong motion I am led
> Into this Wilderness, to what intent
> I learn not yet; perhaps I need not know;
> For what concerns my knowledge God reveals.
> (1.290–94)

The "perhaps" in these lines reverberates, allowing potential significance to his knowledge of his "motions," but it is diminished by the self-effacing affirmation of the fullness of divine knowledge in the Father. The soundness of this willful cancellation of Self, comparable to the iconoclastic reasoning process by which Samson moves from egocentric self-pity disguised as despair to focused action, is reinforced by its demonstration by the weaker-faithed, doubting disciples, Andrew and Simon ("But let us wait," 2.49), and Mary, filled with human "Motherly cares and fears" (2.64) but nevertheless able to turn despair to quiet forbearance: "But I to wait with patience am inur'd" (2.102). These awakened expectations girded by patience widen the scope of the Son's self-emptying and linking of Self to providence and grace, eliciting from the apostles hope in the "deliverance" foreshadowed by Samson and the Israelites: a political deliverance and restoration of the Kingdom of Israel (2.35–36).

In book 2 the Son's deliverance seems to his disciples all too unrealized, suggesting their doubt of the Son's wisdom at retiring to the desert at the moment when the political irons begin to grow hot. Like Samson's Danite "friends," they must learn to reinterpret biblical deliverance to understand the new heroism: God administers justice and mercy, it is true, but they need to learn more firmly the Father's heavenly proclamation that "Mercy first and last shall brightest shine" (*Paradise Lost*, 3.134) even if Andrew and Simon already possess sufficient trust to put down incipient doubt. If the violence of deliverance of Samson is appropriate—and revisionist critics have questioned that appropriateness—Samson's is not the deliverance which the Son proposes. Yet unlike the foolish deliverance of slaughter sought by the wayward chorus in *Samson Agonistes*, the human "chorus" in *Paradise Regained* mirrors the Son's ready acceptance of divine will even before the Son has moved fully into public ministry; the disciples, like the Son, open themselves to trust in the Son's judgment and providence. This element of trust links Samson at his peripeteia, whatever the source of his "motions," to the ready acceptance of God's will seen in the Son, Mary, Andrew, and Simon.

Despite these points of comparison with *Samson Agonistes*, however, *Paradise Regained* extends far beyond the relatively simple issue of trust. What constitutes the focus and developmental pivot in *Samson Agonistes*, is, in *Paradise Regained*, assumed and surpassed in the first two books. The at least partially tragic effect of *Samson Agonistes* is superseded by the comic tenor of the epyllion. Yet these contrary effects do not determine the entire works. The tragic sense of catastrophe among the Danites, frightened by God's expression of wrath and too fearful to embrace the freedom providence offers them, does not finally determine the nature of Samson's act, just as the disciples' occasional losses of faith, not recorded by Milton, do not determine the Son's virtue. But whatever the judgment passed on Samson and his people, the Son offers a model of withstanding the force of evil in its most damaging form—its plays on the passions and human psyche. This is not the place to observe in detail the dexterity of language exercised by both Satan and the Son, and, in any event, other studies have already attended to many of its important features.[9] But issues raised in book 1 of how to interpret reality and text recur as the Son punctures the surface realities of wordly position and lures to the passions. How easily the Son in his divinity dispenses with the crux of responsibility felt so weightily by Samson, countering Satan's invitation to save David's throne by casting down Rome, the Son "unmov'd" responds:

> What wise and valiant man would seek to free

> These [Israelites] thus degenerate, by themselves
>   enslav'd,
> Or could of inward slaves make outward free?
> (4.143–45)

Nowhere does the question of interpretation come to a point of crisis more than in book 4, when the Son hears Satan's most dangerous ploy—the exercise of wisdom and eloquence as apt means of asserting his kingship as God's Son. Satan's argument might seem likely to appeal to a scholar and practitioner of humane studies; the Son, as noted above, has given over his youthful hopes of providing military deliverance to offer "persuasion" through "winning words" as the means of conquest in his "kingdom" (1.221–22). The object of this persuasion, the advancement of the people, is appropriated by Satan as the ostensible object of practical wisdom embodied in the teaching of Plato, Aristotle, and Homer:

>   teachers best
> Of moral prudence, with delight receiv'd
> In brief sententious precepts, while they treat
> Of fate, and chance, and change in human life,
> High actions, and high passions best describing.
> (4.262–66)

To this high and serious matter Satan appends the rhetorical means of achieving "delightful" teaching:

> Thence to the famous Orators repair,
> Those ancient, whose resistless eloquence
> Wielded at will that fierce Democraty.
> (4.267–69)

As the most delectable bait, Satan offers the prospect of "sage Philosophy" (272) linked to Socrates and the Delphic oracle that sanctioned his truth. Armed with a conventional vision of advancement from prudence to wisdom, Satan hopes to lure the Son to "revolve" within himself this sum of learning, pointedly in opposition to the scriptural "revolving" the Son had performed in book 1. With a condescension perhaps born of frustration, Satan suggests that studying secular philosophies in the desert or "at home" (281) will "mature thee to a Kingdom's weight" (282), playing on the political principle that governing oneself is the prelude to effective governance of a commonwealth: "These rules will render thee a King complete / Within thyself, much more with Empire join'd" (4.283–84). The implication, of course, is that the Son is incompletely aware of himself, much less of empire-building or governing the world.

The Son "sagely" (285) rewards this implied ignorance with flat denial (4.291–308) and follows it with a stinging indictment of classical philosophy rooted in the self-professed ignorance of Socrates and the perversions of reality sustained by subsequent philosophers rooted ultimately in the conviction of human pride and an overestimation of human ability:

> Who therefore seeks in these
> True wisdom, finds her not, or by delusion
> Far worse, her false resemblance only meets,
> An empty cloud.
> (4.318–21)

In this Milton strips away the customary humanist icons dedicated to the glorification of classical writers at the expense of scriptural and spiritual truth, and he pursues relentlessly the point that fundamental truth lies only in what is most divinely, most immediately inspired. Having mocked philosophy, the Son dismisses the life of the scholar. Many of the books of the wise

> are wearisome; who reads
> Incessantly, and to his reading brings not
> A spirit and judgment equal or superior
> (And what he brings, what needs he elsewhere seek)
> Uncertain and unsettl'd still remains,
> Deep verst in books and shallow in himself,
> Crude or intoxicate, collecting toys,
> And trifles for choice matters, worth a sponge.
> (4.322–29)

Like philosophy, scholarship may turn to self-serving flattery. Satanic influences upon human learning diminish when the classical tradition, derived from the biblical, is trivialized as the "ridiculous" (342) feigning of gods and themselves, "Ill imitated" (4.339):

> As varnish on a Harlot's cheek, the rest,
> Thin sown with aught of profit or delight,
> Will far be found unworthy to compare
> With Sion's songs, to all true tastes excelling,
> Where God is prais'd aright, and Godlike men,
> The Holiest of Holies, and his Saints;
> Such are from God inspir'd, not such from thee;
> Unless where moral virtue is express'd
> By light of Nature, not in all quite lost.
> (4.344–52)

Finally, the Son turns the force of rhetoric upon rhetoric itself, praising biblical rhetoric at the expense of Satan's greatest source of pride: the Son punctures the professed idealism of classical orators who considered themselves at "The top of Eloquence, Statists indeed, / And lovers of thir Country" by appending the doubtful "as may seem" (4.354 –55) to qualify the degree or existence of their professed patriotism. Classical rhetors, together with Satan himself, are described as far below the prophets, the latter

> divinely taught, and better teaching
> The solid rules of Civil Government
> In thir majestic unaffected style
> Than all the oratory of Greece and Rome.
> In them is plainest taught, and easiest learnt,
> What makes a Nation happy, and keeps it so,
> What ruins Kingdoms, and lays Cities flat;
> These only, with our Law, best form a King.
> (4.357–64)

This passage has naturally drawn the attention of critics for vilification or defense, mostly, as Shawcross observes, for the wrong reasons.[10] Milton does not condemn learning wholesale; rather, he seeks to re-found it on the authority and example of scripture and on methods of reading, speaking, and writing rooted in inspiration. Although not prepared to banish completely the "light of Nature," the Son points to the exercise of internal judgment—a reader in communion with the Spirit and a text—as the truest means of producing meaning: "A spirit and judgment equal or superior" to the subject matter is required if learning is to be possible. But, then, as Milton parenthetically observes, what good is the matter itself ?

At this moment the Son affirms not silence, as Fish has argued, but a redirection of the energies of language away from those activities—learned as well as sordid—which deceive or at best waste one's time.[11] Instead, the Son asserts, people should turn to inspired language, "our Prophets," as the immediate means of enlightenment and moral or civil improvement (4.356 – 64). This affirmation of spiritual language cancels out the Son's own language of self-questioning (the soliloquizing tendency of the newly proclaimed Son), and most certainly the love of argument and debate favored by Satan.[12] Far from silent, the Son increasingly in book 4 speaks with firmness and resolve, and his speech increasingly participates in the firmness of scriptural accounts. The words he directs to Satan move from direct response to outright rejection and command, and he offers unheeded imperatives to an evil that responds in increasingly paltry and burlesque ways: "Get thee behind me" (4.193); "Tempt not the Lord thy God" (4.561), he commands, and the once formidable-seeming Satan becomes alternately fawning, terrified, imprudently bold, and, finally, a living, though ridiculous and insignificant, pratfall.

The Son's acquisition of the language of command in book 4 does not negate but rather supports his earlier commitment to the use of persuasion. The central qualifier in book 1, one recalls, is the determination to strive to use "winning words" with those whose hearts are "willing," while those who remain "stubborn," "wilfully misdoing" are to be subdued (1.221–26). The stubbornness of Satan becomes increasingly apparent to an audience in book 4 as pretexts, useless continuations, and ridiculous threats replace his earlier arguments, now shattered. Conversely, the Son increasingly assumes the voice of the heavenly Son in *Paradise Lost* when, called to action against the rebels, he puts on his Father's terrors, hating whom he hates (*Paradise Lost,* 6.734 –35). Indeed the Son in *Paradise Regained* serves the dual role of destroyer and deliverer in the case of Satan, echoing Samson's destruction of the Philistines. Like the catastrophic Samson, the triumphant Son turns into himself to turn out to the world; he negates the value of material goods, policy, governance, and learning only to refound them in a new world order rooted in the Bible and one's inward light. Although the debate concerning the final state of Samson's soul has not yet been resolved—and in my view may not be resolvable—the overriding pattern of relationship between the two works, published together in 1671, is one of continuity rather than contrast—a continuity centered in the pattern of transformation, of the energizing of central figures for providential good despite the essentially disparate characters of the rude and uncivil Samson and the refined, genuinely learned, and inspired Son.

Notes

1. See Arthur E. Barker, "Calm Regained through Passion Spent: The Conclusions of the Miltonic Effort," *The Prison and the Pinnacle*, ed. Balachandra Rajan (Toronto: University of Toronto Press, 1973), 47–48, who wisely observes that *Paradise Regained* and *Samson Agonistes* can be seen as "companionable" "if we can sufficiently suspend our disbelief, and ask relevant questions and stay for answers that will prove more challengingly complex than simply resolutionary." In the same volume see Rajan's " 'To Which Is Added *Samson Agonistes*—,' " 102–10. John T. Shawcross, in "The Genres of *Paradise Regain'd* and *Samson Agonistes*: The Wisdom of Their Joint Publication," *Composite Orders: The Genres of Milton's Last Poems*, ed. Richard S. Ide and Joseph A. Wittreich (Pittsburgh: University of Pittsburgh Press, 1983), volume 17 of *Milton Studies,* 225–48, and in *"Paradise Regain'd": "Worthy T'Have Not Remain'd So Long Unsung"* (Pittsburgh: Duquesne University Press, 1988), 102–15, anticipates the profound contrasts drawn between the two works by

Wittreich in "'Strange Text!': 'Paradise Regain'd . . . To which is added *Samson Agonistes*,'" *Poems in Their Place: The Intertextuality and Order of Poetic Collections*, ed. Neil Fraistat (Chapel Hill: University of North Carolina Press, 1986), 164–94. See also Wittreich's *Interpreting "Samson Agonistes"* (Princeton: Princeton University Press, 1986), 231.

2. Stanley Fish, "Inaction and Silence: The Reader in *Paradise Regained*," *Calm of Mind: Tercentenary Essays on "Paradise Regained" and "Samson Agonistes" in Honor of John S. Diekhoff*, ed. Joseph A. Wittreich (Cleveland, Oh.: The Press of Case Western Reserve University, 1971), 45. See also Fish's response to Wittreich's revisionist views of *Samson Agonistes* in "Spectacle and Evidence in *Samson Agonistes*," *Critical Inquiry* 15 (1989): 556–86, and David Loewenstein's in "'Casting Down Imaginations': Milton as Iconoclast," *Criticism* 31 (1989): 268–70.

3. Fish, "Inaction," 30.

4. John Milton, *Paradise Regained* and *Samson Agonistes, John Milton: Complete Poems and Major Prose*, ed. Merritt Y. Hughes (New York: Odyssey Press, 1957). All references to Milton's poetry and prose are to this edition and are cited parenthetically in the text. On the Son's self-comprehension see Hugh MacCallum, *Milton and the Sons of God: The Divine Image in Milton's Epic Poetry* (Toronto: University of Toronto Press, 1986), 241–43.

5. On this distinction see Christopher Grose, *Milton and the Sense of Tradition* (Toronto: University of Toronto Press, 1986), 127–30.

6. Grose, *Milton*, 126; see Matthew 3.16–17; Mark 1.1–13; Luke 3.1–4.13; John 1.19–42 for Milton's scriptural authorities. Ashraf H. A. Rushdy, "Of *Paradise Regained*: The Interpretation of Career," *Milton Studies* 24 (1989): 254–55, sets out a similar comparative approach for Satan's temptations and the Son's "biographies" and "autobiography."

7. Shawcross, "*Paradise Regain'd*," 107.

8. MacCallum, *Milton and the Sons,* 232.

9. Fish, "Inaction"; Leonard Mustazza, *"Such Prompt Eloquence": Language as Agency and Character in Milton's Epics* (Lewisburg, Pa.: Bucknell University Press, 1988), 131–52.

10. Shawcross, "*Paradise Regain'd*," 112–13.

11. Fish, "Inaction," 41–42.

12. The evidence that the Son soliloquizes qualifies Mustazza's observation that the soliloquy "is employed only by the sinful, isolated, alienated individual who is incapable of genuine, meaningful converse with others" (*"Such Prompt Eloquence,"* 16–17): one hopes this does not apply equally to the Son!

Authorial Providence and the Dramatic Form of *Samson Agonistes*

JANE COLLINS

Many commentators on the dramatic form of *Samson Agonistes* have begun by dividing it into acts and scenes to liken it to Greek tragedy.[1] Milton, in his preface to *Samson Agonistes*, suggests the work could be five acts but also implies that these divisions are not essential to his use of drama.[2] At the other extreme, John Shawcross has argued that *Samson Agonistes* is to be read as a poem and not a drama; that although Milton's work has many elements of extant Greek plays, "it is not a drama in the generic meaning of that word" and that the dramatic poem would be made "ineffectual by the belief that we have seen an 'imitation' of human action."[3] However, I believe Milton uses the generic meaning of *drama* to offer the reader interpretive keys to *Samson Agonistes* and, in at least three ways, dramatic form qualifies the literal content of the poem: first, as a form that relies on the interplay of human voices without the presence of a controlling, authoritative narrative voice; second, as a form that carries expectations of a physical component because of its association with staged presentation; and third, as a form that has its roots in ritual and communal ceremony. Milton uses these three attributes of dramatic form to illuminate what, I believe, he saw as a tragic flaw in his characters and in his time—the self-serving interpretation of events as signs of divine providence without rigorous interrogation of their meaning. In other words, the action that *Samson Agonistes* "imitates" is not physical; but rather Milton, playing against reader expectations of physical action, throws into relief acts of interpretation that have become thoughtless rituals rather than profound explorations of divine will.

In *Samson Agonistes*, Milton uses dramatic form stripped to its bare bones. There are no scenes or acts; and other than the names of the characters, there is only one stage direction given and that only tersely creates the setting—"The Scene before the Prison in Gaza." This conspicuous authorial absence suggests which aspect of drama best informs the reader about the poem: Milton presents an interplay of human voices vying to be the ultimate interpreters of events not seen but discussed.

The reader of Milton's closet drama, who has only the characters' interpretive acts to illuminate the author's purpose, is in a situation akin to that of Puritans in Milton's day (including Milton himself) who looked for providence—the presence of a divine author—in the events of their day. They tried to discern God's intention in an exegetical act similar to our own search for Milton's purpose when we read his dramatic poem. The conclusions drawn in both cases rely upon interpretive rigor. For Milton, rigorous interpretation was not only an act of faith but the sincerest path to salvation. In *Christian Doctrine*, he concludes after years of scriptural study: "In religion as in other things, I discerned, God offers all his rewards not to those who are thoughtless and credulous, but to those who labor constantly and seek tirelessly the truth."[4] As readers of *Samson Agonistes* then, in order to receive Milton's rewards, we are meant to labor and seek its truth rather than passively accept the conclusions of any or all of the characters. Milton uses dramatic form to create a reader who must seek his truth through careful weighing of evidence: the reader is forced to weigh not the validity of an action, but rather the soundness of meanings assigned to it by dramatic characters.

The lack of authorial commentary in drama is particularly affecting in closet drama, which is deprived of the chance of becoming concrete through a staged interpretation. Milton chose a form for retelling the Samson legend that offered only a proliferation of points of view. The dearth of immediate physical action in Milton's drama focuses our attention on the mental and spiritual action that makes up the poem. As a drama not to be performed, *Samson Agonistes* has been deprived of its physical strength, as if shorn of its locks. Ironically, the loss of its physical presence does not incapacitate Milton's drama but changes its emphasis and meaning: it is wholly dependent upon the interpretive acts of its characters.

The captive Samson, in order to understand his fate and in response to questions and challenges from other characters, interprets his past actions, examining his failures as well as his divinely inspired acts. The debate over how readers should understand Samson's explication of his life has been heated. Irene Samuel argues that Samson is not of a saintly character and his "absolute understanding of anything we may question."[5] Wendy Furman, responding to Samuel, asserts that such a reading is ironic whereas the text, which she reads as a Christian tragedy, is not.⁶ Yet there is unmistakable irony in the Samson character Milton has put at the center of a closet drama; throughout the poem, Samson privileges physical action over speech. Even examining his conscience, Samson must do so in physical terms. He tells the chorus:

> of what I now suffer
> She was not the prime cause, but I my self,
> Who vanquisht with a peal of words (O weakness!)
> Gave up my fort of silence to a Woman.
> (233–36)

Samson attempts to make silence, the antithesis of speech, into a concrete entity—a "fort." Although the chorus have challenged Samson to account for a number of rueful acts, Samson takes responsibility only for the misdeed at which he was caught, which is, ironically, a speech act—telling a secret: "my crime, / Shameful garrulity" (490–91). Samson attempts to physicalize speech when he describes Dalila's artful interrogation to discover where his strength lay:

> Yet the fourth time, when mustring all her wiles,
> With blandisht parlies, feminine assaults,
> Tongue-batteries, she surceas'd not day nor night
> To storm me over-watch't, and wearied out.
> (402–5)

The scourge of the Philistines seems to describe language as overpowering his body: he was besieged by speech and lost the battle. Samson conceals his mental frailty behind a confusion of martial and carnal imagery.

It is precisely by presenting a character so antithetical to speech in a drama that is only speech that Milton forces the reader to explore the inconsistency. The physical nature of drama and of the heroic Samson character exerts pressure on the dephysicalized closet drama: Milton uses this tension to challenge the traditional meanings of both the form and the hero. The reader Milton creates must examine the carnal hero and the form that supposedly offers its audience physical relief through catharsis. *Samson Agonistes* is talk without action; deeds are not done but described. Action could have been portrayed or described in stage directions, but Milton chose to omit these. By stripping *Samson Agonistes* of spectacle, Milton plays on the reader's expectation of spectacle and the communal relief it offers to a theater audience.

An illustrative comparison can be made with the kind of physical action in a 1600 drama, Marcus Andreas Wunstius's *Samson, A Sacred Tragedy*, that relies on the effects of stage directions and direct portrayals of physical action. When Samson first appears in Wunstius's drama, he is brought on by the stage direction "(Enter Samson, carrying the gates of Gaza)."[7] Although the staging involved must have been challenging, this play shows the physical reality of Samson's acts. The immediateness of these imitations of violence is strikingly different from the descriptions of actions past in *Samson Agonistes*, many of which are recounted by a witness rather than a participant. Perhaps the most telling example of the differences between these two uses of dramatic form is the scene at the pillars. Wunstius portrays Samson's act; Milton, however, portrays the characters' describing and then assigning meaning to the act. In Wunstius's version we are at the pillars with Samson and hear his final prayer:

> O God, high ruler of the angel hosts,
> While in my wretchedness I call upon Thee
> With my last words, grant favour to my prayer:
> Punish through me the sinful mockeries
> Heaped on Thy godhead by this impious crew!
> (*Sacred Tragedy*, 46)

Wunstius leaves no doubt about Samson's purpose in his final act and follows this speech with the deaths on stage of the Philistines who cry out "Alas, we die!" (46). In Milton's drama, we learn of Samson's final moments from an eyewitness who describes what he has seen. Samson is led to the pillars

> which when Samson
> Felt in his arms, with head a while enclin'd,
> And eyes fast fixt he stood, as one who pray'd,
> Or some great matter in his mind revolv'd.
> (*Samson Agonistes*, 1635–38)

Milton has not clearly told the reader that Samson is responding to a call from God or even praying for God's guidance. The reader is given interpretations, not answers, and is challenged to interrogate not motives, but the characters' explications of them. Milton's Samson may have been divinely inspired in his final act, but that is a conclusion that the reader must draw. However, the chorus, with little hesitation or thought on the matter, declare that this act is God's will and, moreover, a good sign for the Danites. It is not Samson's act that Milton foregrounds but the chorus' self-serving interpretation of it.

Milton chose the closet drama as a means of interrogating a biblical story that had become a religious symbol before and during the Puritan revolution. Writing after the failure of that revolution, Milton's poem does not simply restate and reinforce the Puritan interpretation of the Samson story, but rather interrogates the story and argues against simple interpretations of God's will and of human responsibility. Milton's choice of dramatic form to retell this story argues against critics who maintain that *Samson Agonistes* is a Puritan call to arms. Rather, Milton's *Samson Agonistes* interrogates the actions of Puritans who, instead of searching tirelessly for God's will, accept the meaning they find most convenient or conducive to their ends. In Milton's drama, it is the Danite characters—the chorus, Samson, and Manoa—who produce, adapt, and adopt interpretations of divine providence.

The chorus, attempting to assign a positive meaning to Samson's acts, align him with two other Old Testament figures, Gideon and Jeptha. All three figures appear in the Old Testament Book of Judges, and in the New Testament Hebrews 11.32, as righteous warriors. In the seventeenth century, the stories of Samson, Gideon, and Jephtha were commonly used by Puritan preachers as a religious justification for war. In a sermon published in 1629, entitled *Bible Battells*, Richard Bernard invokes these three heroes to boost morale amongst the army of the faithful, claiming "there is nothing more for the encouragement in any action than to have conscience satisfied in the lawfulness thereof."[8] Yet, a satisfied conscience is much less strenuous than the perpetual search for truth that Milton urges in *Christian Doctrine*. By listing Samson with Gideon and Jephtha, the chorus attempt to set a precedent for their situation and thereby make it familiar and easily comprehensible. Stanley Fish describes the chorus' action as making "the present into something that has already happened, an event at once predicted and rendered intellectually manageable by a formula ready and eager to account for it."[9]

For the chorus, interpretation has taken on aspects of ritual ceremony: it becomes an established form for ordering words, a set of actions made habitual through repetition. The kind of intellectual sloth exhibited by the chorus is antithetical to Milton's position, and he gives an interpretive key in the final lines of the chorus' description of these exemplary heroes:

> Had not his prowess quell'd thir pride
> In that sore battel when so many dy'd
> Without Reprieve adjudg'd to death,
> For want of well pronouncing Shibboleth.
> (286–89)

The chorus suddenly burst into rhyme, calling into question their interpretive practice. Milton in a note on *Paradise Lost* describes rhyme as "the Invention of a barbarous Age, to set off wretched matter and lame Meeter."[10] The rhymes of the chorus create a sing-song quality that trivializes "the matter" of their statement. Their analysis becomes a trite recitation or catechism made easier to memorize with simple rhymes, implying that these Old Testament stories have been turned into convenient truths rather than being scrupulously examined for their divine truth.

Robert Beum claims that Milton's return to rhyme in *Samson Agonistes* is not surprising and that Milton gives the chorus by far the greatest number of rhyming lines to set "the chorus apart from direct involvement in the action—[to distinguish] an aloof and philosophical entity"; Beum sees the chorus as having a double function: "omniscient voice" marked by the use of rhyme, and "active participant" when speaking without rhyme.[11] However, the chorus' analysis of Samson's acts is not without self-interest; they are of Samson's tribe and their interpretation of his acts as divine providence consoles them and assures them that God favors the Danites. The Danite interpretation of Samson's divine inspiration can be compared with that of Puritans, after the failed revolution, who wanted assurances that the actions of the New Model Army had been justified and that they remained beloved of their God. Beum correctly argues that the rhyming passages are mostly interpretive, but where he argues that Milton uses rhyme to give those interpretations "dignity and power,"[12] I propose that the rhyme calls these self-serving interpretations into question. It is not surprising then that at the point when the chorus want to heroicize Samson, they break into the heroic couplet so popular on the Restoration stage.

Moreover, the chorus' rhyming couplets illuminate the process of creating a political slogan: making a complex issue into a pithy, memorable phrase. Samson's reply to the chorus is aptly "Of such examples add mee to the roul" (290). Milton, through the use of four lines of simple rhyme, has presented and made questionable a basic human activity—simplifying information for the comfort of easy understanding. He has presented a characteristic form of interpretation not for adoption but rather for interrogation.

Jackie DiSalvo argues that Milton's use of these Puritan battle themes aligns him with the New Model Army and gives the entire poem a specific political purpose: "to give those already engaged the good conscience he thought so necessary to a successful revolution, and to those faltering the stirring example of Samson, fighter for God and liberty."[13] I would argue that Milton did not want to "give" good conscience but rather urged the investigation of such trivial summations. He is arguing for introspection that would lead to an enlightened conscience. Joseph A. Wittreich points out that by the seventeenth century there were conflicting images of Samson, and with the failure of the Puritan revolution, its heroic imagery came under close scrutiny:

> it was now more evident than ever that the Lord's battle would not be fought out in history but was to be waged in every Christian. The true exemplar of Christian warfare, therefore, was not Samson but Christ; and the scene of the battle was not at the pillars but in the wilderness.[14]

The Danite characters look only to external signs of providence, ignoring their own interpretive responsibilities.

The chorus' desire to totalize or complete the Samson story is unsatisfying and leaves the reader uncomfortably watching the Danites try to tidy up and organize the range of interpretive possibilities opened by Samson's life and ultimately by his final act. Milton uses the dramatic form, which since its Greek origins has been associated with ritual and communal values, to point out the limitations of such ritualizing. In his preface to *Samson Agonistes,* Milton claims "Aeschulus, Sophocles, and Euripides" to be his models for tragedy, and it is Greek theater's presentation of mythological subjects that illuminates Milton's dramatization of what can be called a Christian myth. Roland Barthes, writing on the structure of Greek theater, notes that mythology

> had been the imposition of a vast semantic system upon nature. The Greek theater seizes upon the mythological answer and makes use of it as a reservoir of new questions: for to interrogate mythology is to interrogate what had been in its time a fulfilled answer.[15]

This interrogation seems to describe exactly the way Milton's poem has addressed the Christian mythology that was so important to the Puritan revolution: *Samson Agonistes* creates new questions about the Samson myth and how such a myth is assigned meanings. However, Milton not only interrogates the fulfilled answers assigned to a Christian myth, but by calling into question the desire to find, and then cling to, ready answers, he challenges his reader to abandon "fulfilled answers" and to read vigilantly for answers more difficult and elusive but also more rewarding.

Milton's description of how to best read and interpret the scriptures offers a program for reading *Samson Agonistes*. He claims that a knowledge "of what comes before and after the passage in question, and comparison of one text with another" are "requisites" for informed interpretation (*Complete Prose Works*, 6:582). Wittreich points out that in the Judges narrative the tribe of Dan receives a fate as severe as that of the Philistines.[16] The fate of the Danites in the biblical narrative makes the speeches of Manoa and the chorus after Samson's death ironic because the Danites do not gain their freedom but continue to serve under the Philistian yoke and are eventually erased from the twelve tribes of Israel. In response to the chorus' rhyming elegy of Samson, Manoa proclaims:

> To Israel
> Honour hath left, and freedom, let but them
> Find courage to lay hold on this occasion,
> To himself and Fathers house eternal fame;
> And which is best and happiest yet, all this
> With God not parted from him, as was feard,
> But favouring and assisting to the end.
> (1714–20)

A reader familiar with biblical history would realize that Manoa's reading of the event is wrong in some details, highly questionable in others, yet ironically correct in one; his house does achieve eternal fame, or infamy, depending upon one's interpretation of Samson's final act. The reader of *Samson Agonistes* interprets the Danites' conclusions with the knowledge of repercussions unknown to Manoa and the chorus, watching the Danites create the myth that will be used to yield up a number of "answers" for the Puritans.

The chorus and Manoa mythologize even the very recent past, preferring nostalgia to the harsh realities of the present in which drama always remains. Actions past are actions completed and therefore more easily interpreted, so it is only when Samson is dead that a definitive interpretation can be made with any certainty that he will not undermine it with an impetuous act. Manoa comforts the chorus, saying:

> Nothing is here for tears, nothing to wail
> Or knock the breast, no weakness, no contempt,
> Dispraise, or blame, nothing but well and fair,
> And what might quiet us in a death so noble.
> (1721–24)

The Danites want some peace and quiet after the riot of Samson's life; they avoid any deeper exploration of Samson's actions and, more damningly, of their own role in history. The Danites are willing to search for signs of providence in the past or look forward to events divinely predicted, but the present is more problematic.

Before his death, Samson berates the Danites for their weakness and rejects responsibility for their slavery. In a particularly insightful passage he notes:

> But what more oft in Nations grown corrupt,
> And by thir vices brought to servitude,
> Then to love Bondage more then Liberty,
> Bondage with ease then strenuous liberty.
> (268–71)

Samson's countercharges presage the later interpretive acts of Manoa and the chorus. He disparages the Danites' acceptance of the Philistian yoke, but within the dramatic whole of *Samson Agonistes*, the physical is enveloped by the mental and spiritual bias of the closet drama. Samson sees their bondage as physical, but more poignantly in the context of the entire work, it is mental and spiritual. The Danites will succumb to the intellectual servitude of a totalized, simplistic vision of history and divine providence; they lack the courage and rigor to struggle against convenient interpretations, preferring mental security to an uncertain fight to break the banal chain of platitudes encircling them. Their communal values simply amount to the desire to maintain a satisfied conscience. The Danites cement this accusation of servitude by answering Samson with the rhyming references to Gideon and Jephtha discussed earlier.

The final words of the drama spoken by the chorus epitomize the communal desire for the fulfilled answers of myth. In fourteen rhyming lines made of two quatrains (abab cdcd) and an unusual sestet (efefef), Milton makes use of the reader's expectations of the sonnet form in much the same way as he has for the dramatic form:

> All is best, though we oft doubt,
> What th' unsearchable dispose
> Of highest wisdom brings about,
> And ever best found in the close.
> Oft he seems to hide his face,
> But unexpectedly returns
> And to his faithful Champion hath in place
> Bore witness gloriously; whence Gaza mourns
> And all that band them to resist
> His uncontroulable intent;
> His servants he with new acquist
> Of true experience from this great event
> With peace and consolation hath dismist,
> And calm of mind all passion spent.
> (1745–58)

The chorus' poetic strategy is not to challenge or question the content of the quatrains but to create a simple rhythm in the sestet that will carry them effortlessly into the future. Moreover, the preceding quatrains have not really set up a problem to be solved. It is hard to imagine the turn or twist we expect in the sonnet form in a poem that mostly agrees with itself from start to finish. The Danites are not really addressing an issue as much as breathing a collective sigh of relief. This sense of relief begins with the first line of the sonnet and is the focus of the first quatrain. The chorus are reiterating their preference for actions that are past as interpretive subjects. Divine providence is "best found in the close." The chorus express some apprehension about reading God's will unambiguously with phrases like "oft we doubt," "Oft he seems to hide his face," "unsearchable dispose," "uncontroulable intent," and "unexpectedly returns." Despite all the undercurrents of doubt, the chorus are determined to put God back in their corner. Their interpretation sweeps all problems out of sight and foresees an idyllic future. They are settling back into a comfortable understanding of their responsibilities. God has "dismist" them, let them off the hook. Ominously, the chorus have also chosen a word that means "to send away," "to discard or remove." The peace and consolation they find in rationalizations and unchallenged acceptance of a simplistic interpretation will not last long. Calm of mind may be a dangerous state of apathy and disinterest. It is certainly not the interpretive strategy Milton valorized in *Christian Doctrine*.

By ending his closet drama with this speech, Milton offers the chorus as a "negative example," to use Wittreich's description of Samson, not of physical actions against enemies but of interpretive acts that are destructive of the Self.[17] The meaning of the chorus' ritualized interpretation and their catharsis in Samson's death relies on the pressure Milton has created through his use of dramatic form: the reader is being warned against an easy, convenient reading of the text. Whereas Shawcross argues that "as poem, *Samson Agonistes* makes clear that Milton's intention was to achieve reader internalization of the poem,"[18] I argue that Milton's use of dramatic form attempts the same effect, not by fulfilling the reader's expectations for drama but by undermining and unsettling them and thereby forcing a more attentive reading—one that Milton could not describe scornfully as "credulous."

Notes

I would like to thank Scott Zaluda and Joseph Wittreich for their helpful comments on early drafts of this essay.

1. William Riley Parker, *Milton's Debt to Greek Tragedy in "Samson Agonistes"* (Baltimore: Johns Hopkins University Press, 1937), 17, maintains that "at least in respect to formal division, Milton's drama is purely and unassailably Greek" and divides *Samson Agonistes* into an introduction followed by five episodes with choruses and a final *exodus*. Anthony Low, *The Blaze of Noon: A Reading of "Samson Agonistes"* (New York: Columbia University Press, 1974), aligns the five acts with the stages of Christian redemption. In addition, Mary Ann Radzinowicz, *Toward "Samson Agonistes": The Growth of Milton's Mind* (Princeton: Princeton University Press, 1978), 89, describes it as "planned in five acts into which it can be divided."

2. Milton writes "Division into Act and Scene referring chiefly to the Stage (to which this work was never intended) is here omitted. It suffices if the whole Drama be found not produc't beyond the fift Act." All references to Milton's poetry are to *The Complete Poetry of John Milton*, ed. John T. Shawcross, rev. ed. (New York: Doubleday, 1971) and are cited parenthetically in the text.

3. John T. Shawcross, "The Genres of *Paradise Regain'd* and *Samson Agonistes*: The Wisdom of Their Joint Publication," *Composite Orders: The Genres of Milton's Last Poems,* ed. Richard S. Ide and Joseph A. Wittreich (Pittsburgh: University of Pittsburgh Press, 1983), volume 17 of *Milton Studies,* 234–39.

4. John Milton, *The Complete Prose Works of John Milton,* ed. Don M. Wolfe et al. (New Haven: Yale University Press, 1953–82), 6:120. All references to Milton's prose are to this edition and are cited parenthetically in the text.

5. Irene Samuel, "*Samson Agonistes* as Tragedy," *Calm of Mind: Tercentenary Essays on "Paradise Regained" and "Samson Agonistes" in Honor of John S. Diekhoff,* ed. Joseph A. Wittreich (Cleveland, Oh.: The Press of Case Western Reserve University, 1971), 244.

6. Wendy Furman, "*Samson Agonistes* as Christian Tragedy: A Corrective View," *Philological Quarterly* 60 (Spring 1981): 169–81.

7. *Samson, A Sacred Tragedy,* in Watson Kirkconnell, *That Invincible Samson: The Theme of "Samson Agonistes" in World Literature* (Toronto: University of Toronto Press, 1964), 25. All references to this edition are cited parenthetically in the text.

8. Richard Bernard, *The Bible Battells or the Sacred Art Military for the Rightly Waging of War According to Holy Writ* (London, 1629), 25.

9. Stanley Fish, "Spectacle and Evidence in *Samson Agonistes*," *Critical Inquiry* 15 (1989): 560.

10. Shawcross, *The Complete Poetry,* 249–50.

11. Robert Beum, "The Rhyme in *Samson Agonistes*," *Texas Studies in Language and Literature* 4 (1962): 182.

12. Beum, "Rhyme in *Samson,*" 182.

13. Jackie DiSalvo, "'The Lord's Battells': *Samson Agonistes* and the Puritan Revolution," *Milton Studies* 4 (1972): 45.

14. Joseph A. Wittreich, *Visionary Poetics: Milton's Tradition and His Legacy* (San Marino, Calif.: Huntington Library, 1979), 198.

15. Roland Barthes, "The Greek Theater," *The Responsibility of Forms: New Critical Essays on Music, Art and Representation,* trans. Richard Howard (New York: Hill and Wang, 1985), 68.

16. Wittreich, *Interpreting "Samson Agonistes"* (Princeton: Princeton University Press, 1986), 98.

17. Wittreich, *Visionary Poetics,* 268.

18. Shawcross, "Genres," 238.

Part V
Spokesperson for Tradition and Change

Comus:
Milton's Re-Formation of the Masque

J. ANDREW HUBBELL

As Stephen Orgel demonstrates, the specific function of the masque is to represent the social order, making particular reference to the monarch as the regal head of both the masque and society. Since the masque proposes to create a political fiction that would glorify the establishment, the praise of the court is an inherent element of the genre.[1] Political issues are thus inseparable from formal ones, and a study of Milton's deviations from the masque traditions will reveal the political agendas within *Comus*.

During the two decades before *Comus*, Ben Jonson united the loosely connected art forms that he had inherited from earlier court entertainment writers. Drawing on a fourteenth-century tradition, Jonson engaged his aristocratic audience in his artistic productions, achieving a special intimacy between the ideal world of the masque and its audience.[2] The masque's dialogue between audience and representation created a self-reflexive system that glorified what it dramatized, which was always the king and the aristocratic values of absolute monarchy.

Although Jonson constantly experimented with the structure, a certain standardized form was developed, beginning with the descent of a divine or symbolic figure whose opening address set the stage for the antimasque. In the later masques (after 1610) Jonson used the antimasque as a counterpoint to the established social fictions of the aristocratic audience. Thus he would present a primitive, uncultured society in the antimasque as a challenge to the contemporary aristocratic society. But to the Christian, aristocratic audience, the antimasquers' argument presented no challenge, revealing only "the deformity of their minds," symbolized in the grotesque masks they traditionally wore.[3] Since the audience's very existence denied the antimasque claims, no drama was involved in the transition to the main masque's perfection; it was only a matter of coordinating the development from discord to harmony. Most often the transition was accomplished by a rapid shift in scenery made possible by Inigo Jones's intricate machinery. But rather than violating dramatic conventions, the literal *deus ex machina* functioned as the core metaphor for the whole masque. From the perspective of the antimasquers, their society seemed a utopia, but from the audience's perspective, this utopia was false. The *deus ex machina* represented the step out of the framework of the antimasque and into the framework of the audience, or from limited to omniscient perspective. Rather than presenting wrong and right, the masque moved from ignorance to knowledge, from deformity to perfection, from chaos to order, which the audience both participated in and directed. In the virtuosity of the evening's performance, the audience achieved a greater awareness of its own ethos through variations on themes with which it identified.

Since aristocratic values centered around the king, and his presence both obviated and evoked the main masque, the transformation that resolved the antimasque and generated the main masque was officially ascribed to his symbolic power. By invoking the symbolic power of the king, the poet grounds his ideal world in the central figure of the real world. Whatever properties the ideal carries are drawn from what already exists in reality. The fundamental myth that the main masque revels and dances attempt to establish is that aristocratic values bring permanence and stability to the world. Theoretically, a hierarchical system founded on the divine right of the ruler tied society to the everlasting, immutable truths of God. The masque draws the king into its fiction in order to generate a myth that is ultimately directed toward validating his own existence.

However, despite its claim to have transcended history, the masque was inherently a part of history, being commissioned for a particular occasion, and existing, like all performing arts, within a set time period. Both Steven Orgel and Angus Fletcher concur that Jonson's fear of the ephemerality of court entertainments led him to emphasize the masque's literary qualities. As a ceremonial performance, the masque was tied to the particular moment, but as a literary monument, it had the same claim to permanence as Shakespeare's sonnet, "Not marble nor the gilded monuments." But Jonson's assertion that his poetry achieves what the masque spectacle cannot conflicts with the genre's inherent presumption that transcendent power is drawn from the king. There is thus a submerged tension between Jonson's claim for the immortalizing power of his verse and the regal myth he invokes in it.

Angus Fletcher suggests that the king and the poet are empowered through mutually exclusive myths, and when they are joined within the same discourse, primacy becomes a serious contention.[4] The rhetorical structures of the genre may acknowledge the primacy of the king's myth, but the very existence of those structures asserts the primacy of their creator, the poet.

In the masque, confrontation with absolutist ideology enlightened the primitive antimasquers, dramatizing the accord between divine truth and the Stuart social order. But on another level, the masque's mimetic representation of an idealized vision of the court transcends the actual world of the court. The poet, not the king, illuminates the ideal, utopian vision, revealing his superior ability to lead society toward an ideal world despite his subordinate status. This contradiction between the poet's myth and the king's myth, which every masque writer was forced to confront and only imperfectly resolved, betrays the precariousness of the political myth at the time.

In *Comus* Milton changed the masque's primary function from honoring the king to honoring the poet, thus making explicit what Jonson had only implied—that the poet's myth is superior to the king's. Angus Fletcher's argument that "the central action of *Comus* is the overthrow of one magician by another" implies a political interpretation that Fletcher fails to develop.[5] If the "magic-users" are identified as the king and the poet and the masque is seen as a battle between their two conflicting myths, then the reading has radical implications.

While Cedric Brown acknowledges that the masque advocates reforms, he claims that Milton's sense of decorum would not have allowed him to make any more radical statement about his own powers as a poet or the failure of the aristocracy.[6] Drawing support from *Lycidas* written three years later, Brown claims that Milton was plagued by serious doubts about his intended vocation in the prelacy at the time he wrote *Comus*, and the doubts account for the spirit of reform in the masque. In his view, the masque hints at Milton's future Puritan radicalism and displays his desire to unite poetry with preaching, but does not make the kind of radical statement that he does in *Lycidas* three years later.[7]

While Fletcher and Brown are hesitant in this matter, Michael Wilding and David Norbrook read Milton's masque as strongly revolutionary. Norbrook's short essay narrates the development of the masque genre in the context of the growing influence of Puritan moral reform, placing *Comus* at the turning point in the conflict between Royalists and Puritans. In Milton's masque, Comus, the villain, speaks for the establishment, while the Lady speaks for the Puritans. The dramatic conflict in the masque represents a Puritan questioning of aristocratic ideology, and Milton attempts to re-formulate masque conventions in light of a Puritan apocalyptic ideology.[8] But this analysis leaves unexamined how Milton's growing disenchantment with his chosen vocation in the Royalist Anglican church and his desire to use his poetic talents productively would necessarily influence his generic re-formulations.

Wilding argues that Comus represents the contemporary state of politics, religion, and society, but he does not recognize the significance of representing contemporary England in the antimasque—a change that I argue is the masque's strongest ideological statement.[9] In the Jonsonian tradition, the representation of England belonged in the main masque where it was acknowledged to be the ideal society. Milton's reversal of this tradition overturns the fundamental precept of the masque—praise of the absolute monarchy. By moving the absolutist ideology to the antimasque and replacing it with a celebration of the self-aware poet, Milton resolves the basic tension between the king and the poet and turns the masque into a vehicle for prophecy. Although he retained the superficial structure of the Jonsonian masque, its purpose was radically changed from the glorification of society to its restructuring.

Imitating Jonsonian tradition, Milton constructs a primitive, uncultured society in his antimasque. Comus, cast as the traditional protean figure of misrule, presides over a primitive, decadent society. He enters the masque carrying a "Charming Rod in one hand, his Glass in the other," which is suggestive, as Wilding notes, of the ball and scepter held by the king.[10] Comus also aspires to make the Lady his queen, taking her back to his "stately Palace" where he expresses the aristocratic ideology of conspicuous consumption, public display, and hierarchy:

> Beauty is nature's brag, and must be shown
> In courts, at feasts, and high solemnities
> Where most may wonder at the workmanship;
> It is for homely features to keep home.
> (745–48)[11]

Additionally, the drunken feasting at the castle parodies the royal banquets given on great occasions, as the "Midnight shout and revelry" parodied the aristocratic entertainments that usually followed the meal. *Comus* itself would probably have followed such a celebration feast, and the audience was thus presented with an imitation of itself as a class in the antimasque, though few may have recognized that fact.

Consistent with the English practice of uniting secular and spiritual leadership in the king, Comus is also cast as a high priest. Besides leading the invocation and religious services, Comus administers the sacrament with his enchanted glass, an obvious parody of the communion cup. He also claims that the Lady's argument is "mere moral babble, and direct / Against the canon laws of our foundation" (807–8). This statement reflects the way the establishment appropriated certain biblical texts or religious traditions in order to perpetuate its own existence and prevent the impetus of reform, a practice Milton would argue against in his prose tracts. By constructing Comus as the king and high priest, Milton is able to use the antimasque as a forum for critiquing the establishment, rather than, as was traditional in Jonson, as a way to bring the aristocratic audience to a greater awareness of the vital purpose that hierarchy served.

In contrast to Comus's chaotic world, the Lady presents a code of self-discipline and order. The Lady is presented as a figure of chastity, and Milton conceives of chastity as the ability to control and order the desires and functions of the human body, protecting the divine light of reason from the temptation of the senses. The Lady's ability to resist evil is attributed by her elder brother to her chaste character: "'Tis chastity, my brother, chastity: / She that has that is clad in complete steel" (420–21).[12] Even with all his art, Comus is incapable of influencing the freedom of her mind, and her arguments are consistently shown to be superior to his: "She fables not, I feel that I do fear / Her words set off by some superior power" (801–2). Both her singing, which "might create a soul / Under the ribs of Death" (562–63), and her rhetoric are witnesses to "something holy lodge[d] in that breast" (246–47). Chastity or self-discipline, in addition to making her art beautiful, also gives her philosophy a moral grounding. Thus it seems that art and morality are mutually dependent, and that style of discourse constructs and is constructed by a moral sense.

In her debate with Comus, the Lady counters Comus's hedonism with her own philosophy of temperance:

> Impostor, do not charge most innocent nature,
> As if she would her children should be riotous
> With her abundance; she, good cateress,
> Means her provision only to the good
> That live according to her sober laws
> And holy dictate of spare Temperance:
> If every just man that now pines with want
> Had but a moderate and beseeming share
> Of that which lewdly-pamper'd Luxury
> Now heaps upon some few with vast excess,
> Nature's full blessings would be well dispens't
> In unsuperfluous even proportion,

> And she no whit encumber'd with her store,
> And then the giver would be better thank't,
> His praise due paid, for swinish gluttony
> Ne'er looks to Heav'n amidst his gorgeous feast,
> But with besotted base ingratitude
> Crams, and blasphemes his feeder.
>
> (762–79)

This passage condemns the absolutist establishment, praising the superiority of the Puritan ethic. But ironically, the Lady is herself one of the aristocracy, both in the masque fiction as well as in reality. Thus, while *Comus* manifests the conventional movement from an inferior to a superior set of values, those values and the people who establish them have been radically changed. Milton's triumphal aristocrats are an entirely new type of leader: reformist, bourgeois, meritocratic.[13]

Alongside this reconceptualization of the aristocratic class, Milton reconstructs the poet. His supreme representation of the poet is the Attendant Spirit, and this figure is portrayed as the controlling power in the masque. In the prologue, he claims authorship of the story:

> And listen why, for I will tell ye now
> What never yet was heard in Tale or Song
> From old or modern Bard, in Hall or Bow'r.
>
> (43–45)

His life amongst "those immortal shapes" (2), suggestive of Platonic forms, constructs an irrefutable authority for his mimetic creation; his words "figure forth" a transcendent truth. By his direction, the dynamics of the masque are kept in motion: the brothers are led out of the wood, the Lady is rescued, the transformation is accomplished, and the children are led home. By ascribing the construction of the didactic, transcendental myth to his own powers, the Spirit, in the vocation of the poet, takes what was traditionally the king's place in the masque. In the Jonsonian tradition, the masque reaffirmed for its audience that aristocratic society, symbolically united in the figure of the king, manifested divine truth. By replacing the royal figure with the poet, Milton shatters this whole tradition.[14]

Discarding the absolutist myth, Milton develops the traditionally muted rival myth of the poet. When Henry Lawes, playing the Attendant Spirit, disguises himself as Thyrsis, he accrues to himself the historical and symbolic meanings of Orpheus, the shepherd-poet.[15] This tripartite role conflates the musician, the divine seer, and the shepherd-poet into one persona. Joining these different parts under one empowering myth, Milton constructs his poet as a divine prophet, a spiritual leader of fundamental importance to society. Beginning his story of Comus, Thyrsis says:

> I'll tell ye; 'tis not vain or fabulous,
> (Though so esteem'd by shallow ignorance)
> What the sage Poets taught by th' heav'nly Muse
> Storied of old in high immortal verse.
> (513–16)

The "sage Poets" had an intimate awareness of transcendent truth, and Thyrsis, through his historical relationship with Orpheus, is constructed as the inheritor of both the wisdom of the ancients and the intimate connection with the "heav'nly Muse." Knowledge of Platonic truth is thus the special power reserved solely for the poet.

Now that the Attendant Spirit has established himself in the tradition of the classical poets, he is in a position to prove his superiority. When Thyrsis plans the rescue of the Lady, he gives the brothers an herb "more med'cinal is it than that Moly / That Hermes once to wise Ulysses gave" (636–37). Whether one interprets the herb as an allegorical representation of the word of God as Cedric Brown does, or the sacrament, the result is the same: Thyrsis is the true preacher, the Christian Shepherd, and the Christian ethos transcends the classical.

Using the knowledge he inherited from Meliboeus, Thyrsis's poetic invocation initiates the transformation scene, that crucial point where the earthly transcendental power was formally recognized. The Jonsonian masque mandated the recognition and inclusion of the royal presence in the transformation of the antimasquers. In Milton's masque, the Lady must be released from Comus's spell.[16] With a song, Thyrsis summons a demigoddess to break the spell:

> as the old Swain said, she can unlock
> The clasping charm and thaw the numbing spell,
> If she be right invok'd in warbled Song,
>   . . . This will I try
> And add the power of some adjuring verse.
> (853–55, 58–59)

Thus the Christian shepherd-poet initiates the transformation with his own poetic power, as that power is the Christian successor and heir to the classical poetic tradition. The power of the absolute monarch is displaced by the power of the poet.

Since Milton has established the poet as the transcendent power, it is only fitting that the main masque celebrate and reaffirm his values in an appropriate form. In both the Trinity Manuscript and the 1637 publication, Milton ends his masque with a didactic eulogy by the Attendant Spirit.[17] Because the poet's special province is the word, it is appropriate for the medium of celebration to be poetry rather than dance or spectacle; and the main masque and eulogy thus represent a poetic revelry, reaffirming the poet's power to translate society into a paradise through words:

> To the Ocean now I fly,
> And those happy climes that lie
> Where day never shuts his eye,
> Up in the broad fields of the sky:
> There I suck the liquid air
> All amidst the Gardens fair
> Of Hesperus.
>
> (976–82)

The poet constructs his own ascension into the paradise of Hesperus and the divine presence of Cupid and Psyche. The chaste union of these two, the god of love and the goddess of the soul, contrasts with the union between Bacchus and Circe; and the offspring of Cupid and Psyche, Youth and Joy, represent the perfection possible by their union.[18] Furthermore, the marriage of Cupid and Psyche also symbolizes the passionate intensity that infuses art within the disciplined control of form. Appropriately, the poet's virtuoso performance ends with a vision of the Platonic form of his art, and elevating that image to the highest point in heaven places his myth in the truth and permanence of the divine.

The last lines of the masque affirm the poet's importance in society; through his awareness of transcendent truth, earthly society can be brought closer to divine perfection. Absolutism, caught in a web of excess, actually retards the progression of society. In his radical transformation of the masque, Milton has boldly taken the irony out of epideictic poetry, making the form a celebration of the self-aware poet.

In the character of the poet, the casting is central to the meaning. In the fiction of the masque, the poet is constructed as the true moral teacher of the young aristocracy. His guidance and knowledge are responsible for the youths' return to the true path, for the Lady's rescue, and for the return of the whole group to their home. Symbolically, he effects the moral and spiritual growth of the political leaders, enabling them to reform English society. In a parallel relationship, Lawes is the teacher of the Bridgewater siblings, and the significance the Spirit accrues to himself reflects onto Lawes. The poet appropriates the myth created about poets, empowering himself as he manifests the myth's grounded reality.

Milton, as the creator of the whole masque, succeeds Lawes as the supreme director and archetypal poet. Whereas Lawes's character claimed the narrator's part, Milton narrates the narrator. In its literary form, his mimetic virtuosity has the potential to affect audiences for all time. The power of his verse immortalizes its creator, and the claims he makes for the poet, he ultimately makes for himself. When the Attendant Spirit says that he was sent "by quick command from Sovran Jove" (41), he means in one significant, obvious sense that he was sent by Milton, the "Sovran" of the masque. Thus Milton has brought the tension between poet and king that was covert in Jonsonian masques out of the closet, decisively subordinating the "magic" of the absolutist to the "magic" of the Christian poet.

This inquiry, rather than closing things off, has only made it clearer that the political issues were much more immediate for Milton in 1633 than critics like John Demaray[19] and Hunter allow, and thus the necessity of pursuing this train of thought further. The length of this essay permits only the suggestion that a fuller study of the agendas in Milton's masque might lead to an examination of Milton's vocational crisis at the time, his questioning about how his poetic talents fit into his political interests and ambitions. The presentation of contemporary England in the antimasque revolutionizes the genre, setting up the even more radical agenda that replaces the king with the poet as the true leader of the nation. In order to validate his own sense of importance in society, Milton proposes the complete restructuring of the social order. The message Milton sends is clear: if the aristocracy wants to lead England to a glorious, golden future, it must follow the only person who can find that future, the poet. To set these ideas in perspective, I would like to close by examining two critics who have argued that in his later poetry, Milton takes the position of the prophet directing his nation toward an apocalyptic future. The changes Milton makes to the masque genre suggest that he was constructing a myth that would allow him to take that position much earlier than either of them suggest.

Both William Kerrigan and Joseph A. Wittreich look at the tradition of prophecy that Milton inherited and molded to his own designs. Although neither one addresses *Comus* at any length, their arguments are so easily adapted to the poem that the neglect is surprising. After examining the transition of the meaning of the word *prophet* from the classical to the Christian, Kerrigan centers the debate over the proper office of this spiritual leader at the crux of the larger religious, economic, and political arguments between Puritans and Royalists.[20] Royalists, fearful of the revolutionary rhetoric inherent in most prophecy, tried to limit its scope to the interpretation of God's word and teaching. Their model was Christ the King leading the world on God's revealed path. By representing the king as the mediating link between God and the world, Royalists could argue that the divine right of kings was sanctioned by the New Testament. Kerrigan argues that Puritans countered by returning to the Old Testament, to Isaiah, Jeremiah, and Micah, for their model of the prophet—although Wittreich claims that the Christ of Revelation was the accepted paradigmatic prophet: a rebel who leads society to a new order by abolishing all orthodoxy.[21] In both cases, however, the resulting image is the same: the prophet was on the margin of society, an observer as well as an actor, who, in a divinely inspired vision, saw the immediate apocalyptic demise of the present institutions and pointed the way to a more righteous future. The prophet's job was to criticize the establishment, to pull down kings and begin the purging revolution. While Milton is not calling for mass destruction in *Comus*, he does suggest the complete restructuring of society. The political criticism in the masque is presented in the prophetic mode: the evolution of antimasque into main masque symbolizes the demise of the present establishment in the apocalyptic future. The future is revealed by the Attendant Spirit, and the audience is instructed to follow him. All through the masque, the Spirit has been the children's spiritual teacher, guiding them through the "perplex't paths of this drear wood" (37). By inheriting the wisdom of the ancients and augmenting it with his divine Christian vision, he is able to transform the world of the masque and return the children to their parents. Through the intricate fusion of fiction and reality, Milton draws this prophet-image to himself, creating a position that would authenticate his sense of divine calling. As the Attendant Spirit of real life, Milton is justified in attempting the compostition of his later epics and tragedy.

Although they are not aware of it, both Kerrigan and Wittreich provide good reasons why Milton's seminal statement about his prophetic stature should be made in the masque. Both critics analyze the structure of Milton's later poetry, concluding that the general pattern mirrors the paradigmatic prophetic mode. Kerrigan notes that prophetic epistemology was traditionally represented as a play unfolding in front of the prophet. He cites the seventeenth-century theorist, John Smith, who proposed that because of the symbolic nature of the prophetic vision and because the prophet was both a participant and an observer, the masque was the appropriate genre for the epistemological metaphor.[22] Furthermore, because the masque was designed to subsume all of history into its allegory and because it manipulated different levels of perspective, it again conformed to the theater of the mind metaphor. To this analysis, Wittreich adds that the mode of prophecy moves toward greater clarity as it relates successive visions.²³ These visions mirror each other, creating the sense of synchronic analogic structures, which duplicate the structure of the active prophetic mind and of the universe itself. The paradigmatic example of the prophetic genre was the Book of Revelation, a visionary poem that created a literary microcosm of the universe by interconnecting all poetic forms. This paradigm is virtually identical to the masque, which moves toward greater clarity through the succession of diachronically represented synchronic perspectives, connected by mirroring and analogy. In addition to operating at a primarily visual level, the masque subsumes many different poetic and artistic genres.

Both critics argue that Milton borrowed from the paradigms of the prophetic mode for all his poetry starting with *Lycidas*. Kerrigan claims that without his claim to prophecy, which was made through his appropriation of prophetic paradigms, *Paradise Lost* would be reduced to the empty verses of a swindler.²⁴ In another sense, without the prophetic element, the Lady or the Spirit's poetry would be reduced to the "barbarous dissonance" of Comus. The similarity between *Comus* and Kerrigan's theater of the mind metaphor on one hand and Wittreich's prophetic poetics from Revelation on the other is so striking that it is difficult to understand why they overlooked Milton's masque. From the argument I have developed in this essay, there is good reason to think that Milton was carefully drawing out the inherent prophetic paradigms of the masque in order to claim a position as a Puritan prophet. Both the rhetorical schemes and the argument trumpet the arrival of a man chosen by God to prepare a nation for its glorious ascent to divine favor.

Notes

This work could not have been completed without the help of Marshall Grossman. I am indebted to him for his insightful comments and encouragement through every step of the way.

1. Stephen Orgel, *The Jonsonian Masque* (Cambridge: Harvard University Press, 1965), 102–3.
2. Orgel, *Jonsonian Masque*, 186.
3. Ibid., 97.
4. Angus Fletcher, *The Transcendental Masque* (Ithaca: Cornell University Press, 1971), 19.
5. Fletcher, *Transcendental Masque*, 24.
6. Cedric Brown, *John Milton's "Aristocratic Entertainments"* (London: Cambridge University Press, 1985), 9.
7. Brown, *"Aristocratic Entertainments,"* 169–70.

8. David Norbrook, "The Reformation of the Masque," *The Court Masque*, ed. David Lindley (Oxford: Manchester University Press, 1984), 94–110.

9. Michael Wilding, *Dragon's Teeth* (Oxford: The Clarendon Press, 1987), chapter 3.

10. Wilding, *Dragon's Teeth*, 67.

11. John Milton, *Comus, John Milton: Complete Poems and Major Prose*, ed. Merritt Y. Hughes (New York: Odyssey Press, 1957). All references to Milton's poetry are to this edition and are cited parenthetically in the text.

12. Milton's concept of chastity has caused more controversy than any other idea in the masque. Some, like E. M. W. Tillyard in *Milton* (London: Chatto and Windus, 1946), William Hunter in *Milton's "Comus": Family Piece* (New York: Whitston, 1983), and Edward Tayler in *Milton's Poetry: Its Development in Time* (Pittsburgh: Duquesne University Press, 1979) trace chastity back to biography. Others, like Malcolme Ross in *Poetry and Dogma* (New Brunswick, N.J.: Rutgers University Press, 1954), are shocked by what they read as a degradation of 1 Corinthians 13's triad—faith, hope, and charity—and think chastity is the masque's major flaw. Still others complain that the portrayal of chastity as protective is ridiculously idealistic (Hunter, *Milton's "Comus,"* 1–2). In the past twenty years, the infamous Castlehaven scandal has become the standard context for interpreting the use and meaning of chastity (see Barbara Breasted, "*Comus* and the Castlehaven Scandal," *Milton Studies* 3 [1971]: 201–24; Leah Marcus, "Justice for Margery Evans," *Milton and the Idea of Woman*, ed. Julia Walker [Chicago: University of Illinois Press, 1988], 66–85; also Hunter, *Milton's "Comus,"* 29ff, and Brown, *"Aristocratic Entertainment,"* who thinks that Milton focuses on chastity not only because he wanted to remind the audience of the earlier scandal, but also because it would dramatize the biblical readings for Michaelmas day [on which day *Comus* was shown] and maintain the pastoral conventions). John Creaser challenges this context in "Milton's *Comus*: The Irrelevance of the Castlehaven Scandal," *Milton Quarterly* 21 (1987): 24–34, claiming that it would have been tactless of Milton to make any overt references to the scandal. Creaser, like both Fletcher and Norbrook, interprets chastity as representative of individual willpower, an important aspect of Puritan ideology. Fletcher also sees an echo of Spenser's Britomart. While I side with Fletcher, Norbrook, and Creaser in this debate, my own reading broadens the meaning of chastity to include poetic as well as moral temperance.

13. I disagree with Wilding's reading of "even proportion" (773) as meaning an "equal distribution of wealth" (58–59). I think that the Lady's speech echoes Aristotle's concept of justice, and thus her ideology is meritocratic rather than, as Wilding suggests, leveling.

14. It might be argued that since the king would not have been present it would have been pointless to follow the traditional practice of making reference to him as the driving force in the masque. But reference to the king was the substance, the raison d'être, of the masque, so it would have been considered highly disturbing to completely discard this important gesture. Since Bridgewater was the king's political stand-in, in the Welsh highlands, it would not have been inappropriate for him to act as the king's symbolic stand-in in the masque—at least not as inappropriate as replacing the royal figure with the poet.

15. In lines 82–91, the Attendant Spirit adopts the disguise of a shepherd-poet. In the lines mentioned, there is a reference comparing the character the Attendant Spirit adopts to Orpheus. See Hughes, *Complete Poems*, 86n; see also Brown, *"Aristocratic Entertainments,"* 114. The reference creates a typological relationship between Orpheus and the Attendant Spirit, and since Lawes, a superior musician himself, plays

the part of the Attendant Spirit, the mythogenic genealogy is grounded in the real world of Lord Bridgewater's court.

16. It would be interesting to explore the ramifications of Milton's metaphor "root-bound" (662) in the context of such Renaissance poetry as Jonson's "To Penshurst," Lanyer's "Cooke-ham," and Marvell's "Upon Appleton House" where trees symbolize the aristocracy. If Milton's metaphor plays on this conventional analogy, then being "root-bound" might signify the hold absolutism has over even those aristocrats who can perceive the hypocrisy and immorality of their culture. Comus's very existence binds these aristocrats to an ideology and to a method of action that they cannot break out of even though they may be able to resist full participation.

17. Brown, *"Aristocratic Entertainment,"* and Hunter, *"Milton's Comus,"* both claim that the Bridgewater Manuscript used as the performance script was considerably changed from what Milton submitted in the Trinity Manuscript. They muse that evidently someone felt that the performance should emphasize the aristocratic performers more than the submitted version did. Both critics interpret the changes as signs of Milton's conservative politics in 1634. I argue that it is more logically consistent to see the changes imposed on Milton's submission as a sign that his aristocratic patrons were disturbed by the radical diminishment of their stature in the masque. For Milton, who changed things back to the way they were in the Trinity and even augmented some of the radical statements in the 1637 edition, the reduction of aristocratic involvement in the main masque allowed the poet to dominate, and this is more consistent with what I take to be his general theme.

18. The union of Bacchus and Circe produced Comus.

19. John Demaray, *Milton and the Masque Tradition: The Early Poems, "Arcades," and "Comus"* (Cambridge: Harvard University Press, 1968).

20. William Kerrigan, *The Prophetic Milton* (Charlottesville: University Press of Virginia, 1974), 88–112.

21. Joseph A. Wittreich, *Visionary Poetics: Milton's Tradition and His Legacy* (San Marino, Calif.: Huntington Library, 1979), 48.

22. Kerrigan, *Prophetic Milton*, 117–18.

23. Wittreich, *Visionary Poetics*, 32–39.

24. Kerrigan, *Prophetic Milton*, 187.

Milton's Vergilian Epigraphs of 1637 and 1645

NATALIE JOY WOODALL

The title page of *A Mask Presented at Ludlow Castle*, published anonymously in 1637, contains an epigraph (presumably supplied by Milton) that was adapted from Vergil's *Eclogus* 2: "Eheu quid volui misero mihi! floribus austrum [/] Perditus."[1] Milton removed this epigraph when he published a volume of his poetry in 1645, and added lines excerpted from Vergil's *Eclogus* 7. The new epigraph, which appeared on the title page of *Poems of Mr. John Milton,* implies a change in philosophy. Though many scholars have commented upon these two epigraphs, no complete analysis of their content and context has been undertaken.[2] I propose that Milton's use of the Vergilian adaptations illustrates his increasing abhorrence of Greek and Roman mythological characters, an abhorrence more clearly and more fully expressed in *Paradise Lost* and *Paradise Regained*.

Because Vergil's *Eclogi* are pastoral poems, immediately a similarity of subject matter between them and *A Mask* can be assumed, since the Stuart court masque regularly featured a pastoral theme, a convention to which Milton also was adhering.[3] Comus, the animal-headed antimasquers, the Attendant Spirit, and Sabrina all had counterparts in earlier masques and/or the pastoral tradition. It is not surprising that Milton should turn to Vergil's *Eclogi* to find an epigraph for his masque. The significance lies, rather, in the identification of the speaker and the context within which the adaptation is employed.

The pertinent lines in *Eclogus* 2 for the first epigraph are: "heu heu quid volui misero mihi? floribus Austrum / perditus et liquidis immisi fontibus apros" (58–59).[4] A literal translation of the first sentence reads: "Alas, alas, what have I wished for miserable me?"[5] The Romans had few punctuation marks, but the interrogative pronoun *quid* clearly indicates that a question is being asked in the first line. The speaker is Corydon, a shepherd who has been "jilted" by his lover, Alexis. The subject of the second sentence continues to be "I," that is, Corydon, shown by the ending on the verb, *immisi*. The masculine participle *perditus*, used adjectivally, modifies the subject and a literal translation is: "I, the lost one, have sent the South Wind over the flowers and the wild boars into the liquid fountains."

Milton emended "heu heu" to "Eheu," a perfectly admissible alteration, except that no longer is this Vergilian poetry. The dactylic hexameter line, used in the *Eclogi*, requires that each line begin with a long syllable. Milton also altered the punctuation so that the first sentence now reads: "Alas[!] what I have wished for miserable me!" The question has become an exclamation. Vergil's *perditus* in the second sentence is clearly a participle modifying the implied subject. Because Milton omits a verb for the second sentence, the reader cannot tell whether *Perditus* is first or third person, but can tell only that *Perditus* is male and singular.

While *perditus* is merely a participle for Vergil, in Milton's text it is altogether possible that *Perditus* is someone's name or nickname. Throughout *Eclogus* 2, Corydon laments his rejection by Alexis. The tone of the poem is that of despair, and Corydon's allusions to the South Wind and the wild boars have been called "proverbs for bringing misery and disappointment on yourself by your own fault or carelessness."[6] In other words, his love for Alexis has so deluded him that he has not noticed the havoc wrought on his pastures by the scirocco, a hot wind that blows in the summer. Likewise, the water in his springs has been made unfit for the sheep to drink by the wild boars that wallow there. Milton's omission of a verb makes it impossible to determine with certitude whether *Perditus* stands in apposition to a verb in the first person or whether the term is the subject of a third person verb. In both cases, nevertheless, *Perditus* has allowed the South Wind to do something to the flowers. The resulting vagueness prompts speculation about the speaker "I" of the first sentence and his possible identification with *Perditus* of the fragment. If the subject of the verb and *Perditus* are the same character, which figures connected with the masque might be identified as *Perditus*?

A popular theory is that Milton alludes to himself. Hanford, for example, says: "A motto, which Milton must himself have chosen, repeats the old deprecation of criticism."[7] Tillyard thinks Milton was "peculiarly conscious of the imperfections of *Comus*" and "would hardly have expressed his fear of public opinion had he felt satisfied with what he had written."[8] Bush's opinion is similar: "Milton must of course have agreed to publication. He must also have chosen the motto (from Virgil's second eclogue), which expressed a perfectionist's reluctance to appear in public before he felt ripe."[9] Finally, Allen comments: "We have failed to notice the apologetic testimony of the Latin motto, or of the variants between the printed poem and the manuscripts which reflect Milton's own dissatisfaction with the work."[10]

If Milton were unhappy with his masque, it is hard to understand why he would agree to its publication. It is rather to be presumed that the masque was well received because Lawes had so many requests for copies of the text. His decision to publish the masque to avoid the necessity for producing more handwritten copies is evidence for this conclusion. As William Riley Parker has remarked, Milton may have hesitated to attach his name to the masque because he desired to avoid further conflict with his father, to whom he had recently written *Ad Patrem* to justify has plan to be a poet rather than a clergyman. Commenting on the epigraph, Parker points out the problem existing between its message and Milton's design for his life: "the quotation, in context, means that the shepherd accuses himself of neglecting his proper business. Still, an ambiguity remains: the pastoral poet who penned the words quoted was eventually to write an epic."[11] According to Parker, Milton was not "neglecting his proper business" by writing *A Mask*. He was actually carrying out his duties in an admirable fashion. In order to become a poet, and thereby to serve God, it was necessary to write and to be published.

John T. Shawcross who has examined the *Epitaphium Damonis* for evidence of homoeroticism with regard to Milton's relationship with Charles Diodati,[12] theorizes that Milton refers to this relationship with Diodati in the epigraph at the beginning of *A Mask*. According to Shawcross, Milton, "the Lady of Christ's College," saw himself as Corydon and Diodati as Alexis. This view posits that Diodati was Milton's counterpart, "one whose sexual life cannot be described but whose rough personality outlines—his excesses, his fickleness in friendship, his sensual nature, his drifting life—would not deny a rather promiscuous homosexuality."[13] Shawcross, who reads Milton's epigraph as identical to Vergil's text, thinks the epigraph in *A Mask* is "Milton's firm farewell to his former liaison with Diodati," but he is unwilling to label Milton a homosexual, saying that his homoeroticism was on the "fringes . . . through religious and ideological repressions of 'natural' attitudes towards sex, highmindedness, and 'female' qualities of appearance, interests, and abilities."[14] Since it is impossible to determine the possible homoeroticism of *Epitaphium Damonis* without firmer evidence as to the sexual orientation of Diodati and more accurate information about his relationship with Milton, Shawcross's use of the epigraph to justify the homoeroticism of *Epitaphium Damonis* is inconclusive.

More recently, Gregory Bredbeck has based his assertive interpretation of *A Mask*[15] on the work of Barbara Breasted and Leah Marcus, both of whom have investigated the sexual scandal associated with the Bridgewater family.[16] He offers no translation of the original Vergilian motto, but uses *it* rather than the Miltonic adaptation as the text for his interpretation, thereby making his conclusion suspect:

> Just a year earlier a nobleman had "made wretched the flower" of a young woman's virginity. Moreover, Bridgewater's relative, Touchet, had managed to "sully the water" of the family lineage through a display of "paederastice" that became memorialized in a series of broadsides."[17]

Bredbeck relies on the theory that Milton's supposed allusions to the Castlehaven scandal in 1634 were repeated in 1637, but his idea, like Shawcross's, is weakened by a failure to base it on the Miltonic adaptation. It cannot be assumed that Milton's text is to be read as identical to the Vergilian, only that Milton had some reason for *not* employing it in its entirety.

Efforts to identify Milton as the speaker of the epigraph, based on modesty or timidity, seem, therefore, to have failed. Lawes's desire to have *A Mask* printed to avoid further handcopying makes it fairly clear that such a fear was unfounded. We might also point to the *Ad Patrem* in which Milton openly expresses his choice of vocation:

> When I too return to my native Olympus, and when
> the changeless ages of eternity stretch forever
> before me, I shall go through the temples of heaven
> crowned with gold, accompanying my sweet songs with
> the gentle beat of the plectrum, wherewith the stars and
> the arch of heaven shall resound.[18]

The poet who sees himself wreathed in gold wandering through Heaven and who asserts that the universe itself will resound with his songs has a high opinion of his talent. The expression of such sentiment must be considered when trying to identify Milton as *Perditus*. In point of fact, he is not lost in any sense of the word. Attempts to locate homoerotic innuendo in the epigraph also lack credibility because the critics base their argument on the Vergilian text instead of the Miltonic.

If we allow for the possibility that Milton is not *Perditus*, based on the foregoing discussion, what other characters can be considered? One "lost" person is the Lady, who has become separated from her brothers in the deep woods as they travel to their new home. Lost in the literal sense of the word, she is subsequently kidnapped by Comus and taken to his palace where the seduction scene occurs. Nevertheless, she cannot be considered "perdit*us*" because she is a woman and, more importantly, because she is ultimately found and restored to her parents.

The only other candidate is Comus himself. In contrast to the Lady, Comus is emotionally or morally "lost" at the end of the masque. And, like the rest of the Vergilian excerpt, he disappears, having failed in his attempt to seduce her. The incomplete second part of the motto "floribus austrum [/] Perditus" may allude to Comus's emotional state as a result of having to abandon the Lady whom he has vowed to make his queen (264–65). Neither conquered nor destroyed when the brothers and the Attendant Spirit dash onto the scene, he simply vanishes. Well drawn, Comus possesses an impressive genealogy created for him by Milton, who makes him the son of Bacchus and Circe (46–59). He exudes a persuasive, genial personality. Even as he tempts the Lady, he realizes her superior goodness and admires her for it. Selfish and intemperate, he still is not the evil being his ultimate "lost" successor, Satan, will be. The alteration of the Vergilian text in the first sentence can be read as Comus's reflection on his failed plan to seduce the Lady, and "What I have wished for myself" may signify unhappiness and a lack of fulfillment. He calls himself *Perditus*, but so great is his grief that he is literally unable to finish the second sentence, actually punning on his nickname. Comus's "lostness" may therefore be associated with the lovesickness Corydon exhibits in *Eclogus* 2. As Corydon philosophically consoles himself at the conclusion of the poem, so Comus lives to "find another lover," since Milton tolerantly allows him to escape the brothers and the Attendant Spirit. Nevertheless, if nothing more serious than an emotional crisis resulting from a failed love affair is implied here, why did Milton delete the epigraph from the masque in 1645? The answer to that question requires an examination of the replacement epigraph.

The second epigraph has received less critical attention than the first. Taken from Vergil's *Eclogus* 7, it appeared on the title page along with Milton's name.[19] In Vergil's text, the shepherd Thyrsis speaks about a fellow shepherd named Codrus: "aut, si ultra placitum laudarit, baccare frontem cingite, ne vati noceat mala lingua futuro" (27–28). A literal translation is: "Or, if he [Codrus] praises beyond what is pleasing, gird the forehead with *baccar* so that his evil tongue may not harm the future prophet." While Thyrsis does not say "my forehead," his meaning is clarified from reading the previous lines. Thyrsis alleges that *too much* praise may actually be harmful,[20] and wreathing the head with *baccar* will ward off evil.[21] Milton's adaptation provides an interesting variation on the original: "Baccare frontem / Cingite, ne vati noceat mala lingua futuro."[22] The emended text reads, "Gird the brow with *baccar*, so that an evil tongue may not harm the future prophet." Shawcross suggests that the second epigraph, like the first, is to be interpreted as identical to the Vergilian original: "Thyrsis (Milton) asks to be wreathed with foxglove to ward off such excessive (envious) praise."[23] No longer, however, does the speaker suggest that too much praise too soon is harmful. He still demands that his head be surrounded with *baccar* to ward off an "evil tongue," but the implication now is that the evil tongue will somehow harm the poet who therefore needs protection. The temptation is to conclude, based on the fact that this epigraph preceded Milton's first collection of poetry, that he feared adverse criticism. Nevertheless, if Milton were worried about negative comments, he might have added the second epigraph to the title page while retaining the first at the beginning of the masque. Its removal leads to speculation that a close connection exists between the two actions and that events occurring between 1637 and 1645 inspired Milton to make these textual changes.

During the years in question Milton was pursuing a heavy schedule of study, particularly in the areas of religion and history.[24] Despite his decision not to enter the clergy, he considered himself dedicated to God, and he believed his scholarly endeavors would somehow serve the Almighty.[25] He composed only three poems at this time, *Lycidas*, *Epitaphium Damonis*, and a sonnet. His notebook shows that in 1640 he was planning a tragedy whose subject was "paradise lost." The political and religious upheavals occurring in the early 1640s turned Milton into a pamphleteer, and within the space of a year, he wrote and published the five antiepiscopal tracts. While he published four anonymously, he did sign *The Reason of Church Government*, and later he would acknowledge *Areopagitica* and the second edition of *The Doctrine and Discipline of Divorce*. He was, as a result, no stranger to adverse criticism, for which reason it is difficult to believe the second epigraph is a deprecation against a negative response to his volume of poetry. Quite the opposite is true: Milton relished pitting his wits and scholarly background against his critics and was eminently qualified to defend himself from the barbs of unappreciative or uncomprehending readers.

Milton's use of *"vati . . . futuro"* has been interpreted to mean that he looked upon his efforts as juvenile, that he asked to be excused for publishing before he had achieved the stature of mature poet.[26] The evidence contained in previously published prose works and in *Epitaphium Damonis* that he had indeed reached poetic maturity makes this argument tenuous. The very fact that he was publishing this volume of poetry clearly indicated that he wanted his efforts to be taken seriously. Among its several translations, the term *vates* can mean both "prophet" and "bard" or "singer." Milton's notebook and his prose works prove that he long planned a *magnum opus*. Originally conceived of as an epic about Britain,[27] it evolved into the Fall of Adam and Eve. His penchant for punning makes it altogether possible that he had both meanings of *vates* in mind here. He "prophesied" the great work and he was its "future singer," in the sense that Vergil sang about Aeneas ("Arma virumque cano").

The problem of the prayer for deliverance from the evil tongue must now be addressed. The importance of the breadth and depth of Milton's religious studies between 1637 and 1645 should not be underestimated. It was commonly thought that Greek and Roman deities and mythological characters were the fallen angels with different names.[28] Milton's extensive research into antiquity and into religion seems to have convinced him of the veracity of that belief.[29] Horrified at discovering how much paganism had crept into Christian observances, he ultimately concluded that only the Bible could be relied upon to provide reliable information.[30] His prose works carefully recorded his progress from pagan writers such as Homer to the philosophers and then to religious thinkers.[31] Milton denied being deluded by pagan ideas but admitted that such delusion was altogether possible for the unwary. His education tract, for example, which lays out a curriculum of several years' duration, reserves many well-known classical writers until near the end of the student's career, as if to say that only then will so firm a moral foundation have been laid that corruption will be difficult if not impossible.[32] It is significant that *Epitaphium Damonis* was Milton's last pastoral, that is, pagan work, and by the time *Paradise Lost* was composed, classical allusions and similes generally were reserved for Satan and his ilk. One telling piece of evidence that Milton ultimately concluded that the pagan deities and creatures were evil is found in the invocation to Urania in book 7 of *Paradise Lost*.

After assuring the reader that Urania is not to be classified with the nine muses of Greek mythology (7.5–7), Milton expresses his fear that he will fall into error without her assistance (15–21). He comments that he has come upon "evil days" and is the object of "evil tongues" (26). He confesses gratefully that Urania visits him in his sleep or upon awakening, and he asks for her continued help in the composition of his poem, imploring her to find him a "fit audience ... though few" for his great effort (31). Lastly, he begs his muse:

> But drive far off the barbarous dissonance
> Of Bacchus and his Revellers, the Race
> Of that wild Rout that tore the Thracian bard
> In Rhodope, where Woods and Rocks had Ears
> To rapture, till the savage clamor drown'd

> Both Harp and Voice; nor could the muse defend
> Her Son. So fail not thou, who thee implores:
> For thou art Heavn'ly, shee an empty dream.
> (32–39)

In contrast to Milton's earlier, apparently tolerant attitude towards the forces personified by Bacchus, the satyrs, and other mythological creatures, he now consciously rejects them, fearful that these spirits of licentiousness and evil may destroy his talent as they destroyed Orpheus, thereby rendering him incapable of finishing his task. Contrasting Urania with Calliope, Orpheus's mother, Milton asserts that his muse is "Heavn'ly," that is, real, while Calliope is a figment of the imagination.

Further evidence is to be found in *Paradise Regained*. In the invocation, Milton asks for inspiration to sing "of deeds / Above Heroic" (1.14–15). Throughout the poem, classical allusions are routinely assigned a negative connotation. For example, conquerors

> Then swell with pride, and must be titl'd Gods,
> Great Benefactors of mankind, Deliverers,
> Worship't with Temple, Priest, and Sacrifice?
> One is the Son of Jove, of Mars the other.
> (3.81–84)

A third example is the banquet scene, wherein Satan tries to make Jesus a character from classical mythology by inviting him to partake of the food served by nymphs, naiads (2.355), "Ladies of th' Hesperides" (357), and young men "of fairer hue / Than Ganymede or Hylas" (352–53). In fact, all of Satan's temptations allude to the heroic, as is seen by his recapitulation:

> Since neither wealth, nor honor, arms nor arts,
> Kingdom nor Empire pleases thee, nor aught
> By me propos'd in life contemplative,
> Or active, tended on by glory, or fame,
> What dost thou in this World?
> (4.368–72)

Jesus' refusal of all things "heroic" sets him apart from Satan and his followers and graphically illustrates Milton's abhorrence of the corruptions that had become part of Christian theology.

Bredbeck agrees that Satan attempts to make Jesus an "epic hero" but goes farther by trying to associate this scene with homoeroticism:

Satan's response [to Belial's suggestion], however, is revealed to be only a rejection of Belial's *limited* notion of sexual temptations, for when the banquet appears it is attended by nymphs, naiads, ladies of the Hesperides and "Tall stripling youths rich clad, of fairer hue / Than Ganymede or Hylas." Through the manipulation of vernacular meaning and pastoral tradition, the temptation invokes a homoerotic component discordant with typical commentaries on the temptation.[33]

The fact is that Satan's recapitulation, quoted above, makes no mention of any sexual temptation at all. Indeed, such allusion, whether overt or covert, would be considered entirely inappropriate, even heretical, to Milton. The care he took to divorce Jesus even from the possibility of heterosexual love indicates his unwillingness to venture into such a sensitive area as the Savior as a sexual being.

Milton's dread or hatred of paganism that developed between 1637 and 1645 and that is revealed in his prose writings of that period may account, therefore, for the decision to remove the first epigraph from *A Mask*. According to this reading, Comus and his animal-shaped antimasquers in 1637 are the precursors of "Bacchus and his Revelers" from whom Milton says, as early as 1645, he needs protection. While calling attention to a lovesick satyr at the beginning of a work whose alleged subject was chastity might be deemed inappropriate, it would, more importantly, be theologically incorrect to a scholar whose research led him to conclude that only the Bible afforded ultimate truth. In the case of *A Mask*, Milton could easily correct his earlier "error" by omitting the epigraph when republishing the text in 1645. The evil tongues to which Milton refers in the early lines of book 7 of *Paradise Lost* are the same ones from which he sought protection in the second epigraph to *A Mask*. Despite the best of efforts, the "demons" assailed the *vates*, causing him to renew the plea first evoked in the 1645 epigraph. Now, however, Milton openly called upon Heaven for assistance, trusting neither to *baccar* nor to anything else not biblically verifiable.

Notes

1. John Milton, *A Mask Presented at Ludlow Castle, John Milton: Complete Poems and Major Prose*, ed. Merritt Y. Hughes (New York: Odyssey Press, 1957). Unless otherwise noted, all references to Milton's prose and poetry are to this edition and are cited parenthetically in the text. The epigraph appears on page 86. A facsimile of the title page of the 1637 edition appears in Geoffrey and Margaret Bullough, *Milton's Dramatic Poems* (London: Athlone Press, 1967), 68.

2. See Don Cameron Allen, *The Harmonious Vision: Studies in Milton's Poetry* (Baltimore: Johns Hopkins University Press, 1954), 31; Douglas Bush, *John Milton:*

A *Sketch of His Life and Writings* (New York: Macmillan, 1964), 49; James Holly Hanford, *John Milton, Englishman* (New York: Crown Publishers, 1949), 65; David Masson, *Life of John Milton* (Gloucester, Mass.: Peter Smith, 1877–96; reprint 1965), 1:640–41; William Riley Parker, *Milton: A Biography* (Oxford: Clarendon Press, 1968), 1:143; E. M. W. Tillyard, *Milton* (London: Chatto and Windus, 1946), 71.

3. See John Demaray, *Milton and the Masque Tradition: The Early Poems, "Arcades," and "Comus"* (Cambridge: Harvard University Press, 1968), 2–3.

4. Vergil, *Eclogus 2, Vergili Maronis Opera*, ed. A. Sidgwick (Cambridge: Cambridge University Press, 1927), 1:81. All references to Vergil's poetry are to this edition and are cited parenthetically in the text.

5. Critics' attempts to translate Milton's version of the epigraph provide interesting reading. Tillyard, for example, offers "Alas, what was I thinking of; unhappy man, I have let the wind blow on my flowers" (*Milton*, 71). Bush translates it quite differently: "Alas what wretchedness I have wished upon myself! In my madness I have let in the south wind upon my flowers" (*John Milton*, 49). Peter Mendes, *John Milton: Odes, Pastorals, Masques*, ed. J. B. Broadbent (Cambridge: Cambridge University Press, 1975), proposes: "O what have I done to myself ? I have loosed the sirocco [sic] onto my flowers" (121). James Holly Hanford, *A Milton Handbook* (New York: Appleton-Century-Crofts, 1961), renders a complete translation of the Vergilian passage: "What, alas, did I purpose to my own destruction, wretched man that I am, when I let the south wind blow upon my flowers and the wild boars trample my clear springs" (165). Masson also translates the entire passage: "Alas! what have I chosen for my miserable self ? Undone, I have let the south-wind in among my flowers" (*Life*, 640–41). Parker makes a slight alteration to Masson's translation: "Alas! what have I chosen for my miserable self ? Ruined, I have let the south wind in among my flowers" (*Biography*, 1:142–43). John T. Shawcross, "Milton and Diodati: An Essay in Psychodynamic Meaning," *Milton Studies* 7 (1975), renders the passage thus: "Alas! What have I brought on my miserable self ? I have let the south wind ruin my flowers" (153).

6. A. Sidgwick, ed., *Vergili Maronis Opera* (Cambridge: Cambridge University Press, 1927), *Eclogus* 2, 1:81,12n, lines 58–59.

7. Hanford, *Englishman*, 65.

8. Tillyard, *Milton*, 71–72.

9. Bush, *John Milton*, 49.

10. Allen, *Harmonious*, 31.

11. Parker, *Biography*, 1:143. See also Christopher Hill, *Milton and the English Revolution* (New York: Viking Press, 1977), 46. Hill sharply disagrees with Parker on the ground that no "real evidence of paternal hostility" exists. Hill thinks some sort of disagreement between Milton and the Egertons between 1634 and 1637 contributed to his decision not to attach his name to the masque, but as Hill himself says, "a great many bricks have to be made with very little straw."

12. Shawcross, "Milton and Diodati," 127–63.

13. Ibid., 152. Curiously, Gregory Bredbeck's discussion (see below) overlooks the homoerotic suggestion afforded by Milton's nickname, "The Lady of Christ's College."

14. Shawcross, "Milton and Diodati," 153.

15. Gregory Bredbeck, *Sodomy and Interpretation: Marlowe to Milton* (Ithaca: Cornell University Press, 1991), 210–13.

16. See Barbara Breasted, "*Comus* and the Castlehaven Scandal," *Milton Studies* 3 (1971): 201–24; see also Leah Marcus, "The Milieu of Milton's *Comus*: Judicial Reform at Ludlow and the Problem of Sexual Assault," *Criticism* 25 (1983): 293–327.

17. Bredbeck, *Interpretation*, 212. Bredbeck's history is inaccurate. According to

Leah Marcus, the assault on Margery Evans occurred in 1631, fully six years before *A Mask* was published. Further, Touchet, Earl of Castlehaven, was a relative only in the most tenuous way. Bridgewater's wife was the sister of Lady Castlehaven.

18. John Milton, "To My Father," *John Milton*, ed. Stephen Orgel and Jonathan Goldberg (Oxford: Oxford University Press, 1991), lines 30–34.

19. Bredbeck seems not to realize that Milton made an alteration in 1645:

> This space is highlighted in the printed editions of the mask, for after the dedication to The Right Honorable John, Earl of Bridgewater, in the 1637 edition, the text inserts the quotation Eheu quid volui mihi [sic]! floribus austrum Perditus, *and the 1645 text follows suit.*" (*Interpretation*, 211; emphasis mine)

20. Thyrsis's entire remark makes clear whose head is to be wreathed:

> Pastores, hedera crescentem ornate poetam,
> Arcades, invidia rumpantur ut ilia Codro;
> Aut, si ultra placitum laudarit, baccare frontem
> Cingite, ne vati noceat mala lingua futuro.
> (*Eclogus* 7, 25–28)

21. *Baccar* is an apparently unidentifiable plant. The term, which cannot be translated, has been variously, and incorrectly, rendered as "ivy" and "foxglove." Servius, quoted in the *Oxford Latin Dictionary*, says: *"baccar herba est, quae fascinum depellit"* ("*Baccar* is a plant which drives away evil").

22. A facsimile of the title page of the 1645 edition of *Poems of Mr. John Milton* appears in Milton, *Complete Poems*, 2.

23. Shawcross, "Milton and Diodati," 154.

24. Parker, *Biography*, 1:145.

25. See *The Reason of Church Government*, 666–67.

26. Parker, *Biography*, 1:290.

27. See *Epitaphium Damonis*, lines 161–78, where he discusses plans for his Arthurian epic.

28. Merritt Y. Hughes, ed., "Introduction," *John Milton: Complete Poems and Major Prose* (New York: Odyssey Press, 1957), 178, 183–84.

29. See *Paradise Regained*, 1.430–64.

30. See ibid., 4.331–64.

31. See *Reason of Church Government*, 668–69, and *Apology for Smectymnuus*, 693–95.

32. See *Of Education*, 636–37.

33. Bredbeck, *Interpretation*, 196–97.

"Nature Taught Art": The Topos of Art and Nature in *Paradise Regained*

PETER M. MCCLUSKEY

Of the "pleasant Grove" where the banquet scene of *Paradise Regained* occurs, Milton writes, "Nature's own work it seem'd (Nature taught Art)" (2.295).[1] This line plays upon a common topos of Renaissance epic poetry, the earthly paradise—a garden or bower—shaped by art imitating nature or by nature imitating art or by both imitating each other.[2] Despite the importance of the art-nature topos in the works of some of the poets who most influenced Milton—notably Ovid, Tasso, and Spenser—his reference to it in *Paradise Regained* 2.295 has attracted little critical attention.[3] Milton evokes the art-nature topos to create a parallel between the "pleasant Grove" (289) where the banquet temptation occurs and the earthly paradises of Tasso and Spenser where similar temptations take place. Yet his use of the topos goes beyond the Renaissance principle of *imitatio*, for Milton adapts the topos to meet the unusual needs of his brief epic.

In order to illustrate the tradition that Milton draws upon and how he manipulates it, I shall examine the art-nature topos as it appears both in the poems that influenced him and in his other works as well. After this necessary survey of background materials, I shall consider how and why Milton uses the art-nature topos in *Paradise Regained* 2.295; also, I shall assess the validity of some earlier interpretations of this line.

The Tradition of the Art-Nature Topos

The association of art and nature with the earthly paradise begins with Ovid. In book 3 of the *Metamorphoses* he describes Gargaphie, Diana's sacred grove, as formed not by art but by nature imitating art:

> arte laboratum nulla: simulaverat artem
> ingenio natura suo.
>
> > (3.158–59)
>
> Formed by no art; with its own talent,
> Nature copied Art.[4]

These lines cleverly reverse Aristotle's statement in *De Mundo* that art imitates nature,[5] and the wit of Ovid's conceit perhaps explains why this passage was admired and imitated by such Renaissance poets as Tasso and Spenser.

Although Milton intimately knew the *Metamorphoses* in Latin, it is likely that he also knew the English translations of both Arthur Golding (1567) and George Sandys (1621).[6] Golding embellishes his translation for the sake of his heptameter, omitting the key words *art* and *nature*: "Not made by hand nor mans devise, and yet no man alive, / A trimmer piece of worke than that could for his life contrive."[7] Although Golding's translation does not accurately express the nature-imitates-art idea, Sandys's version does:"Not wrought by hands; there Nature witty Art / Did counterfeit."[8] This translation provides a good idea of how Milton himself might have rendered these lines in English.

Another of Milton's influences containing the art-nature topos is Torquato Tasso's Christian epic, *La Gerusalemme Liberata* (1580). Although Milton had read the poem in its original Italian, he also knew and sometimes imitated Fairfax's *Godfrey of Bulloigne or The Recoverie of Jerusalem* (1600).[9] In the following passage from Fairfax's translation, Tasso evokes the art-nature topos in his description of Armida's palace:

> So with the rude the polish'd mingled was,
> > That natural seem'd all, and every part
> Nature would craft in counterfeiting pass,
> > And imitate her imitator art.[10]

As in Ovid, nature imitates art; Armida's palace is a place of exquisite natural beauty, yet the imitation of art suggests that something is unnatural about the palace. In fact, Armida's art imitates nature so well that it appears that nature is imitating art. According to A. Bartlett Giamatti, Tasso contrasts Armida's palace with the City (Jerusalem) to symbolize the conflict between duty and the pursuit of personal comfort and satisfaction, that is, the struggle between duty and love.[11] "The City," Giamatti writes, "is the way to eventual inner redemption through physical conflict, Nature the way to immediate inner peace through the avoidance of physical struggle."[12] Although the artificial garden is beautiful, it symbolizes moral shortcomings and false spiritual values.[13]

Spenser makes extensive use of the art-nature topos found in Ovid and Tasso when describing landscapes in *The Faerie Queene* (1590). Anthony E. Friedmann identifies ten separate instances in the epic in which Spenser adapts or imitates the description of Gargaphie.[14] Furthermore, as Robert M. Durling observes, Spenser often imitates, usually modifying, Tasso's treatment of the art-nature topos in Armida's palace.[15]

The following description of the Bower of Bliss, a passage that Walter MacKellar suggests "Milton may have remembered" when he wrote "Nature's own work it seem'd (Nature taught Art),"[16] contains echoes of both Ovid and Tasso:

> One would haue thought, (so cunningly, the rude,
> And scorned parts were mingled with the fine,)
> That nature had for wantonesse ensude
> Art, and that Art at nature did repine;
> So striuing each th' other to vndermine,
> Each did the others worke more beautifie;
> So diff'ring both in willes, agreed in fine:
> So all agreed through sweete diuersitie,
> This Gardin to adorne with all varietie.[17]

Here art and nature struggle against each other, but the results are nevertheless pleasing to the eye. Spenser's debt to Tasso (as well as Fairfax's to Spenser) is evident in the first two lines (the key words *rude* and *mingled* also appear in Fairfax); but, as Durling points out:

> While Armida's garden is entirely factitious, the effect of her magic is to make it seem entirely natural.... Nature seems to have grown into the patterns of landscape gardening of her own accord. In the Bower of Bliss, however, the actual craft of gardening, not magic, is seen working against the actual forces of nature.[18]

The effect of this struggle between art and nature in the Bower of Bliss is "to corrupt men by making it seem that nature itself is wanton."[19] Armida's palace corrupts by pretending to be what the Garden of Adonis actually is, a gift from nature.

The Garden of Adonis, "So faire a place, as nature can devize" (3.6.29), resembles Gargaphie in that it shapes itself through nature's generosity:

> And in the thickest couert of that shade,
> There was a pleasant arbour, not by art,
> But of the trees owne inclination made.
>
> (3.6.44)

Friedmann notes that this passage draws upon two ideas from Ovid's description of Diana's grove: "First, the arbor is a secret, inner shady nook ('antrum nemorale recessu'), and second, there is no art ('arte laboratum nulla'), but there is the appearance of art in nature ('simulaverat artem / ingenio natura suo')."[20]

In *The Allegory of Love* C. S. Lewis states that one of the primary differences between the Bower of Bliss and the Garden of Adonis is Spenser's handling of the art-nature topos: "[Spenser] distinguishes the good and evil paradises by a skilful contrast between nature and art."[21] Spenser repeatedly emphasizes the presence of art in the Bower of Bliss:

> [A]rt striuing to compaire
> With nature, did an Arber greene dispred,
> Framed of wanton Yvie, flouring faire.
>
> (2.6.29)

> they behold around
> A large and spacious plaine, on euery side
> Strowed with pleasauns, whose faire grassy ground
> Mantled with greene, and goodly beautified
> With all the ornaments of *Floraes* pride,
> Wherewith her mother Art, as halfe in scorne
> Of niggard Nature, like a pompous bride
> Did decke her, and too lauishly adorne.
>
> (2.12.50)

> some [grapes] were of burnisht gold,
> So made by art, to beautifie the rest.
>
> (2.12.55)

> The art, which all that wrought, appeared in no place.
>
> (2.12.58)

The antithesis between art and nature culminates in stanza 59 (quoted above), where the distinction blurs and the sterility of the artificial Bower becomes apparent.[22] According to Jean H. Hagstrum, "The bower is evil . . . not because all art is evil but because a work of art has here deceptively replaced nature."[23]

All of the above passages conceivably contributed to Milton's awareness of the art-nature topos. Because of the many occurrences of the topos cited (and doubtless others left uncited as well), it is difficult, if not impossible, to identify, as MacKellar does, a single source for the passage in *Paradise Regained*. Nevertheless, "Nature's own Work it seem'd" echoes Fairfax's, "natural seem'd all," but the parenthetical "Nature taught Art" is without an exact analogue and in fact may be Milton's own contribution to the tradition.

Milton on Art and Nature

In the preface to *The Art of Logic* (1672), Milton briefly considers the relationship between art and nature, and some of his comments may contribute to our understanding of his use of the art-nature topos. Milton explains that "those whose native abilities are active and strong" may omit the logic exercises that he provides, "For art is used for the purpose of aiding nature, not of hindering it; when it is employed too anxiously and too subtly, and especially when it is unnecessary, it blunts rather than sharpens" (7).[24] Milton regards God as the source of all arts: "[T]he primal mover of every art is God, the author of all wisdom" (11). To Milton, logic is an art because it mimics natural reason, "according to that common saying: Art imitates nature" (11).

Milton considers the purpose of any art as "the actual teaching of a useful thing" (13), a goal that cannot be reached "unless nature is adapted to receiving instruction" (15). He accepts the Aristotelian notion that art imitates nature; and he believes that if an art imitates nature for the purpose of "teaching a useful thing," then the imitation of nature is morally acceptable.

In his poetry, however, Milton usually refers to art pejoratively, and when he does make a distinction between art and nature, art invariably suffers. Milton mentions "th'shame of slow-endeavoring art" (9) in his sonnet "On Shakespeare." Comus "excels his Mother [Circe] at her mighty Art" (63) and calls his powers "mine Art" (149). In *Samson Agonistes*, Harapha believes that Samson's strength comes from "spells, and black enchantments, some Magician's Art" (1132–33), but Samson vehemently denies using "forbidden Arts" (1139).

Of the thirteen references to art in *Paradise Lost*, the word always has a negative connotation and frequently refers to Satan and his followers.[25] That Adam and Eve must actively tend their natural paradise is significant, for Milton wants to contrast the natural garden with the artificial paradise the demons build. As in Spenser, there is the same principle of nature being to art what life is to death, what fertility is to sterility, and what spirituality is to corruption.

"Nature's own work it seem'd (Nature taught Art)"

We may now consider how and why Milton evokes the topos of art and nature in *Paradise Regained*. As stated above, "Nature's own work it seem'd" echoes Fairfax's line "natural seem'd all," but "Nature taught Art" lacks an identifiable antecedent; nevertheless, the concatenation of the words *nature* and *art* has parallels in Ovid, Tasso, their English translators, Spenser, and Milton himself. That Milton evokes the art-nature topos in describing the "pleasant Grove" is not unusual, since this topos is, after all, a commonplace in epic poetry.

Yet Milton's use of the topos differs greatly from that of his fellow epic poets. Whereas nature copies art in Ovid, art copies nature in Tasso, and art and nature imitate each other in Spenser, Milton has nature teach art, thus transforming nature's role from the passive one of model to the active one of instructor. This reversal illustrates Milton's comments in *The Art of Logic* on the roles of art and nature: if the proper role of art is to aid nature and to teach useful things, which it does by imitating nature, then nature actually does teach art.

Still, the phrase "Nature taught Art" appearing after the statement that the grove *seemed* natural is puzzling, for readers must determine whether the grove is natural or only appears so. Milton uses the verb *seem* in his poetry as a synonym for *appears*, often to suggest the deceptive difference between appearances and reality.

Milton often employs the word when characters fail to discern the reality underlying deceptive appearances. Satan's first glimpse of Adam and Eve in *Paradise Lost* reveals

> Two of far nobler shape erect and tall,
> Godlike erect, with native Honor clad
> In naked Majesty *seem'd* Lords of all,
> And worthy *seem'd*, for in thir looks Divine
> The image of thir glorious Maker shone.
> (4.288–92; emphasis mine)

Despite seeming lords of all, Adam and Eve are merely caretakers of Paradise, and despite their divine appearance, they prove unworthy of their sacred charge.

Milton also uses the verb *seem* to show appearances intended to deceive. While describing Adam's and Eve's unashamed nakedness, Milton castigates "dishonest shame / Of Nature's works" (4.313–14):

> how have ye troubl'd all
> mankind
> With shows instead, mere shows of *seeming* pure,

> And banisht from man's life his happiest life,
> Simplicity and spotless innocence.
>
> (4.315–18; emphasis mine)

This hypocritical appearance of purity stems from an impurity in human nature resulting from the Fall, and the deception caused by this impurity transforms human happiness and innocence into guilt and shame.

Appearances, however, do not always deceive, and things sometimes are what they seem to be. Milton gives us no reason to suspect the accuracy of this description of Paradise: "so lovely seem'd / That Lantskip" (4.152–53). Likewise, in the statement that Adam and Eve are "Not equal, as thir sex not equal seem'd" (4.296), the word *seem'd* signifies an appearance Milton does not question. Furthermore, we should not doubt that while discussing "celestial Motions" with Raphael, Adam "by his count'nance seem'd / Ent'ring on studious thoughts abstruse" (8.39–40).

In *Paradise Regained* the word *seem* usually carries with it negative connotations. Satan, disguised as a shepherd, "seem'd" to search for a "stray Ewe" (1.315), and he displays his skepticism about Christ's divinity when he says that he "seem'st" to be the one called the "Son / Of God" (1.327, 329–30). Christ, however, recognizes Satan immediately: "I discern thee other than thou seem'st" (1.348). Later Satan fails to impress Christ with the sight of "Huge Cities and high tow'r'd, that well might seem / The seats of mightiest Monarchs" (3.261–62), for Christ serves the mightiest monarch of them all. Nor does Christ admire the oratory of Greece and Rome:

> The top of Eloquence, Statists indeed,
> And lovers of thir Country, as may seem;
> But herein to our Prophets far beneath.
>
> (4.354–56)

The word *seem* occurs several times following the climactic storm scene. Satan, who "glad would also seem" (4.441) that the storm had passed, tells Christ that the tempest was a sign:

> Like turbulencies in the affairs of men,
> Over whose heads they roar, and seem to point,
> They oft fore-signify and threaten ill.
>
> (4.462–64)

After dismissing the signs as "false portents" (491), Christ explains that he has refused Satan's "offer'd aid" because

> I accepting
> At least might *seem* to hold all power of thee,
> Ambitious spirit, and [you] wouldst be thought my
> God.
>
> (4.493–95; emphasis mine)

The word *seem* is important, for Christ cannot permit Satan even the appearance of victory over him.

Because Milton often uses the word *seem* to describe deceptive appearances, the line "Nature's own work it seem'd" invites readers to wonder whether the "pleasant Grove" actually is "Nature's own work," and the echo of Fairfax's "natural seem'd all" makes this invitation even more tempting. If the grove is artificial, the parenthetical clause "Nature taught Art" means that nature taught art so well that the artist's work seems (appears) natural. But if the grove is natural, this parenthetical statement means that nature's handiwork serves as an example to art. Without additional evidence, we are prevented from determining whether the grove is natural or diabolic in origin by the verb *seem* and the ambiguous statement "Nature taught Art."

Few critics address the question of the grove's origin. J. B. Broadbent mentions "the ambivalence of the 'woody scene,' a place which is both nature and art"[26] but does not state whether Satan creates the grove. Northrop Frye, identifying the ambiguous line "Nature's own work it seemed (Nature taught Art)" as "a vestigial survival of the Bower of Bliss, with its triumph of artifice over nature,"[27] offers no evidence to justify his assertion that art triumphs over nature in the "pleasant Grove." MacKellar, in his *Variorum Commentary*, admitting that the word *seem'd* suggests the contrary, says that the grove is natural because the lines following ("And to a Superstitious eye the Haunt / Of Wood Gods and Wood Nymphs" [2.296–97]) "indicate the circumstances in which the scene might be deceptive and evil."[28]

A. S. P. Woodhouse, whose reading MacKellar implicitly favors, believes that the grove is natural and that by admiring it, Christ demonstrates his ability to distinguish between natural beauty and artificial beauty (the banquet offered supposedly as nature's gift). "As in *Comus*," Woodhouse writes, "it is not beauty that is condemned, not natural beauty in its appointed place, but beauty in the service of evil, and specifically, in competition with obedience to God."[29]

Howard Schultz, whom MacKellar also quotes, offers an opposing view on the origin of the "pleasant Grove." Schultz states that the grove is false: "[Milton] tells us in almost as many words that Satan by art built it to look like nature's own work."[30] As evidence for his reading, he points out that the trees that form the grove are too tall for

Judea and that the birds that Christ hears from the hilltop must be singing impossibly loudly. Schultz suggests that the grove is a metaphor for a cathedral, with the banquet representing a service.[31] MacKellar dryly observes, "Of the validity of this unusual interpretation of the scene readers may judge for themselves."[32]

Schultz's argument, while ingenious, is ultimately unconvincing for several reasons. First, the grove, tall trees and all, is not as incongruous as he suggests, for Milton's wilderness clearly includes other natural groves; although Christ awakens on a "grassy Couch" in book 2 (282), Milton mentions "shady vale[s]" and tall trees—oaks and cedars—in book 1 (304–6) and "tallest Pines" and "Sturdiest Oaks" in book 4 (416–17). Second, Milton allows the possibility that the grove may be artificial, but he by no means says in as many words that it is unnatural. Third, Schultz's suggestion that the scene metaphorically represents a cathedral completely overlooks the analogues that the grove and banquet temptations have in Tasso, Spenser, and Fairfax. Although there may be hints of a cathedral in his description of the scene, Milton's primary interest lies in presenting his poem as a Christian epic, echoing and using the conventions of other Christian epics.

The question of whether the garden is natural remains to be answered. Because Milton himself does not directly say whether it is or not, we should consider a third possibility: the description is purposefully ambiguous. Had Milton employed an unambiguous form of the art-nature topos, one that clearly states whether the grove is natural or artificial, Christ's entrance to the grove would be problematic. If it were clear that Satan built the grove, then Christ either is deceived by Satan's handiwork or foresees the test he must face there. The first possibility is unacceptable for an obvious reason—Milton cannot permit Satan even a momentary triumph over Christ. The second possibility is unacceptable because Christ does not know why he is in the wilderness:

> And now by some strong motion I am led
> Into this Wilderness, to what intent
> I learn not yet; perhaps I need not know;
> For what concerns my knowledge God reveals.
> (1.290–93)

If the grove is natural, then Christ does not err in entering it "To rest at noon" (2.292), and Satan's appearance there would be analogous to his presence in Paradise, but Milton does not clearly state that the grove is in fact natural.

Milton wanted the banquet temptation to parallel the temptations that occur within the seductively beautiful bowers of Tasso and Spenser, so he employed a rhetorical commonplace associated with these earthly paradises, the topos of art and nature. Milton's suggestion that the grove only appears natural carries with it sinister connotations strengthening the association with Tasso and Spenser and foreshadows Satan's appearance. But because of the problems, both theological and motivational, with Christ's entering—deceived or otherwise—an artificial grove, Milton could only introduce the topos in such a way that it begs the question of the naturalness of the grove. Nevertheless, the ambiguity allows Milton to avoid the problem that Schultz himself avoids confronting, saying, "It may be a bit pedantic to wonder why Christ is deceived."[33] Milton deliberately clouds the question of whether the "pleasant Grove" is natural in order to use the topos without raising "pedantic" questions. His use of ambiguity to resolve this dilemma reveals both his technical ingenuity and his uncompromising concern for decorum.

Notes

I wish to thank Debora Shuger, Joseph Candido, and especially John Shawcross for their guidance in revising this essay.

1. John Milton, *Paradise Regained*, *John Milton: Complete Poems and Major Prose*, ed. Merritt Y. Hughes (New York: Odyssey Press, 1957). All references to Milton's poetry are to this edition and are cited parenthetically in the text.

2. See A. Bartlett Giamatti, *The Earthly Paradise and the Renaissance Epic* (Princeton: Princeton University Press, 1966) and C. S. Lewis, *The Allegory of Love* (Oxford: Oxford University Press, 1938), 324–30.

3. Most critics concerned with the banquet scene do not mention this line, and those who do either point out a parallel with *The Faerie Queene* 2.12.59 (Northrop Frye, "The Typology of *Paradise Regained*," *Modern Philology* 53 [1956]: 231; Walter MacKellar, ed. *Paradise Regained: A Variorum Commentary on the Poems of John Milton* [New York: Columbia University Press, 1975]) or discuss whether the grove is natural (Arnold Stein, *Heroic Knowledge* [Minnepolis: University of Minnesota Press, 1957]; Howard Schultz, "A Fairer Paradise? Some Recent Studies of *Paradise Regained*," *ELH* 32 [1965]; and A. S. P. Woodhouse, "Theme and Structure in *Paradise Regained*," *University of Toronto Quarterly* 25 [1955]); likewise, critics exploring Milton's use of the art-nature topos (Giamatti; Joseph E. Duncan, *Milton's Earthly Paradise: A Historical Study of Eden* [Minneapolis: University of Minnesota Press, 1972]; and Edward William Tayler, *Nature and Art in Renaissance Literature* [New York: Columbia University Press, 1964]) focus only on *Paradise Lost*.

4. Latin quotations from the *Metamorphoses* are from Frank Justus Miller, ed., *Metamorphoses*, 2 vols., The Loeb Classical Library (Cambridge: Harvard University Press, 1960–64); unless otherwise noted, English translations are my own.

5. Explaining that the universe is composed of contrary principles, Aristotle

observes, "The arts, too, apparently imitate nature in this respect" (*De Mundo*, trans. E. S. Forster, *The Works of Aristotle Translated into English* [Oxford: The Clarendon Press, 1931], 3:396b); Aristotle also mentions the saying when comparing the artificial process of boiling with the natural process of the "concoction" of food (*De Mundo*, 381b).

6. See David P. Harding, *Milton and the Renaissance Ovid*, Illinois Studies in Language and Literature, vol. 30, no. 4 (Urbana: University of Illinois Press, 1946) and Richard J. DuRocher, *Milton and Ovid* (Ithaca: Cornell University Press, 1985).

7. See *Shakespeare's Ovid*, ed. W. H. D. Rouse (London: Centaur Press, 1961), 3:184–85.

8. See *Ovid's "Metamorphoses" Englished: The Renaissance and the Gods* (New York: Garland Press, 1976), 84.

9. "By reading the Fairfax translation of *La Gerusalemme Liberata*, Milton grew interested in its author. He then came to know, probably before the time of his Italian trip, Tasso's masterpiece in the original [Italian]" (Ewald Pommrich, "Miltons Verhaltnis zu Torquato Tasso," [Halle: Erhardt Karras, 1902], 77 [my translation]).

10. See *Jerusalem Delivered*, ed. Roberto Weiss (Carbondale: Southern Illinois University Press, 1962), 26.10.1–4; Fairfax's translation in this edition closely follows the original:

> Stimi (si misto il culto e co 'l negletto)
> Sol naturali e gli ornamenti e i siti.
> Di natura arte par, che per diletto
> L'imitatrice sua scherzando imiti.
> (Torquato Tasso, *La Gerusalemme Liberata*
> [Firenze: Nemi, n.d.], 26.10.1–4).

11. Giamatti, *Earthly Paradise*, 183.
12. Ibid., 184.
13. Ibid., 189.
14. Anthony E. Friedmann, "The Diana-Acteon Episode in Ovid's *Metamorphoses* and *The Faerie Queene*," *Comparative Literature* 18 (1966): 291.
15. Robert M. Durling, "The Bower of Bliss and Armida's Palace," *Comparative Literature* 6 (1954): 335.
16. MacKellar, *Variorum Commentary*, 4:295.
17. Edmund Spenser, *The Faerie Queene*, ed. Thomas P. Roche, Jr. (New Haven: Yale University Press, 1981), 2.12.59; all references to *The Faerie Queene* are to this edition and are noted parenthetically in the text.
18. Durling, "Bower of Bliss," 344.
19. Ibid., 345.
20. Friedmann, "Diana-Acteon," 295.
21. Lewis, *Allegory*, 326.
22. Ibid., 326–27.
23. Jean H. Hagstrum, *The Sister Arts: The Tradition of Literary Pictorialism and English Poetry From Dryden to Gray* (Chicago: University of Chicago Press, 1958), 85.
24. John Milton, *The Art of Logic*, trans. Allan H. Gilbert, *The Works of John Milton*, 18 vols., ed. F.A. Patterson et al. (New York: Columbia University Press, 1931–38), 11:6.
25. *Paradise Lost*, 1.696, 703; 2.272, 410; 3.602; 4.236, 241, 801; 5.297, 770; 6.513; 9.391; 10.312. That most of these references to art are pejorative is clear, but a few require extra scrutiny for their negative meanings to be clear. "If Art could tell [about the Sapphire Fount]" (4.236) implies the limitations of art; "[Nature wantoned] above

Rule or Art" (5.297) suggests that art unduly attempts to restrain nature; Eve uses "Gard'ning Tools as Art yet rude, / Guiltless of fire had form'd" (9.391–92) because the simplest arts, the most innocent, are preferred in Paradise.

26. J. B. Broadbent, "The Private Mythology of *Paradise Regained*," *Calm of Mind: Tercentenary Essays on "Paradise Regained" and "Samson Agonistes" in Honor of John S. Diekhoff*, ed. Joseph A. Wittreich (Cleveland, Oh.: The Press of Case Western Reserve University, 1971), 88.

27. Frye, "Typology," 231.

28. MacKellar, *Variorum Commentary,* 4:124.

29. Woodhouse, "Theme and Structure," 179.

30. Schultz, "A Fairer Paradise," 297.

31. Ibid., 298–99; similarly, Arnold Stein believes "Satan may be the contriver—there is a strong suggestion of this—of the pleasant valley" because of "this quite strange, apparently impossible detail: 'With chaunt of tuneful birds, resounding loud'" (*Heroic Knowledge,* 54).

32. MacKellar, *Variorum Commentary,* 4:125.

33. Schultz, "A Fairer Paradise," 297.

Part VI
Spokesperson for Women

Beneficent Hierarchies: Reading Milton Greenly

DIANE MCCOLLEY

One morning in Paradise, Eve mentions to Adam that they ought to pay less attention to sex and more to taking care of the planet. As Adam's "meet help" (a phrase Milton's God renders "fit help" [8.450][1] in the dressing and keeping of the Garden), Eve knows her place in relation to their subordinates, the earth and its creatures. She shares "dominion" over them with Adam, as in perhaps no other representation of the Hebrew creation story, though both the Anglo-Saxon Genesis and the Junius-Tremellius Bible specifically affirm her partnership.[2] She understands what dominion—derived from *Domino*—is for: to nurture, protect, and encourage the beings in her domain, as does the power who delegates dominion to his representatives. As Adam has explained to her, using the plural pronoun, God has "Conferr'd upon us" this "power and rule" and

>   Dominion giv'n
> Over all other Creatures that possess
> Earth, Air, and Sea.
>   (4.429–32)

They are lords of creation, but the creatures possess the habitats they inhabit. In their calling to dress and keep the Garden of Eden—metonymy for the Garden of Earth of which it is the epitome—Adam and Eve demonstrate what we would now call an ecological consciousness. "Ecology" is the knowledge, or λογοσ, of the house, or οικοσ; by acknowledging that creatures possess (*posse* and *sedere*, to be able to rest in or occupy) their habitations, Adam becomes the first ecologist. Correspondingly, Eve's response to this vocation and the creatures' responses to her model for us the purpose of human dominion in this pendant world. In her innocence and beneficence, "every Beast" is "duteous at her call" (9.521), and "her Fruits and Flow'rs . . . at her coming sprung, / And toucht by her fair tendance gladlier grew" (8.44, 8.46–47).

Eve's proposal on the morning of the Fall to spend some time giving her full attention to tending "Plant, Herb, and Flow'r" (9.206), the nurture and habitat of many creatures, which critics have thought a fallacious whim of feminine vanity,[3] suggests that looking after the Garden of Eden would in the long run enrich the quality of personal life, including erotic life, more than obsession with private gratifications would do. Her argument for freedom of conscience—which both masculinists and feminists have thought a desire for autonomy—recognizes that governments have to serve both the well-being of individual persons, which rigid structures fail to do, and the long-term concerns of all life on earth, which excessive individualism fails to do. Adam and Eve are seeking a balance between personal and ecological relations. In doing so they take part in a hierarchy that transmits beneficence from God to all creatures. That is, although God provides for all and often inspires—breathes into—his images directly through their faculties of reason and imagination, constituting conscience, he also delegates the privilege of beneficence to his creatures through the gradation of their powers: angels as guardians and flaming ministers to human beings, elect human beings such as prophets and poets to other human beings with other talents, and all human beings to each other and to other earthly creatures. These responsibilities raise all transmitters of benefits (whether wisdom, spiritual understanding, knowledge, love, nurture, discipline, challenge, or other opportunities) to the status of hierarchs, or caretakers of sacred things, and give them ways to develop their abilities and distinctions.

This transmission of benefits also yields natural returns. Plants when cared for fruit more freely, providing beauty and nurture. Animals kept wild yet pacific by the natural thaumaturgy of human rectitude present a multiformity of unimaginable otherness within the kinship of flesh, stimulating to the mind and the senses and helpful to the discernment of human identity and potentiality. Humans and angels in a state of grace enjoy returning gratitude and praise, which are primary causes of the arts of music, dance, and poetry, all giving pleasure, understanding, connection, and distinction to their makers.

Paradisal hierarchies are beneficent, flexible, and reciprocal. The purpose of gradation in *Paradise Lost*, from angels to Adam and Eve to the "Creatures wanting voice" (9.199), is not the acquisition of power but the descent of light. Gradation allows diversity of creatures and variety of love, magnanimity and gratitude, responsibility and achievement, humility (from *humus*, earth), and conscience. It resists dualistic polarization, since all of being is contained within the same scale, each species sharing properties with those "below" and "above" it and conferring reciprocal benefits.

Lucifer the light-bearer becomes Satan the adversary[4] by scorning all such service. Not only does he think it "Better to reign in Hell, than serve in Heav'n" (1.263), refuse to bend that stubborn joint the knee (5.782), and scorn singing with "the Minstrelsy of Heav'n" (6.168); he also despises an order in which the greater serves the lesser and thus elicits what he deems a double burden of assistance to others and gratitude for benefits. On Mount Niphates he acknowledges that spontaneous gratitude is no burden after all (4.49–57) but fears being scoffed at if he renounces his boasts (79–86). Service to the later-born he irately rejects:

> Man [God] made, and for him built
> Magnificent this World, and Earth his seat,
> Him Lord pronounc'd, and, O indignity!
> Subjected to his service Angel wings,
> And flaming Ministers to watch and tend
> Thir earthy Charge.
>
> (9.152–57)

Unlike a genuine leader, Satan feels himself impaired by service to others, whether above or below him on the scale of divinity and nature, and strikes out in both directions hoping to wound God by destroying that "earthy Charge." By seducing Eve and Adam to seek benefits in the one place where they cannot be found, the fruit of the one admonitory Tree that keeps their untroubled prelapsarian consciences alert,[5] Satan achieves (though imperfectly) his desire to bring sin and death upon human beings and their hierarchical responsibility, the biosphere. His instrument for this corruption is language.

Eve's concern for care of the earth in *Paradise Lost* is both a good in itself and an analogue of Milton's concern for care of language. Both callings are necessary to each other. Language rooted in nature is packed with moral and spiritual implications which observation of nature unfolds.[6] The workings of nature are the root source of metaphor and of a sense of organic connections, and a language aware of these connections cultivates an ecological consciousness. Both poets and earthkeepers benefit from periods of solitary attention as well as sociable cooperation. Both callings are vulnerable, also, to insidious corruption, to be repelled by consultation with "that seasoned life of man, preserved and stored up in books"[7] and with parliaments of colleagues—in the case of Adam and Eve, with the book of nature, angels, and each other. Both poets and earthkeepers are hierarchs entrusted with divine gifts and creative freedom.

In contemplating the transmission of beneficence we may think not so much of movement down a ladder (though the poem contains steps, literal and metaphorical, by which to ascend to Heaven) as of a spread from the most encompassing to the most specific, from Father to Son to spiritual and rational creatures, from angels to human beings, from men and women to particular neighbors of all species.

The Son and the Angelic Choirs: " More Near United"

The epic action of *Paradise Lost* begins with the subordination of the angels to the Son that cost Satan all that pain, and that Abdiel says is really a kind of exaltation "under one Head more near / United" who "One of our number thus reduc't becomes" (6.830–31, 843) and entirely for their good, thus defining the purpose of any legitimate form of authority as a means of raising or authoring—causing to grow.[8] The "higher" or greater beings in heavenly and paradisal hierarchies minister to and raise the "lower." The Son's begetting is a manifestation, not a beginning, since "by him" the Father created the angels "in thir bright degrees" and "to thir Glory nam'd / Thrones, Dominations, Princedoms, Virtues, Powers" (5.835–40); Satan's refusal to accept that he was created, rather than self-authored (5.853–69), is the basis of his rebellion.[9] The Son in Milton's theology is himself subordinate to the Father; otherwise he could not have been exalted or merited exaltation. From Abdiel's point of view, this exaltation exalts those whom it formally places under the Son's leadership: formally, because as their creator the Son is already their superior, but now becomes their leader, and so their servant.

The Exaltation of the Son precipitates two kinds of angelic hierarchies: those that increase the liberty of their members by increasing their opportunities for growth and well-doing and those that restrict them by decreasing those opportunities. Satan ordains and recruits the latter kind by renouncing good and thereby radically limiting the opportunities of his followers. The two kinds of angelic hierarchies become models for human societies. Nimrod, the father of tyrannous political and ecclesiastical hierarchies, will "arrogate Dominion undeserv'd / Over his brethren" (12.27–28), following in Satan's footsteps by accruing power for its own sake and expressing that power in self-glorifying monumental architecture built of the "black bituminous gurge" that "Boils out from under ground, the mouth of Hell" (12.41–42), an anti-environmental engineering feat that issues in the "hideous gabble" of confounded language (12.56). The work imitates the building of Pandemonium under the leadership of Mammon (1.670–731), the archetype of the ecological devastation wrought by that "least erected Spirit" when power-hungry humans

> with impious hands
> Rifl'd the bowels of thir mother Earth
> For Treasures better hid.
> (1.686–88)

Good leadership inspires individual and concerted well-doing, and so liberates. Bad leadership disempowers and so subjects. Hell may not be more hierarchical than Heaven, but the purpose of ruination to which it is dedicated trivializes its members and the arts of civilization. The fallen angels still play and sing ravishingly, but their song is, in more than a polyphonic sense, "partial" because adherence to their party has robbed them of wholeness and of all the genres and topoi of art that inspire, create, admire, praise, and delight in beauty and well-doing. Their arts attempt to soothe and dignify a coterie of vandals dedicated to destruction. Although in Heaven

> Scepter'd Angels . . .
> sat as Princes, whom the supreme King
> Exalted to such power, and gave to rule,
> Each in his Hierarchy, the Orders bright,
> (1.734–37)

Milton's beneficent hierarchies do not appear to have a rigidly fixed internal order.[10] The words *hierarch* and *hierarchy*, rare in *Paradise Lost*, cluster within the scene of the Exaltation:

> on such day
> As Heavn'n's great Year brings forth, th'
>   Empyreal Host
> Of Angels by Imperial summons call'd,
> Innumerable before th' Almighty's Throne
> Forthwith from all the ends of Heav'n appear'd
> Under thir Hierarchs in orders bright;
> Ten thousand thousand Ensigns high advanc'd,
> Standards and Gonfalons, twixt Van and Rear
> Stream in the Air, and for distinction serve
> Of Hierarchies, of Orders and Degrees;
> Or in thir glittering Tissues bear imblaz'd
> Holy Memorials, acts of Zeal and Love
> Recorded eminent.
> (5.582–94)

The blazons serve to distinguish not only established orders but particular acts. The wordplay on "Empyreal" and "Imperial" calls attention both to the exalted position of the angels and their subordination to God. The unexpected limit put on infinity, the "ends of Heav'n," by querying itself invites readers to consider the alternative reading "purposes." The angels, the whole passage declares, have a lot to do, do not always stand and wait, need to be summoned for announcements, and earn "distinctions."

Generically, a group of angels is usually called a choir (as in 3.217); although "each order bright" (6.885) in Milton's epic does much else, heaven is multichoral, and for "pure concent"—right tuning and timing and other activities for which choral singing provides a metaphor— choirs need a choirmaster "whose love their motion sway[s]."[11] These choirs sing and dance for joy and praise and provide formal anthems to celebrate the Father's acceptance of the Son's offer of himself to redeem humankind (3.344–415), the Son's victory over the rebel angels (6.885–906), the "Birth-day of Heav'n and Earth" (7.256), the "Hymenaen" of Adam and Eve (4.711), the Almighty's eschatological pronouncement (10.616–40), and the Nativity of Christ (12.366). But they sing neither ferial nor occasional anthems on the day of the Exaltation and are not hierarchically arranged in choirs around God's throne. In fact, they have to be summoned from the outermost reaches of Heaven and from whatever they are doing there.

After the Father's announcement that he is appointing the Son their collective head, one might expect an elaborate anthem, but instead, as Raphael recounts,

> That day, as other solemn days, they spent
> In song and dance about the sacred Hill,
> Mystical dance, which yonder starry Sphere
> Of Planets and of fixt in all her Wheels
> Resembles nearest, mazes intricate,
> Eccentric, intervolv'd, yet regular
> Then most, when most irregular they seem:
> And in their motions harmony Divine
> So smooths her charming tones, that God's own ear
> Listens delighted.
> (5.618–27)

The arts are not obsequious to the patronage of the Vice-Gerent Son. His love has already made them dancers and musicians, among other things, at their creation, and they dance on this "solemn day" as at any other festival.

Like the angelic hierarchies themselves, defined by both ordination and merit, their members' dance seems both orderly and voluntary. One may read the angelic dance as preordained, like its similitude the starry one, which may also be performed by living spirits; but one may also suppose that the angelic one is like the starry one in its intricacy and regularity but cooperatively and spontaneously choreographed by free though mutually inspired artists like Adam and Eve at orisons. After the dance has quickened appetite, tables appear within the very circles in which the angels stand when they stop dancing, and they enjoy a feast, "communion sweet," not brought by celestial servitors but provided by "th' all bounteous King, who show'r'd / With copious hand, rejoicing in thir joy" (5.637, 640–41). The service that Satan-to-be defines as servitude appears to be a matter of being served as well as serving and of enjoying joy.

Since Milton's angels' dancing and hymning serve as metaphors for all kinds of "harmony Divine" (5.625), including hierarchical relationships, it seems important to know what kind of "solemn music" Milton is likeliest to have had in mind. Being part of an angelic choir is not only a matter of losing one's distinctive voice in a polyphonic blend. In English choral music of Milton's time, structural regularity, like the mystic dance, is eccentric and intervolved, giving place within its order to passages for solo voice and small ensembles, moments when particular voices emerge from the texture, rhythms altering freely to fit the words within the steady pulse, and harmonic freedom, including dissonances. Because, as Milton describes it, the music angels sing is contemporary—including verse anthems,[12] multichoral and antiphonal intervolvement, music both *concertante* (having solo parts within the choral frame) and *concertato* (combining diverse voices and instruments)—we should take the nature of that audible music into account in contemplating Milton's choral hierarchies and their analogy to the harmony of other societies in which each voice has its say.

The Angels and Humankind: "As Friend with Friend"

Moving to the next hierarchical sphere, we find that angels, to Satan's indignation, are ministering spirits to their near-equals, Adam and Eve, who, the Argument to book 2 tells us, are "equal or not much inferior" to them. Specific angelic ministrations to Adam and Eve include Raphael's to their prelapsarian understanding of the War in Heaven, the creation of the world, and the danger issuing from the former to the latter; Uriel's to their safety when he warns Gabriel of Satan's approach; Gabriel's, Ithuriel's, and Zephon's to their freedom from coercion by Satan, who must overcome their waking consciences, not their sleeping fancies or bodily strength; myriads of unnamed others who guard them and whose "songs / Divide the night"(4.687–88); and Michael's to their postlapsarian understanding of redemption, regeneration, and the ongoing war of good and evil.

The equivocation "equal or not much inferior" also applies to relations within the order of humankind. Milton's indignation, in contrast to Satan's, is directed toward those

> who not content
> With fair equality, fraternal state,
> Will arrogate Dominion undeserv'd
> Over [their] brethren.
> (12.25–28)

Even when he seems to have regarded some degree of primacy "deserv'd," Milton brings traditional subordinates far closer than usual to their traditional superiors and also gives them areas of superiority—such as Eve, who has a large share in the government of Eden and sometimes understands it better than Adam since "Among unequals what society / Can sort?" (8.383–84); and despite contrary passages, Adam and Eve are so nearly equal that readers can argue about whether Milton thinks equality is or should be a principle of paradisal life. Milton's paradisal community gives each member equally immeasurable value but nevertheless allows everyone to rise by "degrees of merit" (7.157), and it also recognizes degrees of merit within each degree. The state of original righteousness—where each being is attentive to the goodness, growth, and particular loveliness of each other being and no one seeks power over others, but only the well-being of each—constitutes equality by full appreciation of each member, without an ethic of levelling sameness or a loss of the impulse of admiration.

The paradisal response to discovering superiority of some kind is (like Abdiel's and Eve's) gratitude and (like Adam's) respectful courtesy. When Raphael arrives in Paradise, Adam bows low, though needing no pomp to supplement "his own complete / Perfections" (5.352–53) and

> not aw'd,
> Yet with submiss approach and reverence meek,
> As to a superior Nature.
> (5.358–60)

The recognition of a "superior Nature" does not diminish, but increases, Adam's own "complete / Perfections" and creative powers. Eve's tribute to Adam claiming that she enjoys "the happier Lot, enjoying thee / Preeminent" (4.446 – 47) is a similar courtesy. Though it may be authorial manipulation from a feminist point of view, it is a good model from a humanist point of view for anyone's pleasure in anyone else's genuine talents. Not only Adam, but Milton recognizes superiorities in Eve as well: Adam is her leader, but her attitude toward their subordinates is sometimes superior to his. If Satan had responded to the merits of others as Adam and Eve and Abdiel do, the evil under which the world groans after the Fall could have been avoided.

Spontaneous responses of reverence, admiration, and praise are not only paradisal pleasures but also the fountainhead of the arts. "The chief [poets] both in antiquity and excellency were they that did imitate the inconceivable excellencies of God," Sidney points out, and the lyric voice "giveth praise, the reward of virtue, to virtuous acts."[13] The morning hymn of praise that Adam and Eve mutually improvise in *Paradise Lost* (5.153–208) combines the art of music and language to speak of and for the hierarchy of free creatures whose well-being depends on them.

Milton's unfallen humans, like the angels in their Monteverdian psalms, are in their songs and dialogues sometimes "Sole," sometimes "responsive each to other's note," sometimes "In full harmonic number join'd," as Adam says of the angels who entertain them nocturnally (4.683– 87)—insofar as two people can be. Unfortunately, the one time there is an opportunity for a trio, the conversation with Raphael, Eve does not take a vocal part. But otherwise, paradisal conversation is reciprocal; authority and response shift from speaker to speaker, like leading voices in a duet that would in time, when they had increased and multiplied, become a polyphonic verse anthem.

Humankind and Subordinate Kinds: All the Creatures

The descent of light through reciprocal hierarchies of merit and responsibility in *Paradise Lost* that begins with the relation of the Son to the angels extends to that of humans to the rest of nature. We may detect an implicit analogy between the begetting of the Son and the creation of Adam, to whom the Creator (who is also the Son) brings the animals to receive their names and "pay thee fealty" (8.344). Thomas Traherne's comment on the creation of Man articulates the parallel: "All the rest of the Creatures were without a Head till he was made, in him all were united, and made great in Value."[14] As angels minister to

Adam and Eve, Adam and Eve minister to nature, which they are supposed to dress and keep, georgically dressing the Garden to encourage nature's fruitfulness, and ecologically keeping it to preserve all kinds of lives. This keeping includes government of the animals by example: while Adam and Eve govern themselves, the birds and beasts naturally obey these kindred but superior creatures of flesh.

Milton makes Adam and Eve ecologists by their work and by the language they speak. Before the Fall, and regenerately afterwards, Adam and Eve manifest an ecological form of consciousness, weaving awareness of the cosmos and of the earth as habitat into speech. Their conversations habitually acknowledge the earth, the source of their nurture, their responsibility for it, and the birds, animals, and flowers that share it; their love songs incorporate nature not as decoration and compliment, as in the courtly artifice of pastoral poetry, but with fresh awareness of the thriving beauty that claims their care and redoubles their joy.

In their first conversation (4.411–91), Adam's preliminary topic, the one hieratic Tree, leads to consideration of other trees' "delicious fruit" and of their dominion over those other creatures that possess the habitats they inhabit, then to their own work of praise and "our delightful task / To prune these growing Plants, and tend these Flow'rs" (4.437–38). Eve's response records her first experience of flowers, waters, cave and plain, lake and sky as well as Adam. Adam's next speech (610–33) includes animals (though rather demeaningly) and "pleasant labor" among flowery arbors, green alleys, blossoms and dropping gums that "ask riddance"; for him the work is mainly keeping order. Eve replies lyrically, with a love song (639–56) that links her delight in Adam to seasons, charming birds, herb, tree, fruit, flower, the fertile earth, morning and evening, sun, moon, and stars. Adam answers with an account of cosmic nurture and the spiritual beings who watch and sing (660–88). Their evening prayer (724–35) cites night and day, appointed work, mutual help, uncropt fruit, and future generations to fill the Earth. The next morning Adam calls Eve (5.17–25) to the fresh field, the tended plants, the citron grove, the myrrh, the balmy reed, the bee; after her dream recitation, he mentions "fresh imployments" (125) among groves, fountains and

> Flow'rs
> That open now thir choicest bosom'd smells
> Reserv'd from night, and kept for thee in store.
> (126–28)

Their morning hymn (5.153–208) includes the whole scale of nature in a Benedicite full of prosodically mimetic empathy and also calls the angels to join in, as each morning they join "thir vocal Worship to the Choir / Of Creatures wanting voice" (9.198–99). Their last unfallen conversation (9.201–384), when they "commune how that day they best may ply / Thir growing work" and Eve suggests dividing their labors, concerns their responsibilities toward nature and each other. This habit of reference to other beings nearly dies with the Fall, except that Eve now speaks scornfully of "Beasts" (9.769) and Adam sees in them the destructive appetites he has unleashed upon his offspring (10.706–19). But their sense of active responsibility toward nature reappears after their repentance. At the news of the expulsion, Eve laments the flowers whom she has "bred up with tender hand" (11.276) and at the vision of Noah's ark Adam rejoices (too hopefully) that "Man shall live / With all the Creatures, and their seed preserve" (11.872–73). Raphael's superb creation poem in book 7 enriches their awareness, and ours, of the natural world, and the nature poetry of the narrator in book 4 enriches ours. By creating—inspired by his double muse and prepared by a life of study and prayer—both a narrative and a poetic language that keeps the multitude of creatures before the imagination's eyes and ears, Milton offers a healing measure to the language we speak and the awarenesses it keeps alive. The οικοσ of *Paradise Lost* is the cosmos, and Milton's song is ecoversal. The human in it who most clearly makes practical applications of this ecological conscience is Eve.

Eve makes her proposal for a morning's concentration on their work (9.205–25) in language that, like paradisal language generally, is itself ecological; her thought is full of cause and process and moves from the general "Plant, Herb and Flow'r" to the specific woodbine, ivy, roses, and myrtle. John Leonard, citing Anne Ferry, notes that unfallen Adam and Eve rarely name species (mentioning the exception of Adam in 8.393 and 396) and suggests that the poet refrains from putting names in their mouths because the fallenness of postlapsarian language impedes him from the right naming that was their birthright. On the other hand, as Leonard points out, Milton is not so modest in the case of Raphael, who both names and describes many specific animals: "Adam and Eve look to the unity behind the multiplicity of Creation. Raphael's emphasis is on multiplicity."[15] In her gardening proposal, Eve does name specific flowers, as is appropriate to her immediate concern, just as Adam's naming of the pairing of "Lion with Lioness" and the discrepancy of ox and ape in his request for an equal mate is appropriate to his. Perhaps Milton suggests that Adam and Eve would have grown more Raphael-like, increasingly using the names they have already given the animals and flowers when they first apprehended their natures, through increased experience: particularly the more philosophic Adam through his experience of Eve's habitual attention to "each Flow'r" (9.428) and to the animals whose duteousness "at her call" (9.521) implies that she already uses their names.

Just as their naming comprehends both generality and specificity, their syntax by its comprehensiveness and its hierarchy of coordinate and subordinate clauses expresses the nature of Nature, both in its unity and in the varieties of its relationships. The two compound-complex sentences in which Eve makes her proposal for their morning's work mime the complex interweaving of life. The structure of her suggestion expresses her sense of the consequences of action and inaction, and her argument concerns the long-term, far-reaching relations of human love and work to the health of a complex fabric of beings dependent on human choices.

Adam is more inclined than Eve to stress human superiority and might incline to arrogance without Eve's tempering open-mindedness. He tells Eve that "other Animals unactive range, / And of thir doings God takes no account" (4.621–22), and that their own "smiles from Reason flow, / To brute deni'd" (9.239–40). Yet, in a chronologically earlier conversation, when Adam has asked God for a meet companion, God has replied that he already has "various living creatures" (8.370) to entertain him:

> know'st thou not
> Thir language and thir ways? They also know,
> And reason not contemptibly; with these
> Find pastime, and bear rule.
>
> (372–75)

The reply is jocular, inasmuch as God is really encouraging Adam to recognize the differences between himself and other animals and to seek a fit mate.[16] Adam answers, "Hast thou not made me here thy substitute, / And these inferior far beneath me set?" (381–82). He is right that he finds no help meet for him among the animals and needs "fellowship . . . fit to participate / All rational delight" (389–91), but God's opinion that the animals know and reason is not discredited by that distinction, and one of the meet ways that Eve helps Adam is that her attitude toward them agrees more closely with God's than his. As a result of her empathy, she wins their affectionate obedience; "every Beast" is naturally "more duteous at her call" than the enslaved "Herd disguis'd" to Circe's (9.521–22). The Serpent, a zoological snob, calls the beasts "Beholders rude, and shallow to discern / Half what in thee is fair," but Eve demurs, "for in thir looks / Much reason, and in thir actions oft appears" (9.544–45, 558–59). In fact, she goes too far in this direction when she subordinates her own will to that of a talking snake who is really a powerful demon in disguise, and her defection from stewardship to consumerism begins the devastation of nature by exploitation.

When in their right minds, Adam and Eve meetly help each other find a balance between dominion over nature and respectful care of it. This balance depends on their subordination to reason of those passions and pleasures within themselves that are emblematized by the beasts and flowers and are the very ingredients of virtue. The hierarchy of human faculties corresponds with the scale of nature; both are systems of nurture starting from above, since reason's work of keeping the affections in right tune and the animals in harmony is good for the affections and for the animals. This nurture is reciprocal, as the affections serve the higher faculties and the animals instruct and delight humans, like living poems.

Raphael's ministry to Adam and Eve includes his generous, observant, and empathetic account of the creation of the animals (7.387–498), from "Leviathan / Hugest of living Creatures" (412–13) to "solemn Nightingale" (435) to "Tawny Lion" (464) to

> The Parsimonious Emmet, provident
> Of future, in small room large heart enclos'd,
> Pattern of just equality perhaps
> Hereafter, join'd in her popular Tribes
> Of Commonalty,
>
> (485–89)

and culminating in

> a Creature who not prone
> And Brute as other Creatures, but endu'd
> With Sanctity of Reason, might . . .
> Govern the rest, self-knowing, and from thence
> Magnanimous to correspond with Heav'n,
> But grateful to acknowledge whence his good
> Descends.
> (506–8, 510–13)

"Not Brute and prone" means rational and erect, but here the sociable archangel's diction sounds more like Adam's and Satan's than like Eve's and God's. Nevertheless, Raphael's emphasis with respect to dominion is on magnanimity. Magnanimous "dominion" would draw forth the distinct potentialities and protect the natures of all creatures—not only the "sportful Herd" but also the wilder animals whose forms Satan appropriates to spy on Adam and Eve: the lion with his "fiery glare" and the tiger who proleptically keeps his "couchant watch" as if to seize "two gentle Fawns . . . Gript in each paw" (4.396, 403–8). I do not think as John Leonard does that "The slide from gambolling lion and tiger to beasts of prey feels inevitable" but agree with him that "The newly created lion seizes its nature and being as vigorously as it is to seize its prey in the fallen world."[17] The carnivorous potentiality of the fiercer animals would not have emerged without the Fall, but even when kept willingly in check in response to human government, their wildness has a salubrious intensity.

Milton's introduction of "Leviathan" into Raphael's speech, and his description of the wildness of other beasts is not (as Stanley Fish has pointed out[18]) an intrusion of evil into the creation. But neither are Milton's prelapsarian animals entirely domesticated. He grants them some of the awesome wildness that delights their Creator and displays his power and ingenuity in the book of Job and his even-handed providence in the Psalms. Leviathan—whether the "Sea-beast" of 1.200–208, the whale of 7.412–16, or the crocodile with echoes of the mythic dragon he seems to be in Job 41—may be, as Regina Schwartz implies, a piece of uninhibited chaos,[19] but his power in Job is beneficial to humans by his very unhookableness. This is no brute that Adam can easily tame, no invitation to arrogance but a powerful one to wonder. He is included in human dominion, but in a way designed to keep self-satisfaction in check.

The Fall bereaves Adam and Eve of the understanding and self-government that make them capable of dominion over the animals. However, their reeducation begins almost at once. When Michael announces the expulsion, Eve laments the loss of the flowers she has "bred up with tender hand" (11.276), and Michael admonishes her not to "set thy heart, / Thus over-fond, on that which is not thine," but think her home with Adam "thy native soil" (11.288–92). When Adam, beginning to recover his hierarchical responsibility for spiritual wisdom while still much in need of it himself, laments the loss of God's presence, Michael's reply restores the continuity between the Garden of Eden and the rest of the earth and the beneficent subordination of Earth to Heaven, and asserts God's providence and very presence within each creature:

> his Omnipresence fills
> Land, Sea, and Air, and every kind that lives,
> Fomented by his virtual power and warm'd.
> (11.336–38)

Although Adam shows less empathy for subordinate nature than Eve does, he is not to be analogized with Satan. Satan boasts that his mind is fixed; Adam learns. Satan desires to destroy; Adam, apart from his unregenerate speeches of hate and despair, desires to preserve. As part of Adam's visionary postlapsarian reeducation, Michael shows him a battlefield

> Where Cattle pastur'd late, now scatter'd lies
> With Carcasses and Arms th' ensanguin'd Field
> Deserted.
> (11.653–55)

But when "The brazen Throat of War had ceast to roar," rather than resuming the dressing and keeping of the earth, the survivors turn "To luxury and riot," and Adam sees "Peace to corrupt no less than War to waste" (11.713–15, 784). God's response—or the response of a shorn, over-grazed, over-exploited environment, which in the long run is the response of the Maker who made nature's laws to go hand in hand with human responsibility—is to drown "all thir pomp" (11.748); with a sort of ecological justice reminiscent of Ovid's narrative of the first environmental disaster,[20]

> in thir Palaces
> Where luxury late reign'd, Sea-monsters whelp'd
> And stabl'd.
> (11.750–52)

Adam watches "every Beast, and Bird, and Insect small" come in "sevens, and pairs... as taught / Thir order" (11.734–36) into an ark well-provisioned "For Man and Beast" (733) like a miniature Garden of Eden, as he had once watched them approach him diffidently and in pairs to receive names from their human guardian. When the ark comes to rest on dry land and Noah emerges "with all his Train" (11.862), Adam exclaims,

> I revive
> At this last sight, assur'd that Man shall live
> With all the Creatures, and thir seed preserve.
> (11.871–73)

He understands the need for preservation of all the species in a world made hostile to them by his own abdication of his hierarchical responsibility to preserve them, a responsibility he has abandoned by choosing ambition and consumption rather than beneficent care.

Adam's hope that his offspring will preserve the seed of all the creatures rings hollow now in a way that Milton's environmental epic might have mitigated if the Western world had taken his pervasive concern with environmental justice as seriously as it deserves. Milton's poetic language, by its openness and its resonance, its polyphonic multiplicity of voices and the alert, educable consciences of its narrative voice and its unfallen voices, invites readers to choose between magnanimous and grateful responses to the created world and the satanic vandalism of a fixed and envious mind. Adam and Eve before the Fall do the work of earth-keeping and invent the arts of praise, knowing their place in a beneficent hierarchy: "grateful to acknowledge whence [their] good descends" and magnanimous toward all the "Creatures wanting voice" on whose behalf, with empathy for each creature, they sing their marvellous morning Benedicite. If their offspring should come to understand with Milton's Raphael and Adam, and especially with his Eve, humankind's responsibilities as hierarchs, or ministers, to nature, Milton's poem might be an antidote to the ecological devastation that is the slow version of the apocalyptic final conflagration, reviving Edenic consciences and Edenic language for the work of that general rehabilitation of this habitat when, Michael promises Adam, "the Earth / Shall all be Paradise" (12.463–64).

Notes

1. John Milton, *Paradise Lost: A Poem in Twelve Books*, ed. Merritt Y. Hughes (New York: Odyssey Press, 1962). All references to Milton's poetry are to this edition and are cited parenthetically in the text.

2. In *Genesis A* in the eleventh–century Junius Manuscript (Bodleian Library MS. Junius 11) God uses the dual pronoun when giving dominion over the creation to Adam and Eve, so that the "them" of Genesis 1.26 cannot be rendered as a gendered plural. See A. N. Doane, *Genesis A: A New Edition* (Madison: University of Wisconsin Press, 1978). The manuscript was published by Francis Junius in Amsterdam in 1655. The annotation to Genesis 1.26–28 in the Latin Bible for Protestant readers, which Milton used, of Junius and Tremellius states that "qui dominentur" includes "Vir & uxor cum posteris."

3. I have cited and discussed these views in *Milton's Eve* (Urbana: University of Illinois Press, 1983), 141–45.

4. On who uses what names of Satan and when, see John Leonard, *Naming in Paradise: Milton and the Language of Adam and Eve* (Oxford: The Clarendon Press, 1990), chapter 2.

5. Milton uses *conscience* before the Fall to mean something like "unfallen consciousness," as in 8.502. After the Fall Adam's "evil conscience" (10.849) brings terrors. Even Satan has "conscience" or moral consciousness, but in him it "wakes despair" and

> the bitter memory
> Of what he was, what is, and what must be
> Worse.
>
> (4.23–26)

When God promises that the repentant shall receive "My Umpire Conscience, whom if they will hear, / Light after light well us'd they shall attain" (3.195–96), he proposes to restore the moral consciousness that Adam and Eve have lost, though now it will sometimes guide by means of pain.

6. William Shullenberger admirably illustrates this process in his discussion of the seed in "Sorting the Seeds," *Riven Unities: Authority and Experience, Self and Other in Milton's Poetry,* ed. Wendy Furman, Christopher Grose, and William Schallenberger (Pittsburgh: University of Pittsburgh Press, 1992), volume 28 of *Milton Studies.*

> It is little; it is out of all proportion to the scale of the being whose future life it carries. It completes and implicitly originates the organic dynamism of the created order which Raphael has epitomized in the image of a plant: "So from the root / Springs lighter the green stalk, from thence the leaves / More aery, last the bright consummate flow'r / Spirits odorous breathes" (*PL* 5.479–82).
>
> As gardeners, Adam and Eve will gradually come to understand the saving implication of this enigma of the Seed, and their struggle to make sense of it initiates the regeneration of their love and of their hope. (168)

7. John Milton, *Areopagitica, The Student's Milton,* ed. Frank Allen Patterson (New York: Appleton-Century-Crofts, 1933), 733.

8. From *augere,* to grow or increase, with the suffix of agency. Marshall Grossman provides extended interpretation of authority and authorship in *Paradise Lost* in *"Authors to Themselves": Milton and the Revelation of History* (Cambridge: Cambridge University Press, 1987), which disagrees with some of my arguments.

9. John S. Tanner discusses Satan's "fantasy of self-creation" in *Anxiety in Eden: A Kierkegaardian Reading of "Paradise Lost"* (New York: Oxford University Press, 1992), 152–54.

10. Barbara Kiefer Lewalski calls Milton's hierarchies "curiously fluid" ("Milton on Women—Yet Once More," *Milton Studies* 6 [1974]: 6), and Irene Samuel believes that "the poem cannot hinge on just such system as Milton's prose constantly denies" (*"Paradise Lost," Critical Approaches to Six Major English Works: "Beowulf" through "Paradise Lost,"* ed. R. M. Lumianski and Herschel Baker [Philadelphia: University of Pennsylvania Press, 1968], 242); see also *Dante and Milton: The "Commedia" and "Paradise Lost"* (Ithaca: Cornell University Press, 1966), 155–57, 190–95.

11. John Milton, "At a Solemn Musick," lines 6 and 22, *John Milton: "Samson Agonistes" and Shorter Poems,* ed. A. E. Barker, Crofts Classics (Arlington Heights, Ill.: AHM Publishing Corporation, 1950), 20–21.

12. Seventeenth-century English "verse" anthems and services employ solos and small ensembles alternating with antiphonal and full choir passages. The beginnings of genre precede the *concertante* style of Venetian music that culminated in Monteverdi and can be performed by smaller and more modestly equipped ensembles.

13. Sir Philip Sidney, *An Apology for Poetry,* ed. Forrest G. Robinson (Indianapolis, Ind.: Bobbs-Merrill, 1970), 18, 47.

14. Thomas Traherne, *Meditations on the Six Days of the Creation* (1717), intro. George Robert Griffy, The Augustine Reprint Society, Publication Number 119 (William Andrew Clark Memorial Library. Los Angeles: University of California, 1966), 67.

15. Leonard, *Naming,* 256, 263; Anne Ferry, *Milton's Epic Voice: The Narrator in "Paradise Lost"* (Cambridge: Harvard University Press, 1963), 76, 81.

16. Hugh McCallum makes this point in *Milton and the Sons of God: The Divine*

Image in Milton's Epic Poetry (Toronto: University of Toronto Press, 1986), 122, and Leonard discusses it in *Naming*, 25–28.

17. Leonard, *Naming,* 262–63.

18. Stanley Fish, *Surprised by Sin: The Reader in "Paradise Lost"* (Berkeley: University of California Press, 1967), 151; qtd. by Leonard, *Naming,* 267–68.

19. Regina M. Schwartz, *Remembering and Repeating: Biblical Creation in "Paradise Lost"* (Cambridge: Cambridge University Press, 1988), 23, 29, 31. Robert Alter in his powerful account of the Book of Job calls the description of Leviathan "a marvelous fusion of precise observation, hyperbole, and mythological heightening of the real reptile" who is "impervious to every hook and snare and every scheme of being subjected to domestication" (*The Art of Biblical Poetry* [New York: Basic Books, 1985], 107–8).

20. *Metamorphoses*, book 1. Whereas Ovid describes the flooding of cottages and groves as well as palaces, Milton defines the flood as the washing away of a civilization devoted to pomp and luxury.

"Grateful Digressions" and "Casual Discourse": Eve's Rapport-Talk

JOAN F. GILLILAND

Why does Eve leave the scene at the beginning of book 8 of *Paradise Lost*, having sat silent through most of book 5 and all of books 6 and 7? An obvious reply is the practical one that, although she seems forgotten by everybody (including the reader), Milton needs to get her off stage so that Adam and Raphael can talk about her, as they do a little later. Raphael has been telling the story of the War in Heaven and then of the creation of the world. Now Adam turns the talk to the nature of the universe, and Eve, rising from "where she sat retir'd in sight," goes "forth among her Fruits and Flow'rs, / To visit how they prosper'd" (8.41, 44 – 45).[1] To a modern ear the explanation of her departure does not sound very convincing, especially with its piling up of negatives:

> Yet went she *not* as *not* with such discourse
> Delighted, or *not* capable her ear
> Of what was high; such pleasure she reserv'd,
> Adam relating, she sole Auditress;
> Her husband the Relater she preferr'd
> Before the Angel, and of him to ask
> Chose rather: hee, she knew, would intermix
> Grateful digressions, and solve high dispute
> With conjugal Caresses, from his Lip
> Not Words alone pleas'd her.
> (8.48–57; emphasis mine)

Despite the disclaimer that Eve is perfectly capable of understanding and would simply prefer not to listen right now, these lines appear incredibly sexist, on a par with the married Pamela's Latin lessons with Mr. B. Is this episode yet another example of Milton's supposed bias against women? Diane McColley considers her departure one of the "gracious errands" that briefly take her away from Adam:

> her "fair tendance" of "her Nurserie" (8.47,46) is no trifle. Nature responds to her as she and Adam respond to each other, and as the children they prepare for might have responded, with glad growth.[2]

Joseph A. Wittreich believes that Eve departs "knowing full well when the discourse extends beyond appropriate boundaries."[3] Unlike Adam, "she knows when it is time 'to know no more,'" as Raphael has noticed when he remarks that she "*sees* when thou art *seen* least wise" (8.578; Wittreich's emphasis).[4] The "clichés of culture," the stereotypical idealizations of the silent woman, "are observed only to be broken."[5]

An approach to Eve's attitude toward language through linguist Deborah Tannen's concept of women's "rapport-talk" and men's "report-talk" may shed some further light on the way Eve acts as well as the way she speaks. Tannen's thesis, popularized in *You Just Don't Understand: Women and Men in Conversation*, holds that women and men have very different conversational styles, styles that become apparent and clearly differentiated in childhood. She does not argue for the superiority of one or the other; they are "*different but equally valid.*"[6]

According to Tannen, "For most women, the language of conversation is primarily a language of rapport: a way of establishing connections and negotiating relationships."[7] Words do much more than relay facts and information. Even studies of children's language find little girls engaging in talk that tends to build consensus, that creates symmetry among the participants. This kind of conversation is not public; it takes place within the home and in the private sphere.[8] And it is the kind of talk that Eve clearly prefers. She wants to converse with Adam, not listen to a factual lecture in a formal situation. So when Adam requests information (of a sort that she has earlier asked for too) and "by his count'nance seem'd / Ent'ring on studious thoughts abstruse" (8.39–40), Eve decides to "visit" "her Fruits and Flow'rs." Their response is almost human, for they "touch't by her fair tendance gladlier grew" (47). She chooses to build her relationship with them, as she "preferred," "chose," and "reserv'd" for herself the "pleasure" of being "sole Auditress" in the prospective discussion with Adam in which she plans to participate actively. As Maureen Quilligan points out, "What Eve gains in going away is a topic for the meet and mutual conversation that Milton had deemed . . . the sole basis of a fit marriage."[9]

In contrast to the rapport-talk that women prefer, Tannen says,

> For most men, talk is primarily a means to preserve independence and negotiate and maintain status in a hierarchical social order. This is done by exhibiting knowledge and skill, and by holding center stage through verbal performance such as story telling, joking, or imparting information.[10]

This, without the joking, is exactly the kind of asymmetrical report-talk that Adam and Raphael engage in, though Adam knows his own place in the hierarchy and is careful not to overstep proper limits even while he maintains his status. Raphael has told his stories, and he partially answers Adam's question, an only slightly more sophisticated version of Eve's wondering in book 4 why the moon and stars shine at night when no one is awake to see them. Then Adam takes his turn to impart information and hold center stage, telling a story that Raphael has not yet heard—about Adam's own awakening to consciousness and the creation of Eve.[11]

The adversarial nature of the verbal performances is most clearly evident at the end of book 8 when Raphael reproves Adam's uxoriousness and Adam not only defends his love for Eve but neatly turns the tables by inquiring about love among the angels. Perhaps Raphael is embarrassed. Perhaps the "Celestial rosy red" of his smile is nothing more than "Love's proper hue" (619) and not a blush at all. Perhaps Raphael has been trying Adam, as God did when he questioned the need for a companion. Certainly Adam defends his position eloquently in both situations. Raphael seems satisfied with Adam's response, for he does not press the point further. Thus, Adam has proved himself a worthy adversary in the contest of words. Like the polemical Milton, he has demonstrated his skill and his fitness for a place in the male social order.

Is Eve then inferior because she moves away from what becomes a somewhat confrontational discussion between Raphael and Adam? In any culture, men's language has higher status. For example, in a society where men speak through proverbs and metaphors, indirection is valued, while women's directness is taken as showing their inferiority.[12] In Western culture, men have traditionally viewed women as talking too much, though studies have shown that in mixed groups men talk far more than women.[13] Eve speaks very little before the Fall (as would have been appropriate for a Renaissance woman), but she also has little to say afterward. One reason for the perception that women talk excessively is the notion that they tend to discuss supposedly trivial things and personal matters, seeking connection rather than information.[14] And we, men and women alike, usually assume that Adam's desire for report-talk is somehow better. The narrator of *Paradise Lost* supports this assumption about what is preferable even while asserting that Eve is not "not capable . . . Of what was high," that she can indeed understand and engage in report-talk about the things that really matter.

Yet while report-talk is given authorial blessing, Raphael reproves Adam's desire for knowledge—"Solicit not thy thoughts with matters hid" (8.167)—and bids him,

> joy thou
> In what he gives to thee, this Paradise
> And thy fair Eve.
>
> (170–72)

And Adam himself, like Milton in the divorce tracts, has spoken of Man's (here clearly the human male's)

> desire
> By conversation with his like to help,
> Or solace his defects,
>
> (417–19)

in other words, rapport-talk that builds relationship. In his defense of his love for Eve, Adam places great value on her speech, along with her behavior: "what she wills to do or say, / Seems wisest, virtuousest, discreetest, best" (549–50); "Wisdom in discourse with her / Loses discount'nanc't" (552–53); and sexual intercourse matters less to him than "Those thousand decencies that daily flow / From all her words and actions" (601–2).

What does the reader actually see (or hear) of Eve's rapport-talk before her silent departure in book 8 and the ensuing discussion between Adam and Raphael that sets the scene for the Fall? This talk is of necessity with Adam, for having lost the illusory companion mirrored in the pool, Eve has no female friends with whom to converse. Though she talks like a woman, she lacks the experience of interacting in a same-sex group. Her description of her image clearly reflects her desire for relationship, for connection with another:

> A Shape within the wat'ry gleam appear'd
> Bending to look on me, I started back,
> It started back, but pleas'd I soon return'd,
> Pleas'd it return'd as soon with answering looks
> Of sympathy and love.
>
> (4.461–65)

In Adam and Eve's first appearance in *Paradise Lost*, as they are seen through Satan's eyes, the two are shown talking. Of course their conversation has an expository purpose, since it is through eavesdropping that Satan learns of the couple's situation and his opportunity, but the words have the further function of cementing the relationship of the two and of establishing that relationship for the larger audience, the reader of the poem. Adam's authoritative position is established and maintained, certainly. He speaks first in book 4, and he speaks last, in reply to Eve's question about the moon and stars; the very possession of information to dispense "sends a metamessage of superiority."[15] As Tannen says,

> Since women seek to build rapport, they are inclined to play down their expertise rather than display it. Since men value the position of center stage and the feeling of knowing more, they seek opportunities to gather and disseminate factual information.[16]

Eve tactfully gives Adam the opportunity to instruct when she asks her childlike question about the heavenly bodies: "But wherefore all night long shine these, for whom / This glorious sight, when sleep hath shut all eyes?" (4.657–58). Adam's explanation that they "Shine not in vain" (675) is kindly and factual, for "Millions of spiritual Creatures walk the Earth" (677), he informs her.

Still, much of Adam and Eve's prelapsarian talk is unnecessary as far as maintaining superiority and conveying information are concerned. The exchange about the heavens takes place as they "talking hand in hand alone . . . pass'd / On to thir blissful Bower" (689–90). Their lengthy titles of respect and praise for each other are purely epideictic, as is their praise of God in their evening and morning songs. Eve already knows of the prohibited Tree of Knowledge that Adam discusses; Adam already knows of Eve's creation and their discovery of each other. Neither possesses factual information hitherto denied the other. Eve talks about her awakening to consciousness and her first experiences because she likes to discuss these events with him: "That day I oft remember, when from sleep / I first awak't" (449–50). Presumably they have discussed all this before in like circumstances—part of the "bliss on bliss" (508) that so torments the prying Satan.[17]

Even Adam's "*let us* ever praise him [God] and extol / His bounty" (4.436–37; emphasis mine) is cast in the language of consensus preferred by women rather than delivered as a command to his spouse. When they continue to their bower talking and join in their evening prayer "unanimous" (736), they reaffirm their connection with God, with each other, and with the "ceaseless praise" (679) of the "Celestial voices" (682) that they have often heard hymning the Creator's glory. None of this is the showing off and the maintaining of status—

the asymmetry—that report-talk entails. Rather, their last words in book 4 are spoken together, unanimously, and to God, before they move into their "shady Lodge" (720).

Trouble enters the garden that night with Satan. When women engage in what Tannen calls "troubles talk," they seek reassurance and comfort, not the objective solution to the problem that men often think they should provide.[18] The point is neatly made in a "Cathy" comic strip when Cathy is distraught over an unsuccessful hairdo. Her boyfriend has ready answers: "Wear a hat. Call the salon. Make them fix your hair. Crisis over? What's the big deal?" She slams the door on him with "Men: all solution, no sympathy." But prelapsarian Adam is not so unfeeling. He does offer an explanation in terms of faculty psychology for Eve's disturbing dream, but he precedes and follows it with sympathy. "The trouble of thy thoughts this night in sleep / Affects me equally" (5.96–97), he says, and he reassures her, reminding her of nature's "bosom'd smells" (127) that are "kept for thee in store" (128). And he says "*let us* to our fresh imployments rise" (125; emphasis mine), again using the language of consensus rather than command.

Numerous explanations have been offered for Eve's proposal in book 9 that she and Adam work apart, but the language of her proposal merits the attention it has begun to receive.[19] First Eve states the problem: the work of tending the garden is becoming too much for just two people. Then she offers an idea, but in a very tentative way, and that only after she asks Adam for his suggestions:

> Thou therefore now advise
> Or hear what to my mind first thoughts present,
> Let us divide our labors, thou where choice
> Leads thee, or where most needs.
>
> (9.212–15)

She does not pause here for Adam to "advise," but he could easily break in since she has given him the opportunity. Her suggestion is the result of "first thoughts," she says, not offered as a developed and coherent plan. She uses the consensus-building "Let us." She also presents Adam's choices first, though her next words indicate that she has already decided where she wants to go: "while I / In yonder Spring of Roses intermixt / With Myrtle, find what to redress till Noon" (9.217–19). All this is cast indirectly, as suggestion and possibility. As Tannen points out concerning the indirect approach, "if you get your way because others happened to want the same thing, or because they offered freely, the payoff is in rapport. You're . . . happily connected to others whose wants are the same as yours."[20]

At the end of her proposal Eve provides a reason for dividing the labor:

> For while so near each other thus all day
> Our task we choose, what wonder if so near
> Looks intervene and smiles, or object new
> Casual discourse draw on.
>   (9.220–23)

Joan Blythe has suggested that Adam is too quick to bring closure to the discussion: maybe Eve just wants to talk about working separately.[21] Such a continued conversation would maintain the sense of rapport and connection so important to Eve. Or is Eve tiring of rapport-talk, of "casual discourse," even while she uses its strategies to persuade Adam to her way of thinking? He seems to think so when he says, "But if much converse perhaps / Thee satiate, to short absence I could yield" (247–48), after he has spoken of talk as "Food of the mind" (238). He goes on to urge the dangers of working apart and her need for his protection, objections to which she responds with more direct arguments. But she does not comment on his idea that she is "satiate[d]" with "much converse." Perhaps she is. Tannen finds

> that male-female conversations are more like men's conversations than they are like women's. So when women and men talk to each other, both make adjustments, but the women make more. Women are at a disadvantage in mixed-sex groups.[22]

Surprisingly, Tannen reports "that women want more time away from their partners than men do." One reason is that "when women are with partners, they make more adjustments and accommodations, buying harmony at the cost of their own preferences."[23] Milton would probably say that this is as it should be, for in the *Doctrine and Discipline of Divorce* it is "man" who needs "an intimate and speaking help, a ready and reviving associate in marriage."[24] Yet the responsibility for sustaining the "meet and happy conversation" that is "the chiefest and the noblest end of marriage"[25] may be wearying, and Eve may actually need a break.

When Satan successfully tempts Eve in book 9, it is the only time in *Paradise Lost* that she is shown actually conversing with anyone besides Adam, though she does speak very briefly in public situations after the Fall. In her account of her first moments of life, a voice speaks to her, and Adam calls, but she says nothing. In her dream, as she narrates it, she is spoken to but does not reply. Has she in fact been silent? Or does she (or the author) consider her own words not worth reporting? When Raphael visits, he greets her ceremoniously as "Mother of Mankind" (5.388), but her reply, if any, is not recorded. "A while discourse they hold" (395), we are told, until Adam invites the angelic guest to join in eating human food, but which individuals comprise the antecedent of "they" is uncertain. Apparently even before lunch she is a silent auditor while her husband does the speaking in a formal situation.

When Eve leaves her discussion with Adam and meets the serpent, she is "not unamaz'd" (9.552) that the creature can speak at all and also that he is "To me so friendly grown above the rest" (564). Eve's conversational style calls for building relationships and establishing connections, and she proceeds to do just that with the serpent, just as she has all but conversed with the flowers. When he imparts false information mixed with flattery, the "amaz'd unwary" (614) Eve engages in friendly discussion at a time when recalling and asserting humankind's dominant position in the earthly hierarchy is what Adam probably would have done in her place, and what she should be doing.

After Eve's fall, "casual discourse" and "grateful digressions" cease, at least for a time. Eve's approach to Adam on her return is not one of building relationships and establishing connections but of placing herself higher in the scheme of things. Knowledge is power, she knows. She wants, she says, to render herself "more equal" (9.823) and even "sometime / Superior" (824–25), and her speeches are designed to further that aim even after she decides that "Adam shall share with me in bliss or woe" (831). She is playing the masculine game of establishing a dominant position, and she is the dispenser of information as she recounts her amazing adventure with the talking serpent and the marvelous tree. For once, Eve is the one with more knowledge and expertise, however faulty, as she says, "On my experience, Adam, freely taste, / And fear of Death deliver to the Winds" (988–89). This is report-talk, and the imperative forms that Eve uses certainly do not imply consensus; they suggest that she knows best.

When Eve and Adam are judged in book 10, we hear her speak in public for the first time (the second is her spontaneous lament), for an individual answer is required. Now she cannot leave the public talk to her husband. The brevity of her response—"The Serpent me beguil'd and I did eat" (10.162)—makes an impressive contrast to Adam's lengthy explanations and excuses, excuses that blame not only Eve but also, indirectly, God—"This Woman *whom thou mad'st* to be my help" (137; emphasis mine). In case the reader misses the point, the authorial voice stresses it by describing her as "not before her Judge / Bold or loquacious" (160–61). Not only is fallen Eve's brief response decorous for a woman, but its acceptance of responsibility already marks the movement toward repentance and reconciliation that she sets in motion for the couple.

In book 10, too, Eve's silence after she and Adam realize the enormity of what they have done contrasts strikingly to Adam's torrent of words. His long soliloquy (10.720–844) seems endless and gets nowhere, running in circles of blaming himself and everybody else, including God. Furthermore, this speech represents only a sample of his "sad complaint" (719) that goes on all night as he lies "on the cold ground" (851): "Thus Adam to himself lamented loud / Through the still Night" (845–46). Then after an authorial summary of his complaints, he resumes for a while longer: "Why comes not Death" (854). In the course of these laments he is worried about his relationship with God and with his descendants, who will justly blame their ancestor—"For this we may thank Adam" (736)—but he is doing nothing to set those relationships right. And for Eve he has only reproach, both before and after she breaks in upon his gloom and falls at his feet: "Out of my sight, thou Serpent" (867).

It is silent Eve, the peacemaker, who reestablishes connection with Adam and brings about reestablishment of the couple's connection with God. She accepts guilt and insists on Adam's forgiveness, stressing her need for his help: "thy gentle looks, thy aid, / Thy counsel in this uttermost distress" (10.919–20). Her troubles—very serious ones indeed—evoke Adam's real sympathy in spite of himself, and he responds with "peaceful words" (946) that begin to blend rapport-talk and report-talk:

> *let us* no more contend, nor blame
> Each other . . . but strive
> In offices of Love.
> (958–60; emphasis mine)

So it is as Adam adopts some of Eve's language as well as her desire for peace and harmony that the two are reconciled first with each other and then, as prevenient grace does its work, with God. In book 11 they return to the prayers the reader has heard earlier, now not only prayers of praise but prayers of contrition and true repentance. Perhaps part of the education of Adam is education in conversation.

Silent Eve has the last word at the end of *Paradise Lost*, as Diane McColley has pointed out.[26] Adam has been told to share with her what he has learned through his vision and through Michael's description of the future: "Let her with thee partake what thou hast heard, / Chiefly what may concern her faith to know" (12.598–99). As in book 8, Adam is cast as the authoritative dispenser of information.

But he has no chance to impart facts, for she tells him at once that "God is also in sleep" (611) and she has already learned what he intends to reveal. She knows. And the blazing sword cuts off any possibility of reply. For the sake of the poem's formal symmetry, it might be appropriate for Adam's words to end the human talk in *Paradise Lost*, as they begin and end his talk with Eve in book 4. But for the sake of conversational symmetry, it is even more appropriate that Eve have the last speech as she and Adam move out into the world hand in hand, however wandering and slow their steps, to maintain and create relationships.[27]

Further, Eve has been promised that she will bear to Adam "Multitudes like thyself" (4.474). The future belongs to her descendants, including the second Eve and the second Adam: perhaps they will even talk as she does. Milton suggests this possibility in *Paradise Regained* when the Son, recalling his youthful desire for "victorious deeds" and "heroic acts" (1.215, 216),

> Yet held it more humane, more heavenly, first
> By winning words to conquer willing hearts,
> And make persuasion do the work of fear;
> At least to try, and teach the erring Soul.
>   (221–24)

It is immediately after he reflects on this conclusion that Jesus meditates on his mother's intuitive "soon perceiving" of "These growing thoughts" (1.227) and her revelation of his ancestry. Though the poem is concerned with his great confrontation with Satan, it ends in a return to the domestic sphere where women use rapport-talk to build consensus and relationship: "hee unobserv'd / Home to his Mother's house private return'd" (4.638–39). Possibilities for rapport-talk along with report-talk lie in the future, then, with Eve's final words of harmony and reconciliation in *Paradise Lost*:

> This further consolation yet secure
> I carry hence; though all by mee is lost,
> Such favor I unworthy am voutsaf't,
> By mee the Promis'd Seed shall all restore.
>   (12.620–23)

Notes

1. John Milton, *Paradise Lost, John Milton: Complete Poems and Major Prose*, ed. Merritt Y. Hughes (New York: Odyssey Press, 1957). All references to Milton's poetry are to this edition and are cited parenthetically in the text.

2. Diane McColley, *Milton's Eve* (Urbana: University of Illinois Press, 1983), 114.
3. Joseph A. Wittreich, *Feminist Milton* (Ithaca: Cornell University Press, 1987), 92.
4. Wittreich, *Feminist Milton*, 92.
5. Ibid., 102.
6. Deborah Tannen, *Women and Men in Conversation* (New York: Ballantine, 1990), 15.
7. Tannen, *Women and Men*, 77.
8. Ibid., 77–79.
9. Maureen Quilligan, *Milton's Spenser and the Politics of Reading* (Ithaca: Cornell University Press, 1983), 232.
10. Tannen, *Women and Men*, 77.
11. Walter J. Ong remarks that "by the advent of the New Criticism the verbal world had strikingly downgraded ceremonial combat," *Interfaces of the Word* (Ithaca: Cornell University Press, 1977), 288. But ceremonial combat had a major place in Milton's verbal world and, as Tannen demonstrates, has survived beyond the New Criticism.
12. Tannen, *Women and Men*, 277.
13. Ibid., 75.
14. Ibid., 78.
15. Ibid., 62.
16. Ibid., 125.
17. Marshall Grossman says of Eve's speech to Adam in 4.635–56,

Eve uses language both to perform and to represent the round of pleasant and varied repetitions that denotes the passing of time in Eden, and she suggests that even this benign temporality is transcended by the eternal conversation of man and woman, a conversation Adam and Eve begin in their love and extend indefinitely through the race that love is to found.

(*"Authors to Themselves": Milton and the Revelation of History* [Cambridge: Cambridge University Press, 1987], 89)
18. Tannen, *Women and Men*, 100–102.
19. For example, Joan Heiges Blythe discusses the grammatical structures of Eve's and Adam's language in "Sex-Marked Objects of Desire in *Paradise Lost*," Fourth International Milton Symposium, Vancouver, B.C., 5 August 1991. McColley surveys and summarizes the critical positions, *(Milton's Eve)*, 140–45.
20. Tannen, *Women and Men*, 225–26.
21. See Blythe, "Sex-Marked Objects."
22. Tannen, *Women and Men*, 237.
23. Ibid., 294.
24. Hughes, *Complete Poems*, 709.
25. Ibid., 707.
26. McColley, *Milton's Eve*, 217.
27. Wittreich discusses Eve's speech, cast as a sonnet, (*Feminist Milton*, 105–9). He notes that the prophetic quality of her words is reminiscent of the Quaker emphasis on women's equality, including the ability to prophesy (108).

Discourse and Danger: Women's Heroism in the Bible and Dalila's Self-Defense

HOPE PARISI

Continuing to beset discussions of Dalila as hero in *Samson Agonistes* is critics' ever-mindfulness of a distinction between Renaissance *heroism*, a self-determined and public brand of action, and *mediation*, agency that points to others, and others' projects, rather than to oneself.[1] But Dalila's prototypes are biblical. In recent years, women readers of the Bible have questioned the assumption that ancient Israel was patriarchal in the same sense that characterizes feminists' uses of the term today. They urge readers to "uncover ideology not only in biblical narrative, but perhaps even more in the commentaries and traditional interpretations which so shape our reading of these texts."[2] It is possible that the twentieth century has created a "problem of patriarchy,"[3] the erroneous assumption that modern gender asymmetry is merely a continuation of women's oppression in biblical culture, one that blockades the same venues for women's agency and accords to the same scale. But before the exile, ancient Near Eastern culture often blurred the boundaries between heroism and mediation for women. One finds the Bible harboring scriptures and traditions that negotiate its own discourses of patriarchy.[4] Dalila is modeled after a woman, though Philistine, of pre-exilic bearing. While Dalila's attempt at reconciliation with Samson marks her as a seventeenth-century (female) mediator, what she says belies her identity as a displaced *hero* of biblical spirit.

Very simply, a woman's heroism in the seventeenth century depended upon humility, chastity, and obedience. Embodying these virtues, a woman fulfilled her role to uphold the family structure; i.e., to clear and maintain the channels for achievement by men in the public realm. Part of her new status in marriage owed to her role and privilege of fostering the "little church" environment of her Protestant home; she mediated as a domestic minister. But in doing so, she was no more than living the allegories of the Middle Ages wherein *consolatio* figures, such as Beatrice and Lady Philosophy, entered and egressed only according to a male protagonist's need of them. As personifications of the divine *numen*, such prototypes were idealized, respected for the spiritual truths that stirred repentance.[5] But in the case of seventeenth-century women, the guilt of Eve was never far behind. The responsibility to promote reconciliation, between man and God or man and family, could only preoccupy women and modify their resistance to being edged out of the public realm.

One of the ways in which the seventeenth century emphasized women's harmonizing role was by referring to Old Testament heroines, putative prototypes of womanly virtue. However, communicating these stories as exempla was often complicated and frequently entailed two related projects: ambiguating the morality of these women and/or covering over details that attested to women's occasional public agency in biblical times. Catalogues of worthy women— both in literature and art—often included Judith, Jael, and Esther. However, it is only Esther, because of her chastity and wifely decorum, who escapes comparatively unscathed from the ambivalence with which her more violence-prone counterparts are represented.[6] Like Esther, Judith and Jael lead campaigns to rescue their people. Judith and her maid enter an Assyrian camp, proffering to betray the Israelites' valuable secrets. Once received by her host Holofernes, Judith brutally slays him. Similarly, Jael takes part in battle by driving a tent peg into the temple of Sisera, the commander of Jabin's Canaanite army. Among Renaissance depictions of Judith that seem to bear fewer traces of misogyny, Judith stands for truth or justice—concepts that drive the focus away from the literary personage and toward the object of some nationalist interest: perhaps a king or a besieged city. In other, less favorable, portrayals, Judith's sexuality is the focus, her *true* weapon. Jael also regularly appears in catalogues of worthy women simultaneous to her featuring in print series denoting the power of women.[7] Nonetheless, according to the caption to one Renaissance print of the Jael story, "Nothing is as evil as a woman's malice."

As an overplayed element in these stories' retellings, female sexuality diverted attention away from the fact that these women of Hebrew Scripture took on a greater share of public agency than Protestant guidelines for household government could sanction. Despite the ploys that the women use to make contact with their victims, the biblical record does not condemn them for furthering these actions with their sexuality. As Nehama Aschkenasy notes of Judith and Jael, these stories point to the infractious desires of the male antagonists. Ahasuerus sends Vashti, Esther's predecessor, to death when he cannot fetishize her publicly. Holofernes plays the fool in his undue attention to Judith's beauty. And Sisera no sooner gains a polite intimacy with Jael, denoted by his respectful demeanor once inside her tent, than he oversteps his boundaries by commanding her in a "masterly" voice.[8] ("Stand in the door of the tent" [Judges 4.20]).[9] In each story, the narratological perspective assures us that God is on the woman's side. Esther's story contains no less than three injunctions to rejoice. Her prayer, rendered fully in the pre-Christian Greek, evinces God's favor since what she asks for ("Frustrate their plot and make an example of him who started it all" [The Rest of Esther, C:22]) comes to embed the tale's irony and names the cause of celebration. In the Judith text, the agent of focalization (as I will describe it later) is clearly the woman herself: it is she who sees, who speaks, and who acts. The frequent ironies spoken by Judith continue to draw the reader into sympathy with her.[10] In the case of Jael, her conquest is celebrated within the victory ode of Deborah, in its own way a record of the threat against women in climates of war that in turn justifies their public action.[11]

In feminist exegesis, attention has turned to the history of texts' reception. Betsy Merideth, writing on betrayal by biblical women, enlists Jonathan Culler and Wolfgang Iser to make the point that any interpretation of a text is more a reading of the *reader* than of the text itself. She asks, "How do our readings and received interpretations reflect and then replicate cultural values and norms?" The treacherous woman as a topos in the Bible develops only when readers presume the narrator to be cuing identification with the man.[12] As I have noted, even figures such as Judith and Jael, supposedly "right" with Israel, solicit scorn in that they move past the bounds of acceptable female behavior. To cite another example, when Renaissance artists were not representing Judith as a hag, they often figured her handmaiden, Abra, as wretched instead. At the same time, these artists were particularly adept in depicting graphically the pain in Holofernes' face at the moment of decapitation, but left Judith expressionless or, perhaps more accurately, "cool[ly] deliberat[e]" in the act.[13] Such representations demonstrate that it was easier for male artists to identify with the man's state, no matter how much the "victim" deserved his anguish.

The Judges' narrative in Delilah's case suggests something different. According to Merideth, a deeper level of identification is embedded within the narrator's point of view: that of the focalizer—separable from the narrator—through whom the events of the story are seen. For example, when Delilah first chides Samson in 16.10–12 for circumventing her question about his secret, she says, "Behold, thou hast mocked me and told me lies" (16.10). Here "mocked" and "lies" connote a strong sympathy with Delilah since these words could only be selected from her perspective (especially since what Delilah says is true). Texts that identify the focalizing agent without question, as in the case of Judith, clarify for which character the redactor would wish to invoke the reader's sympathies. In narratives where the focalizer shifts from one main character to another, the reader is constrained to resist siding with either or any of them. This is the case with the Samson story. Frequently, Delilah emerges as focalizer. Evidence includes the preponderance of active verbs that stem from Delilah's agency (seeing, sending, calling for, making Samson sleep, having him shaved, among others); the steady progression with which Delilah acts on her own terms, undirected by the Philistines; and not least of all, the candor of Delilah's speech. Delilah has made her purposes clear to Samson all along, repeating three times, "Tell me, I pray thee, wherein thy great strength *lieth*, and wherewith thou mightest be bound to afflict thee" (16.6; emphasis mine).[14]

Thus a cautionary word goes out to readers of Milton's Dalila *not* to reinforce what might be Protestant writers' and thinkers' interpretive misunderstandings, especially since the opportunity Milton gives Dalila to present her case leaves open the question whether his text conforms to their readings. Milton's text encourages one to read Dalila in relation to *two* sets of prototypes: Old Testament women who enter the public arena and their skewed renderings in seventeenth-century literature and iconography. An ancient Near Eastern intercessor for her people, Dalila mediates in a way that conflicts with the domestic "strategies" proper to seventeenth-century women. As the stories of Judith, Jael, and even Delilah suggest, Renaissance notions of (public) heroism and (private) mediation merge in female agency by numerous biblical women. A woman's sphere of influence did not end at the threshold. Repeatedly, the Bible depicts the woman venturing out into the public realm or inviting its dignitaries into her abode. In instances where the woman is solicited by men for help, the course of her activity is often left to her device.[15] Moments in which women initiate saving action, as with Judith and Deborah, argue the case for women's public agency even more strongly. As for Delilah's agency, a reader may argue, as Merideth does, that more than following the Philistines' directives, she creates some of her own.

In *Samson Agonistes*, Dalila's attempt at reconciliation bears the strains of her effort as an ancient Near Eastern woman to accommodate herself to the repressive family structure of Milton's day. By setting Dalila's "crime" within the public-private split ("Being once a wife, for me thou wast to leave / Parents and countrey" [885–86]),[16] Samson would force a choice from which worthy women of the Bible were often exempt, especially in moments of political crisis.[17] During these times, biblical women constituted their identity as wives and nationalists simultaneously. Mordecai tells Esther that it is perhaps *because* of her Jewishness that providence obtains for her the opportunity of marrying a king. Likewise, Judith, Jael, and Deborah all save while existing in some relationship to marriage. Although a widow, Judith arrays herself in the style "when her husband Manasseh was alive" (Judith 10:3), thus resurrecting her identity as a *wife*. Following her lead, the widows Tamar and Ruth deceive father figures in the interest of perpetuating their husbands' line of descent, an inherently national interest. Instead of merely being subsumed by a husband's identity, female mediators in the Bible, absenting male agency, often could assume his public strength.

Critics unsympathetic to Dalila use the "wavering" (732) and disparate quality of her arguments to support her culpability.[18] But according to Mieke Bal, coherence is "[something] which readers desire much more than texts exhibit." What Milton criticism traditionally has read as the self-incriminating nature of Dalila's discourse finds an analogue in the prejudicial readings characterizing the Book of Judges in both popular and scholarly opinion. Bal writes, "The book is taken as a whole, its topic is determined, and the individual stories are subordinated to it." The topic? The "illustrious men" who answered God's call.[19]

In much the same way, readers of *Samson Agonistes* subordinate Dalila's defense to Samson's claims to be God's viceregent. Arguments against Dalila work only if the reader has first forged a whole out of the equally fragmentary bits of evidence that now discredit or now support Samson's relation to divine commission. Dalila's guilt emerges not so much from deduction as from a deliberated act of presupposition.[20] Protecting the coherence of Samson's heroism, our theories mimic the members of the chorus, who throughout the play psychologically contend against disparateness of explanation themselves. Overhearing "hideous noise" (1509) from the arena, the chorus once again are challenged to discern coherence, which Manoa threatens: "Of ruin indeed methought I heard the noise, / Oh it continues, they have slain my Son." The chorus immediately respond: "Thy Son is rather slaying them" (1515–17). The warning they issue to impede each other's hasty investigation of the event alerts us to our own predilection for closure on Samson's probity: "Best keep together here, lest running thither / We unawares run into dangers mouth" (1521–22). To be "safe," we are to keep reading Samson's regeneration coherently.

That the reader might reconceive Dalila's self-defense, I suggest allowing the chorus to implicate us as misguided hermeneuts. Their hastiness to square the relationship between Samson's past and present mirrors our own forcefulness in conjoining *Samson Agonistes* to (conventional conceptions of) its biblical source. The chorus provide a model of reading to be avoided: not that of rendering coherence, which is unavoidable, but rendering it unself-consciously.

Just as Bal notes that conventional readings of the Judges' narrative presuppose the protagonist's reciprocal relationship to divine favor, so critics of *Samson Agonistes* proceed backwards from a history of received readings favoring the Judges' Samson: the overdetermined suppression of Samson's prayer, and the chorus' implicit trust in it, serve as fulcrums that jettison the critic back and back, forcing the apprehension of beginning and intermediate events in terms of "overfamiliar" and "deadened" endings.[21] Bal extends such retrospection to the concept of characterization. The common idealization of Samson as hero plays out Bal's "retrospective fallacy"; i.e., "the projection of an accomplished and singular named character onto previous textual elements that lead to the construction of that character."[22] Delilah and her counterpart in Milton may be thought similarly overdetermined, judged retrospectively in the interest of keeping their identities as temptresses "coherent."

We can proceed from Bal's insight that coherency is a metaphor for structuration, and go on to structure Dalila's defense coherently as well. The reading I wish to offer of Dalila's arguments corroborates John Ulreich's inclination to see Dalila's intentions as sincere. She approaches Samson according to her stated cause: to seek forgiveness and reunion.[23] What happens in the course of this effort, and how it gets spoken, however, are different matters. Dalila is constrained to speak various discourses, thus seeming inconsistent to many. Still the ambiguities lodged in her speech need not be read misogynistically as an indictment against her sincerity as much as an indication of the difficulty of having to accommodate competing social norms of gender within the speaking subject.[24]

Dalila's motions, right from the start, mark this effort. More than psychological, her speech is "situational."[25] Had she prepared her speech, she might have had assistance from women's detractors in the period's pamphlet debates: She attributes her part in Samson's fall to "womans frailty" (783). Her womanhood renders her "weakness / . . . incident to all our sex" (773–74) and opens her to:

> Curiosity, inquisitive, importune
> Of secrets, then with like infirmity
> To publish them, both common female faults.
> (775–77)

These admissions align her with conventions Renaissance women invoked to gain a semblance of authority to speak at all. Various studies on the preconditions for women's foray into the public world contextualize Dalila's slew of apologetics.[26] The Renaissance prohibition against a woman's speech embedded all the other injunctions against her public agency. The learned woman who entered debate, the woman writer, the female partaker in rhetorical "intercourse"—each stepped forward from the charge to remain invisible. Any verbal behavior that provoked a woman's notoriety was transgressive. No wonder Dalila approaches Samson with "doubtful feet," "wavering resolution," and "timorous doubt," "dreading [his] displeasure" (732, 740, 733). She knows she is incurring ignominy by breaking the protocol for woman's silence. Her typically female "infirmity / To publish" (776–77) can only call up the association, as old as Proverbs, between woman's sexuality and that "glibbery" detractor of honor, the tongue.[27]

To initiate her case, Dalila employs the strategies that women writers and speakers, from the early Renaissance on, used to lessen the impression of their audacity. Women would preface their rhetoric by admitting to unworthiness and anxiety over breaking with their private roles. Each mode of woman's expression has its examples of women textualizing their own self-diminution. One dedicatory epistle to a volume on women's preaching reads:

> Weakness is entailed upon my sex in general, and for myself in particular, I am a despised worm, a woman full of natural and sinful infirmities, the chiefest of sinners, and least of Saints.[28]

Women petitioners of the civil war years acknowledged their "frail Condition" and attested that they were speaking "not out of any Self-Conceit or Pride of Heart, as seeking to equal ourselves with Men, either in Authority or Wisdom."[29] That women often made reference to a female weakness self-consciously may be judged by an implicit male approval of women's special ways of pleading: the husbands of these women knew the power of "a soliciting temper" where it concerned, say, their release from prison or getting a sequestration order lifted.[30] Women's dissembling had the power to affect important transactions. Men were primed for it, and women responded. Insofar as women could progress as public persons only within male-mediated conventions, we have a new context for interpreting Dalila's words: "To what I did thou shewdst me [i.e., prepared for me] first the way" (781).

While a timorous speaking voice colors much of Dalila's argument, its conventions collect within her opening words especially. Dalila's first approach to Samson bespeaks a tentativeness akin to that with which even the boldest of women writers and speakers would have proceeded:

> With doubtful feet and wavering resolution
> I came, still dreading thy displeasure, Samson.
> Which to have merited, without excuse,
> I cannot but acknowledge; yet if tears
> May expiate....
> My penance hath not slack'n'd, though my pardon
> No way assur'd. But conjugal affection
> Prevailing over fear, and timorous doubt
> Hath led me on desirous to behold
> Once more thy face.
> (732–36, 738–42)

These lines share with women's rhetorical efforts of the period common ways of beginning one's speech: deference to a male audience's anticipated reactions, the woman's willingness to assume guilt, her request for pardon, and the claim that something working almost in opposition to modesty forces her to speak. Through the conventions of femininity, Dalila might offset the bold masculine nature of her approach. Her deference recalls less her biblical namesake, who requests Samson's secret directly, and more the bride of Timna who "wept before him" (Judges 14.16–17) continually. By the contrast, Milton enables his readers to better recognize the independent spirit of Dalila once it eventually surfaces. For now, she accedes to the politics of deference, first with hopes to reconcile with Samson and then to solicit the Philistines for his release (920–21).

Remembering Milton's generally antagonistic relationship to convention, however, we can anticipate that Dalila's arguments to follow will soon erode her reliance on, for the most part, *querelle des femmes* tropes. What next feels like a shift in her argument is really an intensification of the subtext Milton has introduced in her initial words (732–47) and "First granting" speech (766–89): a climate dangerous for women's speaking. Of the years surrounding the events of the mid and late 1640s, women assumed the most liberty to speak during the years of the wars themselves. But with the court of Charles II, the public initiative that women had taken in pamphleteering and petitioning was checked by a male backlash of anger. Libertine literature and art burgeoned in a way unprecedented. Bolstering the phenomenon was the now uncertain political milieu in which men found themselves. As theorists on pornography attest, one of a society's symptoms of (and coping strategies for) political tension is a preponderance of aggression toward those groups with the least defenses. Receiving their cues, women curtailed their political writing and sought their notoriety and efficacy by another channel. Writing about romance, women who were still intent on negotiating power relations between the sexes could continue such work within the private context of love.[31]

Dalila then must write a love story: "And what if Love, which thou interpret'st hate, / . . . Caus'd what I did?" (790, 793). As before, her speech incorporates the clichés of femininity while subtending an awareness of a climate dangerous to women's speaking. But paradoxical to what feels like a softened approach, Dalila moves closer to her biblical prototypes' role as mediator in the public realm. The subtext of violence toward women intensifies. Outright mention of the woman of Timna, a victim of murder, comes in the midst of domestic sweet-talk.

> I saw thee mutable
> Of fancy, feard lest one day thou wouldst leave me
> As her at Timna, sought by all means therefore
> How to endear, and hold thee to me firmest.
> (793–96)

While Milton may, according to Joseph A. Wittreich, "push [Timna] to the basement of his poem"[32] for narrative effect, that basement is not dug so deep as to be inaccessible. The Timna event encapsulates the concern over women's safety present in Dalila's speech from the beginning. Here it occasions, for the first time, Dalila to admit her anxiety outright. "As her at Timna" may not mean simply "as you left her at Timna" but also "as in the same (vulnerable) state in which you left her," that is, a state of susceptibility toward male anger, retribution, and violence. The thought that Samson would be "mutable / Of fancy," while it ennobles Dalila's possessiveness as *lover* and belies her fear of desertion, suggests even more the danger of Samson's impassioned *return*. It was Samson's return to the woman of Timna that incited backlash upon backlash, leading to her and her father's murders. Dalila's desire to "hold thee to me firmest" denotes "jealousie of Love" (791), yes, but it also signals her intention to circumvent Timna's regrettable outcome.

The case Dalila makes for her former "importun[ity]" likewise takes on added resonance.

> No better way I saw then [this]
> To learn thy secrets, get into my power
> Thy key of strength and *safety*.
>
> (797–99; emphasis mine)

The syntax of these lines obscures whether the object of Dalila's concern is safety for Samson or herself. Indeed it is both, and more: if Dalila could "get into [her] power" the secrets of Samson's strength, she would share that strength. In doing so, she would rise from passivity to enablement, a progression that women model as they need to, now and again, throughout the biblical text.

Rereading Dalila's "discourse on love," one notes the profusion of words and ideas related to safekeeping, specifically within domesticity. Dalila wants assurance (800) from "cares and fears" (805) within "loves [safe prison]" (808); i.e., the home. The three-part context of safety *in love* and *at home* points up the disparity between a domesticity meant to shield one (i.e., the husband) from the hostility of the outside world and the hostility inherent within home life for women. One might compare Jael's "inhospitable guile" (989) with Judith's treacherous sexuality: both emblematize in their own way "Matrimonial treason" (959) in that they pervert the contract upon women to provide domestic ease and comfort.[33] In popular imagination, Delilah likewise violates the contract to love rightly. In response, Dalila aligns herself with Jael, but only after building a subtext that discloses the sanctuary of the home environment, real and psychological, as violent for women in general as it was for certain biblical men.[34]

If irony foregrounds points that would otherwise remain in recess, we must underscore the irony of Samson's reactions to Dalila's use of female conventions in light of similar practices by biblical heroines. As I have already indicated, women of the Bible repeatedly use their sexuality to gain political advantage. But instead of condemning them, Scripture seems to contextualize these ploys in light of the measure of the threat weighing against them as women. If Esther is to thwart Haman's murder of her people, she first must approach the king without invoking his anger. So she thoughtfully lays aside "the clothing of a suppliant, and dress[es] herself in splendid attire" (The Rest of Esther, D:1) in a spirit reminiscent of her and the harem members' earlier efforts to be chosen as queen. Once in Ahasuerus's presence, she modifies her defiant posture by "stumbl[ing], turn[ing] pale and faint[ing], keeling over on the maid who went before her" (D:7).[35] She gains closer and closer access to Haman, her and Israel's endangerer, by continuing to evoke conventions of female sexuality.

Much the same, Judith knows that to approach Holofernes is to put her life in danger. The way in which she readies herself to meet the enemy parallels Esther's process: first, she *manufactures* a transformation (as the elders notice, "her face was so transformed and her clothes so different" [Judith 10.6 – 8]). Once inside the camp, the woman must demonstrate deference. Judging from Holofernes' response, Judith prostrates herself before the commander quite dramatically (10.23): "Courage, woman! Don't be afraid. For I have never hurt anyone who chose to serve Nebuchadnezzar, king of the whole world" (11.1). The text leaves the reader to imagine Judith playing up a self-diminutive fear. As with Esther, the decisive moment of the enemy's downfall follows a banquet at which (since she occasions it) the woman presides. In turn, the story of Jael foregrounds providence working both through and against conventions of female behavior. Deborah knows enough that Sisera, when driven from his chariot, will head right toward Jael's tent. Jael "complies": "Turn in, my lord, turn in to me" (Judges 4.18). She presents the sensualized comforts of domestic safety: here warmth, covering, and apropos the banquet theme, a "princely bowl of curds" and drink (5.25). In fact, Jael would *surpass* the standards of feminine hospitality by offering Sisera not just water, which he asked for, but milk.[36] Again, the biblical narrator does not judge the woman. Instead he compels the reader to notice the male antagonist for his misguided attention to conventional feminine assets that for him mean patriarchy's perpetuation.

In *Samson Agonistes*, it is the chorus that present women as wily. Samson's excessive blame of Dalila condones their view. But again, Dalila's speaking of feminine conventions is grounded by inferences to a world of dangerous male anger. Had Samson and the chorus their sway, her own clichés would incriminate her. But Dalila's discourse on love, with its subtext of violence, mirrors her biblical prototypes' acting out of these conventions to the same effect: the return of implication to a male antagonist. Merging public concern with private rhetoric, Dalila aligns herself with contemporaries—both ancient Near Eastern and late seventeenth-century—anxious to right political/sexual imbalances.

By the time of her departure, Dalila is ready to disclose her true "concernments" (969), those behind her more forceful identity as ancient Near Eastern woman. "Why do I *humble* thus my self . . . suing / For *peace*" (965– 66; emphasis mine). From the beginning, Dalila has gestured and spoken in ways that anticipate violent reaction against her. It has been no use. Samson's rage finally threatens "to tear thee joint by joint" (953). Spurred and spurned, Dalila claims outright her right to vindication in the public realm.

> My name perhaps among the Circumcis'd
> In Dan, in Judah, and the bordering Tribes,
> To all posterity may stand defam'd,
> With malediction mention'd, and the blot
> Of falshood most unconjugal traduc't.
> But in my own countrey where I most desire,
> ....
> I shall be nam'd among the famousest
> Of Women.   (975–80, 982–83)

Seventeenth-century injunctions against a woman's notoriety no longer claim her. Neither does the noble charge of accommodation. In the end, Dalila's scriptural prototypes require her to stand outside the gendered heroisms of the seventeenth century. As *haggada*, the biblical *femme forte* contextualizes both Dalila's and Delilah's heroism. The history of their reception, together with Milton's critique, converges in Dalila's own words:

> Fame if not double-fac't is double-mouth'd,
> And with contrary blast proclaims most deeds,
> On both his wings, one black, the other white,
> Bears greatest names in his wild aerie flight.
>   (971–74)

Only the last reason she offers, her compulsion toward public action, does justice to the biblical spirit of female initiative through which we may read her representation.

Notes

I owe thanks to a number of people who read and commented on this paper in its various stages, especially Jackie DiSalvo, Tom Hayes, Marshall Grossman, Bill Shullenberger, and Joseph Wittreich.

1. Criticism has framed the problem of Dalila's heroism in terms of the public-private split. See Joan Bennett, "Liberty under the Law: *Samson Agonistes*," *Reviving Liberty* (Cambridge: Harvard University Press, 1989), 119–60; John Guillory, "Dalila's House: *Samson Agonistes* and the Sexual Division of Labor," *Rewriting the Renaissance: The Discourses of Sexual Difference in Early Modern Europe*, ed. Margaret W. Ferguson, Maureen Quilligan, and Nancy J. Vickers. (Chicago: University of Chicago Press, 1986), 106–22; Jackie DiSalvo, "Intestine Thorn: Samson's Struggle with the Woman Within," *Milton and the Idea of Woman*, ed. Julia Walker (Urbana: University of Illinois Press, 1988), 211–29. For Dalila as agent of regeneration, see Heather Asals, "In Defense of Dalila: *Samson Agonistes* and the Reformation Theology of the Word," *Journal of English and Germanic Philology* 74 (1975): 183–94. Stella P. Revard tries to rescue Dalila from the public-private distinction in terms of

Euripides. See "Dalila as Euripidean Heroine," *Papers on Language and Literature*, 23 (1987): 290–302.

2. Betsy Merideth, "Desire and Danger: The Drama of Betrayal in Judges and Judith," *Anti-Covenant: Counter-Reading Women's Lives in the Hebrew Bible*, ed. Mieke Bal (Detroit: Almond Press, 1989), 62.

3. Carol Meyers, *Discovering Eve: Israelite Women in Context* (New York: Oxford University Press, 1988), 24.

4. Strands of pre-exilic writings within the Bible contribute toward its "heterogeneity," its ability to resist ideological coherence. Following, even when one turns to stories like Judith and Esther, part of *post*-exilic tradition, a basis yet exists for negotiating the Bible's patriarchal discourses. That post-exilic authors were often re-presenting earlier material in their work is another encouragement for reading the Bible dialogically. Most recently in Milton studies, Gregory Bredbeck has applied the idea of negotiation to seventeenth-century discourses of homosexuality. See *Sodomy and Interpretation: Marlowe to Milton* (Ithaca: Cornell University Press, 1991), esp. chapter 5.

5. Carolyn Asp, "Shakespeare's Pauline and the *Consolatio* Tradition," *Shakespeare Studies* 11 (1978): 152.

6. H. Diane Russell, *Eva/Ave: Women in Renaissance and Baroque Prints* (Washington, D.C.: National Gallery of Art, 1990), 33.

7. Russell, *Eva/Ave*, 155. Such representations were contemporary to her figurings as a prototype of the Virgin Mary.

8. Nehama Aschkenasy, *Eve's Journey: Feminine Images in Hebraic Literary Tradition* (Philadelphia: University of Pennsylvania Press, 1986), 172, 171.

9. All references to the King James Version are cited parenthetically in the text. My source for the apocryphal Judith and Greek additions to Esther (denoted by letter) is the Anchor Bible, gen. eds. W. Albright and D. Freedman, 43 vols. (New York: Doubleday, 1964 –), also cited parenthetically in the text.

10. Merideth, "Desire and Danger," 75.

11. Danna Nolan Fewell and David M. Gunn, "Controlling Perspectives: Women, Men, and the Authority of Violence in Judges 4 and 5," *Journal of American Academy of Religion* 58 (1990): 403–4.

12. Merideth, "Desire and Danger," 65, 72.

13. Mary D. Garrard, *Artemesia Gentileschi: The Image of the Female Hero in Italian Baroque Art* (Princeton: Princeton University Press, 1989), 298, 291.

14. Merideth, "Desire and Danger," 69–76. The Hebrew *anah* for "afflict" carries connotations, among others, of depressing, humbling, or weakening. The Revised Standard Version (Merideth's source) renders it "subdue."

15. Aschkenasy, *Eve's Journey*, 176–78. Cf. Esther; 1 Samuel 25.17–31; 2 Samuel 14.1–22.

16. John Milton, *Samson Agonistes, The Complete English Poetry of John Milton*, ed. John T. Shawcross (New York: New York University Press, 1963). All references to *Samson Agonistes* are to this edition and are cited parenthetically in the text.

17. See Jo Ann Hackett, "In the Days of Jael: Reclaiming the History of Women in Ancient Israel," *Immaculate and Powerful: The Female in Sacred Image and Social Reality*, ed. Clarissa Atkinson et al. (1985; Boston: Beacon Press, 1987), 15–38.

18. See, for example, Thomas Kranidas, "Dalila's Role in *Samson Agonistes*," *Studies in English Literature* 6 (1966): 125–37.

19. Mieke Bal, *Death and Dissymmetry: The Politics of Coherence in the Book of Judges* (Chicago: University of Chicago Press, 1988), 11, 12.

20. Catherine Belsey's comments on narrative are relevant. When read for clo-

sure, narratives "reinstate" or establish "an order which is understood to have preceded the events of the story" while asserting a "hierarchy of discourses," wherein the "privileged" discourse "places as subordinate all the discourses that are literally or figuratively between inverted commas" ("Constructing the Subject, Deconstructing the Text," *Feminist Criticism and Social Change*, ed. J. Newton and D. Rosenfelt [London: Methuen, 1985], 53). Stanley Fish affirms in a related way the text's problem of closure as spoken by the chorus. See "Spectacle and Evidence in *Samson Agonistes*," *Critical Inquiry* 15 (1989): 556–86.

21. Frank Kermode, *The Art of Telling: Essays on Fiction* (Cambridge: Harvard University Press, 1983), 65. With regard to these moments in *Samson Agonistes*, see Joseph A. Wittreich, *Interpreting "Samson Agonistes"* (Princeton: Princeton University Press, 1986), 66.

22. Mieke Bal, *Lethal Love: Feminist Literary Interpretations of Biblical Love Stories* (Bloomington: Indiana University Press, 1987), 108.

23. John Ulreich, "'Incident to All Our Sex': The Tragedy of Dalila," *Milton and the Idea of Woman*, ed. Julia Walker (Urbana: University of Illinois Press, 1988), 187.

24. Cf. Belsey, "Constructing the Subject," 50: "The displacement of subjectivity across a range of discourses implies a range of positions from which the subject grasps itself and its relations with the real, and these positions may be incompatible or contradictory." Aligning Delilah with Dalila extends the latter's range of subject positions even further, through time.

25. Ann Rosalind Jones applies the term to women's strategies for speaking in the seventeenth century. See "Surprising Fame: Renaissance Gender Ideologies and Women's Lyric," *Poetics of Gender*, ed. Nancy K. Miller (New York: Columbia University Press, 1986), 74–95.

26. See Jones, "Surprising Fame"; Elaine Hobby, *Virtue of Necessity: English Women's Writing, 1649–88* (Ann Arbor: University of Michigan Press, 1989); and Germaine Greer, "Introduction," *Kissing the Rod: An Anthology of Seventeenth-Century Women's Verse*, ed. Germaine Greer et al. (New York: Farrar Straus Giroux, 1988), 1–31.

27. Robert Braithwaite, *The English Gentlewoman* ([London, 1631], qtd. in Jones, "Surprising Fame," 78), proclaims:

> To enter into much discourse . . . with strangers argues lightness or indiscretion: what is said of maids may properly be applied to all women: *They should be seen and not heard.* . . . Women's tongues are held their defensive armor, but in no particular detract they more from their honor than by giving too much scope to that glibbery member.

See also Proverbs 5.3–5.

28. Susanna Parr, *Susanna's Apology to the Elders* (London, 1659), sig. A2r–v, qtd. in Hobby, *Virtue of Necessity*, 44.

29. ". . . Petition . . . Feb. 4th 1641," *Harleian Miscellany* (1746), 7:568–69, qtd. in Patricia Higgins, "The Reactions of Women with Special Reference to Women Petitioners," *Politics, Religion, and the English Civil War*, ed. B. Manning (New York: St. Martin's Press, 1973), 210–11.

30. A friend writes one woman's husband to assure him: "it would not be amiss if [your wife] can bring her spirit to [such a temper] and can tell how to use the juice of an onion sometimes to soften hard hearts." (The husband responds that the gravity of the circumstances is enough to produce the tears.) Apparently, the friend's advice reflected the practice of "sages" who so "instruct [their] wi[ves]" (F.P. Verney, *Memoirs of the Verney Family* [London, 1892], 2:239–40, qtd. in Antonia Fraser, *The Weaker Vessel* [New York: Vintage, 1985], 214–16).

31. Hobby, "Surprising Fame," 85–88.

32. Wittreich, *Interpreting Samson*, 65.

33. Esther figures as a transgressor of the domestic code as well in that the repeated banquets she arranges for Ahasuerus include Haman, whom she eventually has executed.

34. James Turner articulates the rhetoric of anger that runs through the divorce tracts, thus implying the danger for women who either failed or disappointed their husbands' expectations that marriage provide their solace and comfort. See *One Flesh: Paradisal Marriage and Sexual Relations in the Age of Milton* (Oxford: Clarendon Press, 1987), 194–215. David Loewenstein also alludes to Milton's impassioned rhetoric in these tracts. But insofar as Loewenstein's study concerns more the simultaneously "poetic, theatrical, and liberating" quality of Milton's prose writing, he does not treat the implications of such anger for women that Dalila may represent. See *Milton and the Drama of History: Historical Vision, Iconoclasm, and the Literary Imagination* (New York: Cambridge University Press, 1990), esp. chapter 6.

35. Although these actions feature only in the Greek additions, Renaissance art shows familiarity with them. See Garrard, *Artemesia*, 76.

36. Aschkenasy, *Eve's Journey*, 171.

Contributors

DAVID BOOCKER is Assistant Professor of English at Tennessee Technological University. He has published an article on John Heywood and has articles forthcoming on the Irish-American poet James McHenry and on the Milton plaque at Vallombrosa. He is currently working on a bibliography of Milton in the American Periodicals, 1800–1850.

STEPHEN M. BUHLER, Assistant Professor of English at the University of Nebraska–Lincoln, has published essays on Miltonic politics in *Milton Studies* and on Ficinian magic in *Renaissance Quarterly*. He is completing a study of Spenser and Renaissance Epicureanism, and is currently examining the role of music in shaping audience responses to film productions of Shakespeare.

JANE COLLINS teaches at Queens College of the City University of New York. Currently, she is writing a dissertation on female readership in Early Modern England.

CHARLES W. DURHAM, Professor of English at Middle Tennessee State University, has presented papers on Milton at numerous conferences and published in *Milton Quarterly*. He is codirector of the Southeastern Conference on John Milton and is currently examining the nature of hierarchy in Milton's poetry.

ANGELA ESTERHAMMER is Assistant Professor in the departments of English and Modern Languages at the University of Western Ontario. She has published essays and reviews on Blake, Romanticism, and twentieth-century fiction and is completing a book-length manuscript on speech-act theory and poetic discourse, *Creating States: Studies in the Performative Language of John Milton and William Blake*.

ROBERT THOMAS FALLON, Professor of English at LaSalle University, is the author of *Captain or Colonel: The Soldier in Milton's Life and Art* and *Milton in Government*.

ALBERT W. FIELDS, Professor of English at the University of Southwestern Louisiana, has served as editor of *Explorations in Renaissance Culture*. As managing editor of the Levy Humanities Series, he has edited the published lectures of Cleanth Brooks, Shirley Ann Grau, Peter Gay, and others, and has himself published essays and reviews in the *Milton Encyclopedia, PMLA, PBSA, Southern Humanities Review, Xavier Review*, and *South Central Bulletin*.

JOAN F. GILLILAND was educated at Vanderbilt University and is Professor of English at Marshall University, where she directs the graduate program in English. She has published articles on Milton and Shakespeare and is coauthor of *Reasons for Writing*.

JANE HILES, Assistant Professor of English at Samford University, has published articles on Shakespeare, Faulkner, and Philip Larkin. She is currently working on a book-length study of fictional discourse in Milton's prose, *Plotting the Revolution*, and essays on Bakhtinian "images of language" in *Eikonoklastes* and the digression to Cromwell in Milton's *Second Defense*.

J. ANDREW HUBBELL is a doctoral candidate in English at the University of Maryland at College Park, where he is a teaching assistant. His work in progress includes "Song of Myself: The Triumph of Poetry in *Comus*," "The System of Friendship in *The Faerie Queene*," and "Readers Reading Themselves: The Reception History of Shelley's 'Mask of Anarchy.'"

STEVEN JABLONSKI is Lecturer in English at Princeton University, where he is writing a dissertation on Milton's providentialism and Arminianism, "The Ways of God: Providence and John Milton."

DANIEL T. LOCHMAN received his Ph.D. at the University of Wisconsin-Madison, and is Professor of English at Southwest Texas State University. He has published articles on John Colet and Milton in *Milton Studies, Renaissance and Reformation*, and *Sixteenth-Century Studies*, and is currently working on a book-length study of Colet.

PETER M. MCCLUSKEY is a doctoral candidate in English at the University of Arkansas, where he teaches Honors Freshman Composition. He has presented papers at several conferences, published in *Publications of the Arkansas Philological Association*, and was awarded the 1992 C. Vann Woodward Prize for Non-fiction by the University of Arkansas Press. He is currently working on a dissertation that examines English representations of the Dutch on the Renaissance stage.

CONTRIBUTORS

KRISTIN PRUITT MCCOLGAN is Professor of English at Christian Brothers University. She codirects the Southeastern Conference on John Milton, and has published articles on *Paradise Lost* in *Milton Quarterly, ANQ, Milton Studies,* and *South Central Review.*

DIANE MCCOLLEY, educated at the University of California at Berkeley and the University of Illinois at Urbana–Champaign, is Professor of English at Rutgers University, Camden College of Arts and Sciences. She is the author of *Milton's Eve* and *A Gust for Paradise: The Arts of Eden in the Age of Milton.*

CATHERINE GIMELLI MARTIN is Associate Professor of English at the University of Memphis, where she is completing a book-length study, *The Ruins of Allegory: Tradition and Revision in "Paradise Lost."* She has published essays on literary theory, Renaissance drama, and has articles on *Paradise Lost* in *SEL, Milton Studies,* and *Discourses of Desire.*

ALICE MATHEWS is Lecturer and Assistant Chair of the English Department at the University of North Texas. She directed an NEH Summer Institute, "Roots of Individualism in American Literary Classics," is editor of *CCTE Studies,* has published articles on Milton in *Explicator* and *CCTE Studies* and on Arthur Clough in *Victorian Institute Journal,* and is currently working on a study of the parallels between *Paradise Lost* and *Lord Jim.*

HOPE PARISI received her Ph.D. in English at City University of New York, is currently teaching at Kingsborough Community College, CUNY, and is engaged in a book-length study of Milton's women and narrative voice.

JOHN T. SHAWCROSS is Professor of English at the University of Kentucky. His recent studies of Milton include *"With Moral Voice": The Creation of "Paradise Lost," "Paradise Regain'd": "Worthy T' Have Not Remain'd So Long Unsung," John Milton and Influence: Presence in Literature, History and Culture,* and *John Milton: The Self and the World.* He is currently working on a book entitled *The Uncertain World of "Samson Agonistes."*

SAMUEL SMITH is Assistant Professor of English at Messiah College. He is currently at work on a book examining the politics of Apocalypse in Milton's *Paradise Regained* and an essay on the politics of Apocalypse in Shakespeare's *Macbeth.*

JOHN S. TANNER received his doctorate at the University of California at Berkeley and is Associate Professor of English and Associate Academic Vice-President at Brigham Young University. He edited the *Rocky Mountain Medieval and Renaissance Association Journal* and received a Fulbright Fellowship to Brazil in 1991. His principal scholarly interests are Milton, Shakespeare, and other writers of the English Renaissance, and he has published widely on religion and literature. He is the author of *Anxiety in Eden: A Kierkegaardian Reading of "Paradise Lost."*

NATALIE JOY WOODALL received her doctorate in Classics at SUNY–Albany and is currently pursing postdoctoral work in British Literature at Syracuse University. She has published articles on Greek and Roman literature as well as essays on British and Irish women authors and artists for the *Encyclopedia of the 1890's*.

Index

Achtemeier, Elizabeth, 55–56 n. 11
Addison, Joseph, 8
Aeschylus, 185
Agnew, Jean-Christophe, 45 n. 9
Allen, Don Cameron, 208, 214–15 n. 2
Alter, Robert, 248 n. 19
Anderson, Bernhard W., 55–56 n. 11
Andrewes, Launcelot, 78, 85 n. 25
Anne of Austria (queen regent of France), 103, 108, 109
Apocrypha: Judith, 264, 270; Rest of Esther, 262, 269
Aristotle, 116, 164 n. 29, 174, 204 n. 13, 218, 226–27 n. 5
Arnold, Matthew, 126–35
Asals, Heather, 271–72 n. 1
Aschkenasy, Nehama, 262
Augier, Tene, 102, 103
Augustine, St., 155, 164 n. 29
Austin, J. L., 147, 150

Bacon, Sir Francis, 154, 156
Bakhtin, M. M., 95, 96, 98, 100 n. 21
Bal, Mieke, 264, 265
Barker, Arthur E., 177–78 n. 1
Barthes, Roland, 185
Baschet, Armand, 105, 111 n. 7
Becanus, Joannes, 23
Beecher, Henry Ward, 84–85 n. 21
Beecher, Lyman, 84–85 n. 21
Belsey, Catherine, 272–73 n. 20, 273 n. 24
Benet, Diana Treviño, 13
Bennett, Joan, 9, 46 n. 16, 99 n. 10, 271–72 n. 1
Benson, Auditor, 126
Benveniste, Emile, 148
Bernard, Richard, 183
Berryman, John, 5
Beum, Robert, 184

Bible: Acts, 142, 145; I Chronicles, 97; I Corinthians, 55 n. 8, 115, 204 n. 12; Daniel, 60; Ephesians, 122, 123, 125 n. 21; Ezekiel, 74, 81; Habakkuk, 22; Hebrews, 183; Hosea, 56 n. 12; Isaiah, 75, 117, 124; Job, 56 nn. 13, 15, 244; Joel, 142; John, 22, 56 n. 12, 65, 178 n. 6; I John, 56 n. 12; Judges, 262, 263, 267, 270; I Kings, 58–59; Leviticus, 75, 78; Luke, 9, 22, 57, 75, 178 n. 6; Mark, 116, 178 n. 6; Matthew, 59, 62, 79, 178 n. 6; II Peter, 53; Philippians, 120, 123; Proverbs, 273 n. 27; Psalms, 15, 64, 65, 66, 113; Revelation, 57–66, 74, 79; Romans, 49; I Samuel, 272 n. 15; II Samuel, 100 n. 25, 272 n. 15
Bissell, Benjamin, 27
Blake, William, 15, 142, 152 n. 2
Blythe, Joan Heiges, 255, 259 n. 19
Boehrer, Bruce, 99 n. 10
Brady, Thomas A., Jr., 84 n. 12
Braithwaite, Robert, 273 n. 27
Breasted, Barbara, 204 n. 12, 209
Bredbeck, Gregory, 209, 213, 215 n. 13, 215–16 n. 17, 216 n. 19, 272 n. 4
Bredvold, Louis, 155
Broadbent, J. B., 224
Brooks, Cleanth, 74
Brooks, Gwendolyn, 7
Brown, Cedric, 195, 199, 204–5 n. 15, 205 n. 17
Browne, Sir Thomas, 76
Bullough, Geoffrey, 214 n. 1
Bullough, Margaret, 214 n. 1
Burnet, James, Lord Monbaddo, 6
Burns, Ken, 48
Burns, Robert, 7
Bush, Douglas, 207, 214–15 n. 2, 215 n. 5

INDEX

Cable, Lana, 99 n. 10
Cain, William E., 137 n. 30
Calvin, John, 85 n. 27, 123
Campanella, Tommasa, 85 n. 27
Certeau, Michel de, 148
Chaney, Edward, 71
Charles I (king of England), 8, 9, 77, 87–98, 101, 124, 126
Charles II (king of England), 126, 267
Charles X (king of Sweden), 102
Chatterton, Thomas, 5
Cherry, Conrad, 85 n. 23
Childs, George, 126, 128
Chilon, 163 n. 11
Coffin, Charles, 160
Coleridge, Samuel Taylor, 7, 132, 155
Collett, Jonathan, 28
Cook, Albert, 163 n. 7
Corns, Thomas N., 82, 85 n. 25, 99 n. 10
Cowper, William, 129
Crane, Hart, 5
Cranmer, Thomas, 90
Creaser, John, 204 n. 12
Cromwell, Oliver, 9, 12, 77, 84 n. 18, 103, 104, 105, 112 nn. 8, 9, 10, 11
Cromwell, Richard, 104, 112 nn. 9, 10, 11
Culler, Jonathan, 262

Daly, James, 125 n. 8
Danielson, Dennis, 10, 31, 32, 45 nn. 4, 11, 49, 55 n. 5, 125 n. 13
Dante, 128
Davenant, Sir William, 27
Davies, John, 155
Davies, Stevie, 109
DeBry, Theodore, 27
Demaray, John, 201, 206, 215 n. 3
DeQuincey, Thomas, 132
Dike, Daniel, 57
Diodati, Charles, 208
DiSalvo, Jackie, 184, 271–72 n. 1
Doane, A. N., 246 n. 2
Donne, John, 156, 158
Douglas, Rev. John, 6, 16 n. 3
Dryden, John, 32, 33
Duncan, Joseph E., 226 n. 3
Durham, Charles W., 13
Durling, Robert M., 219
DuRocher, Richard J., 227 n. 6
Dury, John, 60

Egerton, Sir John, Earl of Bridgewater, 204 n. 14, 204–5 n. 15, 215–16 n. 17, 216 n. 19
Eliot, T. S., 5, 6, 7, 56 n. 19, 129
Elizabeth I (queen of England), 77
Elliot, Emory, 65
Empson, William, 10
Epiphanes, Antiochus, 60
Euripides, 185, 271–72 n. 1
Evans, Margery, 215–16 n. 17

Fairfax, Edward, 218, 219, 221, 222, 224, 225, 227 nn. 9, 10
Fairfax, Sir Thomas, 77, 84 n. 18
Farrar, F. W., 126, 127
Fauconberg, Thomas, Viscount, 104
Featley, Daniel, 85 n. 25
Ferry, Anne, 241
Fields, Albert W., 163 n. 7, 164 n. 29
Fish, Stanley, 26, 28, 72, 73, 98, 154, 164 n. 18, 165, 166, 176, 178 n. 2, 183, 244, 272–73 n. 20
Fix, Stephen, 6
Fletcher, Angus, 194, 195, 204 n. 12
Fletcher, Harris, 150
Fletcher, Robert, 133
Forset, Edward, 114, 120
Foucault, Michael, 161
Fowler, Alastair, 119
Fraser, Antonia, 273 n. 30
French, J. Milton, 150
Freud, Sigmund, 15
Friedmann, Anthony E., 219, 220
Friesen, Abraham, 84 n. 12
Frye, Northrop, 224, 226 n. 3
Furman, Wendy, 180

Garrard, Mary D., 274 n. 35
George I (king of England), 105
Gerarde, John, 22, 24
Giamatti, A. Bartlett, 218, 226 nn. 2, 3
Gilson, Étienne, 155, 163 n. 12
Ginsberg, Allen, 5
Godwin, William, 15
Golding, Arthur, 218
Gordon, George, Lord Byron, 7, 132
Graham, Jean, 22
Grandsen, F. W., 45 n. 6
Greenblatt, Stephen, 154
Greer, Germaine, 273 n. 26
Gregory, E. R., 152 n. 2

Grose, Christopher, 178n. 5
Grossman, Marshall, 160, 161, 247n. 8, 259n. 17
Guillory, John, 271–72n. 1
Guss, Donald L., 45n. 8

Haak, Theodore, 102
Hackett, Jo Ann, 272n. 17
Hagstrum, Jean H., 220
Hale, David George, 114, 125n. 11
Haller, William, 57
Hanford, James Holly, 207, 214–15n. 2, 215n. 5
Harding, David P., 227n. 6
Hardy, John Edward, 74
Hartlib, Samuel, 60, 67n. 8
Hawkins, Sir John, 6, 9
Hayley, William, 131
Helgerson, Richard, 99n. 10, 100n. 12
Henry VIII (king of England), 105, 114
Henry, Prince of Wales (son of James I), 77
Heraclitus, 158, 163n. 11
Herbert, George, 145
Heylyn, Peter, 26, 27
Higgins, Patricia, 273n. 29
Hill, Christopher, 32, 67n. 9, 71, 215n. 11
Hobby, Elaine, 273n. 26
Hog, William, 5
Hollander, John, 84n. 18
Hollis, Thomas, 9
Holyoke, Edward, 9
Homer, 127, 174, 212
Hooker, Richard, 155, 158, 164n. 29
Hopkins, Gerard Manley, 15
Hughes, Merritt Y., 204n. 15
Hunter, William B., 109, 121, 201, 204n. 12, 205n. 17
Huxley, Aldous, 7

Iranaeus, St., 121, 122, 125nn. 18, 21
Ireland, William, 5
Iser, Wolfgang, 262
Ivimey, Joseph, 133

Jacobus, Lee A., 56n. 16
James I (king of England), 77, 114, 115
Jameson, Frederic, 9
Johnson, Samuel, 5, 6, 16n. 4, 132, 133
Jones, Ann Rosalind, 273nn. 25, 26
Jones, Inigo, 194

Jonson, Ben, 22, 193, 194, 195, 197, 205n. 16
Jonston, John, 25
Joyce, James, 5
Jubilee Singers, 78
Juhnke, Anna, 10
Julian of Norwich, Dame, 56n. 19
Jung, Carl, 158
Junius, Francis, 246n. 2

Kant, Immanuel, 56n. 15
Kantorowicz, Ernst, 115
Keats, John, 7
Kelsall, Malcolm, 45n. 13
Kermode, Frank, 45n. 6
Kerrigan, William, 13, 47, 52–54, 55n. 8, 56n. 15, 85n. 27, 152n. 2, 201–3
Kierkegaard, Søren Aabye, 53, 54, 56n. 17
Kranidas, Thomas, 272n. 18

Lamb, Charles, 133
Lanyer, Aemilia, 205n. 16
Latimer, Hugh, 90
Lauder, William, 5–6, 16n. 3
Lawes, Henry, 198, 200, 204–5n. 15, 208, 209
Lawry, Jon S., 83
Lawson, John, 125n. 18
Leavis, F. R., 7
Legouis, Pierre, 84n. 18
Leibnitz, Gottfried Wilhelm, 34, 48
Leonard, John, 27, 241, 244, 246n. 4, 247–48n. 16
Lewalski, Barbara, 162, 247n. 10
Lewis, C. S., 47, 220, 226n. 2
Lieb, Michael, 10, 45n. 12, 125n. 11, 158, 161, 163n. 7, 164n. 33
Lloyd, Lodowick, 77, 78
Loewenstein, David, 72, 99n. 10, 100n. 14, 178n. 2, 274n. 34
Louis XIV (king of France), 103, 104, 105, 107, 108, 111n. 5, 112nn. 8, 10, 11
Lovejoy, Arthur, 32, 44–45n. 3, 45n. 4, 49, 55n. 5
Low, Anthony, 189n. 1
Luther, Martin, 57, 85n. 26, 150
Lyttleton, George, 126, 127

Macaulay, Lord Thomas, 129, 133, 134

MacCallum, Hugh, 171, 178 n. 4, 247–48 n. 16
McColley, Diane, 10, 250, 257, 259 n. 19
MacKellar, Walter, 219, 221, 224, 225, 226 n. 3
MacPherson, James, 5
Mackey, Louis, 52
Marcus, Leah, 204 n. 12, 209, 215–16 n. 17
Margoliouth, H. M., 84 n. 18
Márquez Sánchez, Reuben, 9
Martin, Catherine Gimelli, 55 n. 5
Martyr, Peter, 27
Martz, Louis, 21, 24, 28, 156
Marvell, Andrew, 76, 77, 101, 205 n. 16
Mary II (queen of England), 108
Mason, William, 15
Massenius, Jacob, 5
Masson, David, 214–15 n. 2, 215 n. 5
May, Thomas, 92, 93
Mazarin, Cardinal Jules, 103, 104, 105, 107, 111 n. 5, 112 nn. 8, 9, 10, 11
Meadows, Philip, 101
Mendes, Peter, 215 n. 5
Meredith, Betsy, 262, 263
Merry, Robert, 7
Milton, Christopher, 150
Milton, John, works of: *Ad Patrem*, 14, 162, 208, 209; *Animadversions*, 76; *Apology for Smectymnuus*, 162, 216 n. 31; *Areopagitica*, 98, 142, 155, 156, 211; *Art of Logic*, 221, 222; "At a Solemn Music," 71–83; *Brief Notes Upon a Late Sermon*, 8; *Christian Doctrine*, 53, 109, 115, 122, 125 n. 11, 133, 142, 144, 155, 158, 159, 161, 164 n. 25, 170, 180, 183, 188; *Doctrine and Discipline of Divorce*, 211, 255; *Eikonoklastes*, 87–98; *Epitaphium Damonis*, 208, 211, 212, 216 n. 27; *First Defense*, 101, 115; *History of Britain*, 142; *Lycidas*, 6, 74, 81, 82, 195, 203, 211; *Mask Presented at Ludlow Castle (Comus)*, 6, 25, 193–203, 206–14, 221, 224; *Of Education*, 63, 67 n. 8, 216 n. 32; *Of Reformation*, 88, 90, 91; *Of True Religion, Heresie, Schism, and Toleration*, 8; "On Shakespeare," 221; *Paradise Lost*, 5, 6, 10, 12, 13, 14, 15, 21–29, 31–44, 47–54, 57, 75, 76, 79, 80, 82, 98, 99 nn. 10, 11, 106–11, 113–24, 129, 130, 131, 132, 134, 135, 143, 147, 153–62, 177, 184, 203, 206, 212–14, 221, 222–23, 226 n. 3, 227–28 n. 25, 231–46, 249–58; *Paradise Regained*, 15, 39, 57–66, 98, 110, 165–77, 206, 213, 216 n. 29, 217–26, 258; *Prolusions*, 141; "Psalm II," 113; *Ready and Easy Way to Establish a Free Commonwealth*, 12, 115–16, 117, 118, 120, 124, 125 n. 12; *Reason of Church Government*, 79, 80, 81, 131, 141–51, 216 nn. 25, 31; *Samson Agonistes*, 6, 9, 56 n. 19, 78, 99 n. 10, 147, 165–77, 179–88, 221, 260–71; *Second Defense*, 12, 54, 101, 143; "Sonnet 16," 9; "Sonnet 19," 54; *Tenure of Kings and Magistrates*, 8, 13, 57, 116–17; *Tetrachordon*, 14; *Treatise of Civil Power*, 8; Trinity Manuscript, 74, 82, 199, 205 n. 17
Miner, Earl, 45 n. 11
Mollenkott, Virginia R., 45 n. 11, 55 n. 5
Monteverdi, Claudio, 247 n. 12
More, Sir Thomas, 154, 156
Mueller, Janel, 125 n. 11
Murphy, Arthur, 6
Mustazza, Leonard, 178 n. 12

Nelson, James G., 133, 134
Nemerov, Howard, 5
Nicholas of Cusa, 75
Norbrook, David, 74, 195, 204 n. 12

Olney, James, 158
Ong, Walter J., 259 n. 11
Orgel, Stephen, 193, 194
Osiander, Andreas, 75
Ovid, 217, 218, 219, 220, 222, 245, 248 n. 20
Owen, John, 124

Pareus, David, 37, 60, 67 n. 5
Parker, Lois, 127
Parker, William Riley, 56 n. 18, 87, 106, 149, 189 n. 1, 208, 214–15 n. 2, 215 nn. 5, 11
Parsons, William, 7
Pater, Walter, 129
Patrick, J. Max, 101
Patrides, C. A., 75, 125 n. 18

Patterson, Annabel, 9
Pausanias, 163 n. 11
Pelikan, Jaroslav, 66 n. 2
Perkins, William, 57, 59, 62, 63
Phocylides, 163 n. 11
Piper, O. A., 55–56 n. 11
Plato, 163 n. 11, 174
Pommrich, Ewald, 227 n. 9
Pope, Alexander, 32, 48
Potter, Lois, 100 n. 20
Pound, Ezra, 7
Purchas, Samuel, 76

Quilligan, Maureen, 250

Radzinowicz, Mary Ann, 55 n. 6, 189 n. 1
Rajan, Balachandra, 177–78 n. 1
Ralegh, Sir Walter, 22, 23, 153
Raleigh, Sir Walter A., 129
Ramsay, Allen, 6
Ranke, Leopold von, 75, 76
Revard, Stella P., 271–72 n. 1
Richardson, Joe M., 85 n. 22
Richardson, Samuel, 47
Ricks, Christopher, 23, 24
Ricoeur, Paul, 56 n. 13
Ridley, Nicholas, 90
Robinson, Mary, 7
Rogers, Samuel, 7
Rosedale, Rev. H. G., 134, 135
Ross, Malcolme, 204 n. 12
Rourke, Constance Mayfield, 84–85 n. 21
Rumrich, John, 26
Rupert, Prince, Count Palatine of Rhine and Duke of Bavaria, 77
Rushdy, Ashraf H. A., 178 n. 6

Salmasius, Claudius, 115
Samuel, Irene, 180, 247 n. 10
Sandler, Florence, 99 n. 10
Sandys, George, 218
Scherer, Edmond, 129–30
Scholes, Percy, 84 n. 18
Schullenberger, William, 10, 247 n. 6
Schultz, Howard, 224, 225, 226, 226 n. 3
Schwartz, Regina, 82, 147–48, 244
Seccombe, Thomas, 77
Sensabaugh, George, 13
Servius, 216 n. 21
Shakespeare, William, 34, 50, 95, 128, 129, 156, 194

Sharpe, Kevin, 135
Sharratt, Bernard, 134
Shaw, George Bernard, 5
Shawcross, John T., 15 n. 1, 16 nn. 4, 5, 56 n. 16, 164 n. 33, 169, 176, 177–78 n. 1, 179, 188, 208, 211, 215 n. 5
Shelley, Percy Bysshe, 7
Sheppard, William, 146
Shumaker, Wayne, 50
Sidney, Sir Philip, 81, 82, 95, 162, 239
Simpson, A. W. B., 146, 147
Smith, Charlotte, 7
Smith, John, 202
Snyder, Gary, 5
Socrates, 163 n. 11, 174, 175
Solon, 163 n. 11
Sophocles, 185
Southey, Robert, 7
Spenser, Edmund, 81, 82, 86 n. 30, 154, 156, 161, 204 n. 12, 217, 218, 219, 220, 222, 225, 226
Stavely, Keith W. F., 45 n. 10, 84–85 n. 21, 99 n. 10
Stein, Arnold, 156, 159, 160, 226 n. 3, 228 n. 31
Stowe, Harriet Beecher, 84–85 n. 21
Strauss, Jakob, 79, 85 n. 26
Strong, William, 122
Summers, Joseph H., 55 n. 6
Svendsen, Kester, 22

Tannen, Debora, 250–58, 259 n. 11
Tanner, John S., 247 n. 9
Tasso, Torquato, 85 n. 27, 217, 218, 219, 222, 225, 226, 227 n. 9
Tayler, Edward, 67 n. 11, 204 n. 12, 226 n. 3
Taylor, Dick, 67 n. 10
Taylor, Thomas, 57, 58, 59, 61, 62, 63, 64
Terrien, Samuel, 56 n. 13
Tertullian, 117
Thales, 163 n. 11
Theognis, 163 n. 11
Thomson, James, 7, 129
Thurloe, John, 105
Tiberius (emperor of Rome), 60, 61
Tillyard, E. M. W., 74, 164 n. 36, 204 n. 12, 207, 214–15 n. 2, 215 n. 5
Touchet, Anne, Lady Castlehaven, 215–16 n. 17
Touchet, Mervin, Earl of Castlehaven, 209, 215–16 n. 17

Traherne, Thomas, 239
Trusler, John, 10
Turner, James Grantham, 274 n. 34

Ulreich, John, 265

Verney, F. P., 273 n. 30
Virgil (Vergil), 128, 206–14
Voltaire, 32, 45 n. 6

"W. J." ("W. I."), 77
Walker, Margaret, 85 n. 22
Walzer, Michael, 114
Webber, Joan, 10, 15 n. 1
Wesley, John, 15
Whaler, James, 24
White, George L., 85 n. 22
Whiting, George W., 135
Wilding, Michael, 195, 196, 204 n. 13
William III (king of England), 108

Williams, Charles, 7
Williamson, George, 163 n. 7
Wilson, Thomas, 87, 89
Wingren, Gustaf, 125 n. 18
Wittreich, Joseph A., 9, 74, 82, 86 n. 30, 131, 177–78 n. 1, 178 n. 2, 185, 186, 188, 201–3, 250, 259 n. 27, 268, 273 n. 21
Wollstonecraft, Mary, 10, 15
Woodcock, Katherine, 128
Woodhouse, A. S. P., 224, 226 n. 3
Worden, Blair, 125 n. 12
Wordsworth, Christopher, 8
Wordsworth, William, 7, 129
Work, Henry C., 85 n. 22
Wunstius, Marcus Andreas, 182

Yalden, Thomas, 8
Young, Edward, 7

Zwicker, Steven, 135